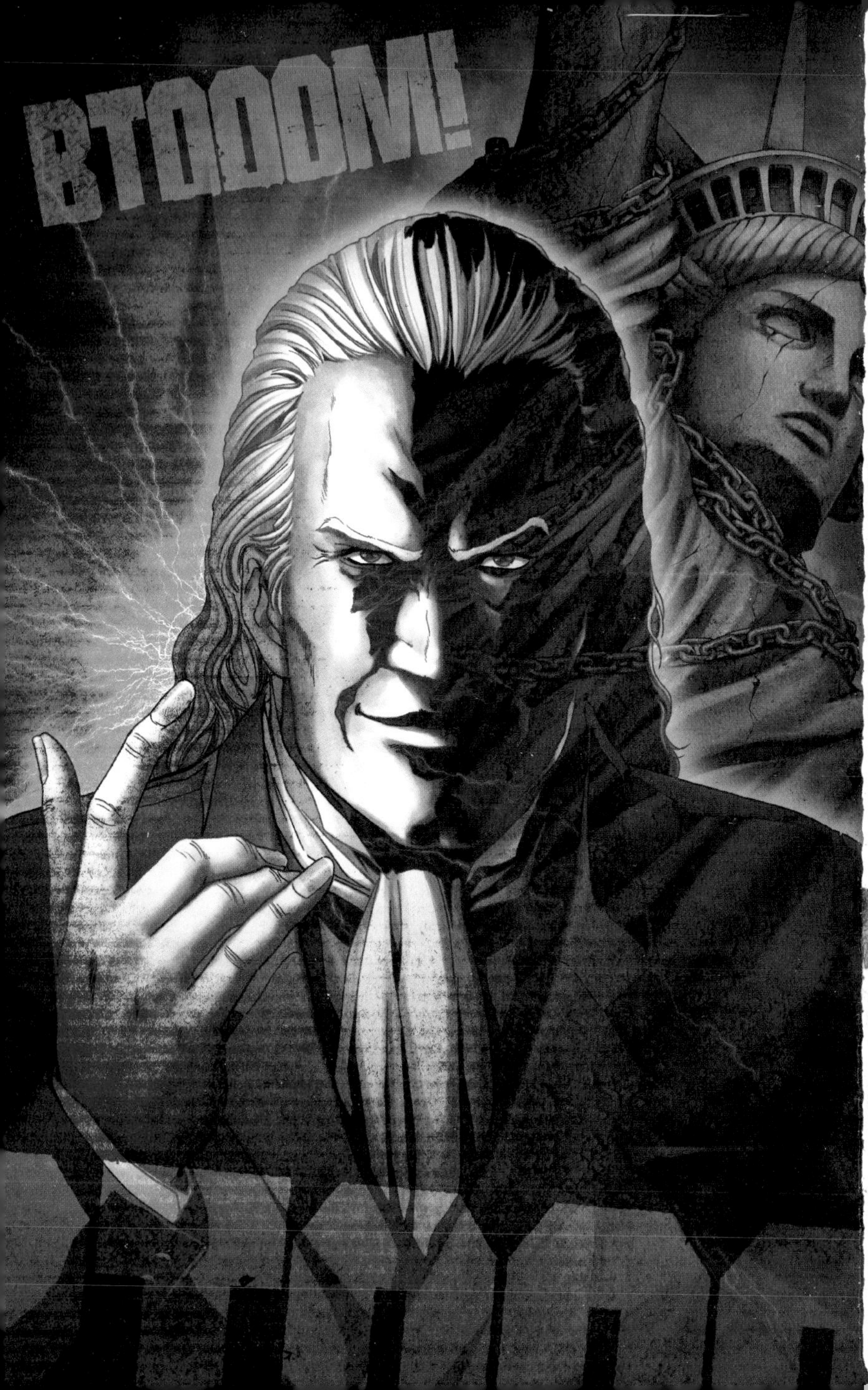
BTOOOM!

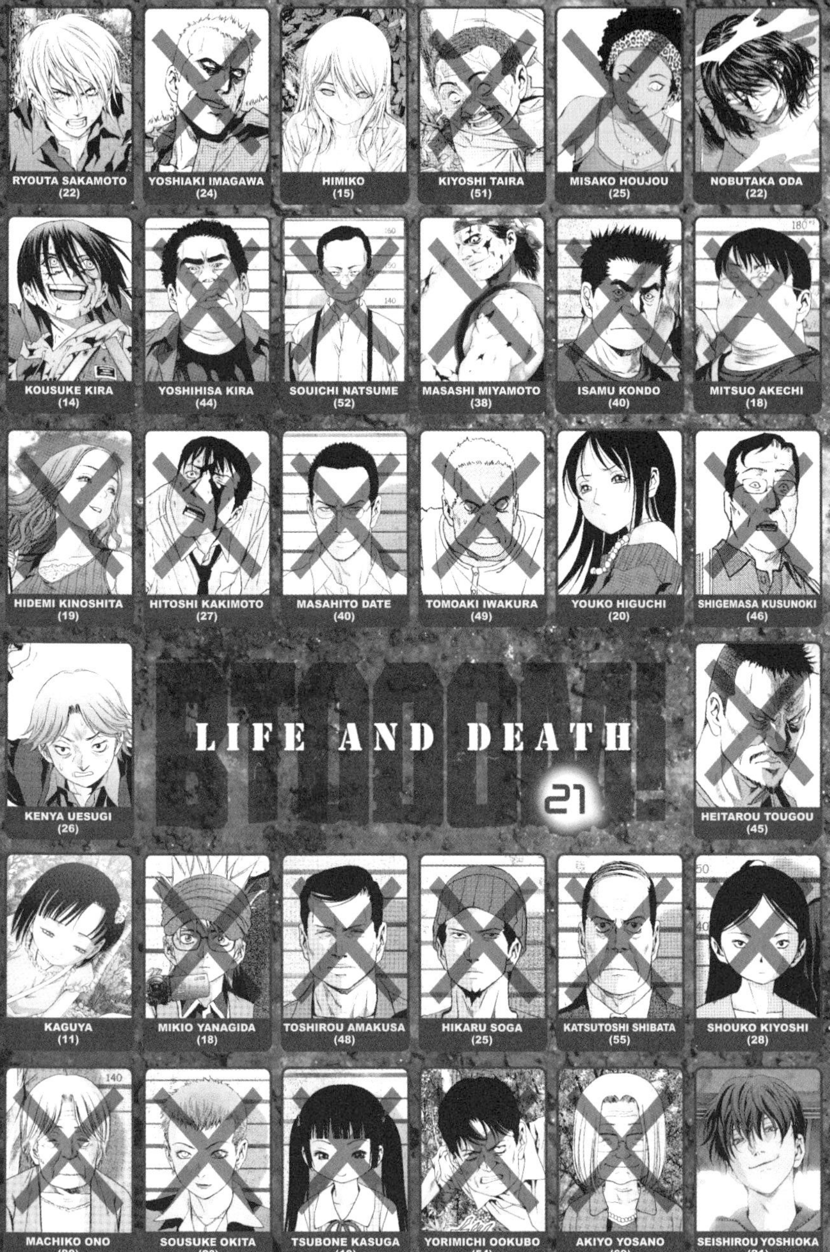
RYOUTA SAKAMOTO (22)
YOSHIAKI IMAGAWA (24)
HIMIKO (15)
KIYOSHI TAIRA (51)
MISAKO HOUJOU (25)
NOBUTAKA ODA (22)
KOUSUKE KIRA (14)
YOSHIHISA KIRA (44)
SOUICHI NATSUME (52)
MASASHI MIYAMOTO (38)
ISAMU KONDO (40)
MITSUO AKECHI (18)
HIDEMI KINOSHITA (19)
HITOSHI KAKIMOTO (27)
MASAHITO DATE (40)
TOMOAKI IWAKURA (49)
YOUKO HIGUCHI (20)
SHIGEMASA KUSUNOKI (46)
KENYA UESUGI (26)
BTOOOM!
LIFE AND DEATH
21
HEITAROU TOUGOU (45)
KAGUYA (11)
MIKIO YANAGIDA (18)
TOSHIROU AMAKUSA (48)
HIKARU SOGA (25)
KATSUTOSHI SHIBATA (55)
SHOUKO KIYOSHI (28)
MACHIKO ONO (80)
SOUSUKE OKITA (23)
TSUBONE KASUGA (19)
YORIMICHI OOKUBO (54)
AKIYO YOSANO (69)
SEISHIROU YOSHIOKA (21)

BTOOOM!

JUNYA INOUE

CHARACTER

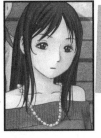

YOUKO HIGUCHI

GENDER: Female
AGE: 20
BLOOD TYPE: A
JOB: Actress
HOME: Kanagawa

Before she was taken to the island, she was active as a popular porn star who went by the name of "Kazuha." She has the uncanny ability to tell when someone's lying. She's a member of Tougou's team and likes strong men. When she made advances on Tougou, he turned her down due to his impotence.

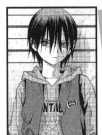

KOUSUKE KIRA

GENDER: Male
AGE: 14
BLOOD TYPE: AB
JOB: Junior high student
HOME: Tokyo

This junior high student harbors a dark, brutal, murderous past. On the island, he blew up his own father and is genuinely enjoying this murderous game of "BTOOOM!". He's always been a big fan of the online version of the game, and his dream is to defeat "SAKAMOTO," a top world ranker. Unfortunately, he keeps failing at it. He joins Tougou's team and has grown up a little by doing so.

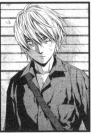

RYOUTA SAKAMOTO

GENDER: Male
AGE: 22
BLOOD TYPE: B
JOB: Unemployed
HOME: Tokyo

After spending every day cooped up in his home gaming online, he suddenly finds himself forced to participate in "BTOOOM! GAMERS," a killing game taking place on a mysterious uninhabited island. As a world ranker in the online third-person shooter "BTOOOM!", he uses his experience and natural instincts to survive and concoct a plan to get off the island along with his comrades, only for it to end in failure. While wallowing in despair, he arrives at the Sanctuary alone, where he teams up with Kaguya and Soga to beat Torio.

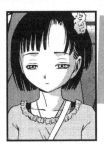

KAGUYA

GENDER: Female
AGE: 11
BLOOD TYPE: AB
JOB: Grade schooler
HOME: Tokyo

A mysterious little girl who came across Sakamoto when he washed ashore. She doesn't speak and uses a tablet to communicate. She's the figurehead of the Order of Moonlight, a religious cult managed by Toshirou Amakusa. She can see dead people. In the Sanctuary, she worked with Sakamoto and Soga to defeat the real villain behind the tragedies, Torio.

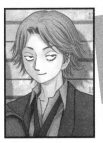

KENYA UESUGI

GENDER: Male
AGE: 26
BLOOD TYPE: AB
JOB: Office worker
HOME: Tokyo

A cowardly and easily flattered young man who used to dream of becoming an actor. He was almost killed by Kira, but he escaped thanks to Higuchi's lie-detecting ability. He was previously a part of Tougou's team.

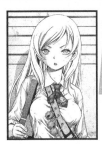

HIMIKO

GENDER: Female
AGE: 15
BLOOD TYPE: B
JOB: High school student
HOME: Tokyo

A foreign high school girl who has teamed up with Sakamoto. She harbors a deep resentment against men after a sordid experience in her past, but after surviving some battles thanks to Sakamoto, she begins to trust him. Her character in the online version of "BTOOOM!" is actually married to Sakamoto's character, and she has fallen in love with the real Sakamoto too.

BTOOOM! 21

LONGER SCHWARITZ

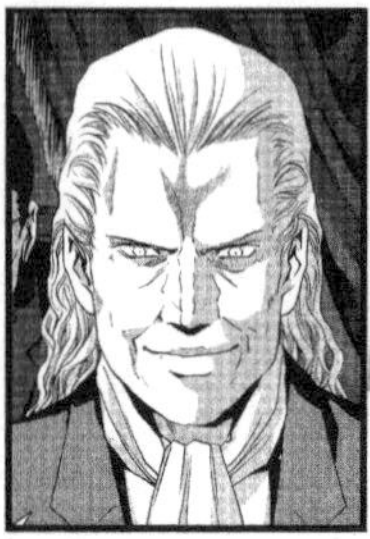

GENDER: Male
AGE: 77
BLOOD TYPE: O
JOB: Capitalist
HOME: New York

A descendant of European aristocracy, he is a man of power who controls the world behind the scenes with his considerable capital. In order to more thoroughly control the online realm, he founds the THEMIS project and has high hopes for "BTOOOM! GAMERS."

TAKANOHASHI

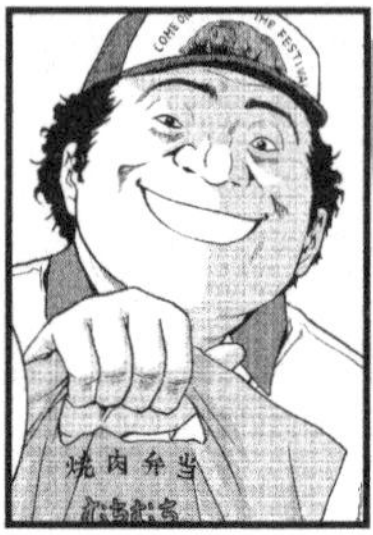
焼肉弁当

GENDER: Male
AGE: 45
BLOOD TYPE: AB
JOB: Game planner
HOME: Hokkaido

An executive staff member at Tyrannos Japan, he is the leader behind all the development of the online and real-life versions of "BTOOOM! GAMERS." He considers Sakamoto a valuable player and debugger. As a result of Sakamoto's plan to hijack the helicopter, Takanohashi's precious game was almost forced to come to a premature end.

SEISHIROU YOSHIOKA

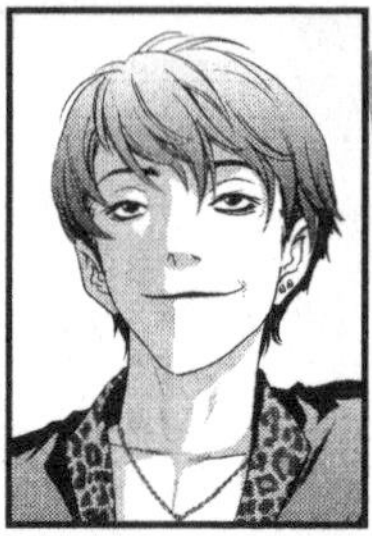

GENDER: Male
AGE: 21
BLOOD TYPE: A
JOB: Musician
HOME: Tokyo

Himiko's childhood friend and the lead vocalist of a popular band. He and his bandmates lured their fans—Himiko's classmates—into his apartment and raped them. He was later arrested. He is the reason behind both Himiko's distrust of men and her nomination for the island.

HISANOBU

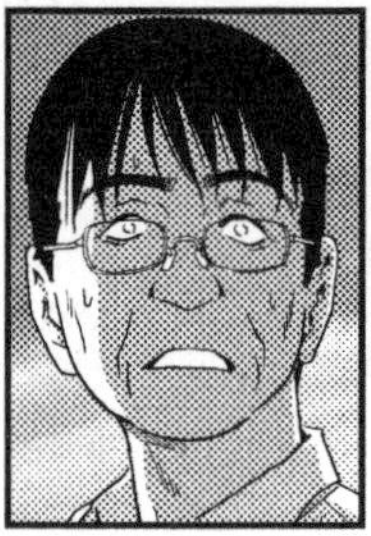

GENDER: Male
AGE: 55
BLOOD TYPE: A
JOB: Unemployed
HOME: Tokyo

Yukie's new husband and Sakamoto's stepfather. He's worried about how much time his stepson spends up in his room and scolds him, only to be attacked. Having just been laid off, he racks up debt because of his praiseworthy efforts to preserve his family's lifestyle. However, Yukie is frail in body and mind and attempts to kill herself. Fate has dealt him an unfair card in life.

TSUNEAKI IIDA

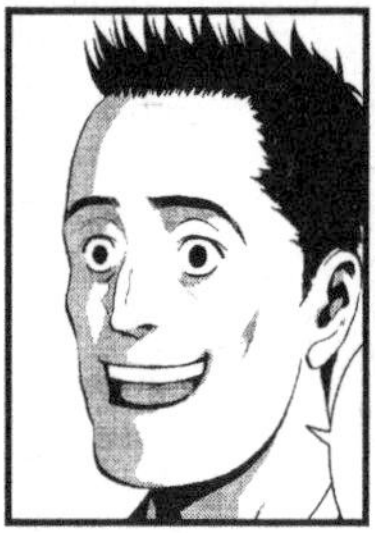

GENDER: Male
AGE: 24
BLOOD TYPE: A
JOB: Programmer
HOME: Tokyo

An employee at Tyrannos Japan and Sakamoto's senpai from college. He's an excellent programmer and works under Takanohashi on the development of "BTOOOM! GAMERS." But he doesn't agree with the inhumane nature of the game and approached Sakamoto with the proposal and strategy to put a stop to the game's development, only for the plan to fall apart.

MATTHEW PERRIER

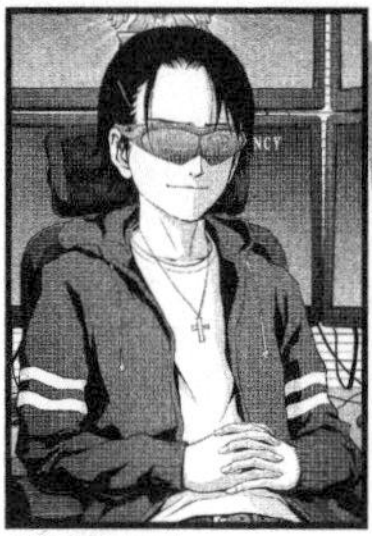

GENDER: Male
AGE: 27
BLOOD TYPE: O
JOB: Ex-NSA programmer, political refugee
HOME: Washington
(location unknown after exile)

A former programmer with the NSA (U.S. National Security Agency), he's a capable hacker and curbed a number of cyber-crimes while with the NSA. But after learning about the government's darker side, he made off with sensitive data about the THEMIS project—in a way, the evidence of their nefarious plans—and defected to another country.

CONTENTS

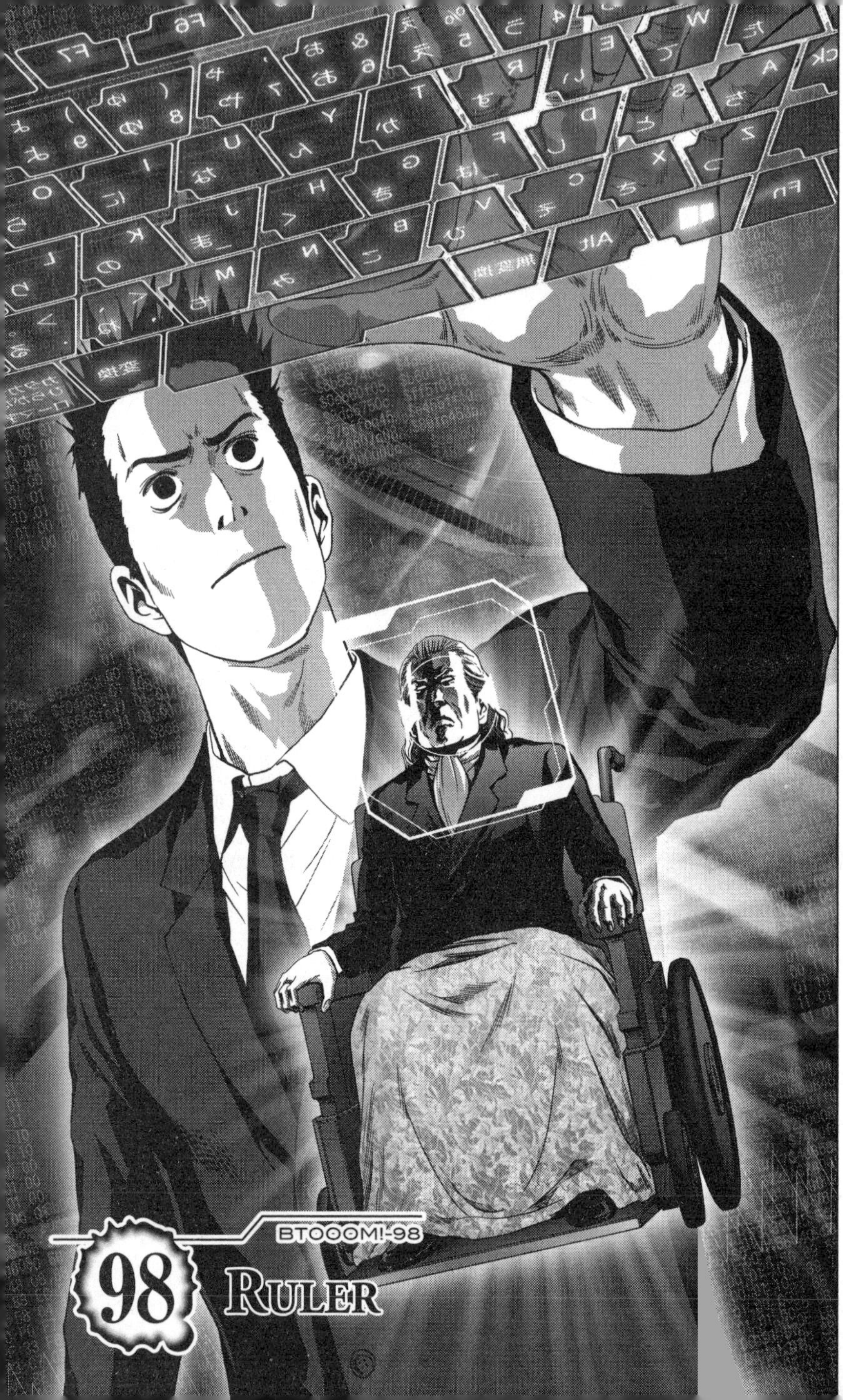
BTOOOM!-98
98
RULER

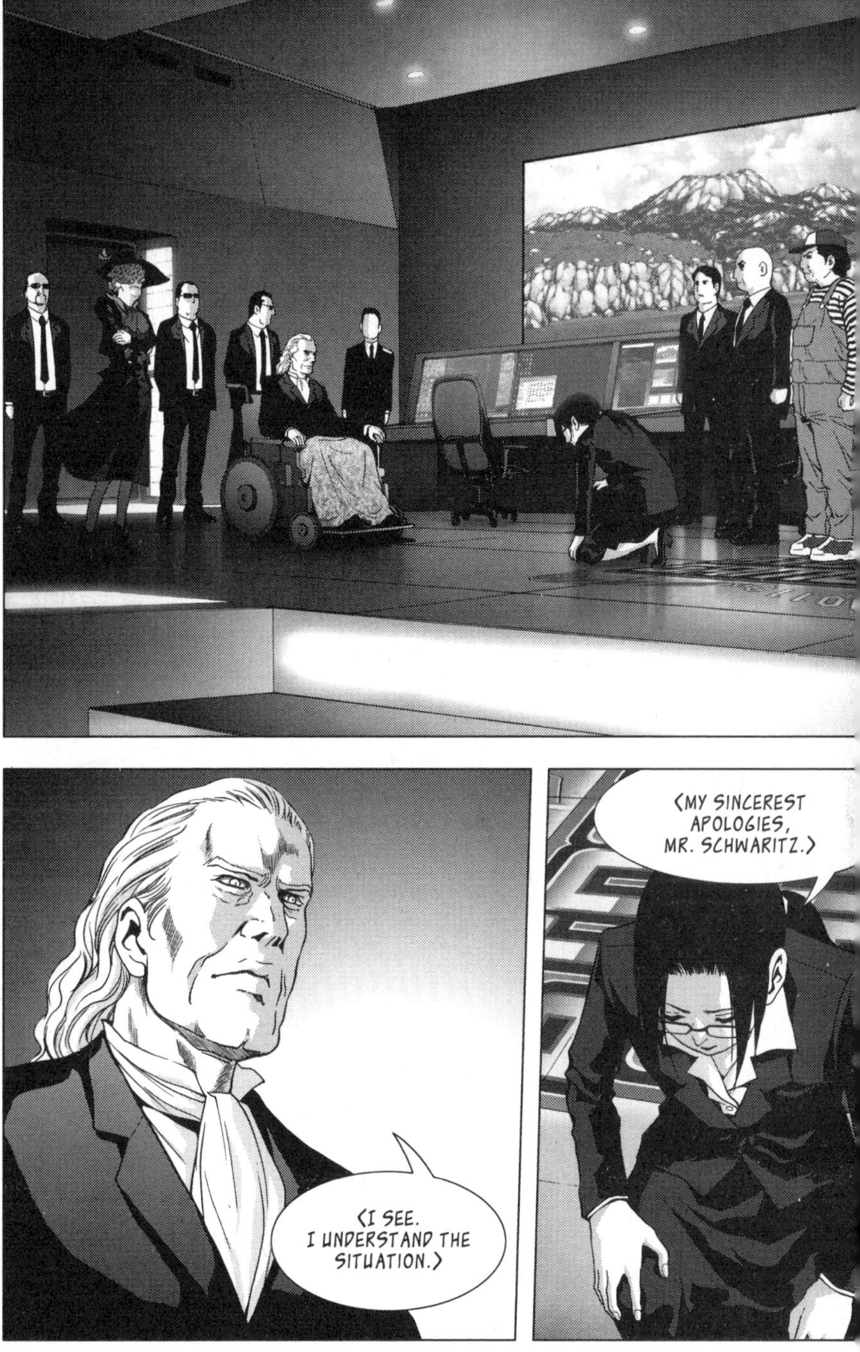
<MY SINCEREST APOLOGIES, MR. SCHWARITZ.>
<I SEE. I UNDERSTAND THE SITUATION.>

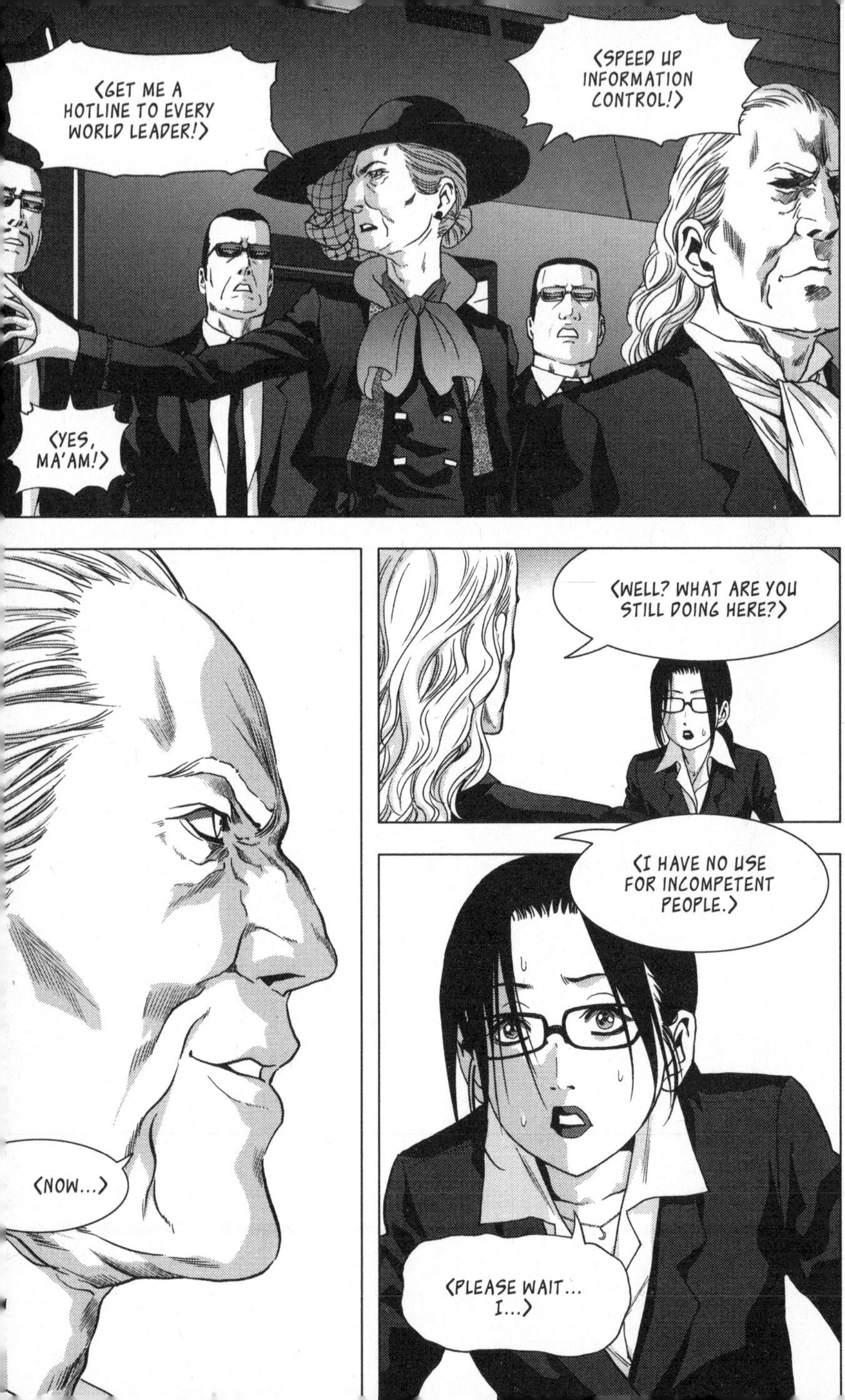
<SPEED UP INFORMATION CONTROL!>
<GET ME A HOTLINE TO EVERY WORLD LEADER!>
<YES, MA'AM!>
<WELL? WHAT ARE YOU STILL DOING HERE?>
<I HAVE NO USE FOR INCOMPETENT PEOPLE.>
<PLEASE WAIT... I...>
<NOW...>

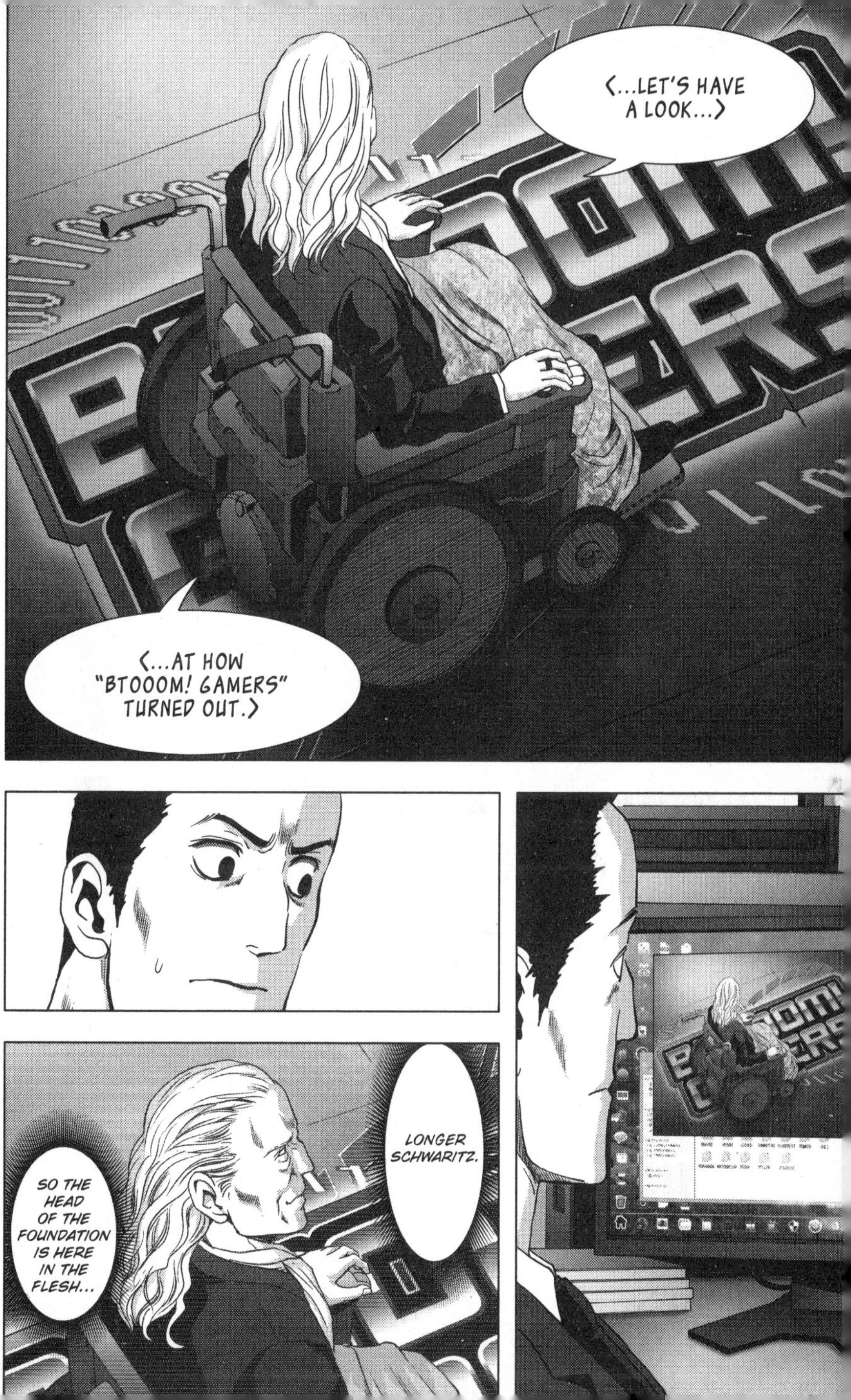
〈...LET'S HAVE A LOOK...〉
〈...AT HOW "BTOOOM! GAMERS" TURNED OUT.〉
LONGER SCHWARITZ.
SO THE HEAD OF THE FOUNDATION IS HERE IN THE FLESH...

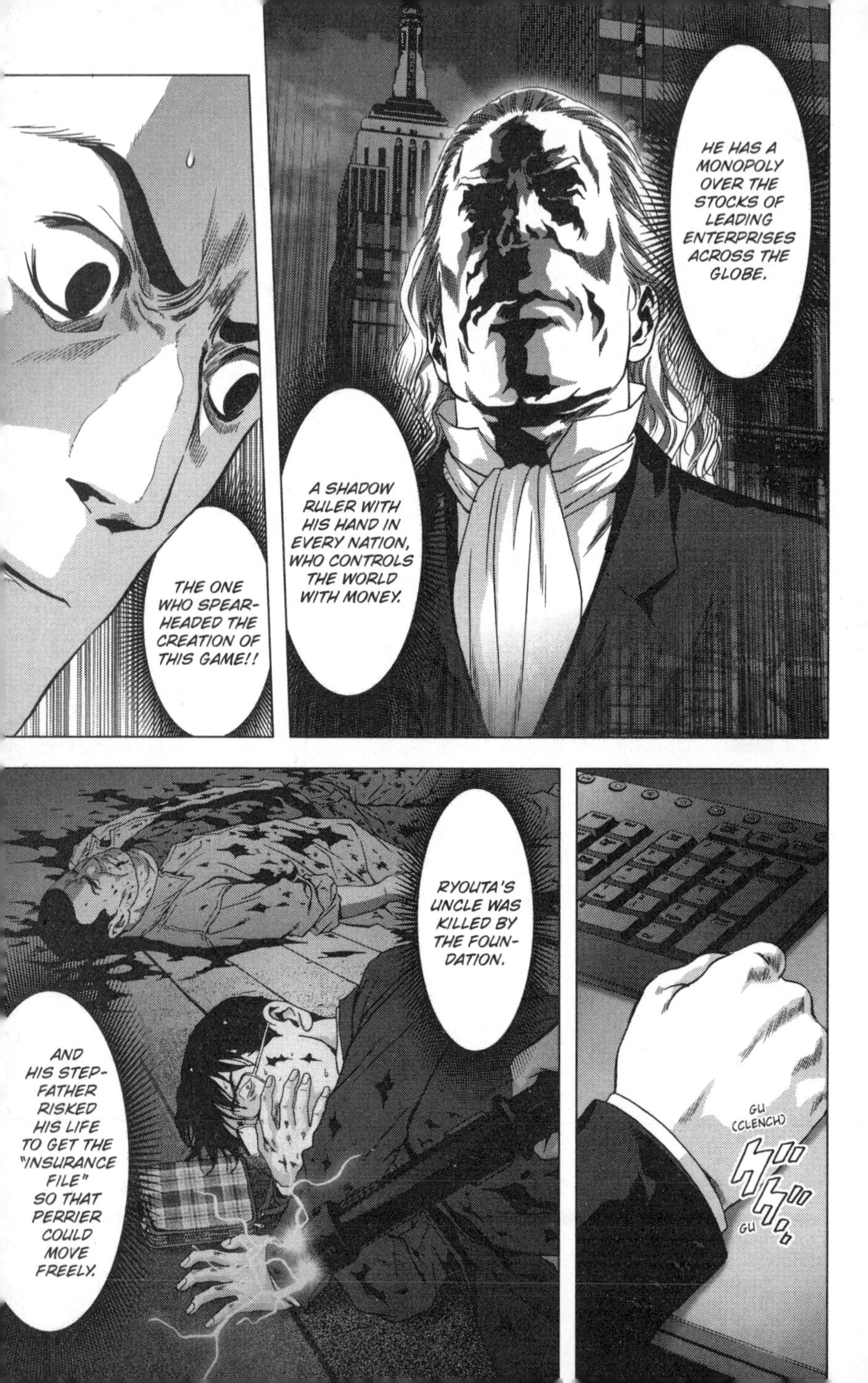
HE HAS A MONOPOLY OVER THE STOCKS OF LEADING ENTERPRISES ACROSS THE GLOBE.
A SHADOW RULER WITH HIS HAND IN EVERY NATION, WHO CONTROLS THE WORLD WITH MONEY.
THE ONE WHO SPEAR-HEADED THE CREATION OF THIS GAME!!
GU (CLENCH)
GU
RYOUTA'S UNCLE WAS KILLED BY THE FOUN-DATION.
AND HIS STEP-FATHER RISKED HIS LIFE TO GET THE "INSURANCE FILE" SO THAT PERRIER COULD MOVE FREELY.

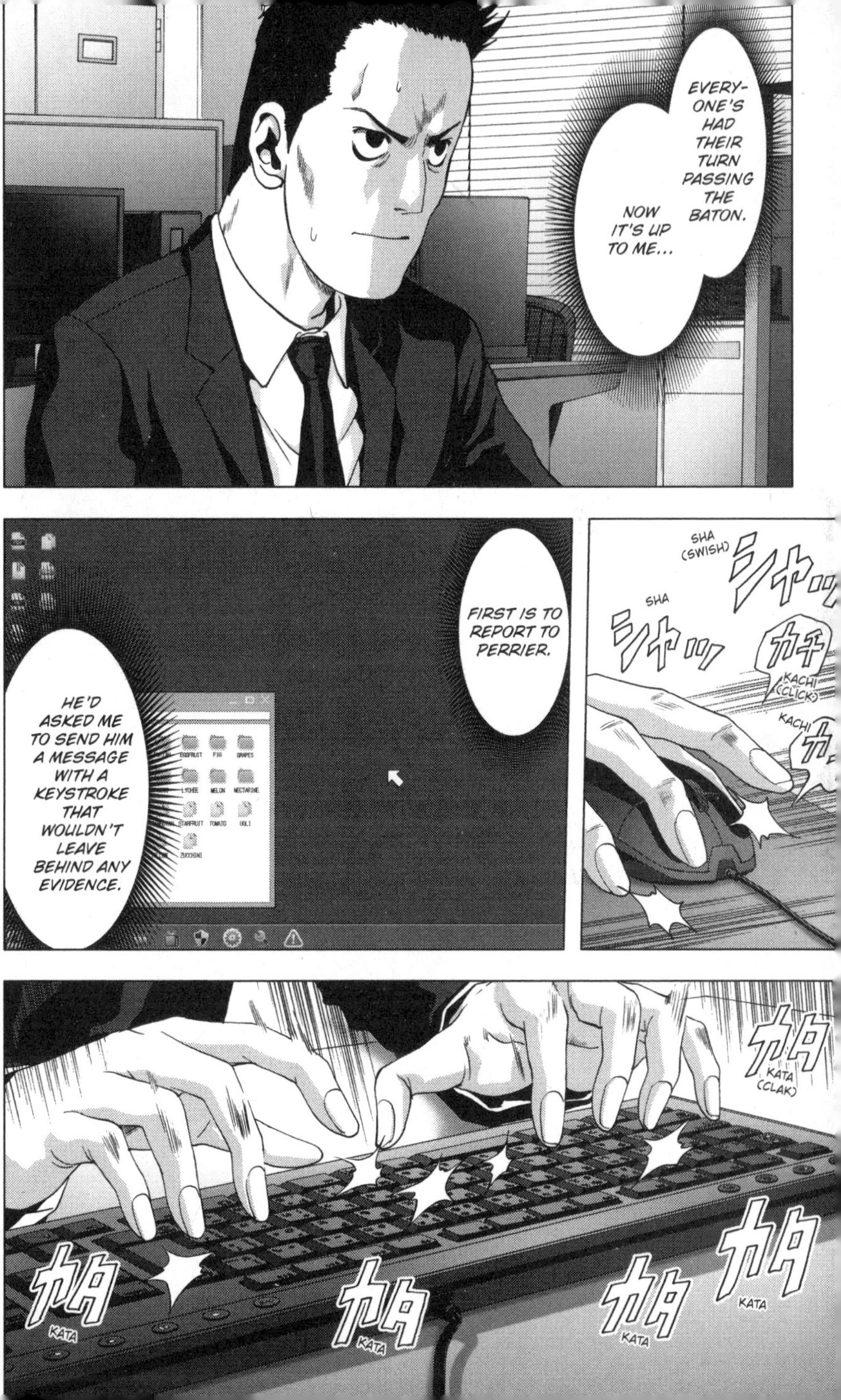
EVERY-ONE'S HAD THEIR TURN PASSING THE BATON.
NOW IT'S UP TO ME...
シャッ
SHA (SWISH)
シャッ
SHA
カチ
KACHI (CLICK)
KACHI
FIRST IS TO REPORT TO PERRIER.
EGGFRUIT
FIG
GRAPES
LYCHEE
MELON
NECTARINE
STARFRUIT
TOMATO
UGLI
ZUCCHINI
HE'D ASKED ME TO SEND HIM A MESSAGE WITH A KEYSTROKE THAT WOULDN'T LEAVE BEHIND ANY EVIDENCE.
カタ
KATA (CLAK)
カタ
KATA
カタ
KATA
カタ
KATA
カタ
KATA

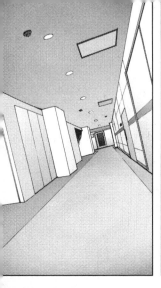
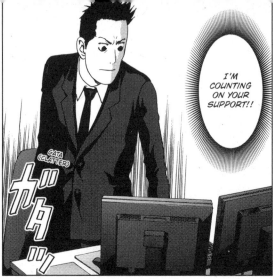

I'M COUNTING ON YOUR SUPPORT!!

GATA
(CLATTER)
ガタッ

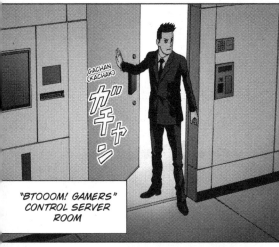

GACHAN
(KACHAK)
ガチャン

"BTOOOM! GAMERS" CONTROL SERVER ROOM

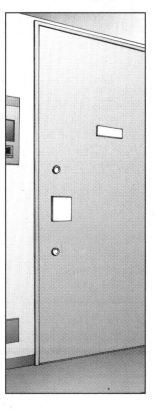

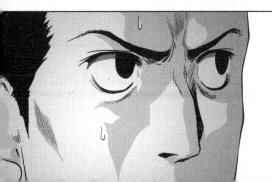

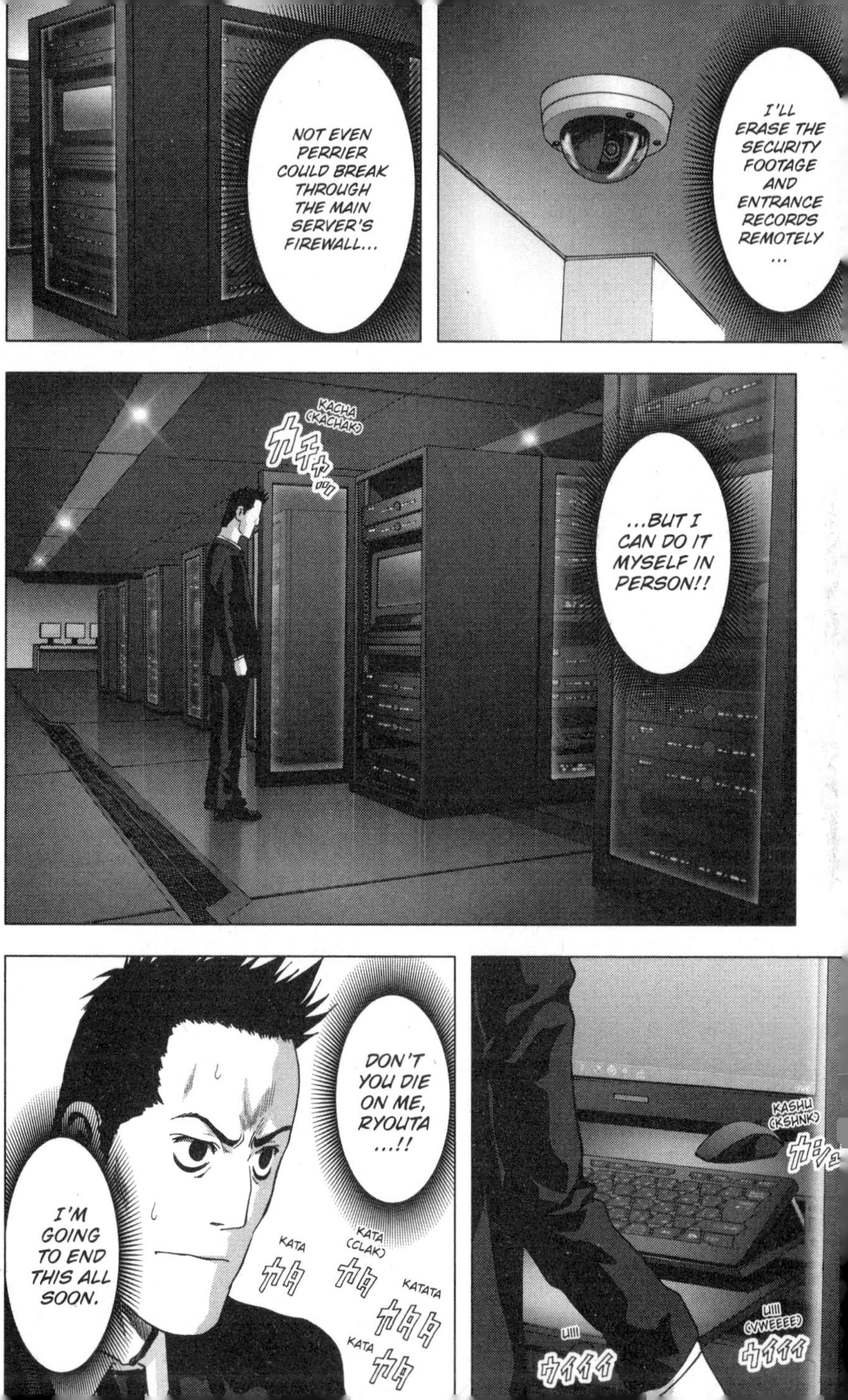
I'LL ERASE THE SECURITY FOOTAGE AND ENTRANCE RECORDS REMOTELY ...
NOT EVEN PERRIER COULD BREAK THROUGH THE MAIN SERVER'S FIREWALL...
...BUT I CAN DO IT MYSELF IN PERSON!!
KACHA (KACHAK)
KASHU (KSHNK)
UIII (VWEEEE)
UIII
DON'T YOU DIE ON ME, RYOUTA ...!!
I'M GOING TO END THIS ALL SOON.
KATA (CLAK)
KATA
KATATA
KATA

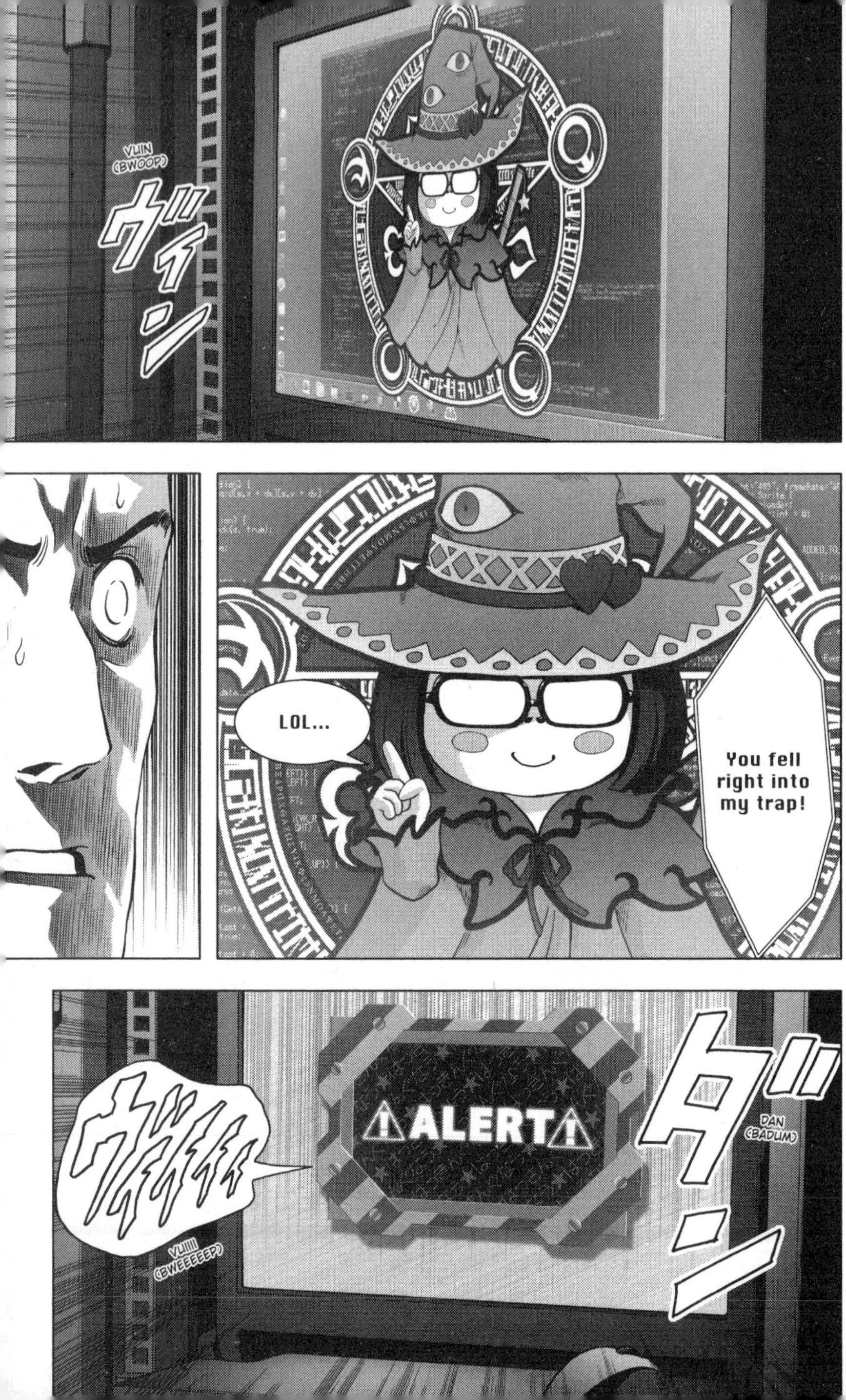
ヴィン
VUIN (BWOOP)
You fell right into my trap!
LOL...
ALERT
ダン
DAN (BADUM)
ヴィィィィ
VUIIII (BWEEEEEP)

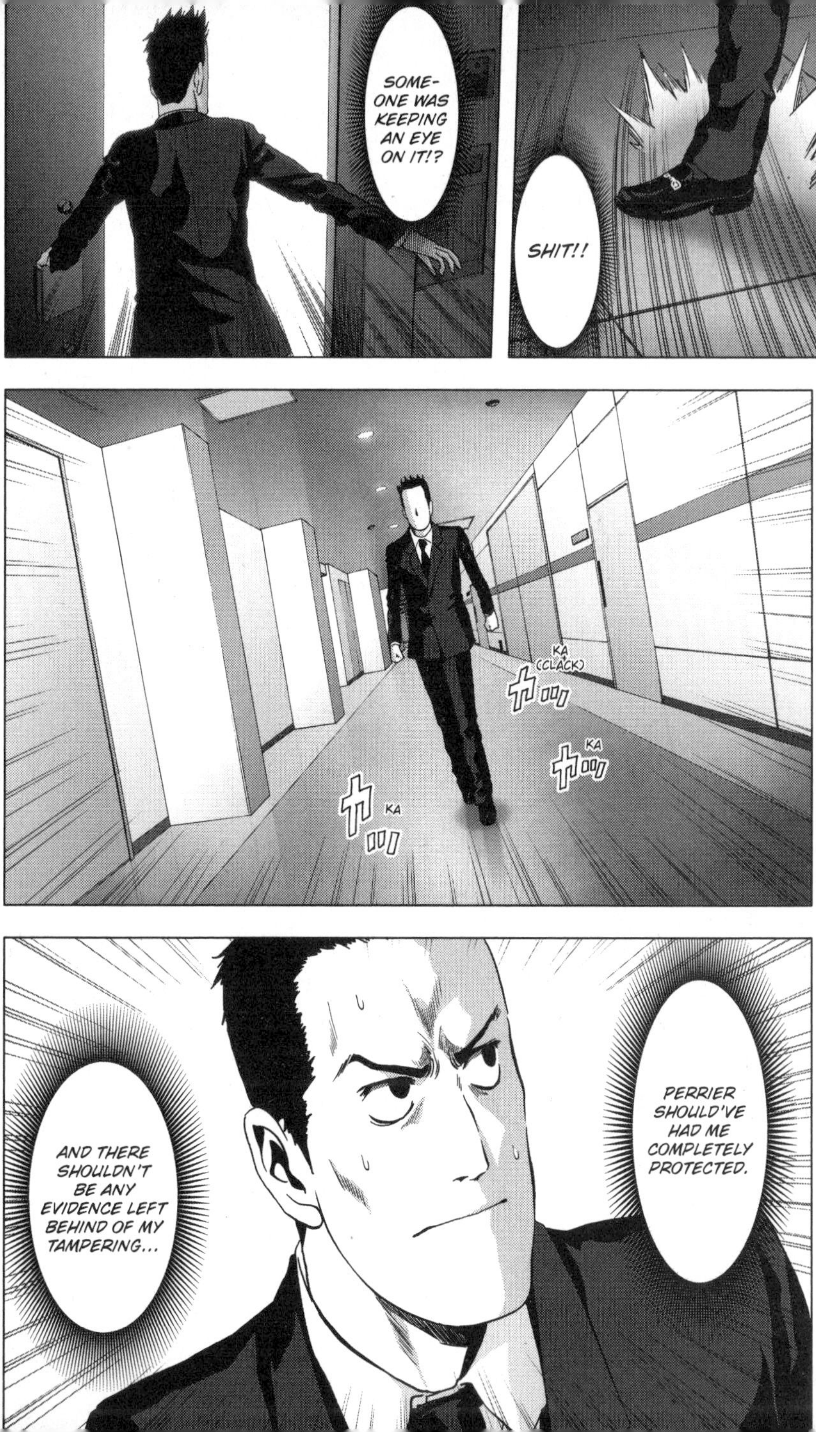
SHIT!!
SOME-ONE WAS KEEPING AN EYE ON IT!?
KA (CLACK)
カッ
KA
カッ
カッ
KA
PERRIER SHOULD'VE HAD ME COMPLETELY PROTECTED.
AND THERE SHOULDN'T BE ANY EVIDENCE LEFT BEHIND OF MY TAMPERING...

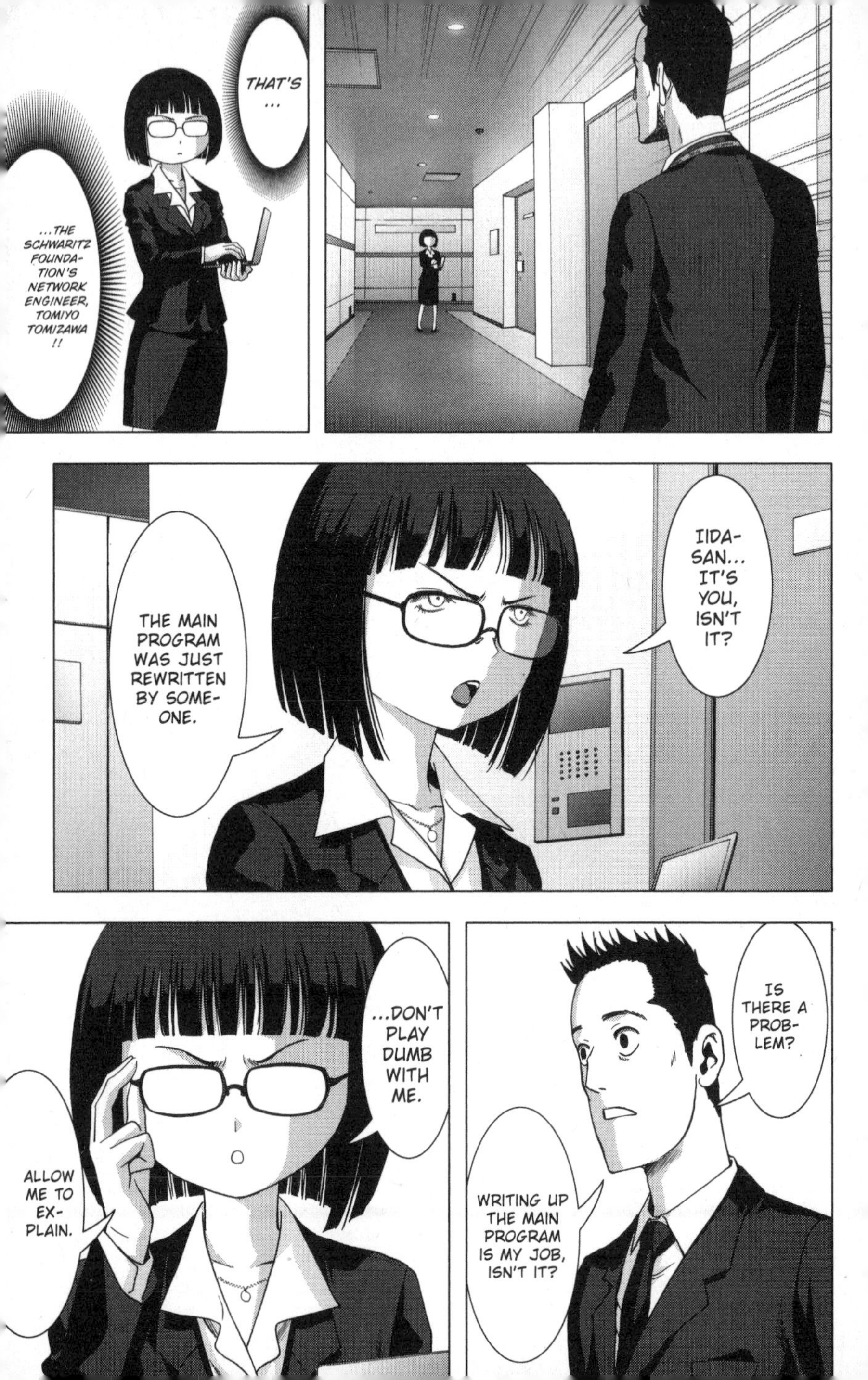
THAT'S ...
...THE SCHWARITZ FOUNDATION'S NETWORK ENGINEER, TOMIYO TOMIZAWA !!
IIDA-SAN... IT'S YOU, ISN'T IT?
THE MAIN PROGRAM WAS JUST REWRITTEN BY SOMEONE.
IS THERE A PROBLEM?
WRITING UP THE MAIN PROGRAM IS MY JOB, ISN'T IT?
...DON'T PLAY DUMB WITH ME.
ALLOW ME TO EXPLAIN.

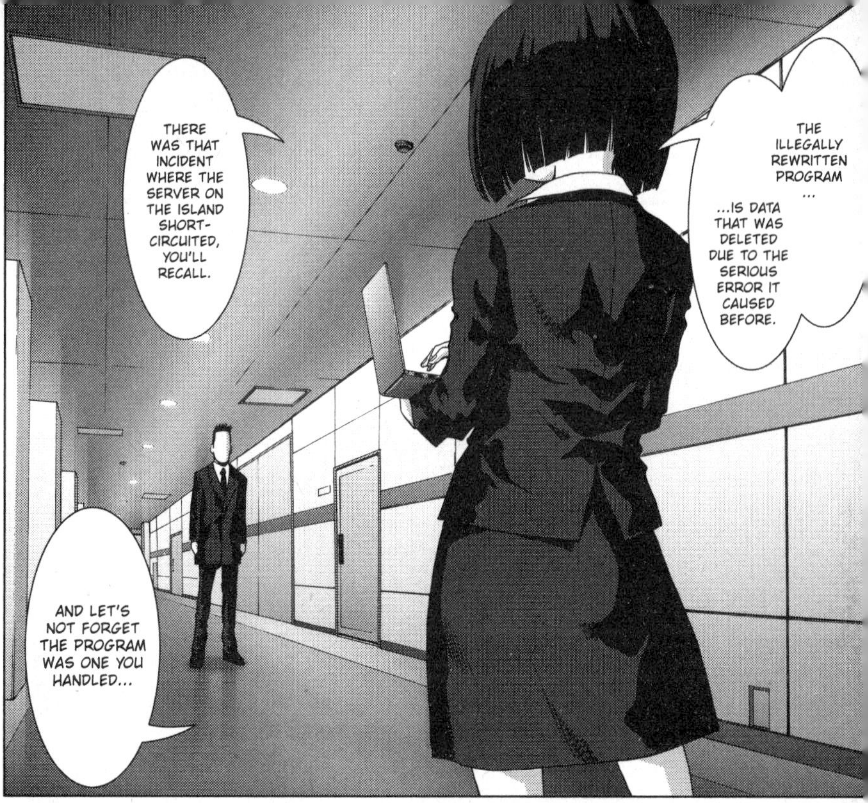
THE ILLEGALLY REWRITTEN PROGRAM ...
...IS DATA THAT WAS DELETED DUE TO THE SERIOUS ERROR IT CAUSED BEFORE.
THERE WAS THAT INCIDENT WHERE THE SERVER ON THE ISLAND SHORT-CIRCUITED, YOU'LL RECALL.
AND LET'S NOT FORGET THE PROGRAM WAS ONE YOU HANDLED...

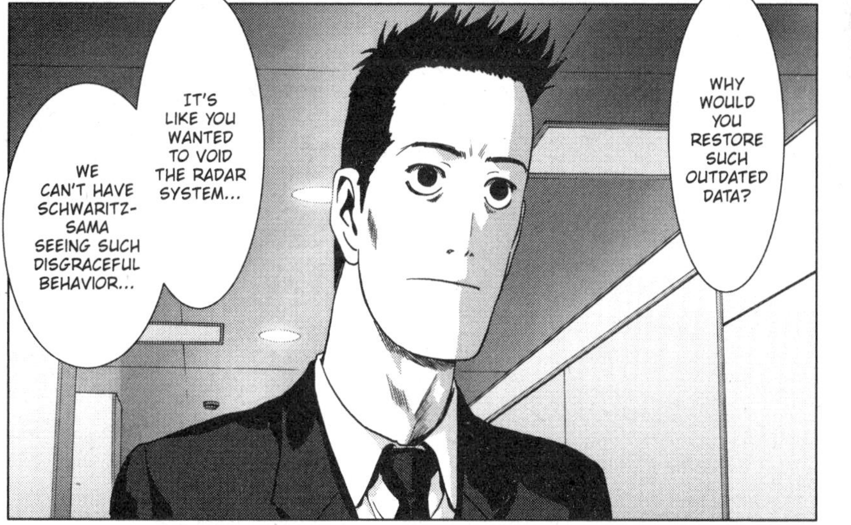
WHY WOULD YOU RESTORE SUCH OUTDATED DATA?
IT'S LIKE YOU WANTED TO VOID THE RADAR SYSTEM...
WE CAN'T HAVE SCHWARITZ-SAMA SEEING SUCH DISGRACEFUL BEHAVIOR...

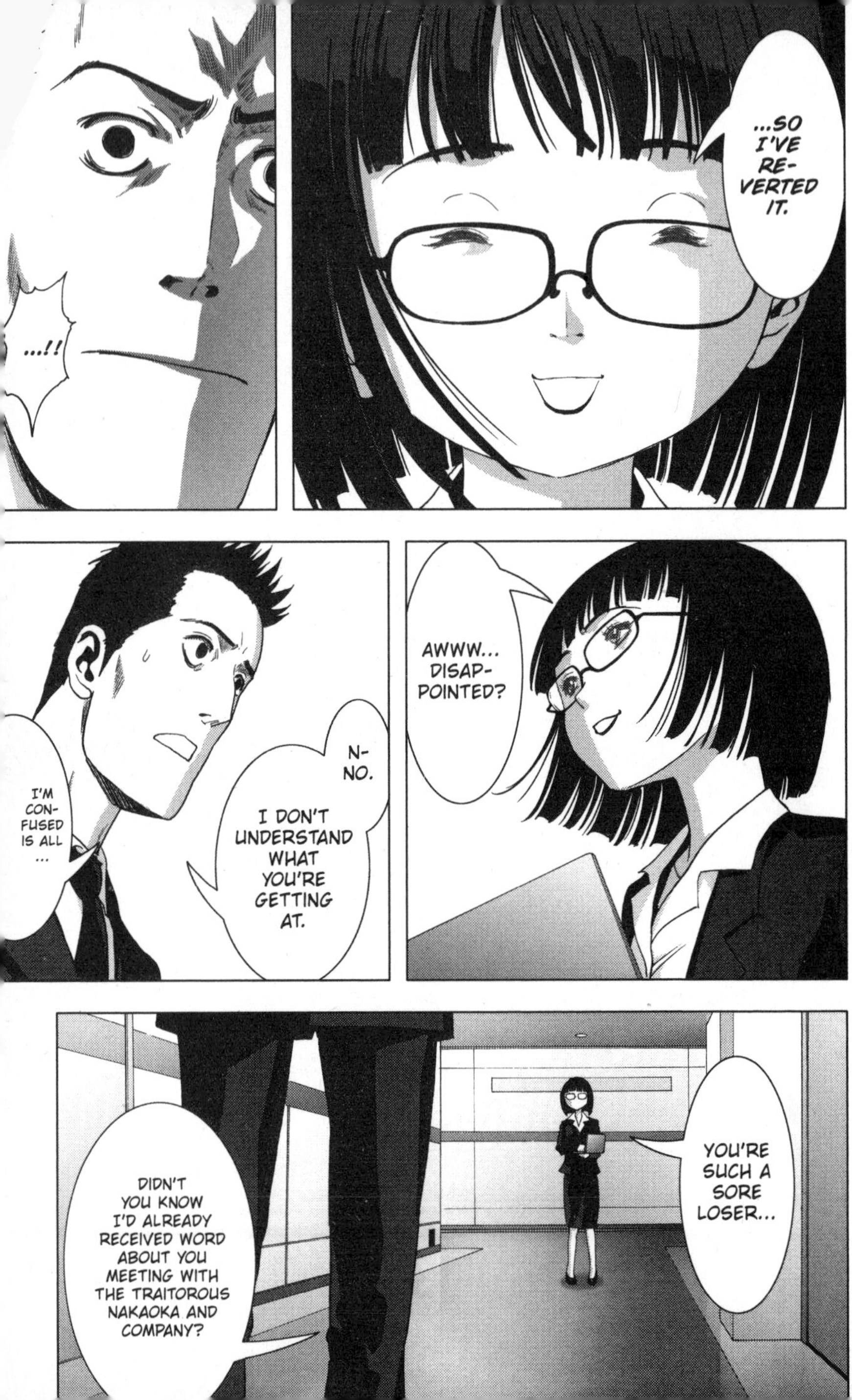
...SO I'VE RE-VERTED IT.
...!!
AWWW... DISAP-POINTED?
N-NO.
I DON'T UNDERSTAND WHAT YOU'RE GETTING AT.
I'M CON-FUSED IS ALL ...
YOU'RE SUCH A SORE LOSER...
DIDN'T YOU KNOW I'D ALREADY RECEIVED WORD ABOUT YOU MEETING WITH THE TRAITOROUS NAKAOKA AND COMPANY?

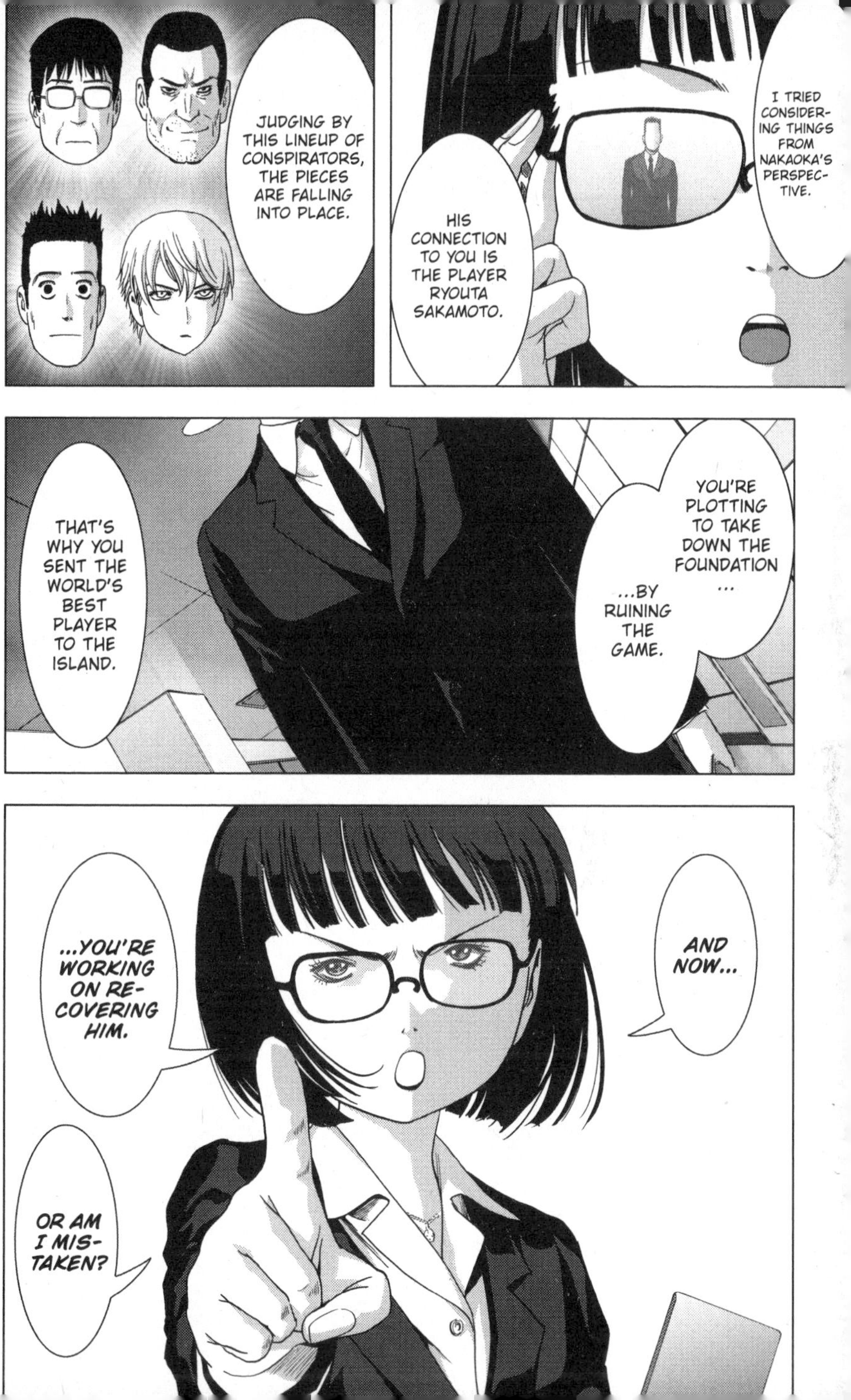
I TRIED CONSIDERING THINGS FROM NAKAOKA'S PERSPECTIVE.
HIS CONNECTION TO YOU IS THE PLAYER RYOUTA SAKAMOTO.
JUDGING BY THIS LINEUP OF CONSPIRATORS, THE PIECES ARE FALLING INTO PLACE.
YOU'RE PLOTTING TO TAKE DOWN THE FOUNDATION ...
...BY RUINING THE GAME.
THAT'S WHY YOU SENT THE WORLD'S BEST PLAYER TO THE ISLAND.
AND NOW...
...YOU'RE WORKING ON RECOVERING HIM.
OR AM I MISTAKEN?

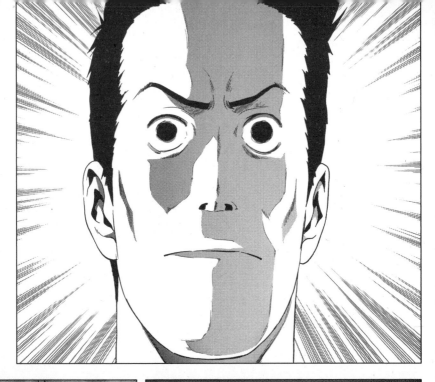

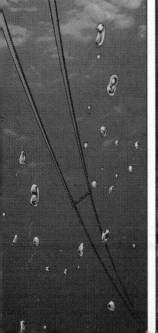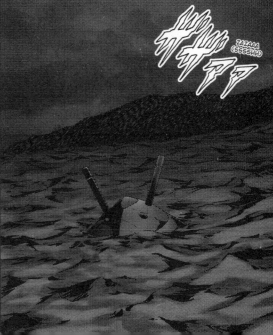

ZAZAAA
(SSSSHH)

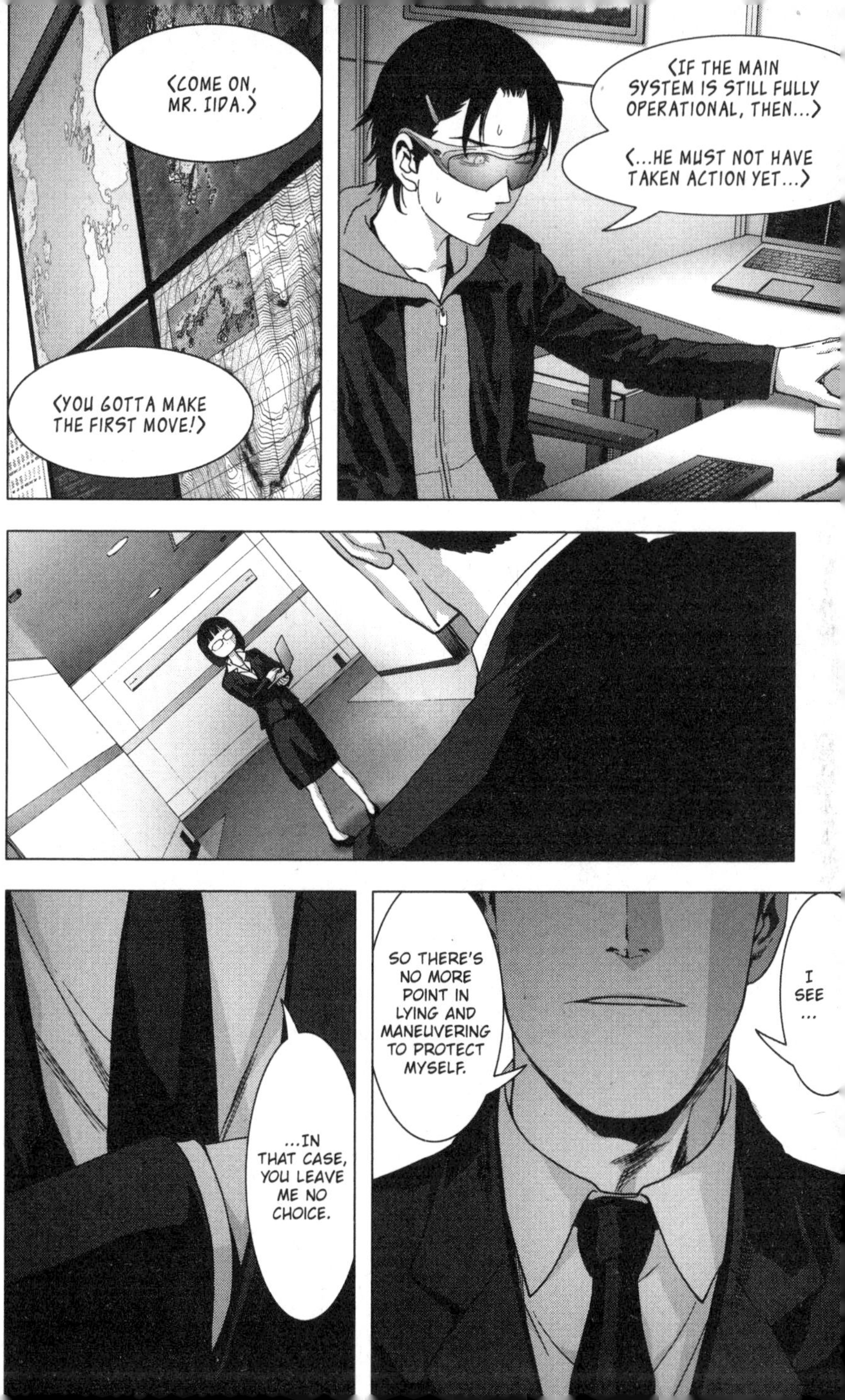
<IF THE MAIN SYSTEM IS STILL FULLY OPERATIONAL, THEN...>
<...HE MUST NOT HAVE TAKEN ACTION YET...>
<COME ON, MR. IIDA.>
<YOU GOTTA MAKE THE FIRST MOVE!>
I SEE...
SO THERE'S NO MORE POINT IN LYING AND MANEUVERING TO PROTECT MYSELF.
...IN THAT CASE, YOU LEAVE ME NO CHOICE.

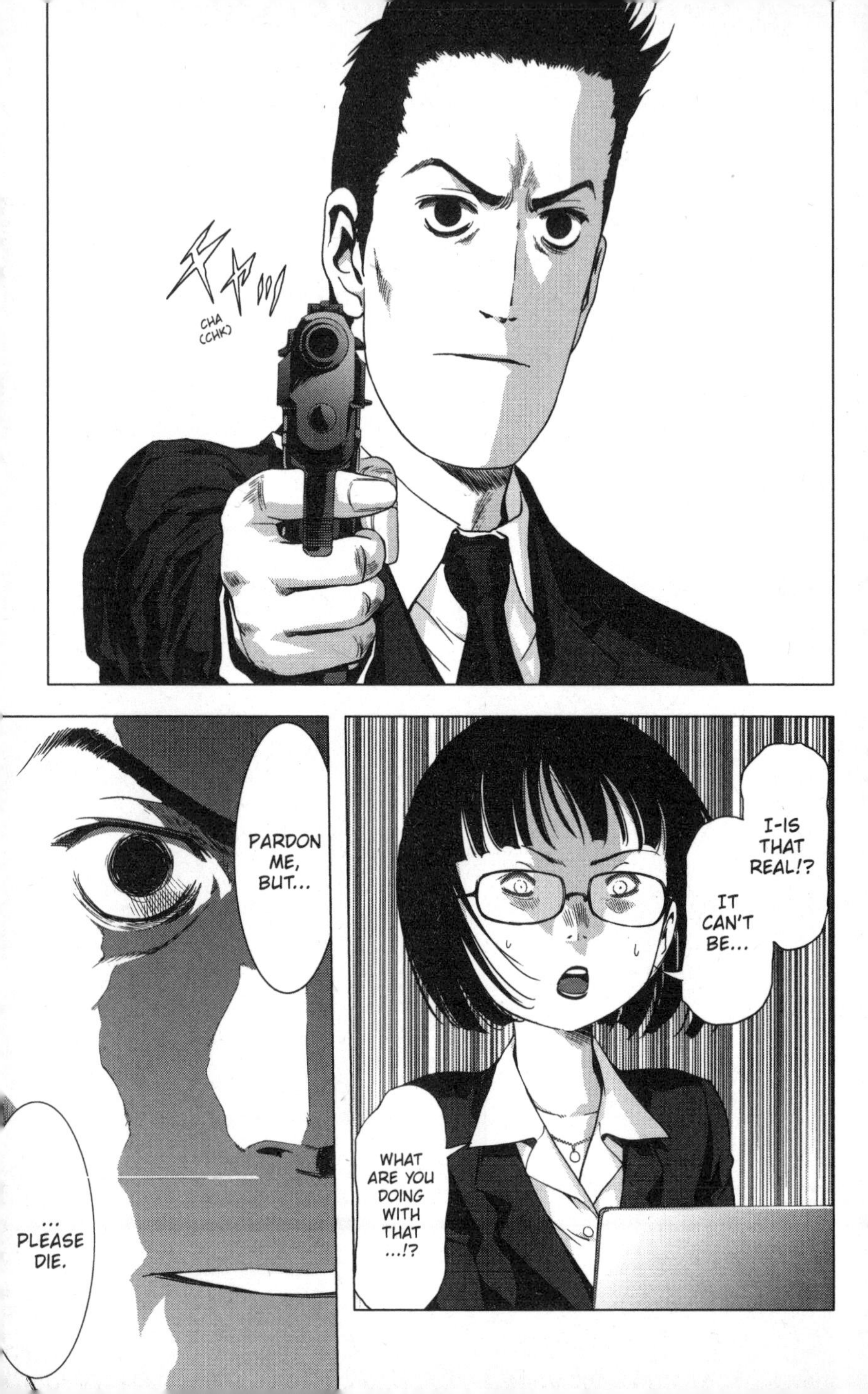
CHA
(CHK)
I-IS THAT REAL!?
IT CAN'T BE...
WHAT ARE YOU DOING WITH THAT ...!?
PARDON ME, BUT...
... PLEASE DIE.

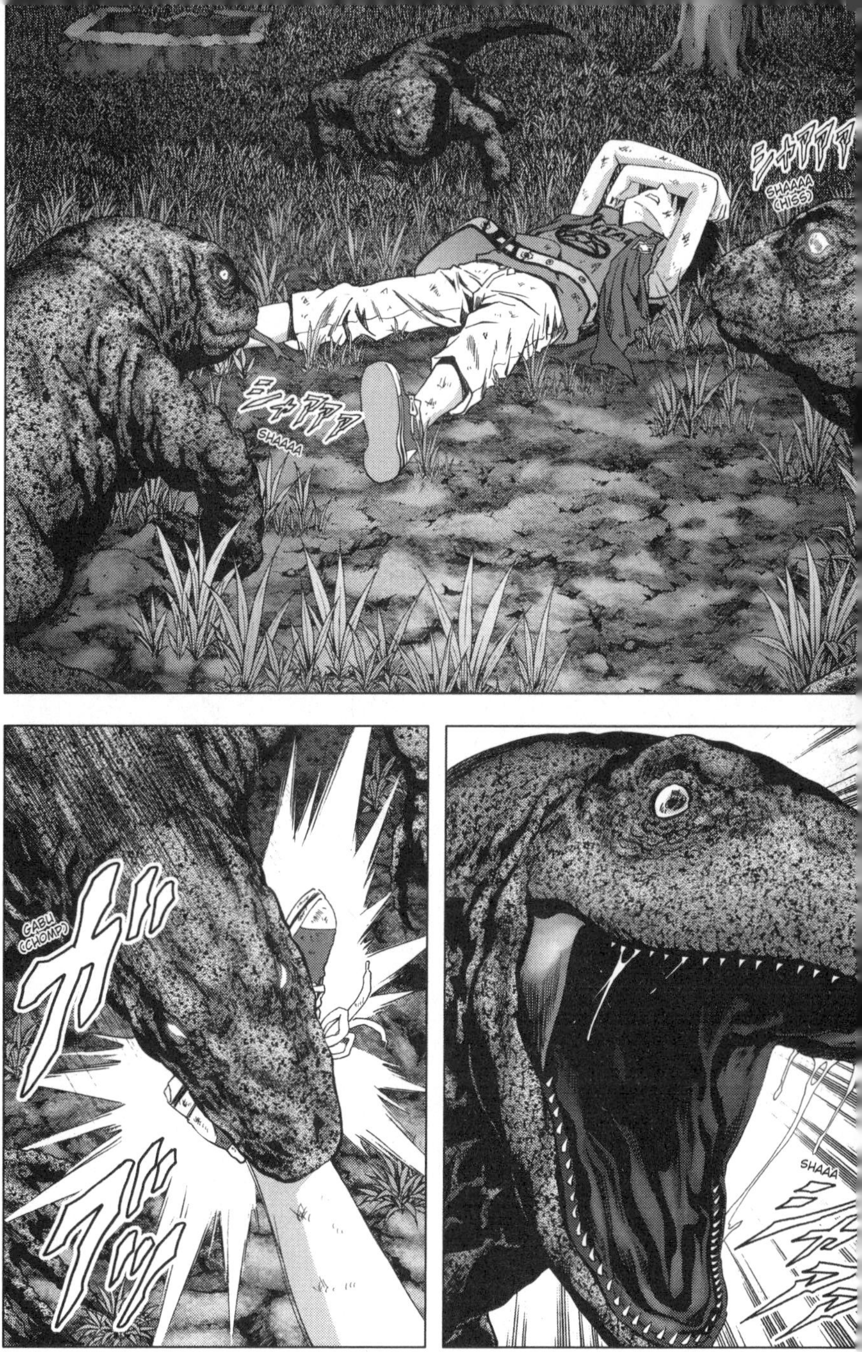
シャアアア
SHAAAA (HISS)
シャアアア
SHAAAA
SHAAA
GABU (CHOMP)

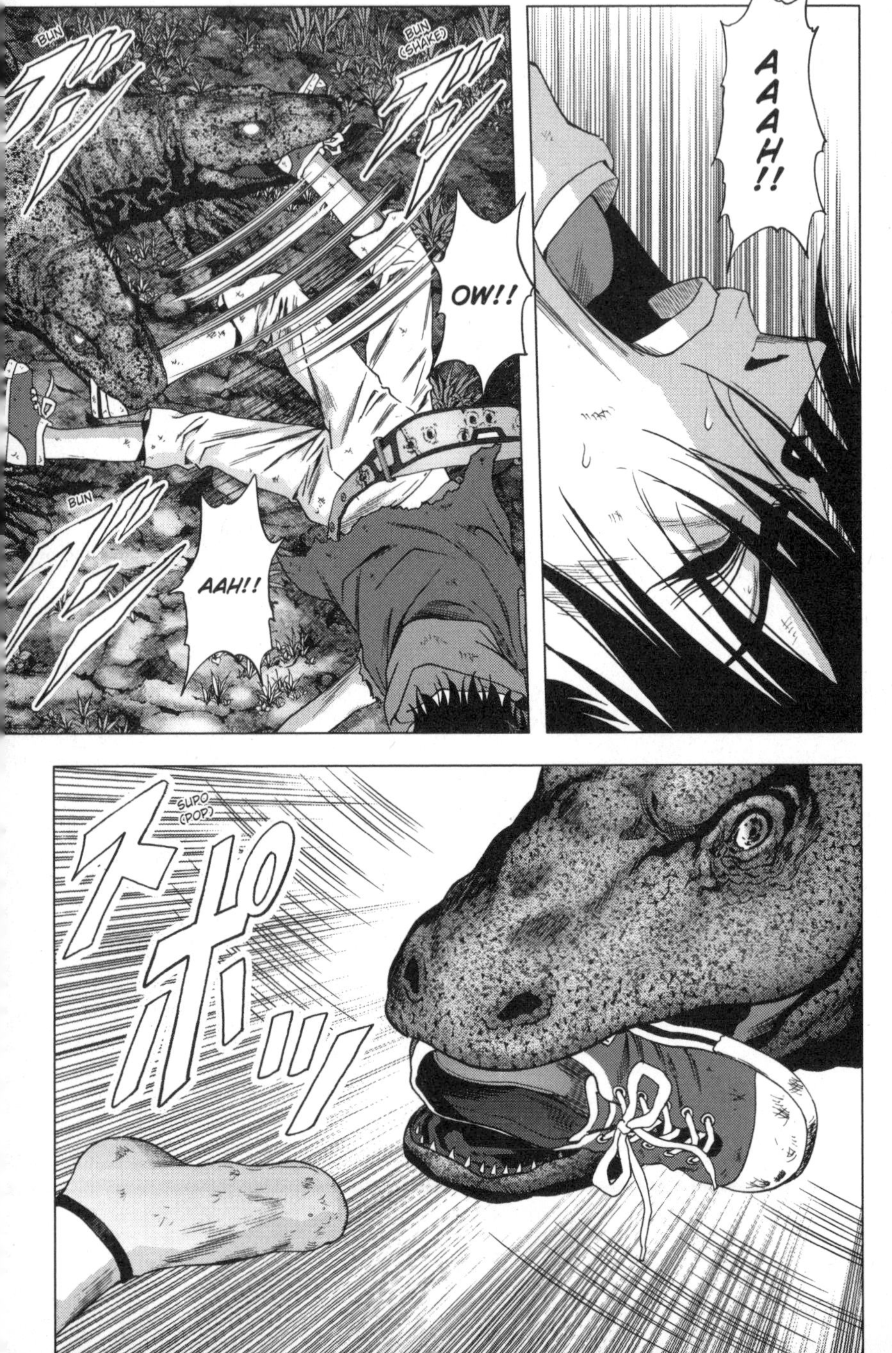
AAAAH!!
BUN (SHAKE)
BUN
OW!!
BUN
AAH!!
SUPO (POP)

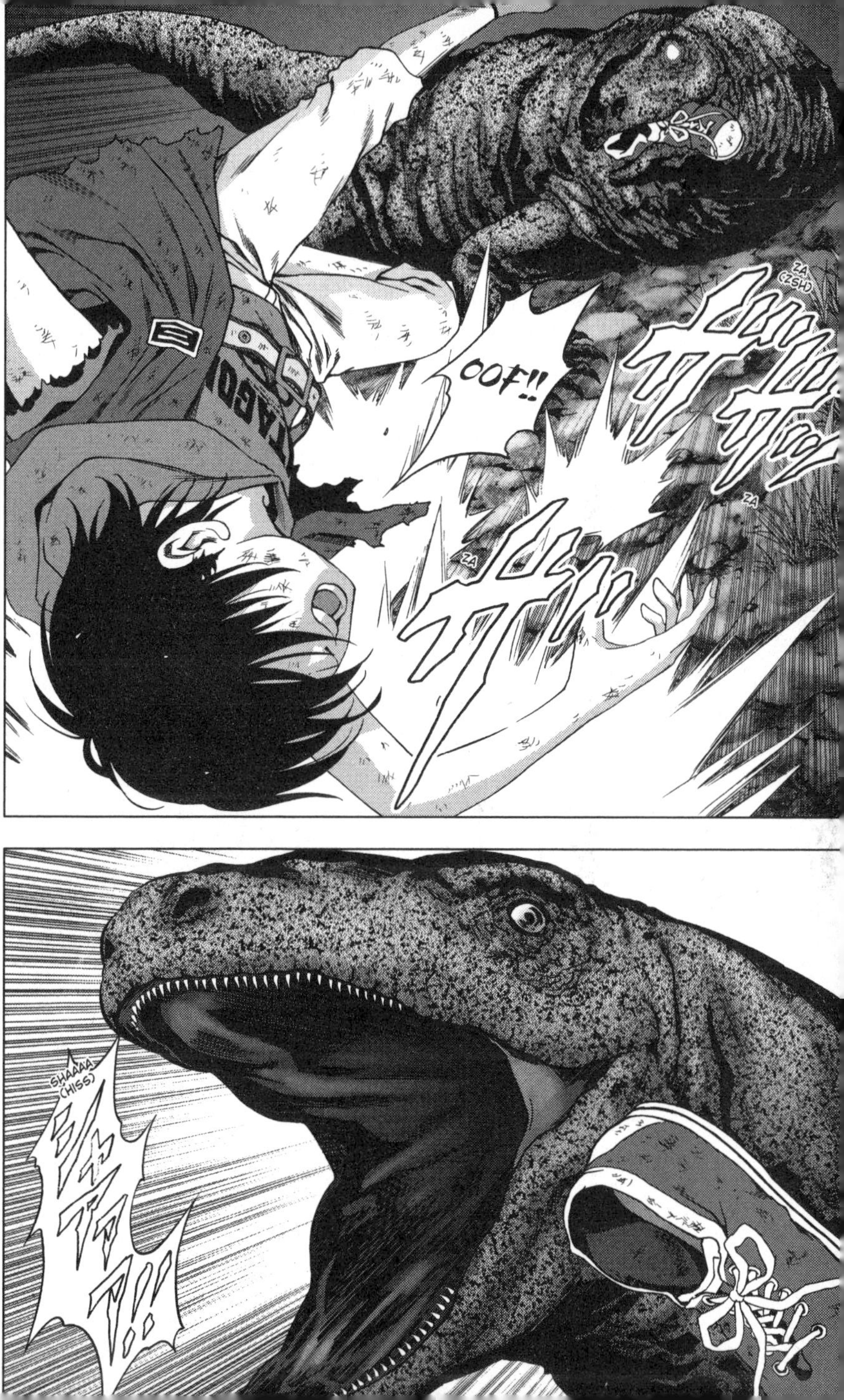
ZA (ZSH)
OOF!!
ZA
ZA
SHAAAA (HISS)

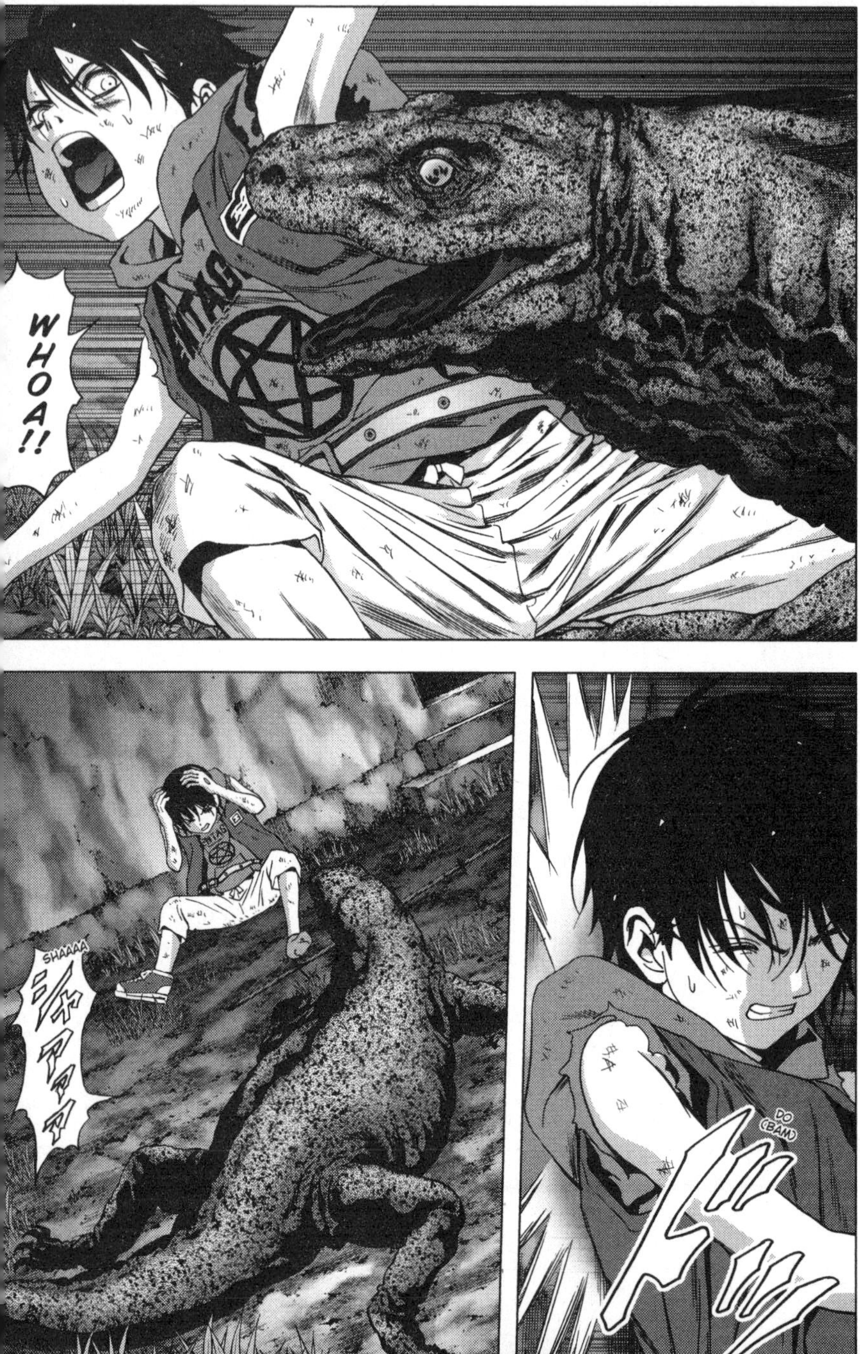
WHOA!!
DO
(BAM)
SHAAAA

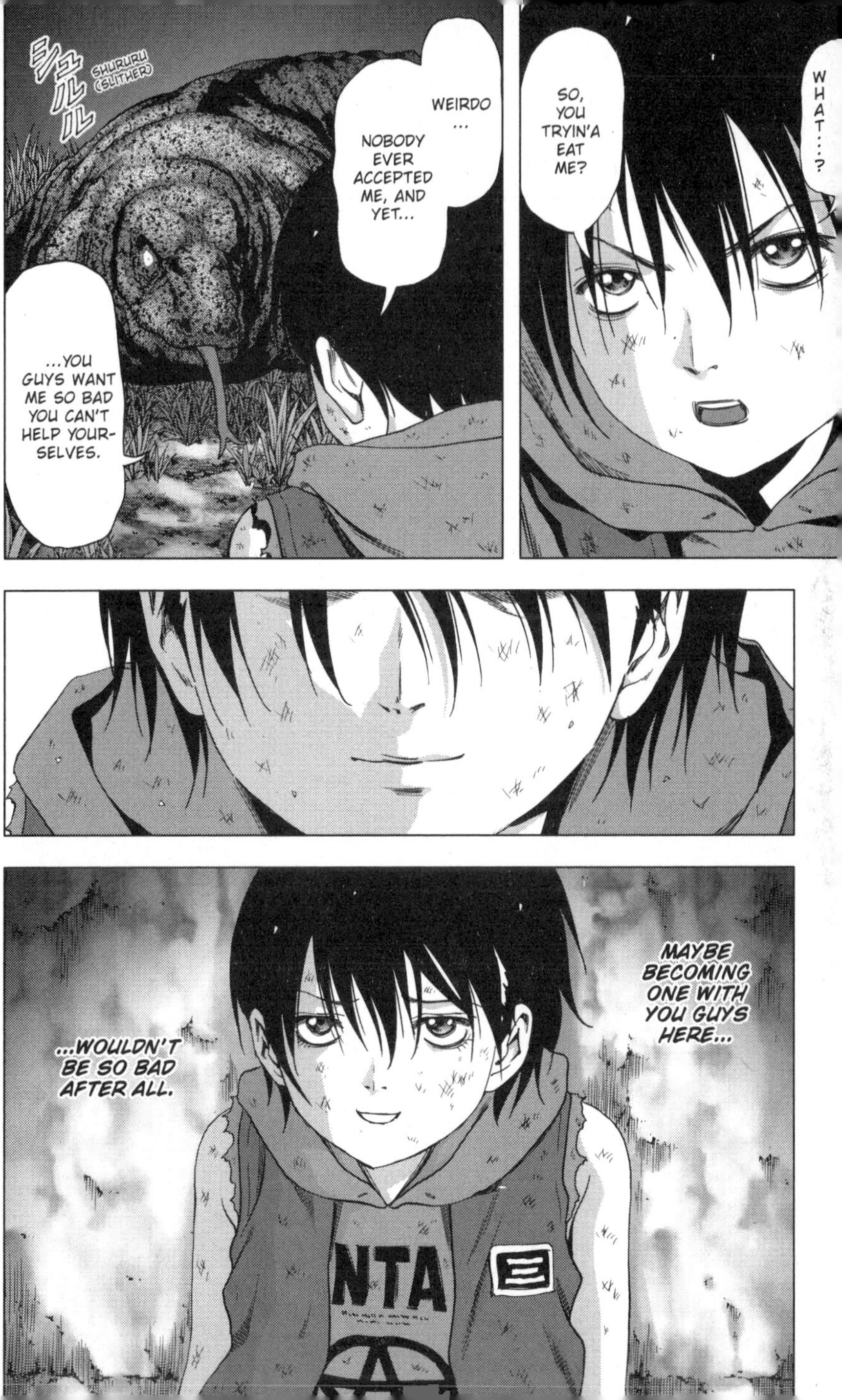
WHAT...?
SO, YOU TRYIN'A EAT ME?
シュルルル
SHURURU (SLITHER)
WEIRDO...
NOBODY EVER ACCEPTED ME, AND YET...
...YOU GUYS WANT ME SO BAD YOU CAN'T HELP YOUR-SELVES.
MAYBE BECOMING ONE WITH YOU GUYS HERE...
...WOULDN'T BE SO BAD AFTER ALL.
NTA

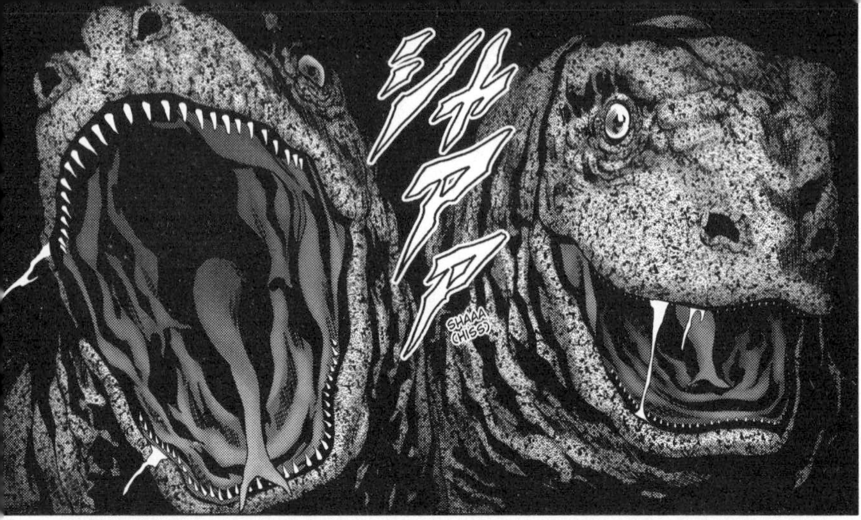
シャアア
SHAAA (HISS)

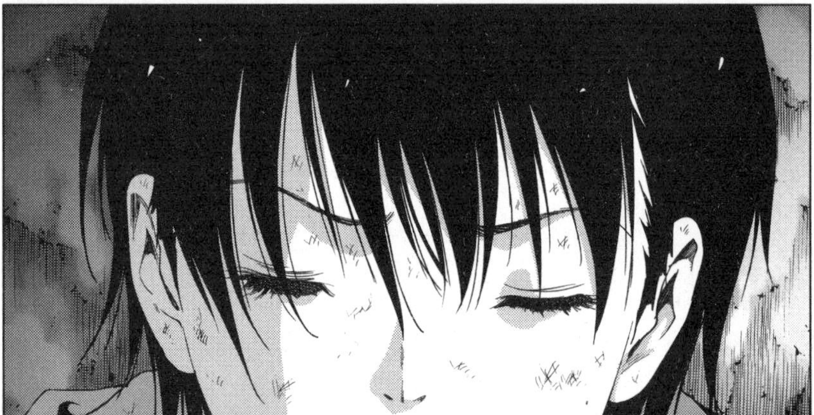

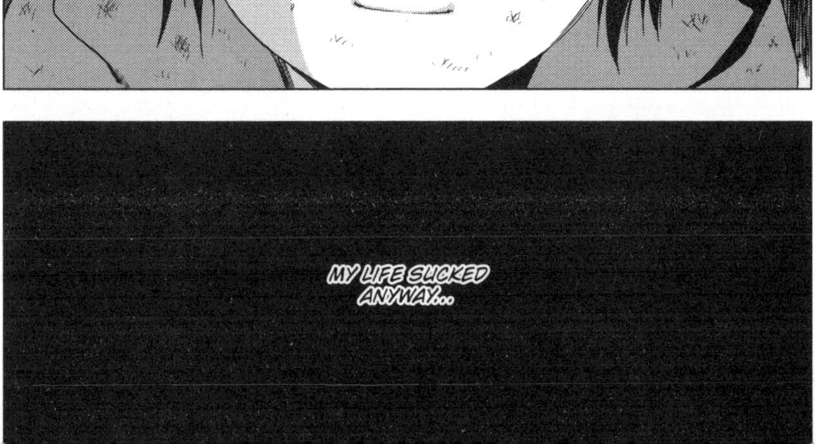
MY LIFE SUCKED ANYWAY...

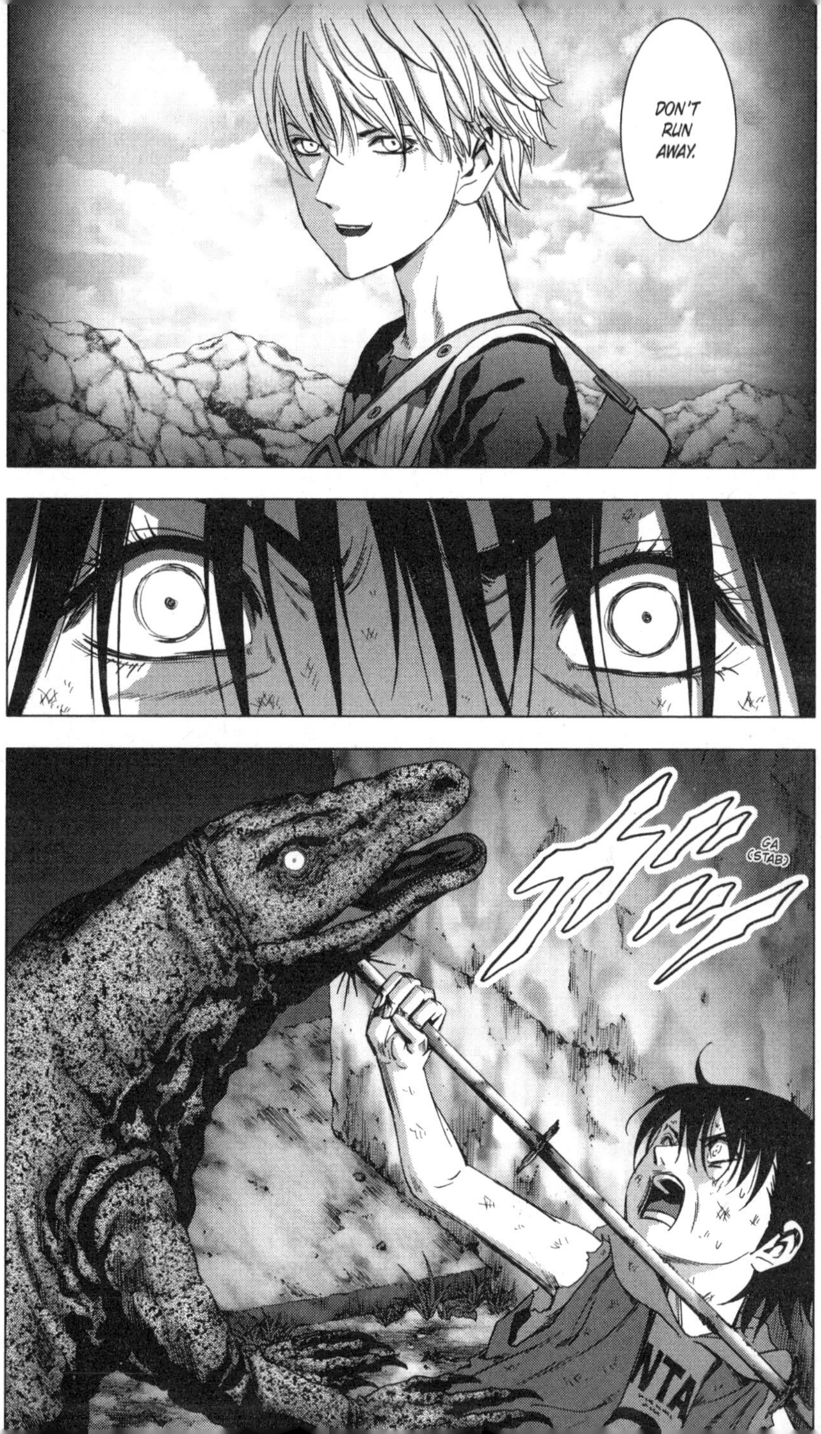
DON'T RUN AWAY.
GA (STAB)
NTA

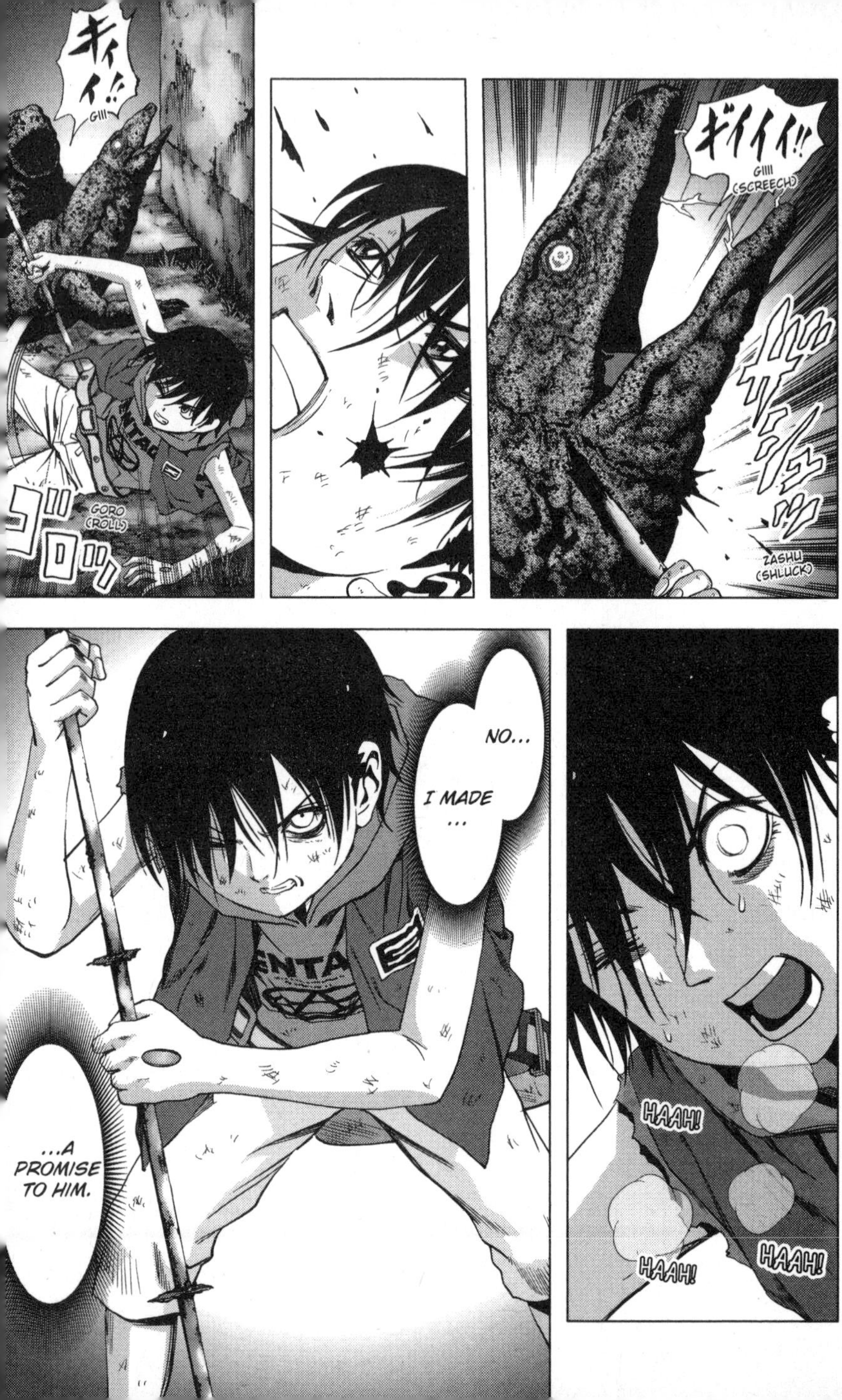
ギイイイ!!
GIII (SCREECH)
ZASHU (SHLUCK)
キィイ!!
GIII
GORO (ROLL)
HAAH!
HAAH!
HAAH!
NO...
I MADE ...
...A PROMISE TO HIM.

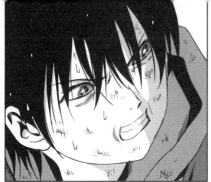

OW!!

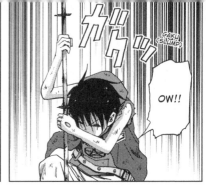

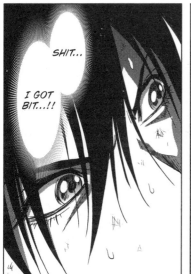

SHIT...

I GOT BIT...!!

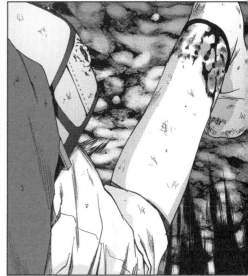

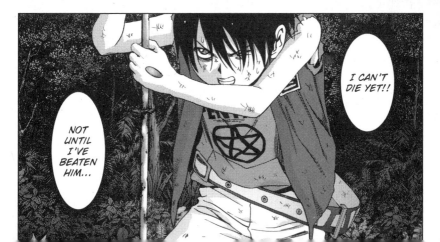

I CAN'T DIE YET!!

NOT UNTIL I'VE BEATEN HIM...

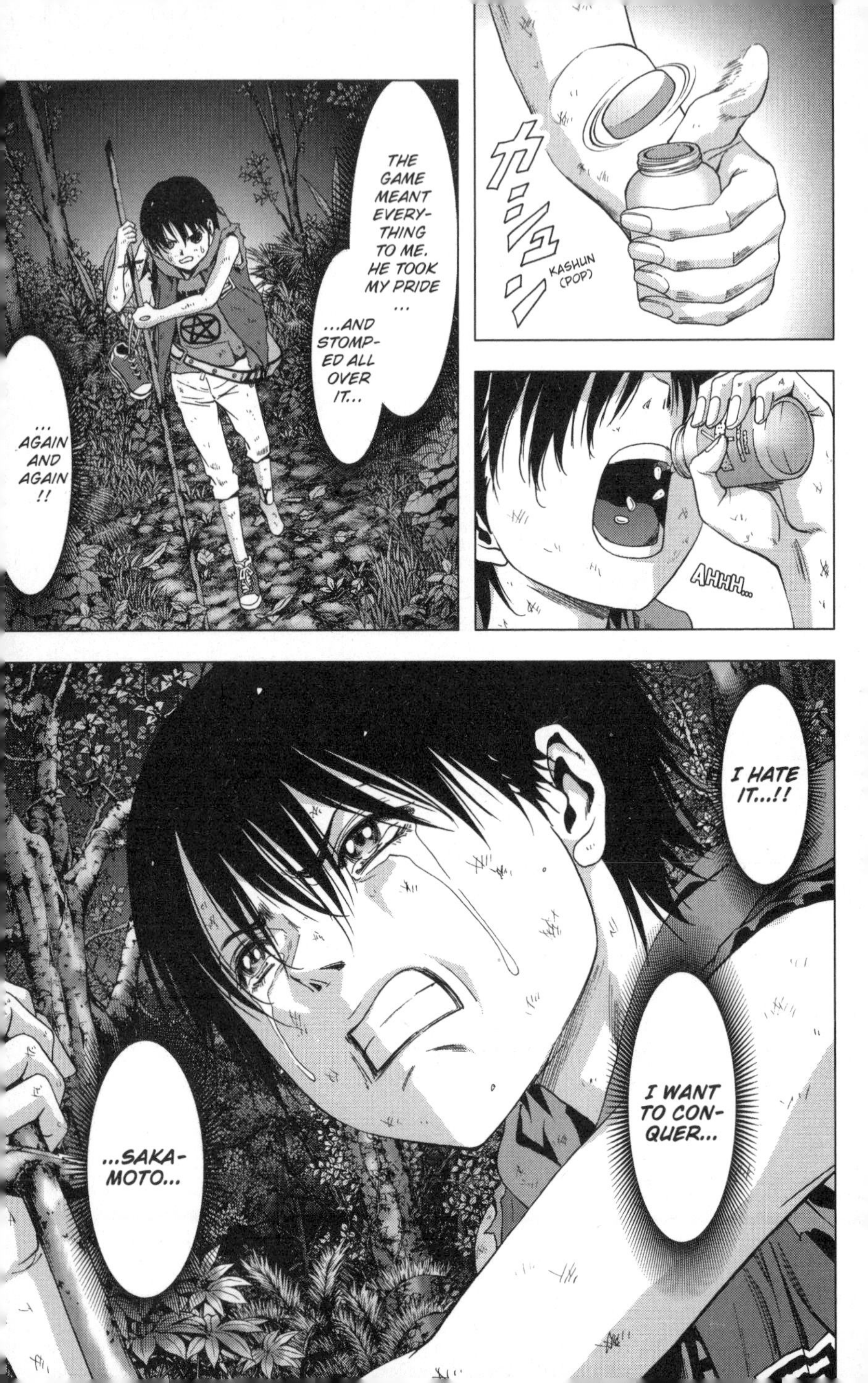
カシュン
KASHUN (POP)
AHHH...
THE GAME MEANT EVERY-THING TO ME. HE TOOK MY PRIDE ...
...AND STOMP-ED ALL OVER IT...
... AGAIN AND AGAIN !!
I HATE IT...!!
I WANT TO CON-QUER...
...SAKA-MOTO...

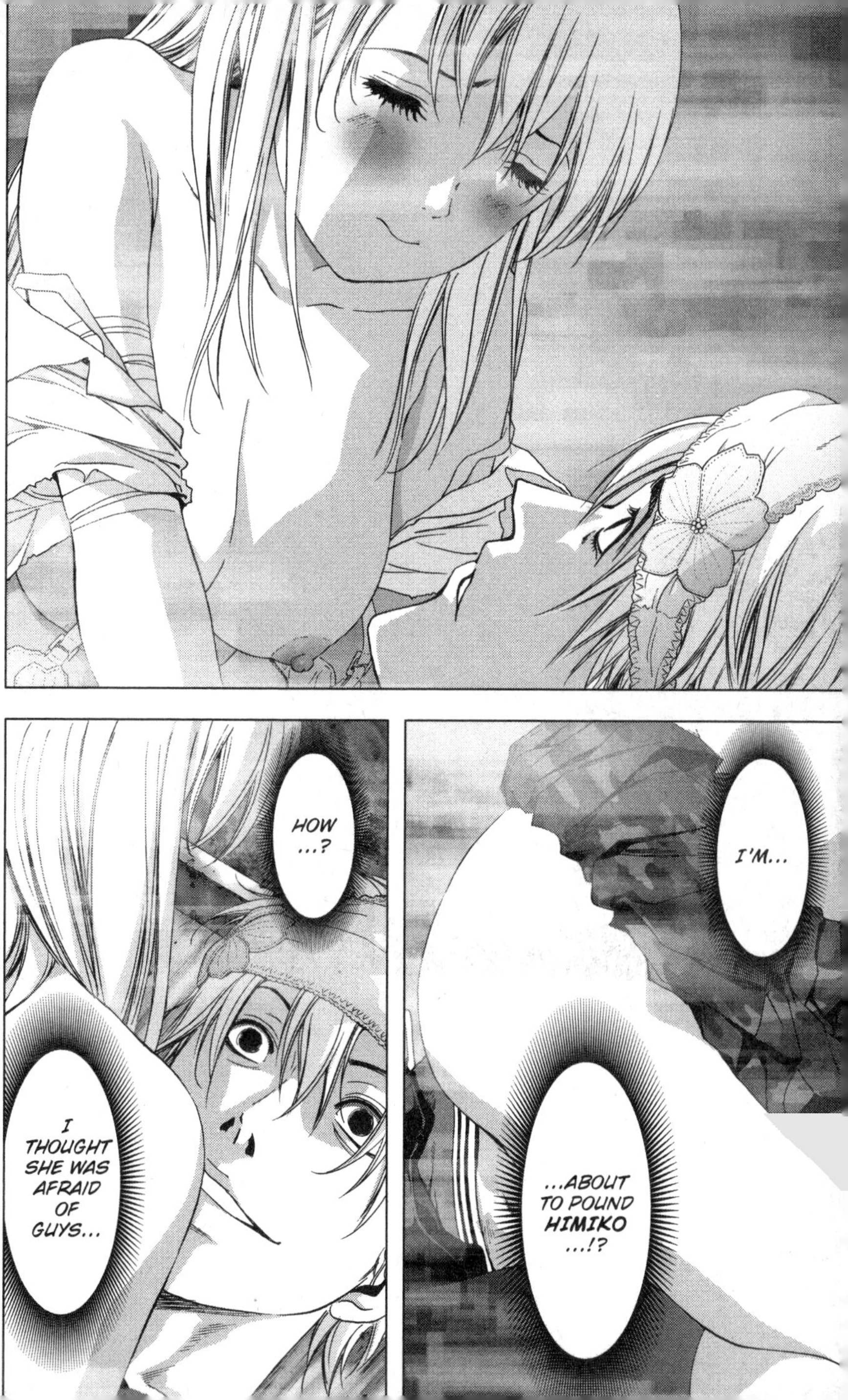
I'M...
...ABOUT TO POUND HIMIKO ...!?
HOW ...?
I THOUGHT SHE WAS AFRAID OF GUYS...

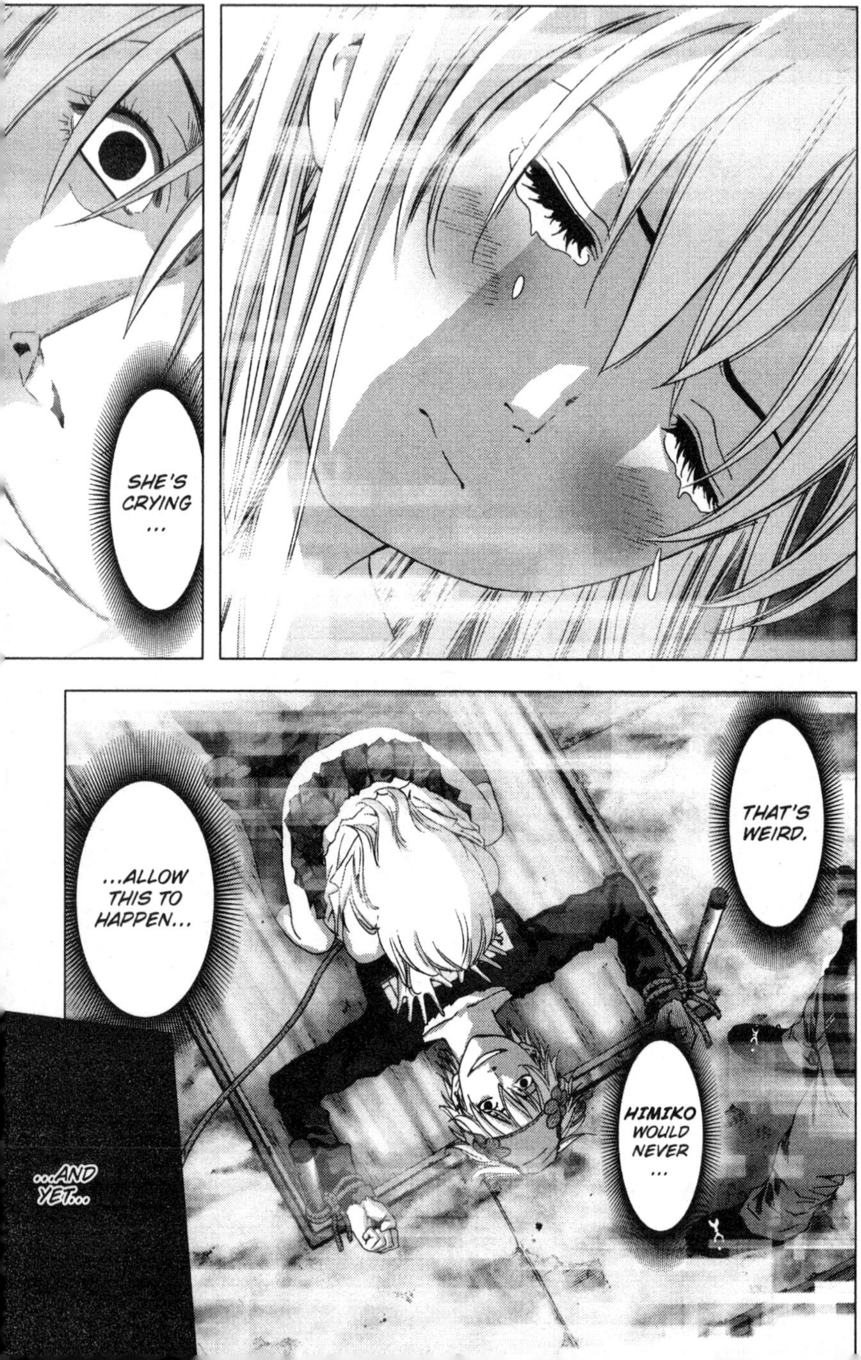
SHE'S CRYING ...
THAT'S WEIRD.
HIMIKO WOULD NEVER ...
...ALLOW THIS TO HAPPEN...
...AND YET...

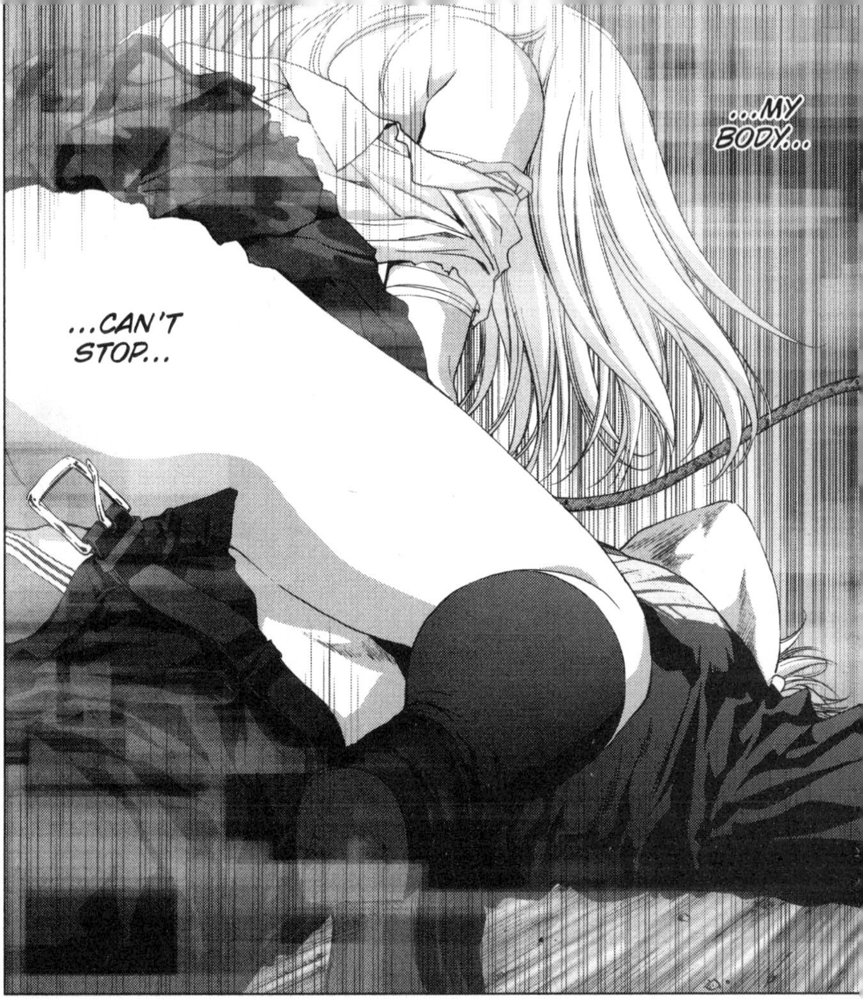
...MY BODY...
...CAN'T STOP...
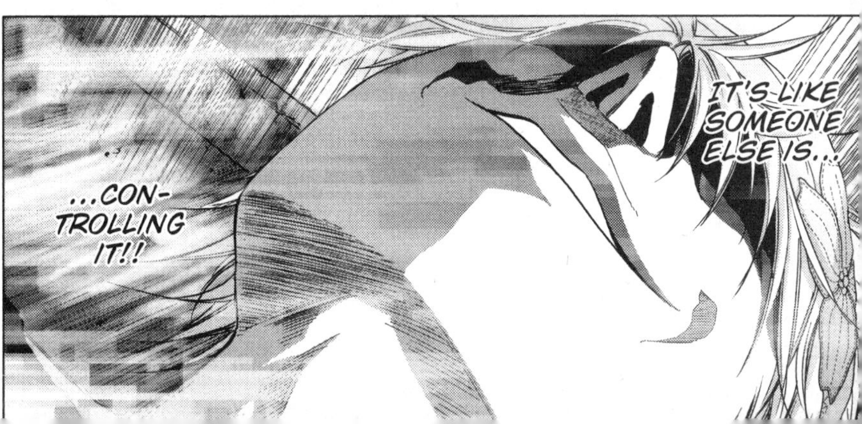
IT'S LIKE SOMEONE ELSE IS...
...CON-TROLLING IT!!

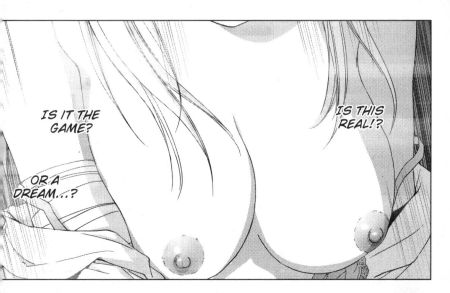

IS IT THE GAME?

IS THIS REAL!?

OR A DREAM...?

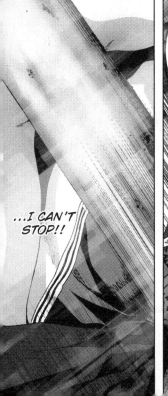

...I CAN'T STOP!!

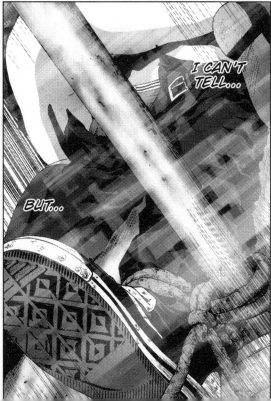

I CAN'T TELL...

BUT...

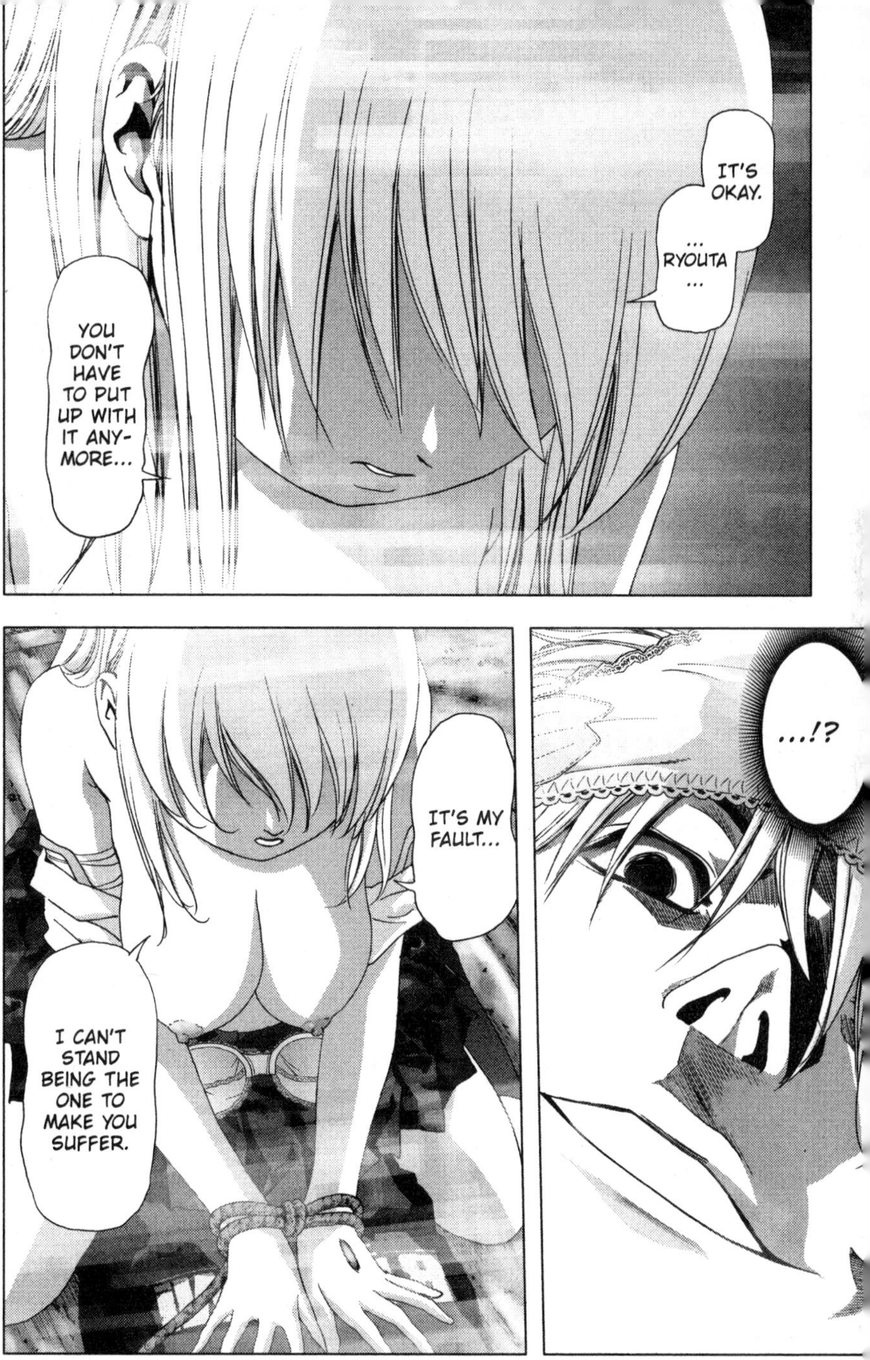
IT'S OKAY.
... RYOUTA ...
YOU DON'T HAVE TO PUT UP WITH IT ANY-MORE...
...!?
IT'S MY FAULT...
I CAN'T STAND BEING THE ONE TO MAKE YOU SUFFER.

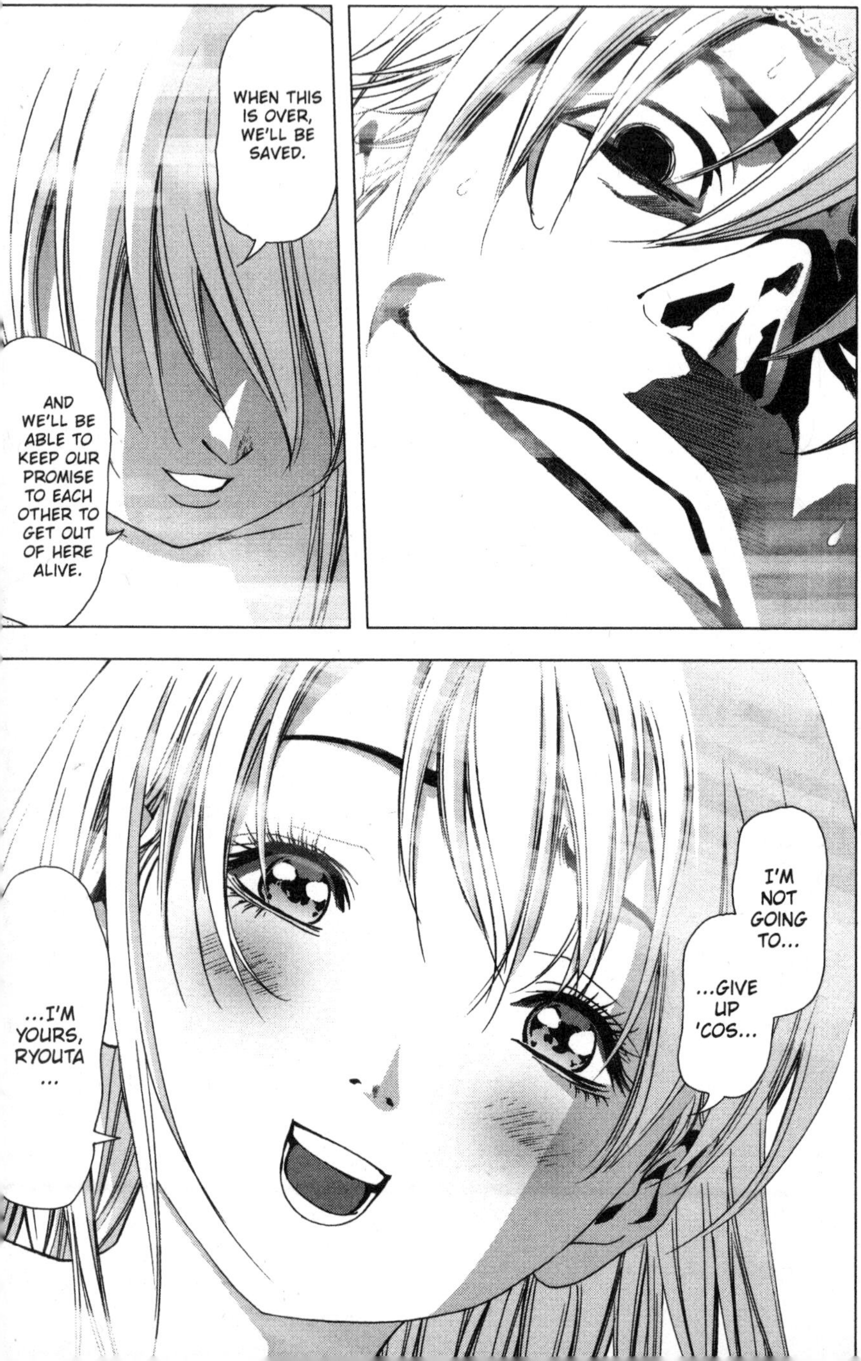
WHEN THIS IS OVER, WE'LL BE SAVED.
AND WE'LL BE ABLE TO KEEP OUR PROMISE TO EACH OTHER TO GET OUT OF HERE ALIVE.
I'M NOT GOING TO...
...GIVE UP 'COS...
...I'M YOURS, RYOUTA ...

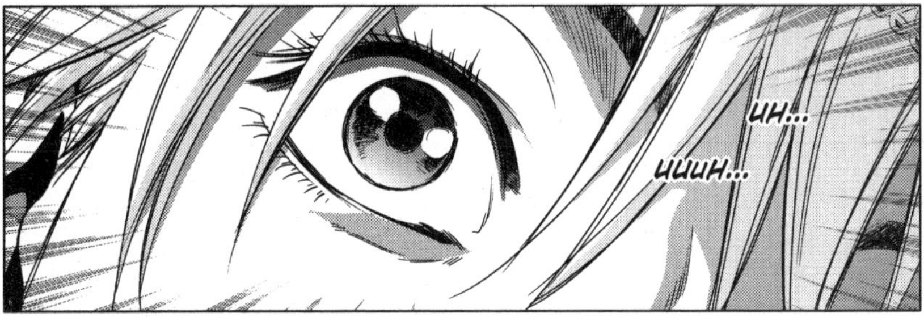
UH...
UUUH...
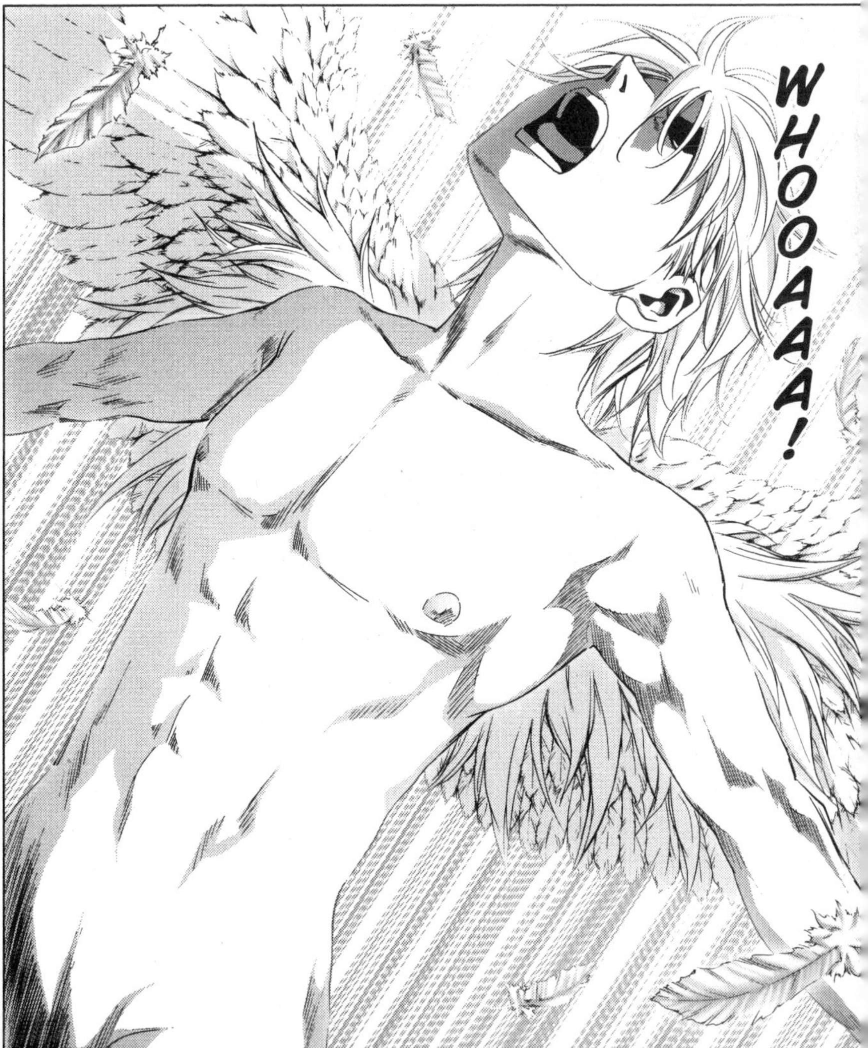
WHOOAAA!

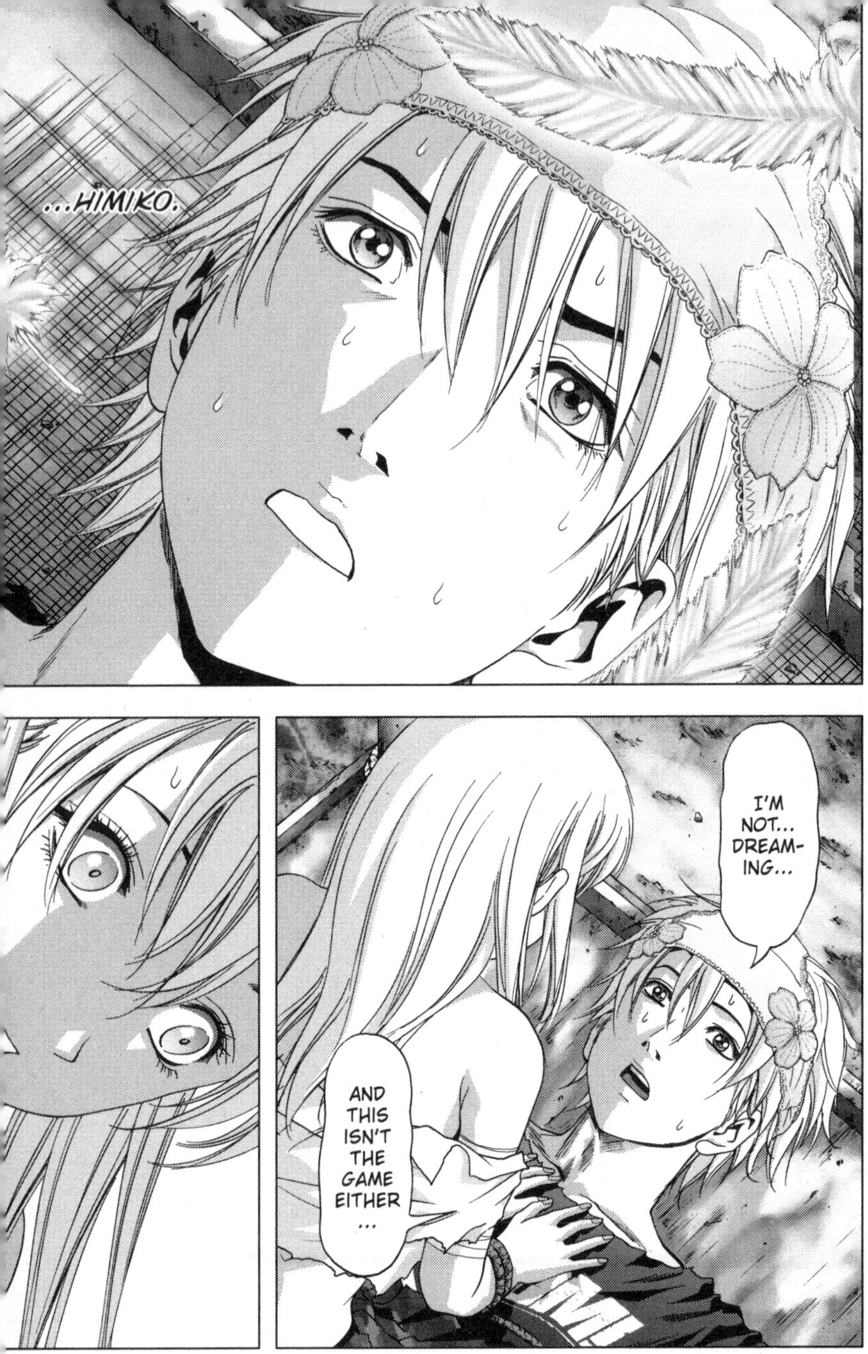
...HIMIKO.
I'M NOT... DREAMING...
AND THIS ISN'T THE GAME EITHER ...

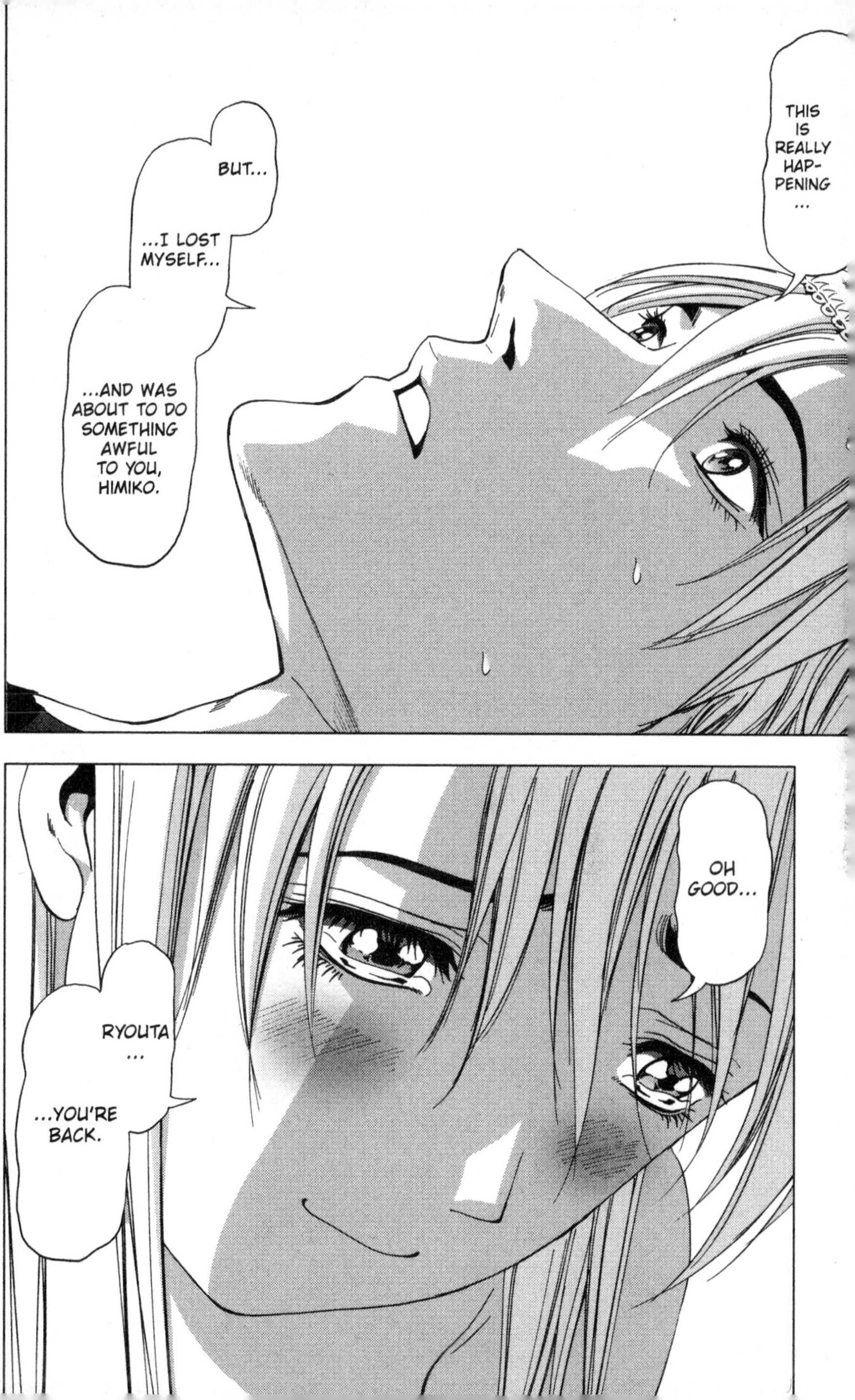
THIS IS REALLY HAP-PENING...
BUT...
...I LOST MYSELF...
...AND WAS ABOUT TO DO SOMETHING AWFUL TO YOU, HIMIKO.
OH GOOD...
RYOUTA...
...YOU'RE BACK.

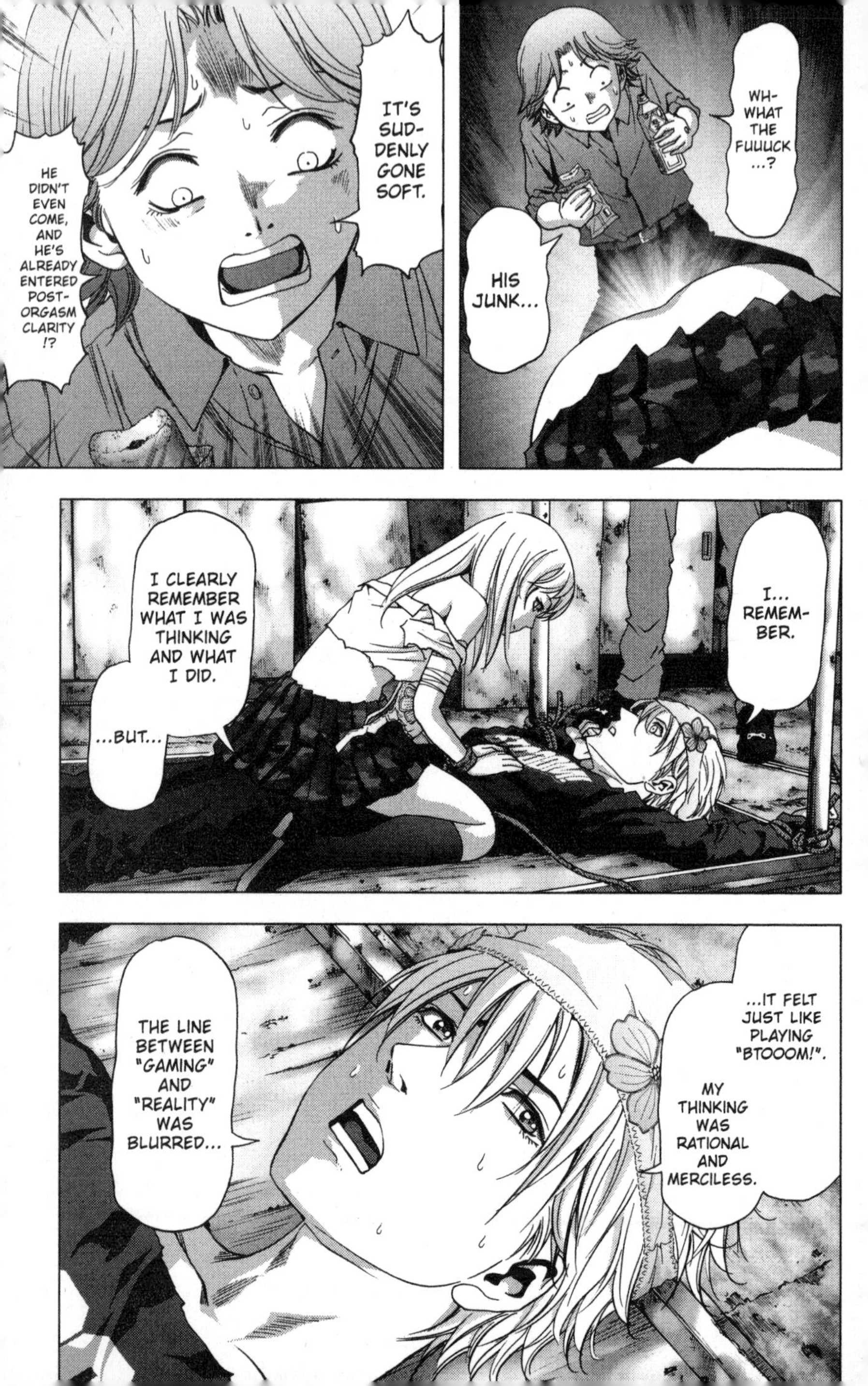
WH-WHAT THE FUUUCK...?
HIS JUNK...
IT'S SUD-DENLY GONE SOFT.
HE DIDN'T EVEN COME, AND HE'S ALREADY ENTERED POST-ORGASM CLARITY!?
I... REMEM-BER.
I CLEARLY REMEMBER WHAT I WAS THINKING AND WHAT I DID.
...BUT...
...IT FELT JUST LIKE PLAYING "BTOOOM!".
MY THINKING WAS RATIONAL AND MERCILESS.
THE LINE BETWEEN "GAMING" AND "REALITY" WAS BLURRED...

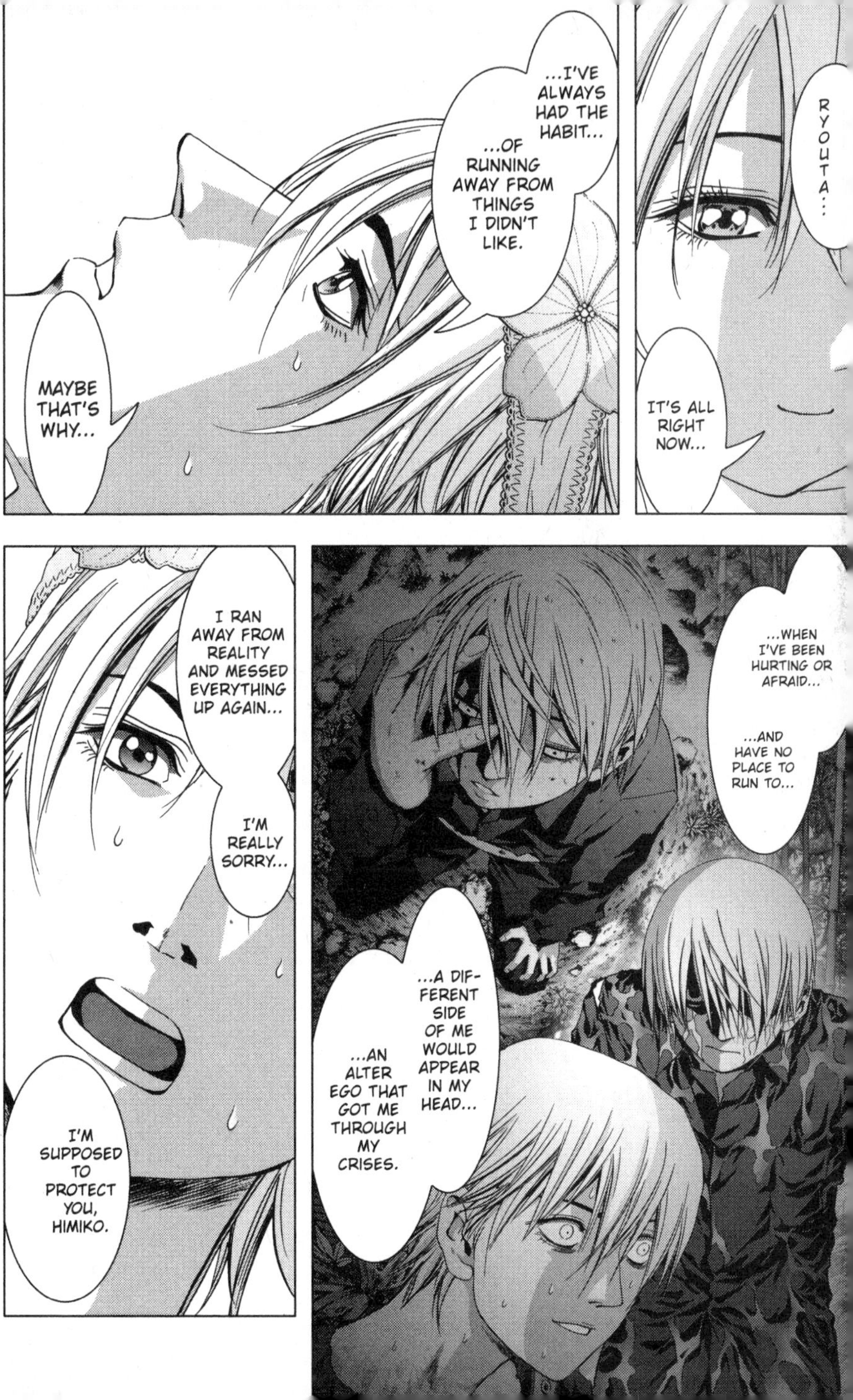
RYOUTA...
IT'S ALL RIGHT NOW...
...I'VE ALWAYS HAD THE HABIT...
...OF RUNNING AWAY FROM THINGS I DIDN'T LIKE.
MAYBE THAT'S WHY...
...WHEN I'VE BEEN HURTING OR AFRAID...
...AND HAVE NO PLACE TO RUN TO...
...A DIF-FERENT SIDE OF ME WOULD APPEAR IN MY HEAD...
...AN ALTER EGO THAT GOT ME THROUGH MY CRISES.
I RAN AWAY FROM REALITY AND MESSED EVERYTHING UP AGAIN...
I'M REALLY SORRY...
I'M SUPPOSED TO PROTECT YOU, HIMIKO.

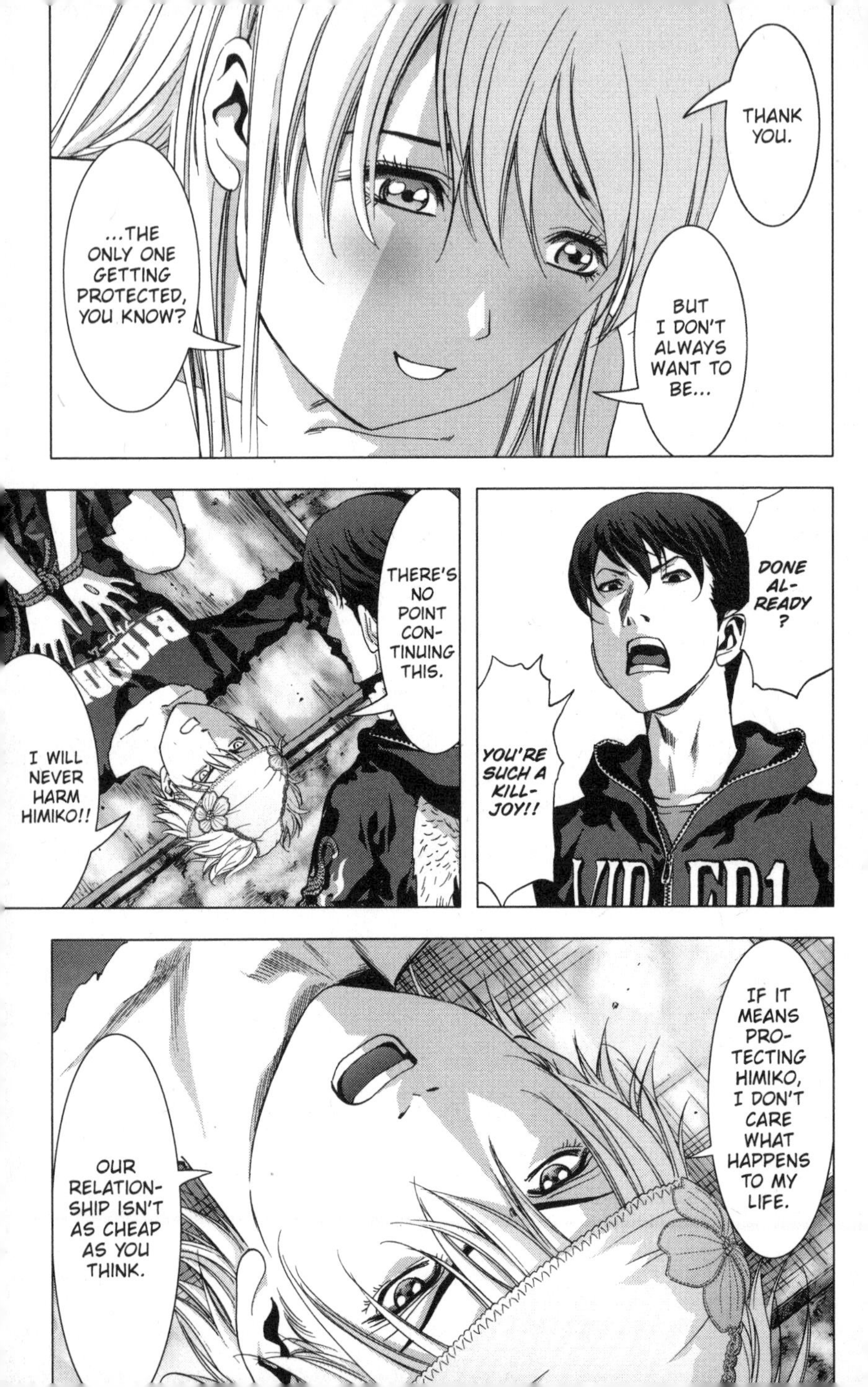
THANK YOU.
BUT I DON'T ALWAYS WANT TO BE...
...THE ONLY ONE GETTING PROTECTED, YOU KNOW?
DONE AL-READY?
YOU'RE SUCH A KILL-JOY!!
THERE'S NO POINT CON-TINUING THIS.
I WILL NEVER HARM HIMIKO!!
IF IT MEANS PRO-TECTING HIMIKO, I DON'T CARE WHAT HAPPENS TO MY LIFE.
OUR RELATION-SHIP ISN'T AS CHEAP AS YOU THINK.

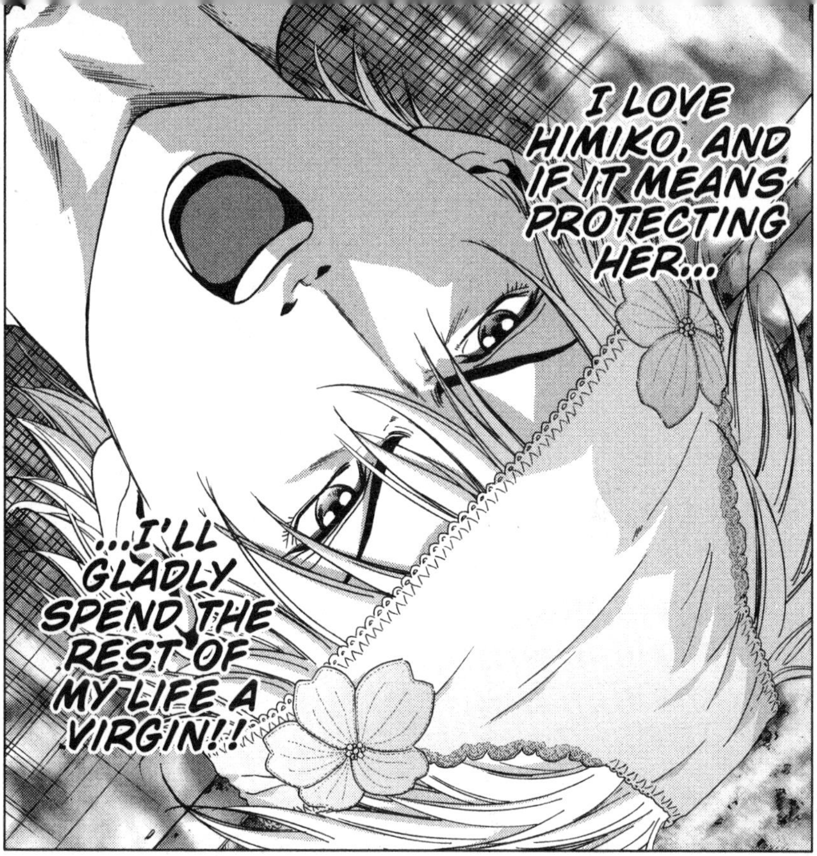
I LOVE HIMIKO, AND IF IT MEANS PROTECTING HER...
...I'LL GLADLY SPEND THE REST OF MY LIFE A VIRGIN!!

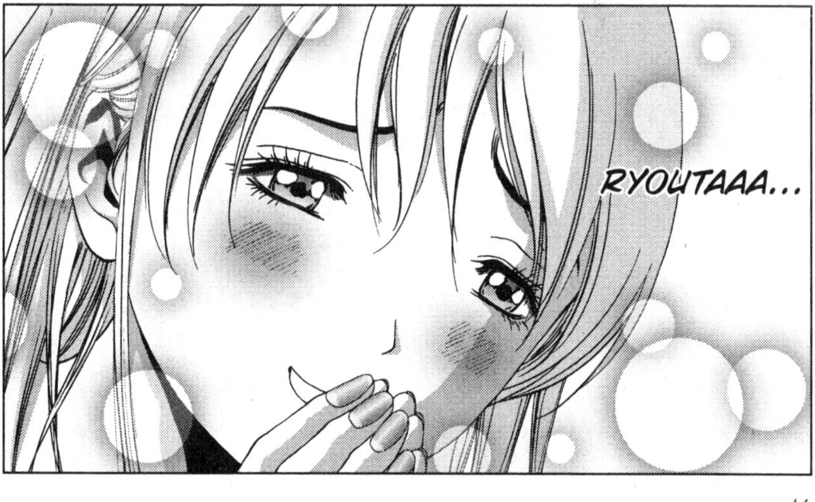
RYOUTAAA...

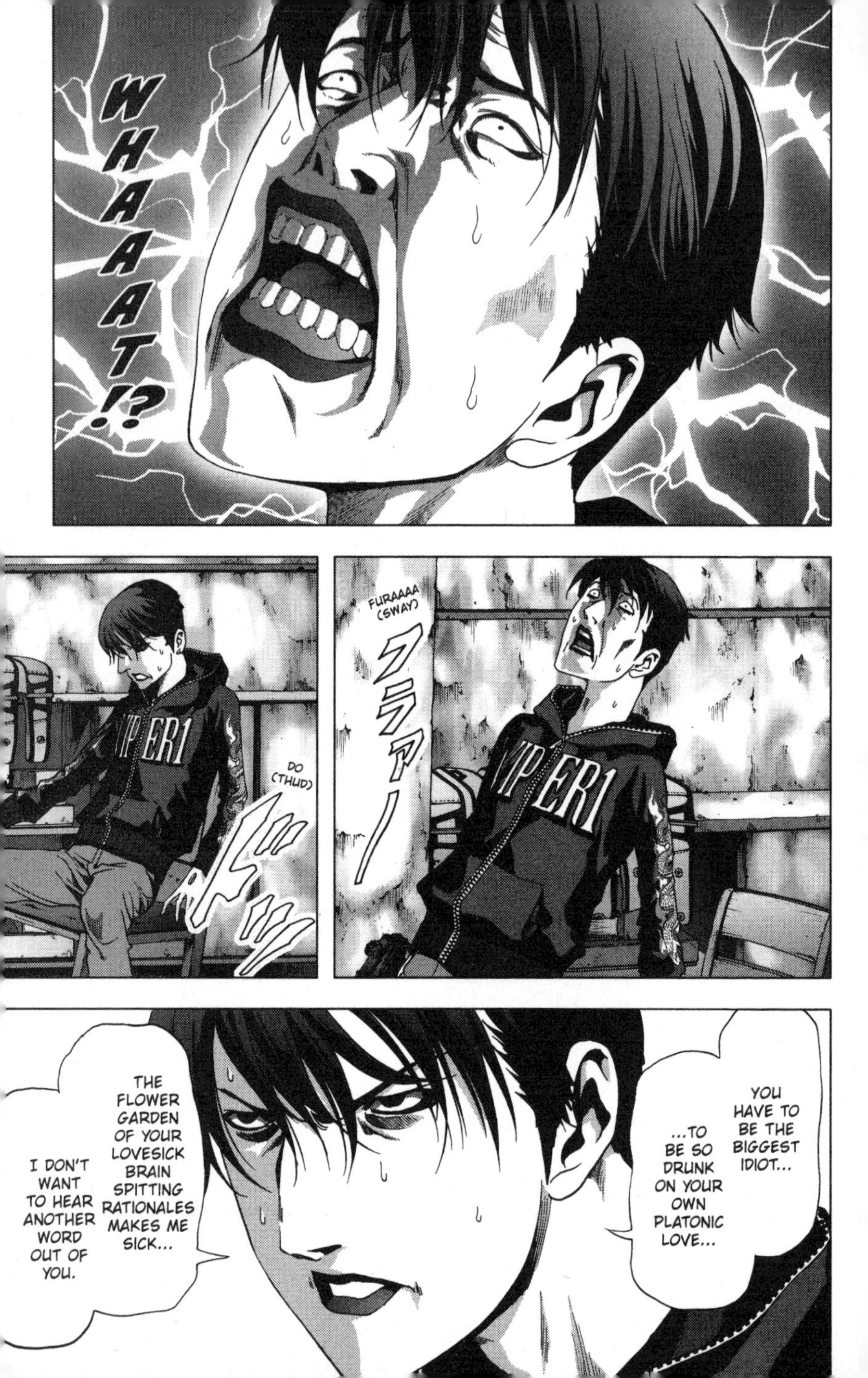
WHAAAAT!?
FURAAAA (SWAY)
フラァー
DO (THUD)
YOU HAVE TO BE THE BIGGEST IDIOT...
...TO BE SO DRUNK ON YOUR OWN PLATONIC LOVE...
THE FLOWER GARDEN OF YOUR LOVESICK BRAIN SPITTING RATIONALES MAKES ME SICK...
I DON'T WANT TO HEAR ANOTHER WORD OUT OF YOU.

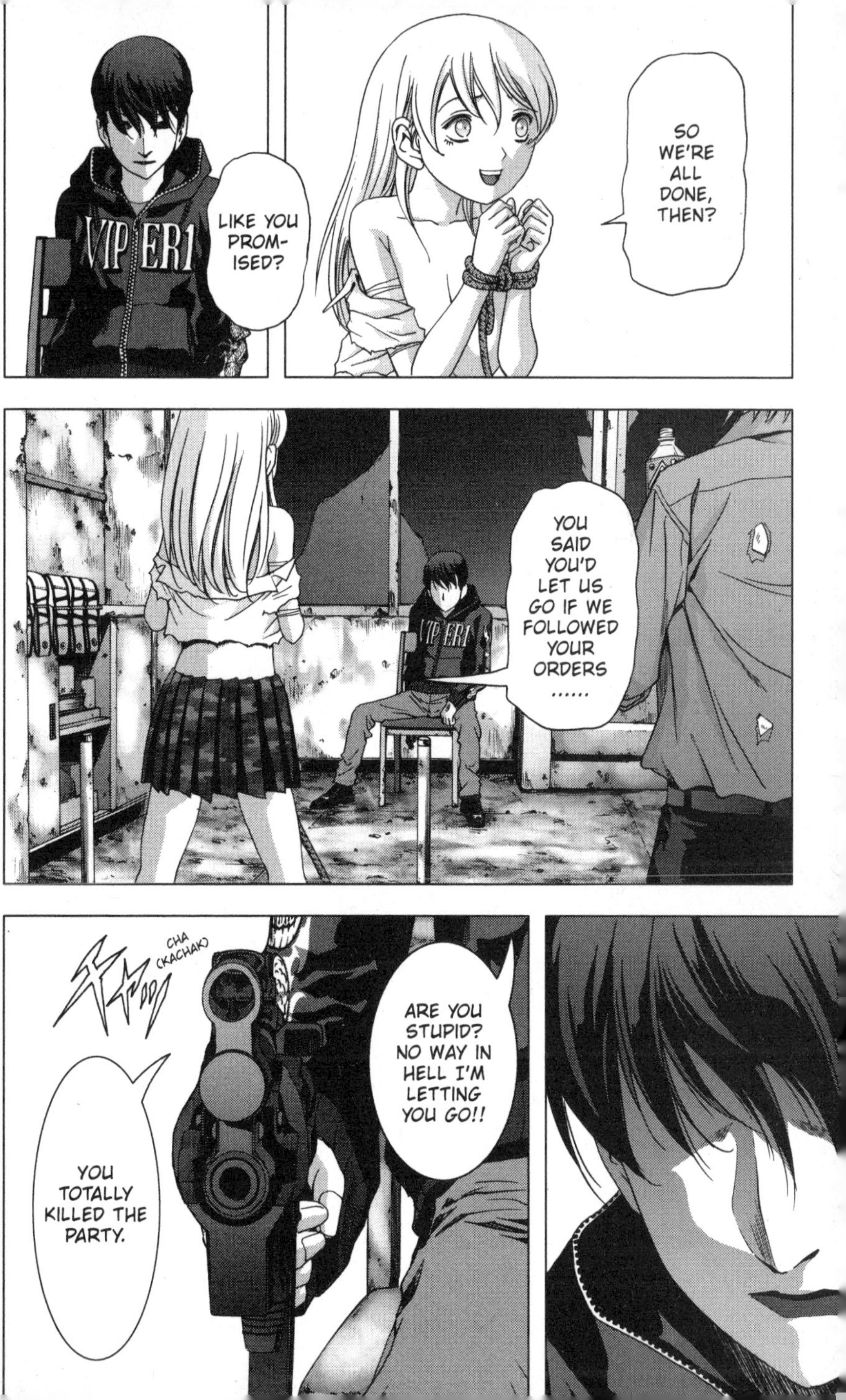
SO WE'RE ALL DONE, THEN?
LIKE YOU PROM-ISED?
YOU SAID YOU'D LET US GO IF WE FOLLOWED YOUR ORDERS ......
ARE YOU STUPID? NO WAY IN HELL I'M LETTING YOU GO!!
CHA (KACHAK)
YOU TOTALLY KILLED THE PARTY.

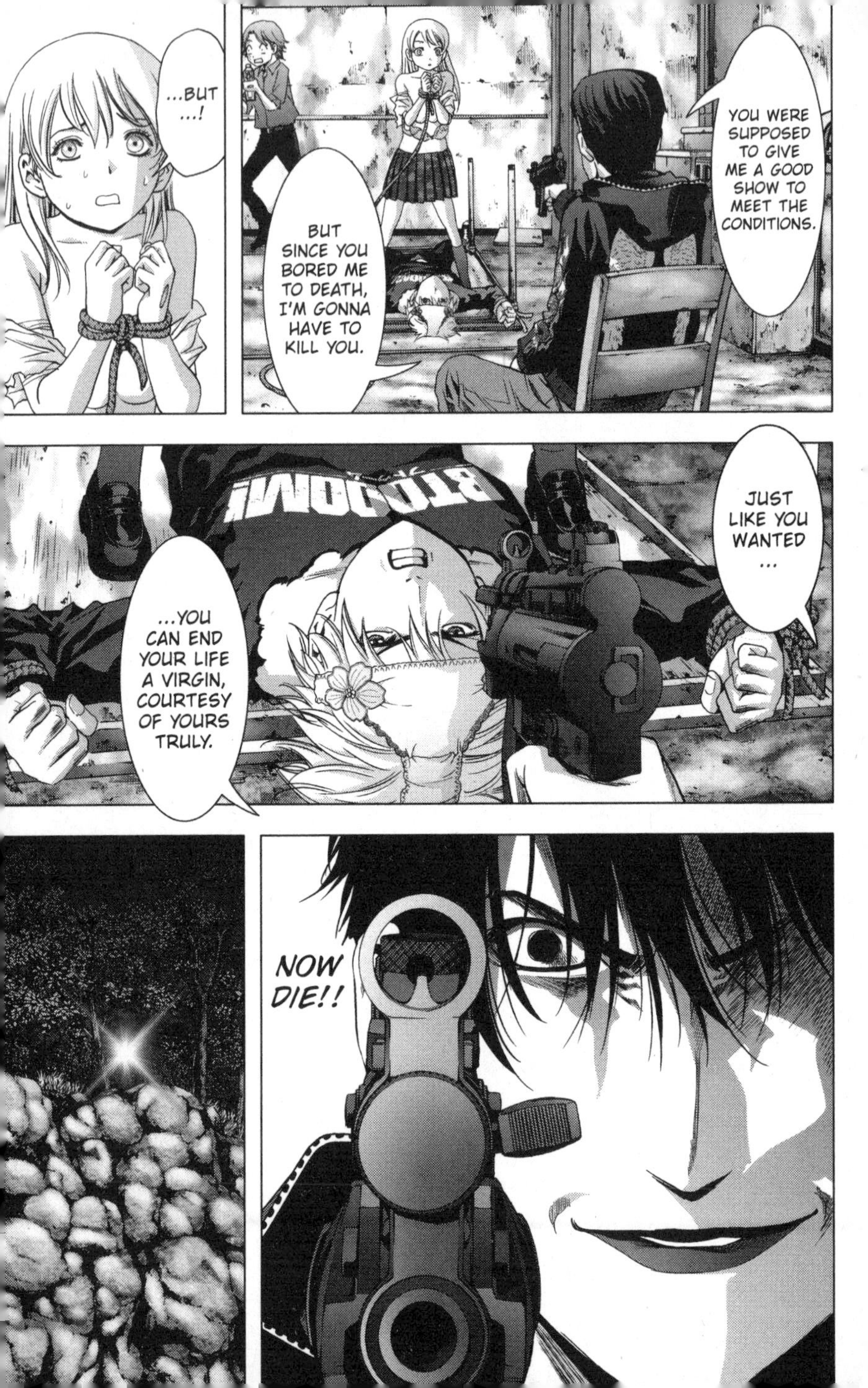
YOU WERE SUPPOSED TO GIVE ME A GOOD SHOW TO MEET THE CONDITIONS.
BUT SINCE YOU BORED ME TO DEATH, I'M GONNA HAVE TO KILL YOU.
...BUT ...!
JUST LIKE YOU WANTED ...
...YOU CAN END YOUR LIFE A VIRGIN, COURTESY OF YOURS TRULY.
NOW DIE!!

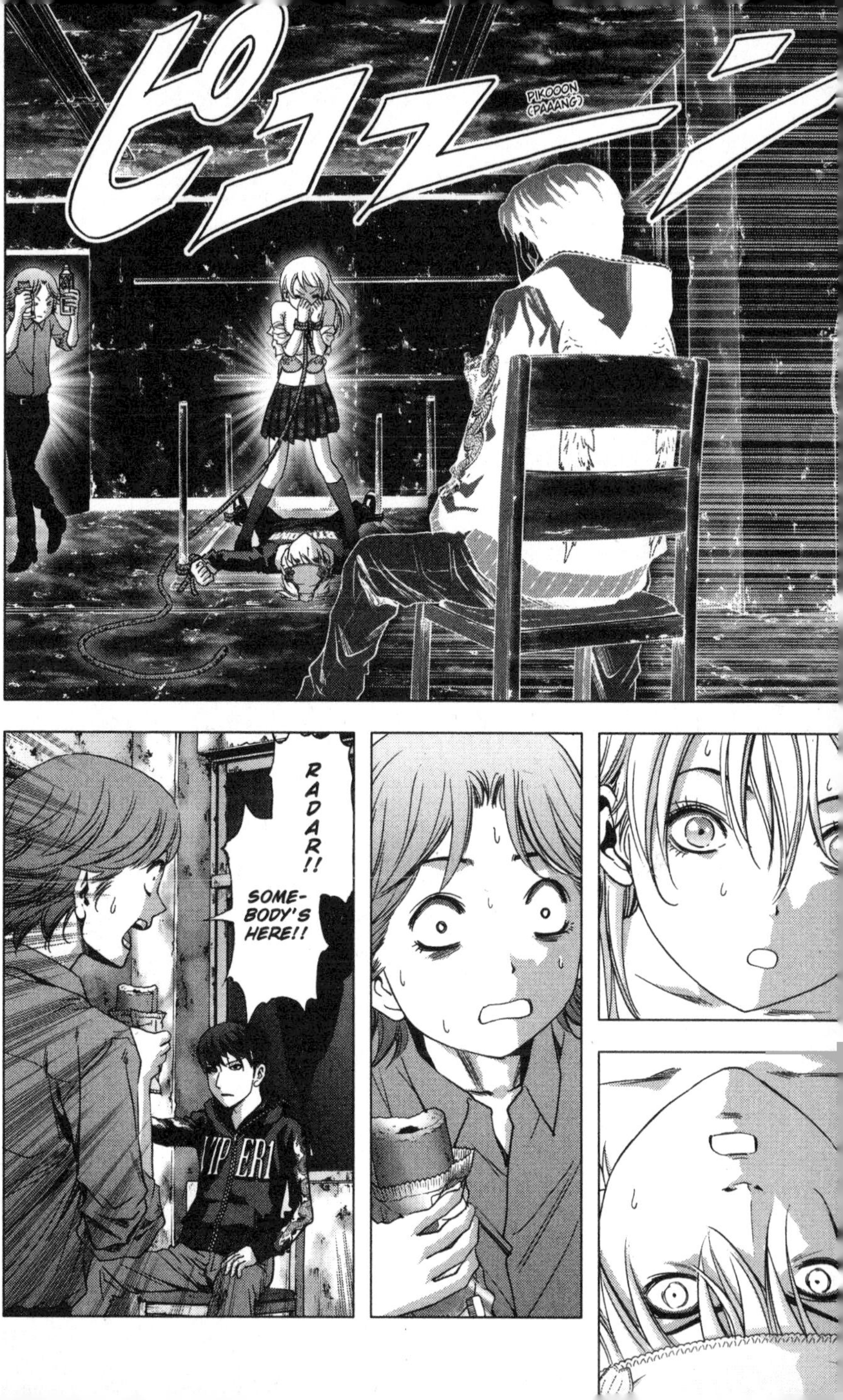
ピコーーン
PIKOOON (PAAANG)
RADAR!!
SOME-BODY'S HERE!!
VIPER1

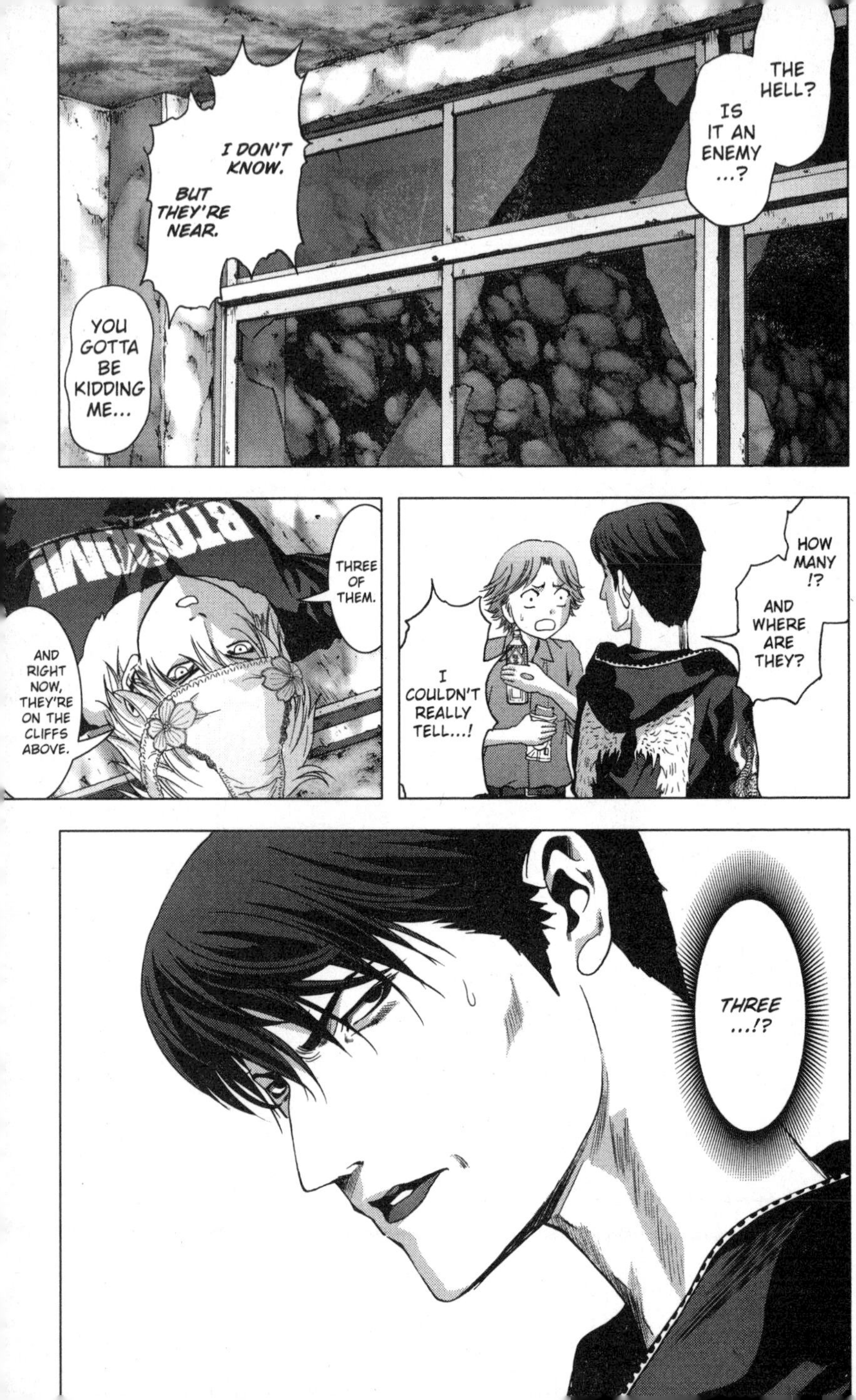
THE HELL?
IS IT AN ENEMY...?
I DON'T KNOW.
BUT THEY'RE NEAR.
YOU GOTTA BE KIDDING ME...
HOW MANY!?
AND WHERE ARE THEY?
I COULDN'T REALLY TELL...!
THREE OF THEM.
AND RIGHT NOW, THEY'RE ON THE CLIFFS ABOVE.
THREE...!?

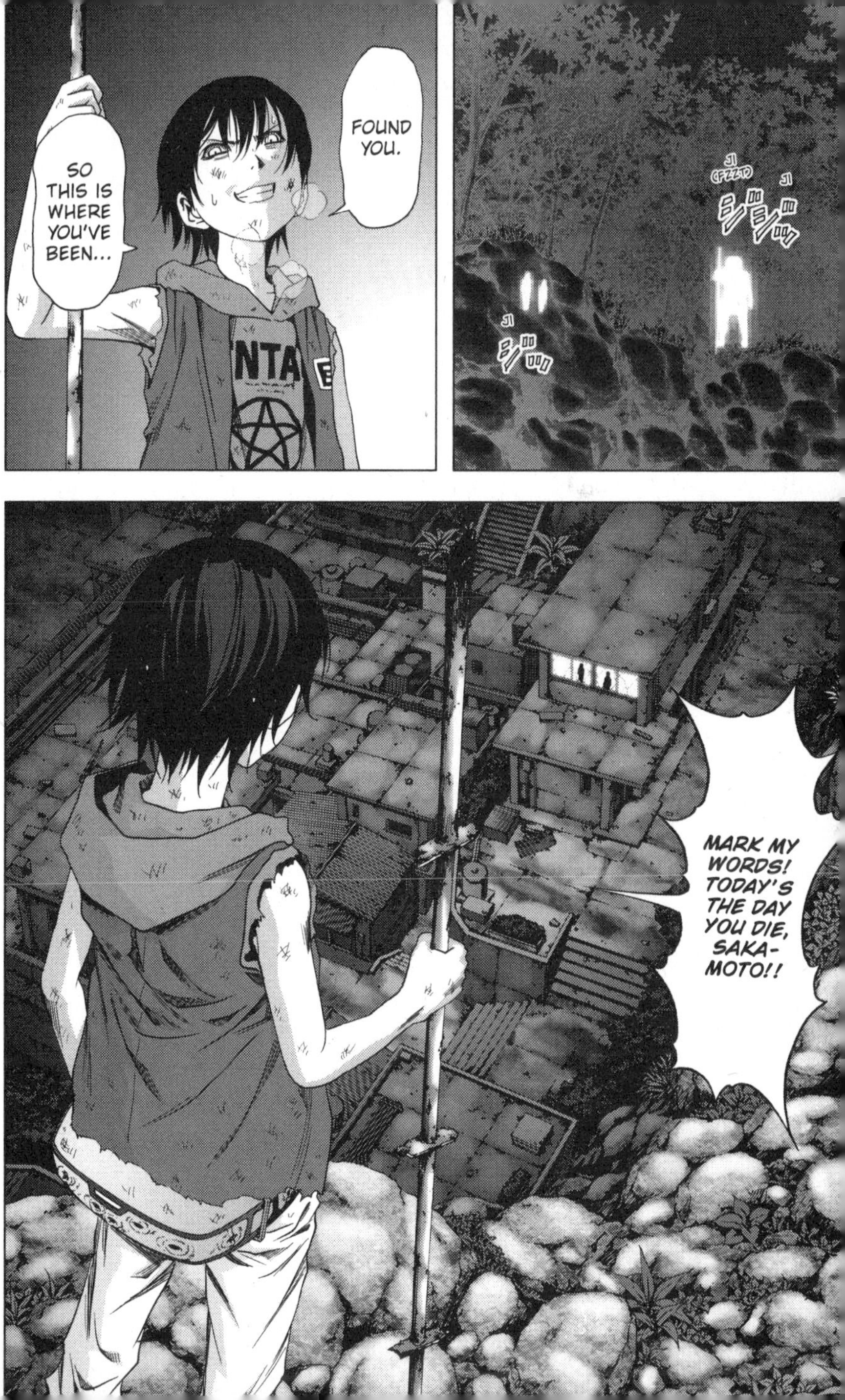

JI (FZZT) JI
JI
FOUND YOU.
SO THIS IS WHERE YOU'VE BEEN...
MARK MY WORDS! TODAY'S THE DAY YOU DIE, SAKA-MOTO!!

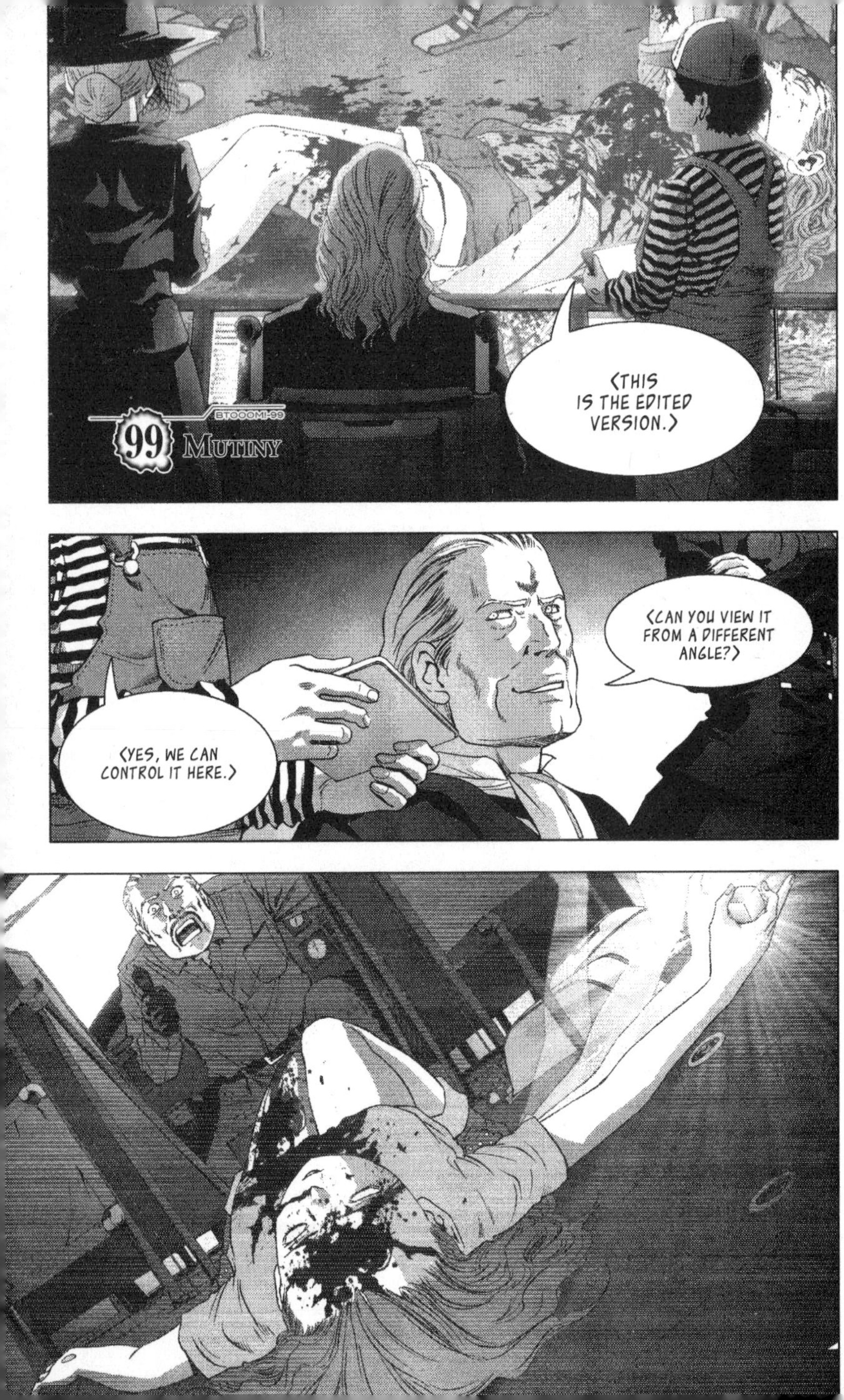
BTOOOM!-99
99 MUTINY
<THIS IS THE EDITED VERSION.>
<CAN YOU VIEW IT FROM A DIFFERENT ANGLE?>
<YES, WE CAN CONTROL IT HERE.>

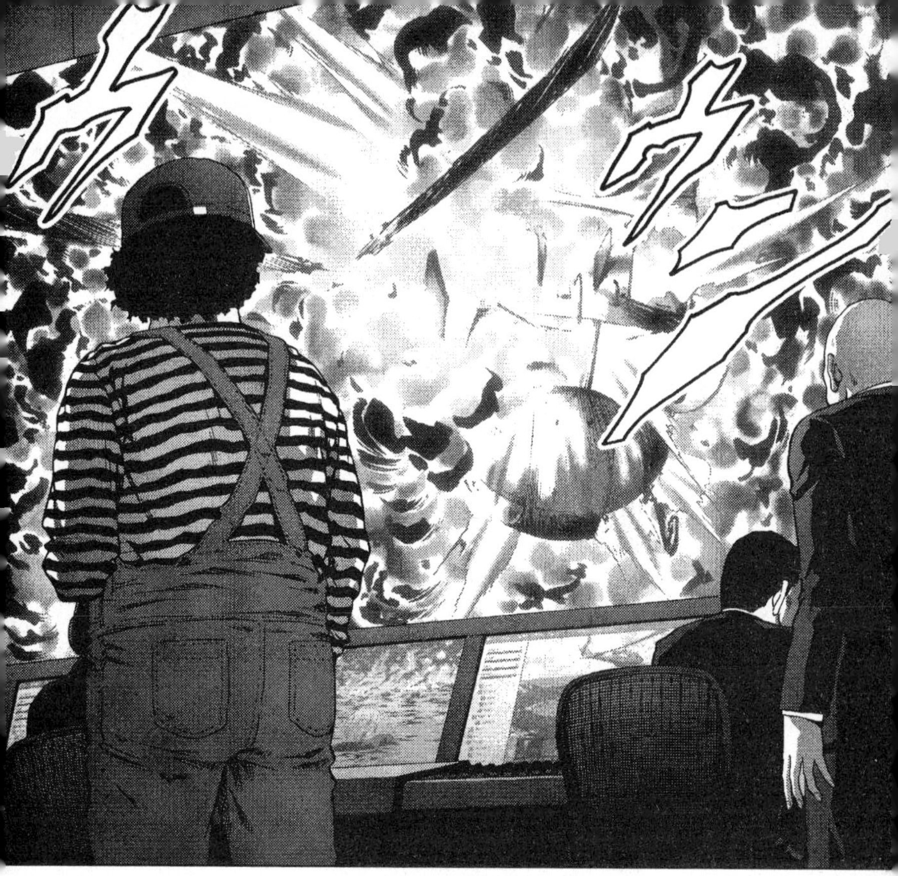

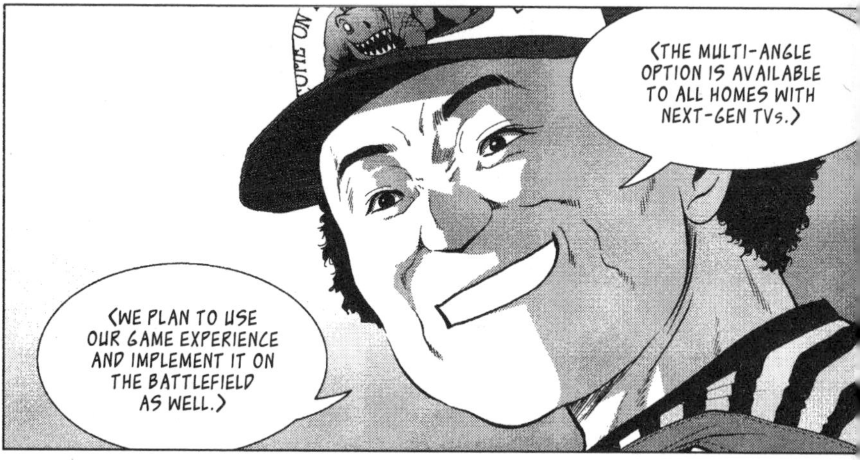
⟨THE MULTI-ANGLE OPTION IS AVAILABLE TO ALL HOMES WITH NEXT-GEN TVs.⟩
⟨WE PLAN TO USE OUR GAME EXPERIENCE AND IMPLEMENT IT ON THE BATTLEFIELD AS WELL.⟩

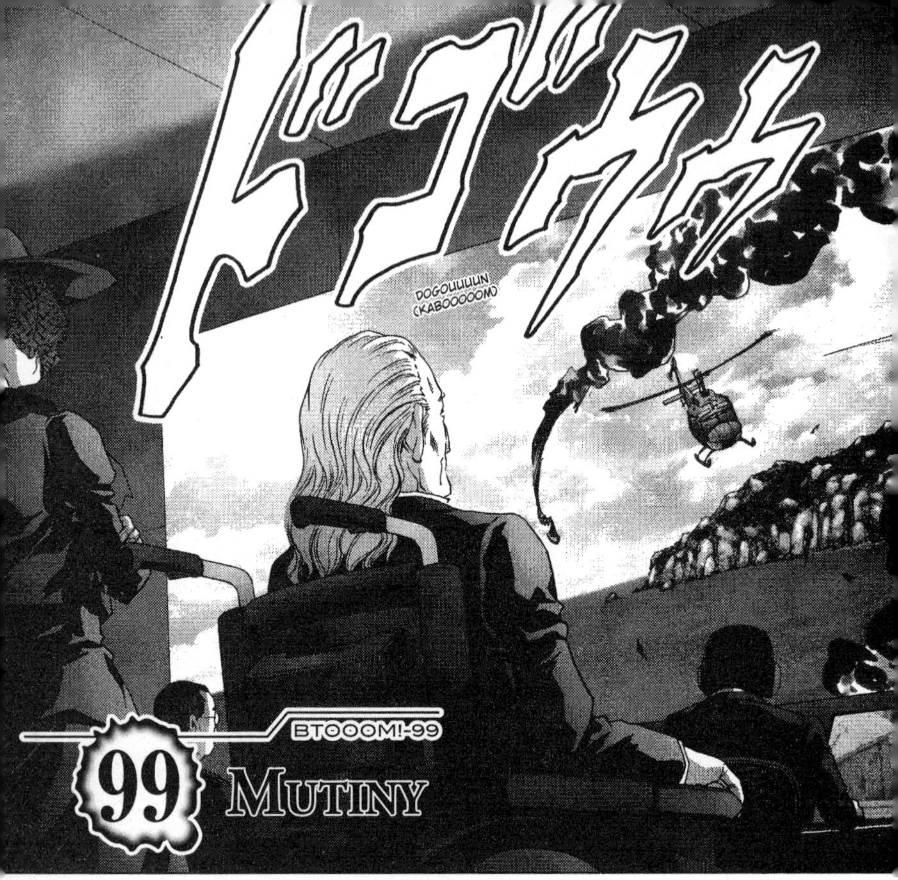
ドゴゥゥ
DOGOUUUUN (KABOOOOOM)
BTOOOM!-99
99 MUTINY

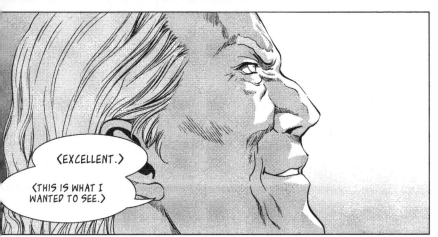

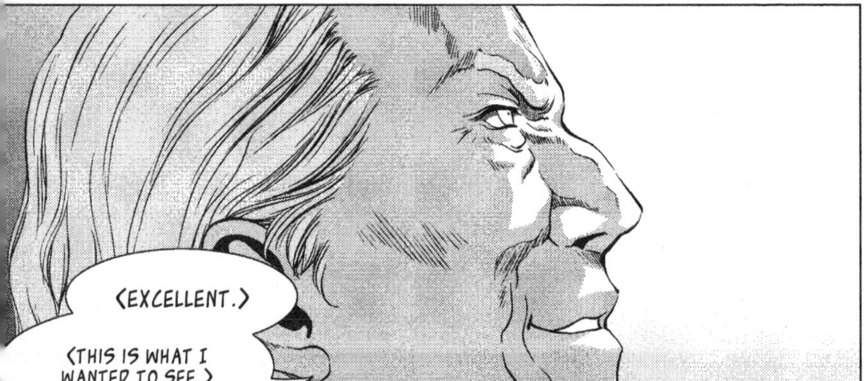
<EXCELLENT.>
<THIS IS WHAT I WANTED TO SEE.>

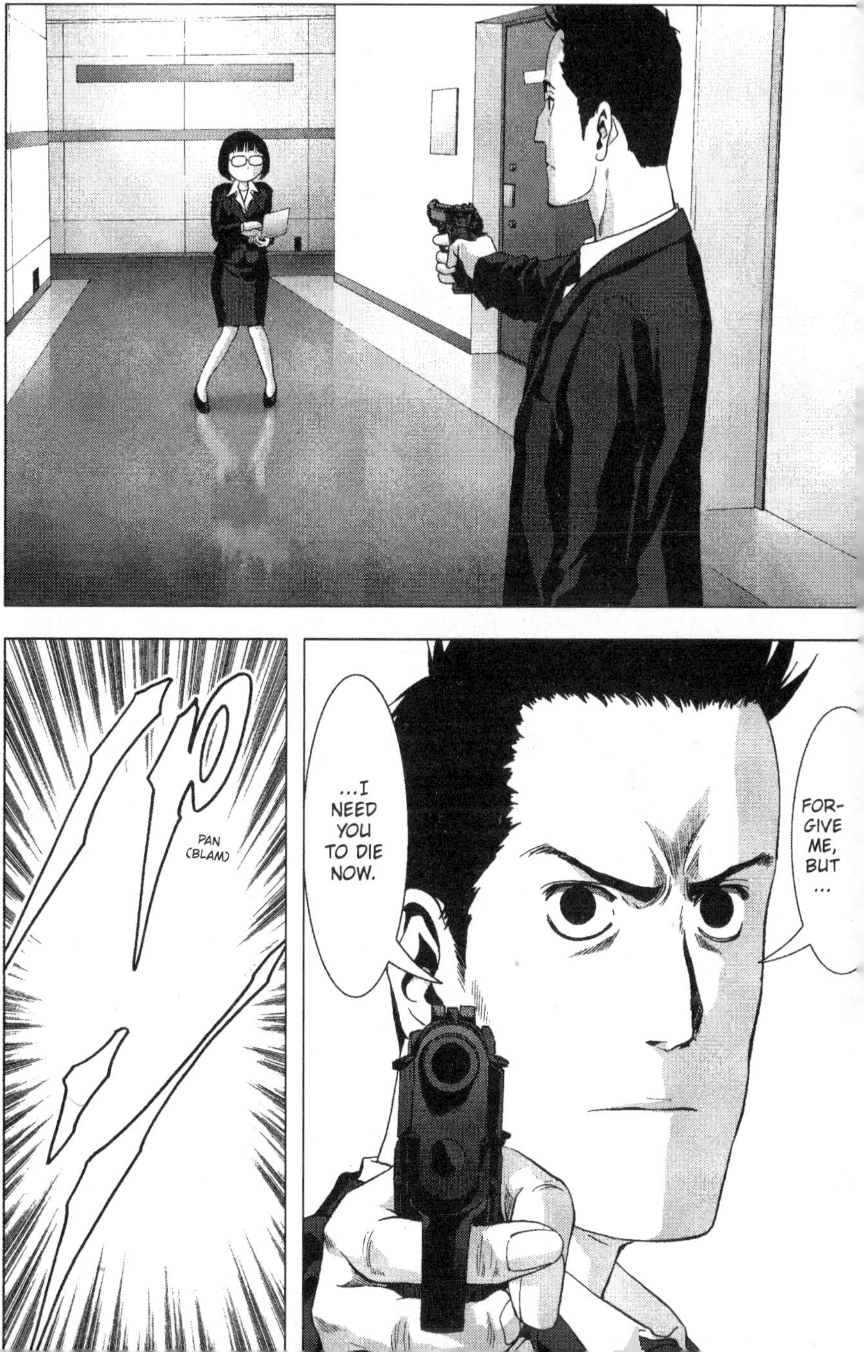
FOR-
GIVE
ME,
BUT
...
...I
NEED
YOU
TO DIE
NOW.
PAN
(BLAM)

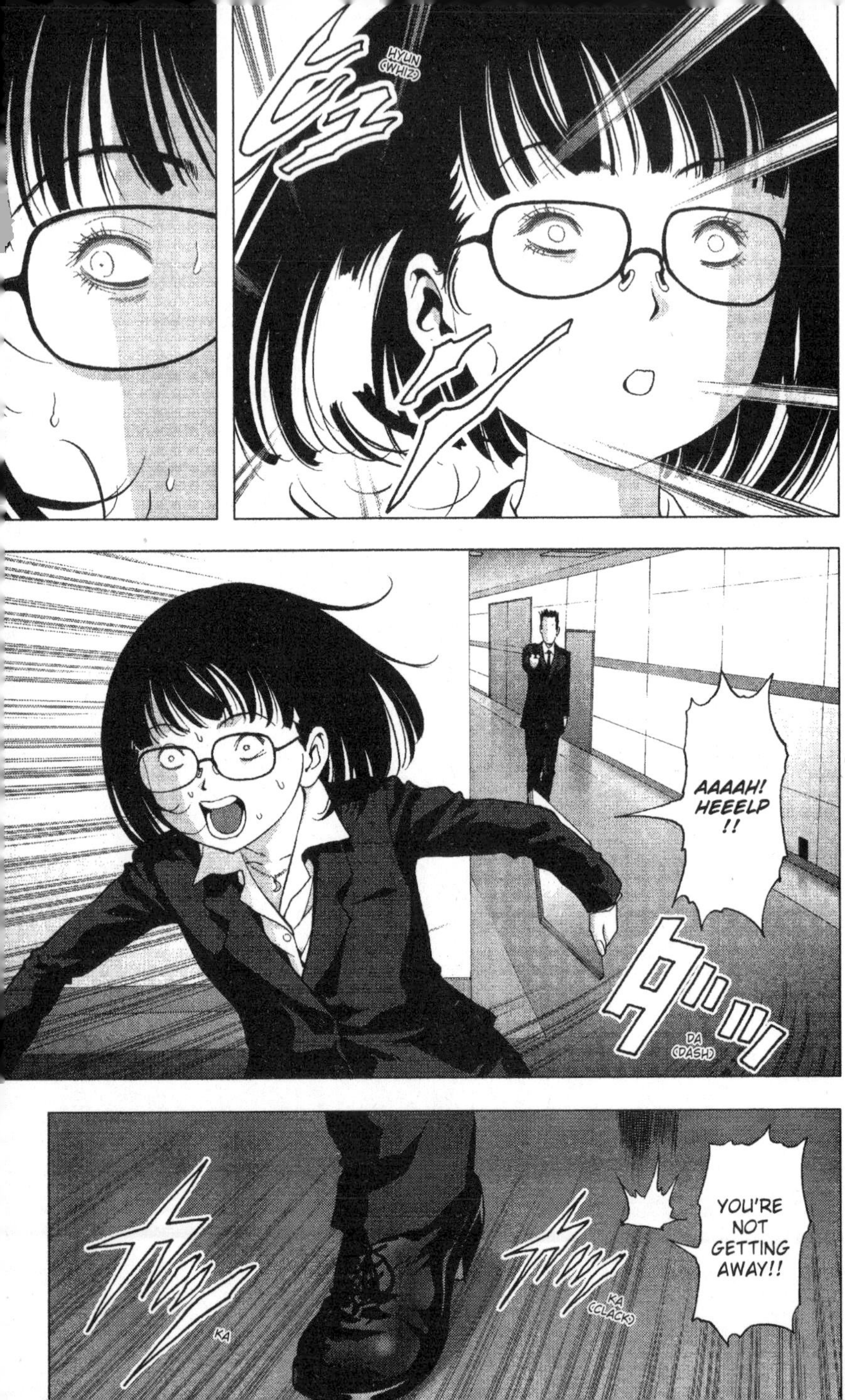
HYUN (WHIZ)
AAAAH! HEEELP !!
DA (DASH)
YOU'RE NOT GETTING AWAY!!
KA (CLACK)
KA

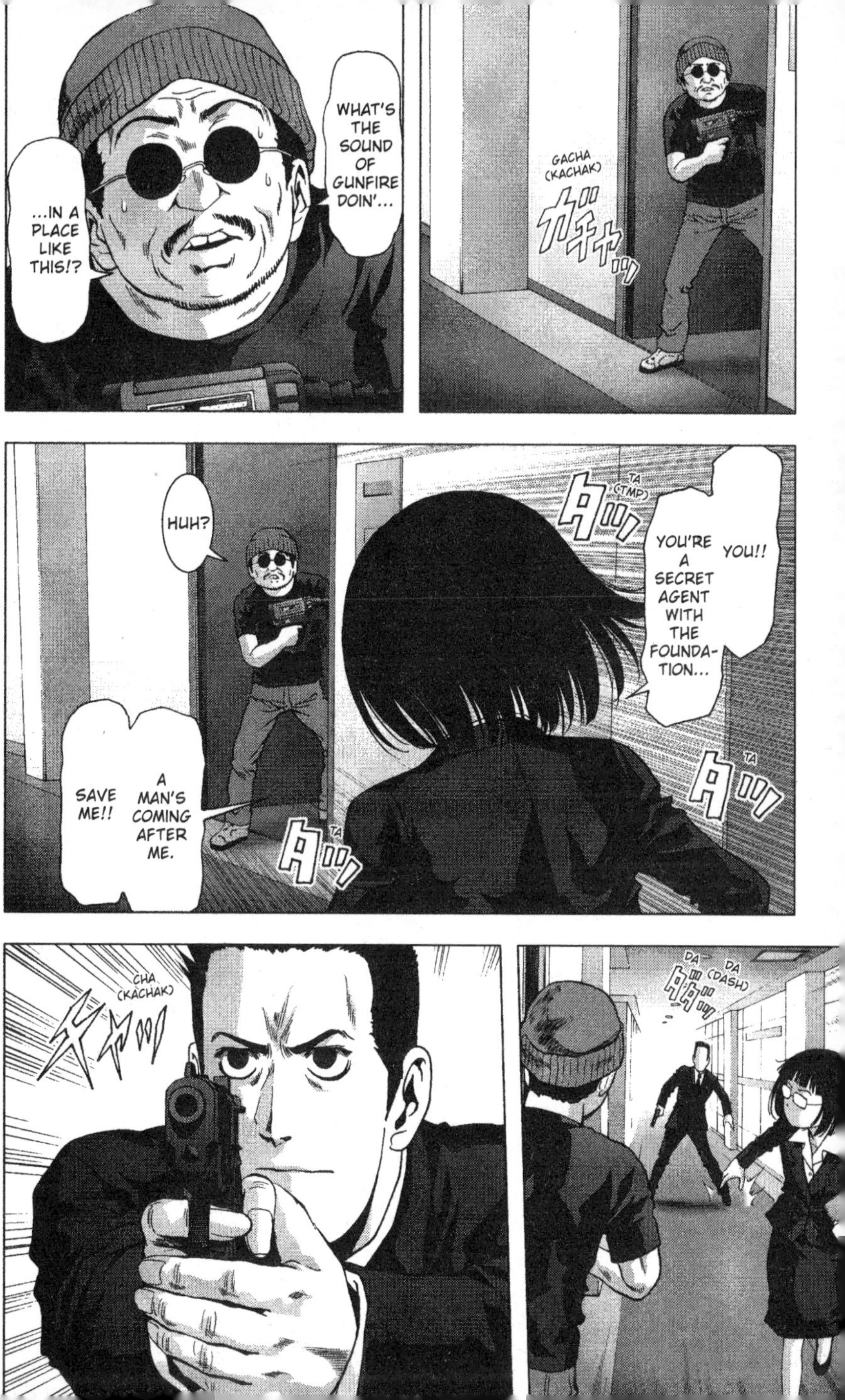
GACHA (KACHAK)
WHAT'S THE SOUND OF GUNFIRE DOIN'...
...IN A PLACE LIKE THIS!?
TA (TMP)
YOU!!
YOU'RE A SECRET AGENT WITH THE FOUNDATION...
TA
HUH?
A MAN'S COMING AFTER ME.
SAVE ME!!
TA
DA DA (DASH)
CHA (KACHAK)

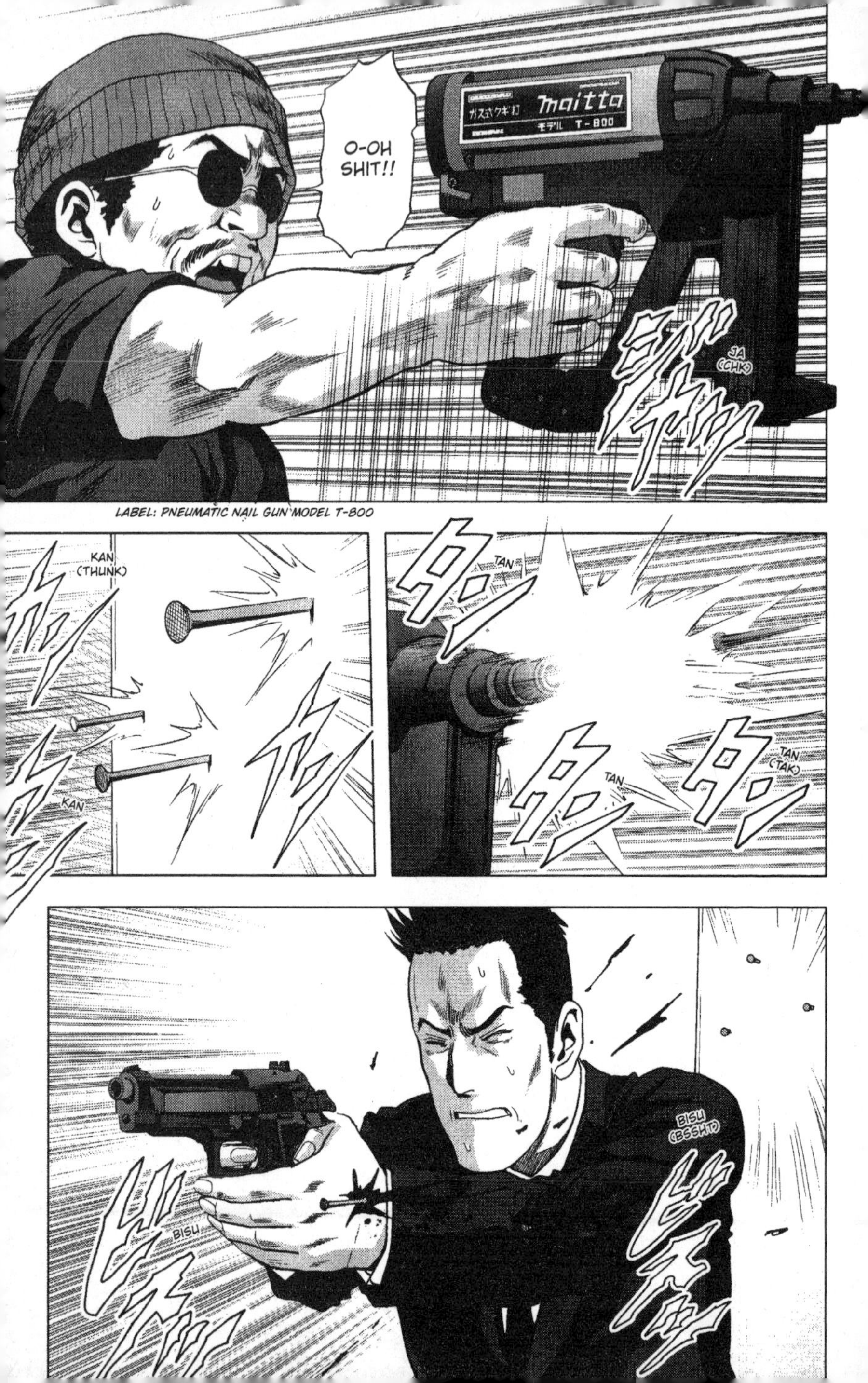
O-OH SHIT!!
ガス式クギ打
maitto
モデル T-800
JA (CHK)
LABEL: PNEUMATIC NAIL GUN MODEL T-800
TAN
TAN (TAK)
TAN
KAN (THUNK)
KAN
BISU (BSSHT)
BISU

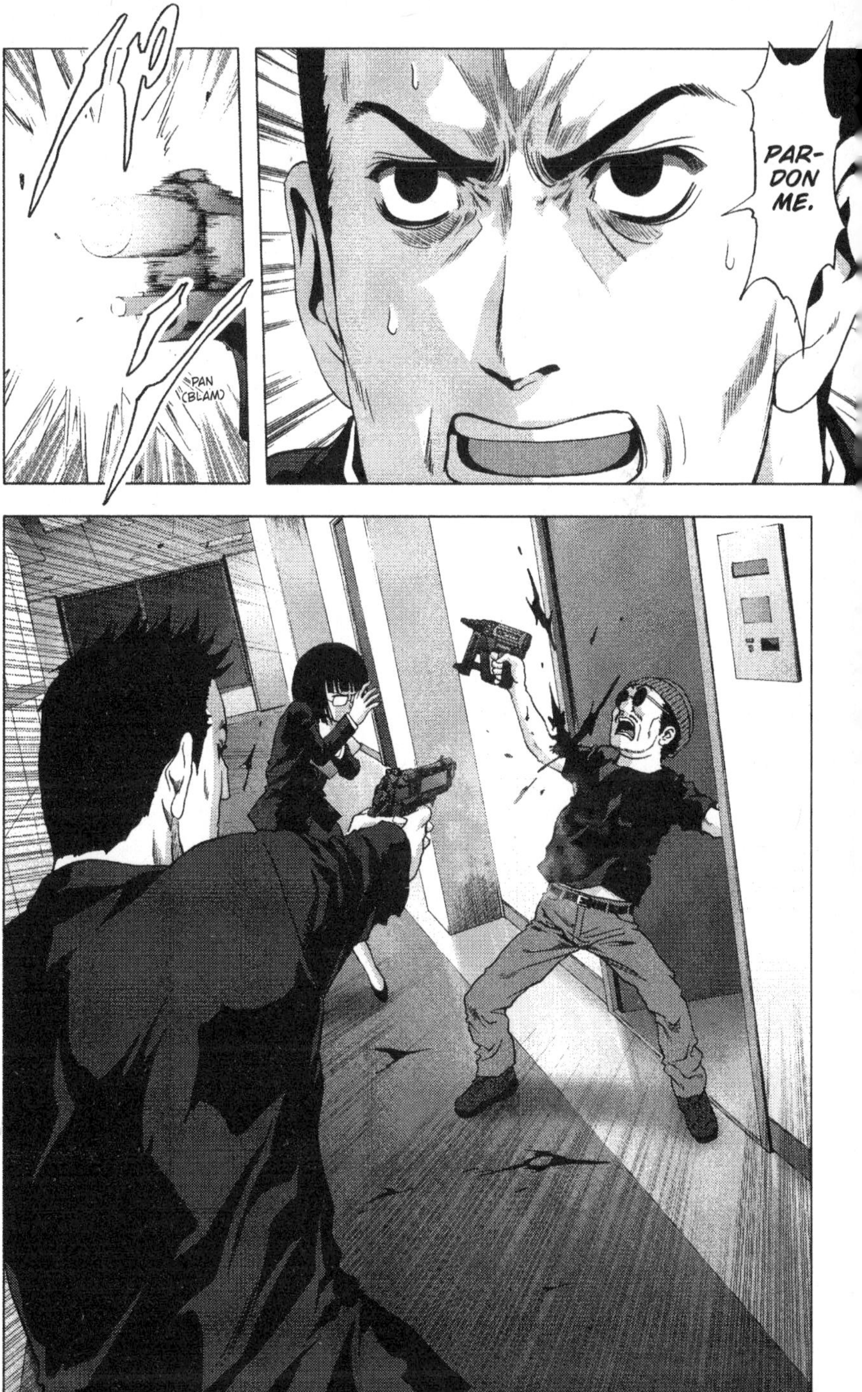
PAR-
DON
ME.
PAN
(BLAM)

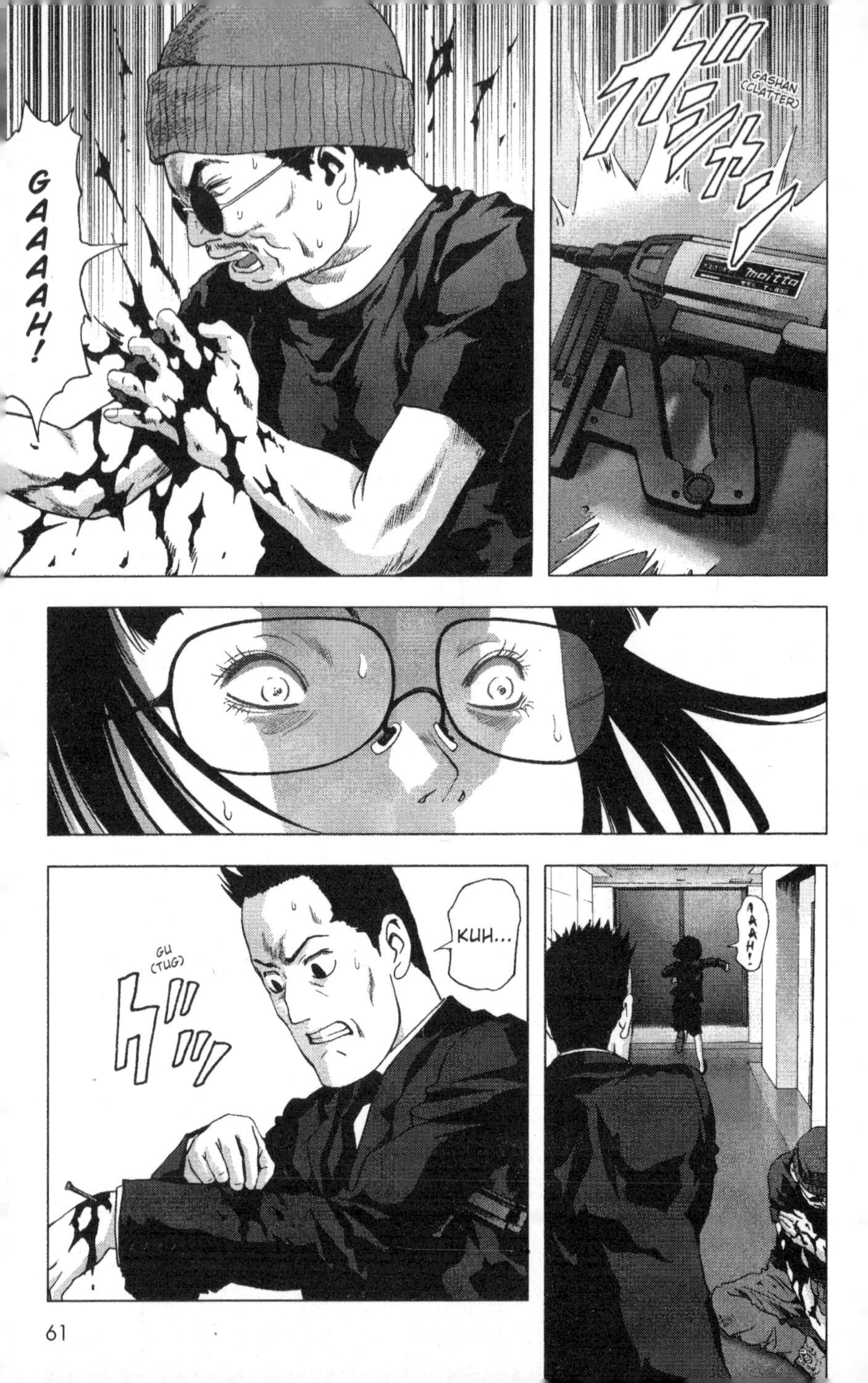
GASHAN (CLATTER)
maitta
GAAAAAH!
KUH...
GU (TUG)
AAAH!

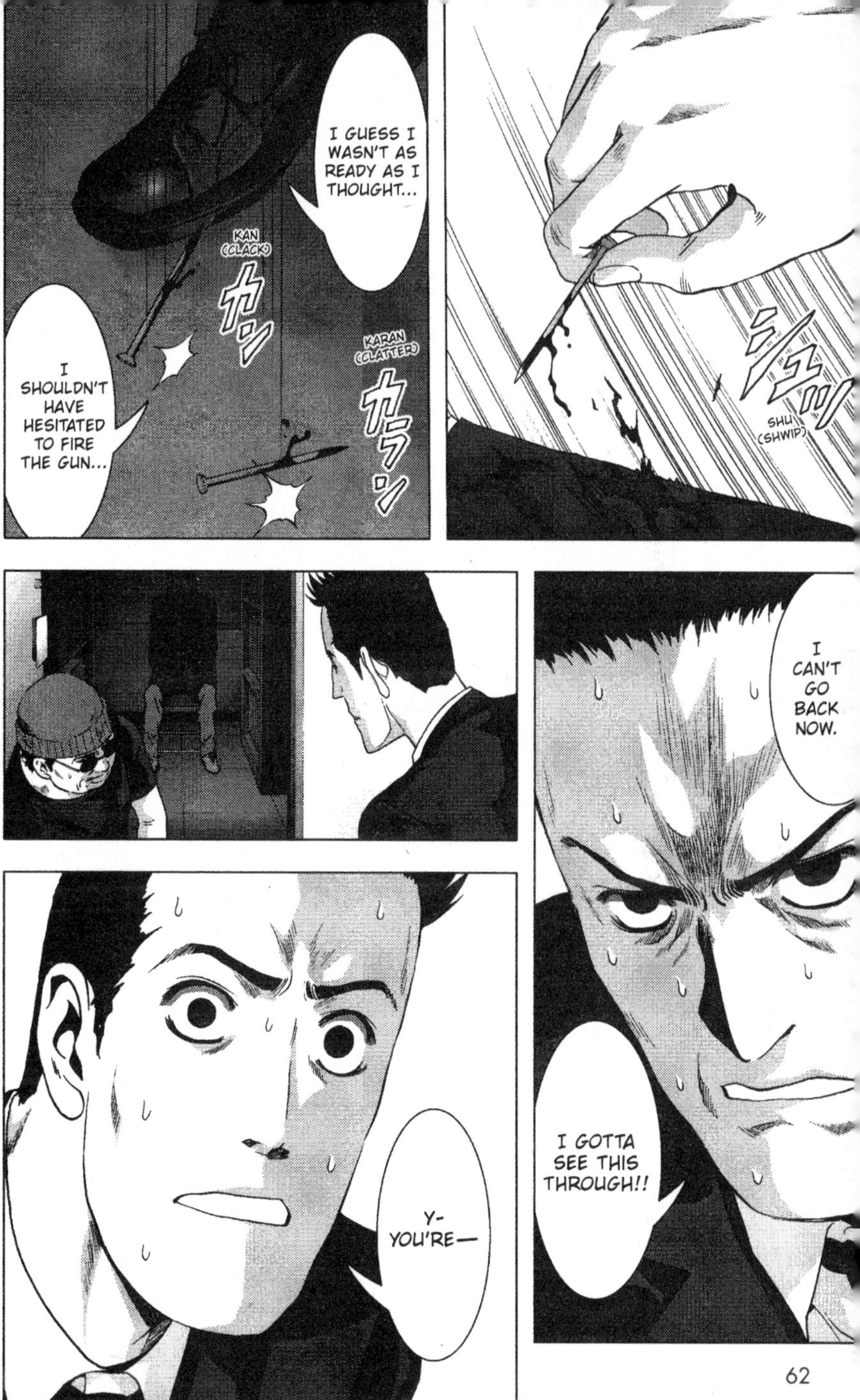

シュッ
SHU (SHWIP)
I GUESS I WASN'T AS READY AS I THOUGHT...
KAN (CLACK)
カン
KARAN (CLATTER)
カラン
I SHOULDN'T HAVE HESITATED TO FIRE THE GUN...
I CAN'T GO BACK NOW.
I GOTTA SEE THIS THROUGH!!
Y-YOU'RE—

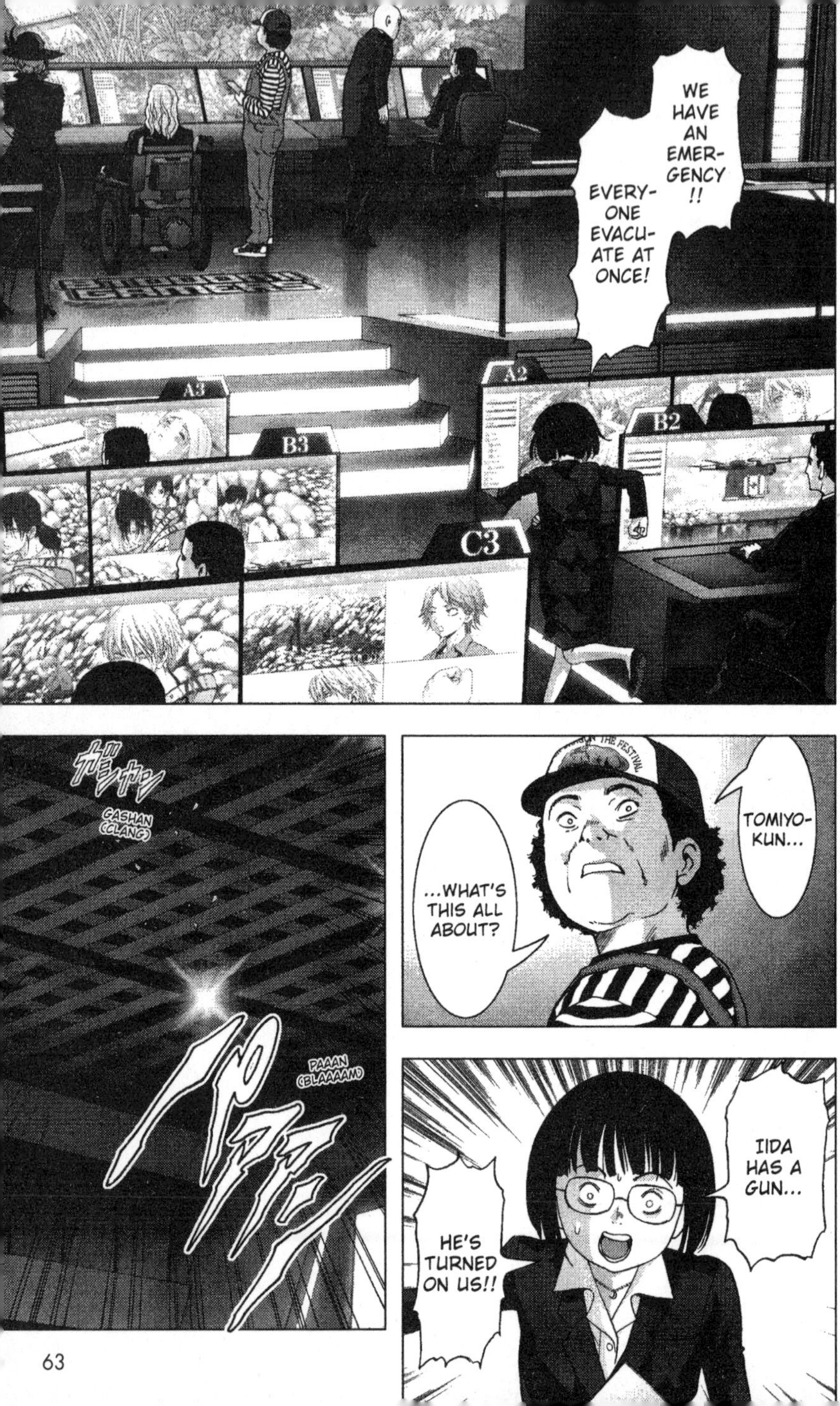
WE HAVE AN EMERGENCY!!
EVERYONE EVACUATE AT ONCE!
TOMIYO-KUN...
...WHAT'S THIS ALL ABOUT?
IIDA HAS A GUN...
HE'S TURNED ON US!!
GASHAN (CLANG)
PAAAN (BLAAAAM)

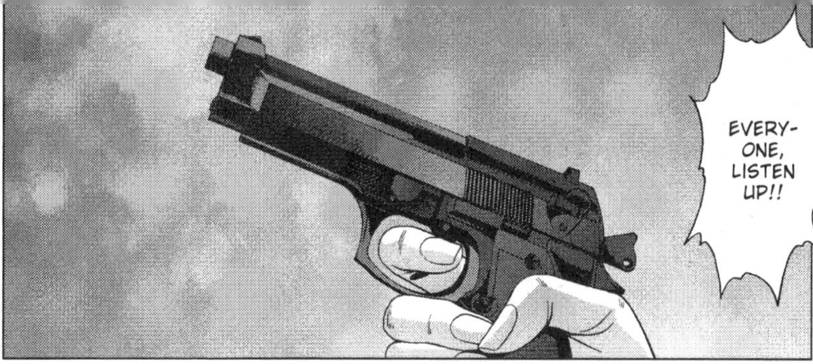
EVERY-ONE, LISTEN UP!!
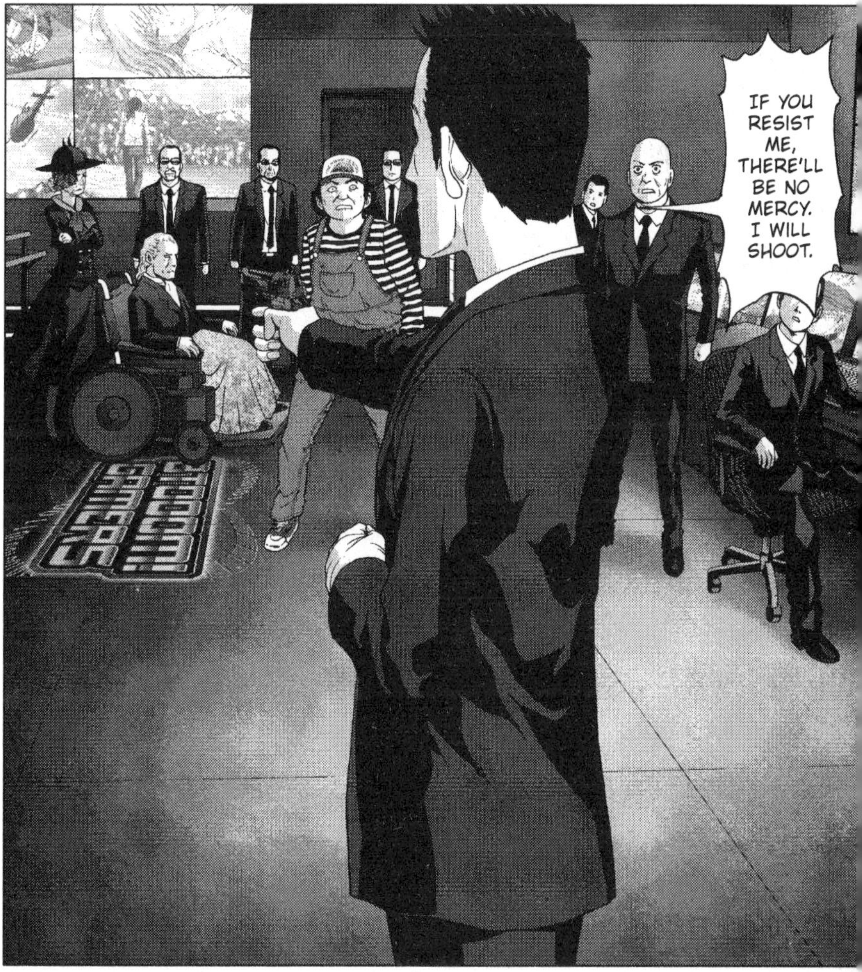
IF YOU RESIST ME, THERE'LL BE NO MERCY. I WILL SHOOT.

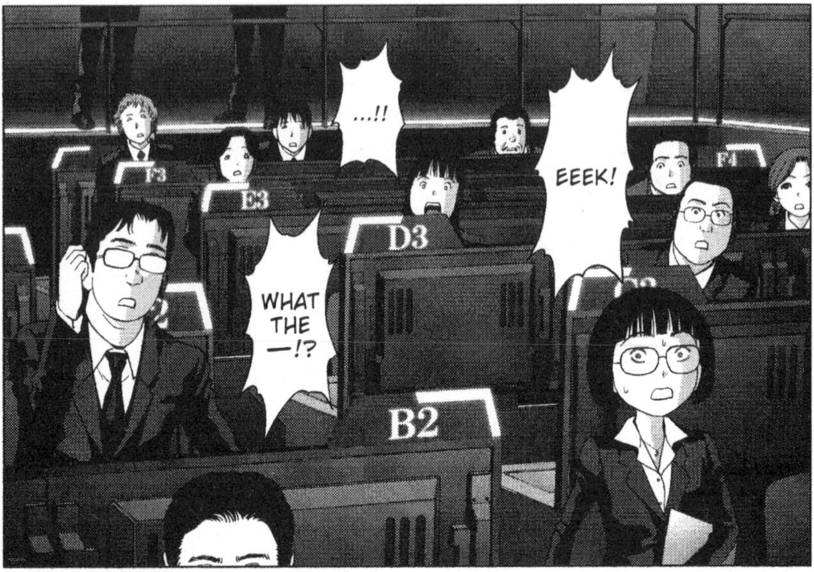
EEEK!
...!!
WHAT THE —!?

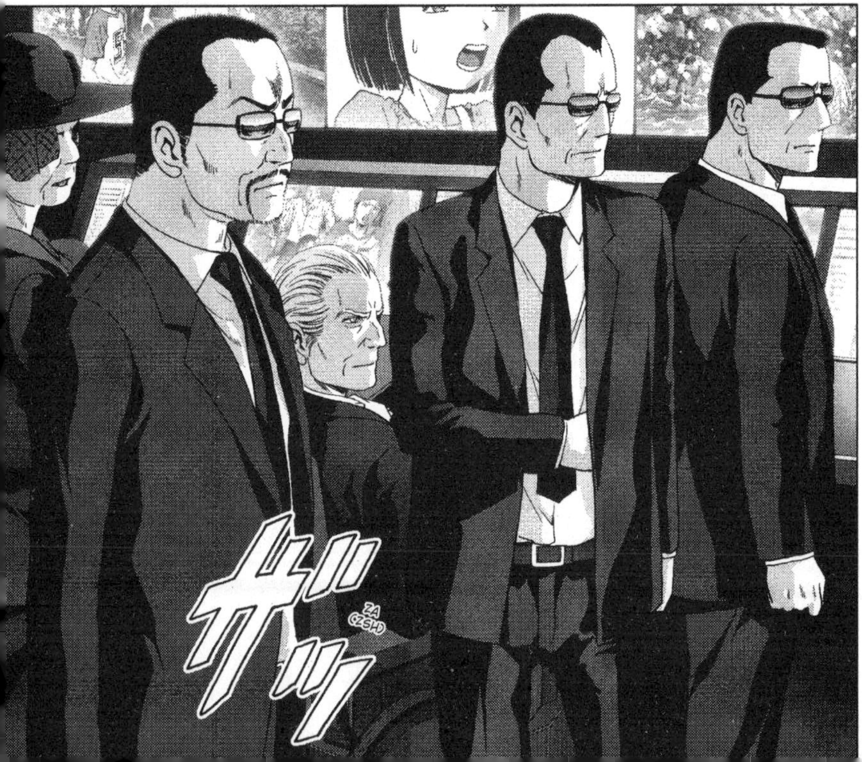
ザッ
ZA
(ZSH)

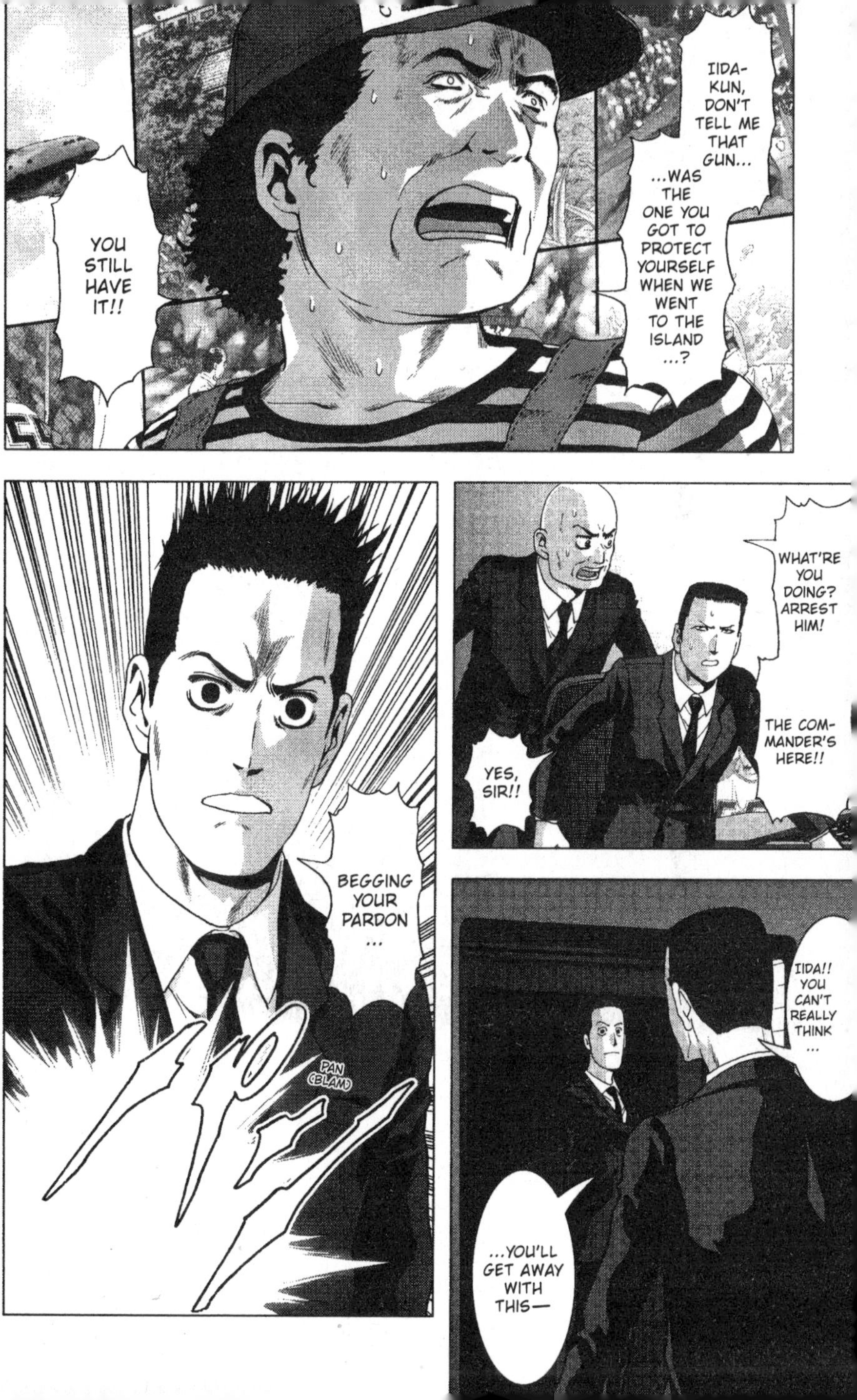
IIDA-KUN, DON'T TELL ME THAT GUN...
...WAS THE ONE YOU GOT TO PROTECT YOURSELF WHEN WE WENT TO THE ISLAND ...?
YOU STILL HAVE IT!!
WHAT'RE YOU DOING? ARREST HIM!
THE COMMANDER'S HERE!!
YES, SIR!!
IIDA!! YOU CAN'T REALLY THINK ...
...YOU'LL GET AWAY WITH THIS—
BEGGING YOUR PARDON ...
PAN (BLAM)

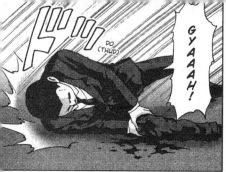

DO (THUD)

GYAAAH!

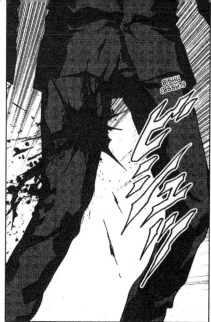

BISHU (BSSH!)

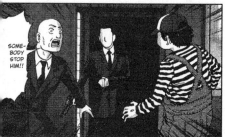

SOME-
BODY
STOP
HIM!!

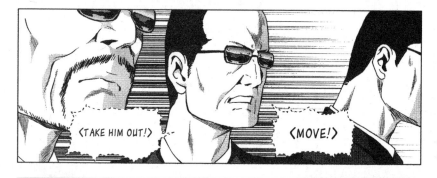

〈TAKE HIM OUT!〉

〈MOVE!〉

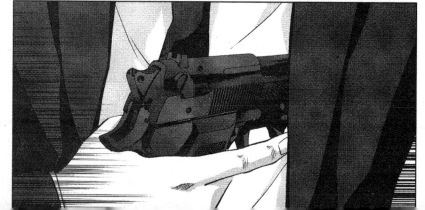

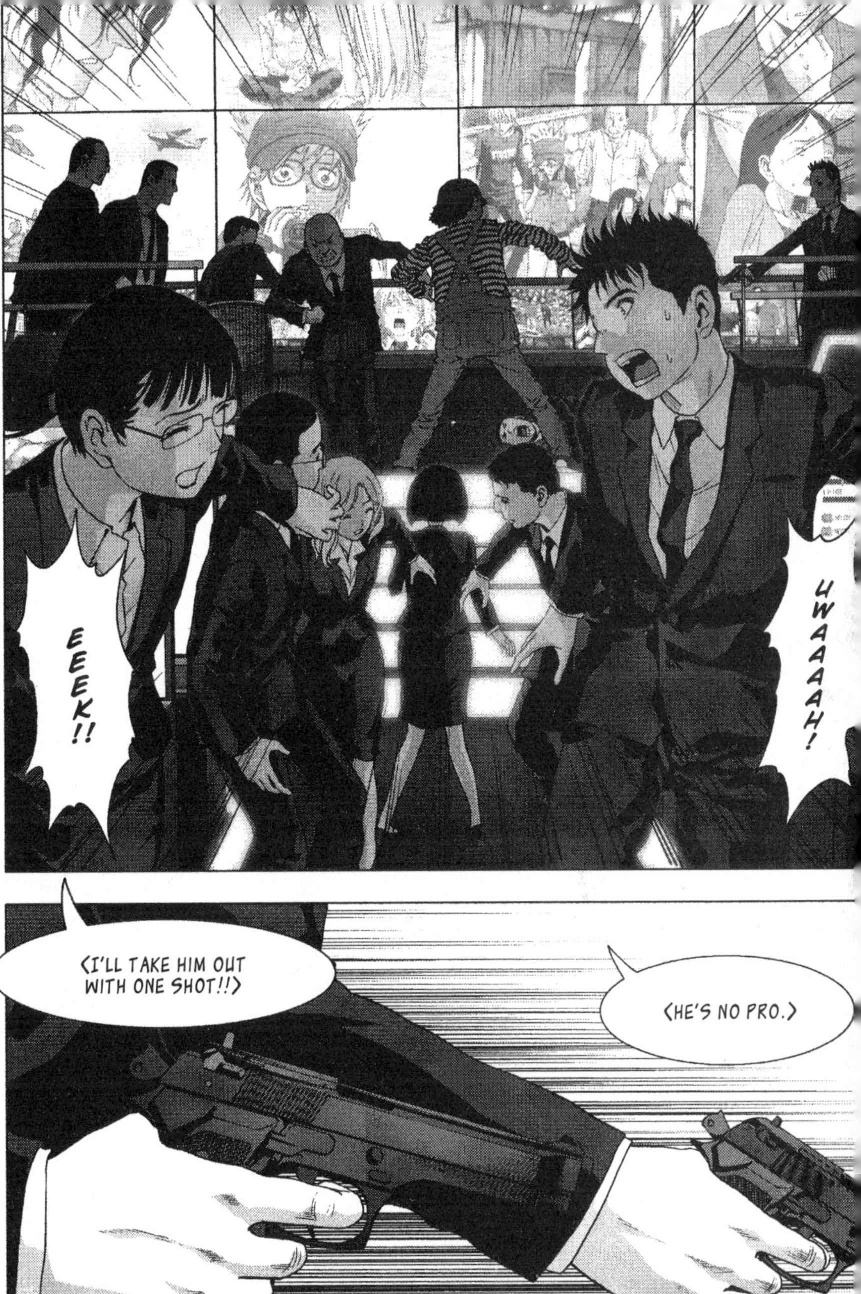
UWAAAAAH!
EEEK!!
〈HE'S NO PRO.〉
〈I'LL TAKE HIM OUT WITH ONE SHOT!!〉

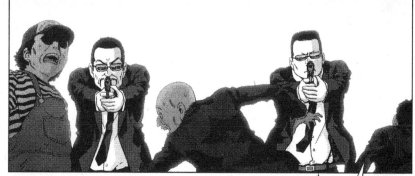

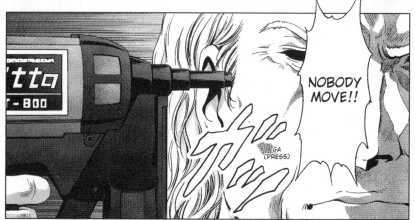

NOBODY MOVE!!

GA
(PRESS)

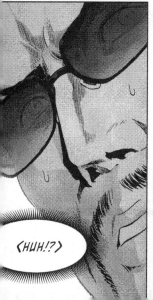

〈HUH!?〉

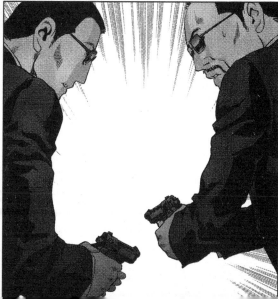

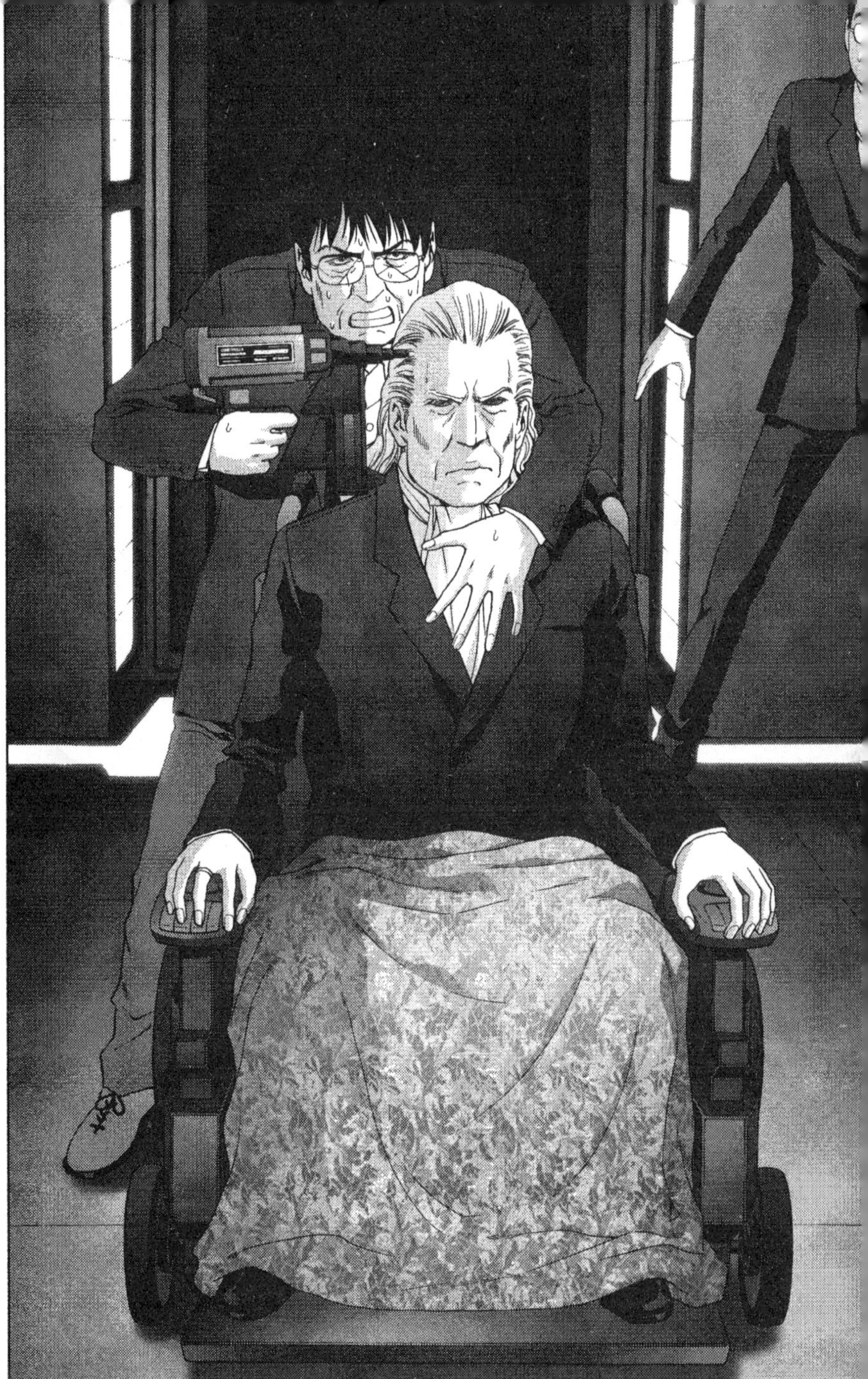

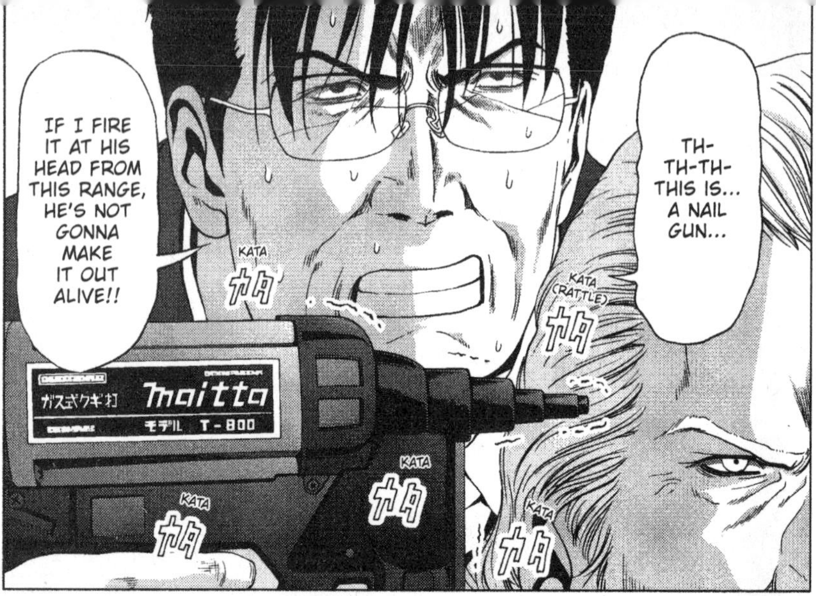
TH-TH-TH-THIS IS... A NAIL GUN...
KATA (RATTLE)
KATA
IF I FIRE IT AT HIS HEAD FROM THIS RANGE, HE'S NOT GONNA MAKE IT OUT ALIVE!!
KATA
ガス式クギ打
maitta
モデル T-800
KATA
KATA
KATA
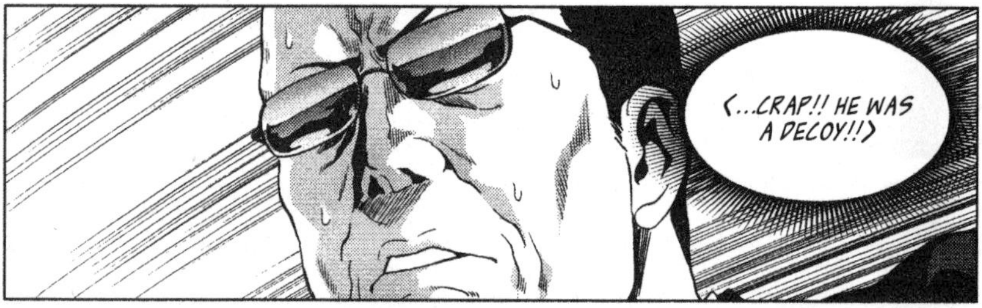
〈...CRAP!! HE WAS A DECOY!!〉
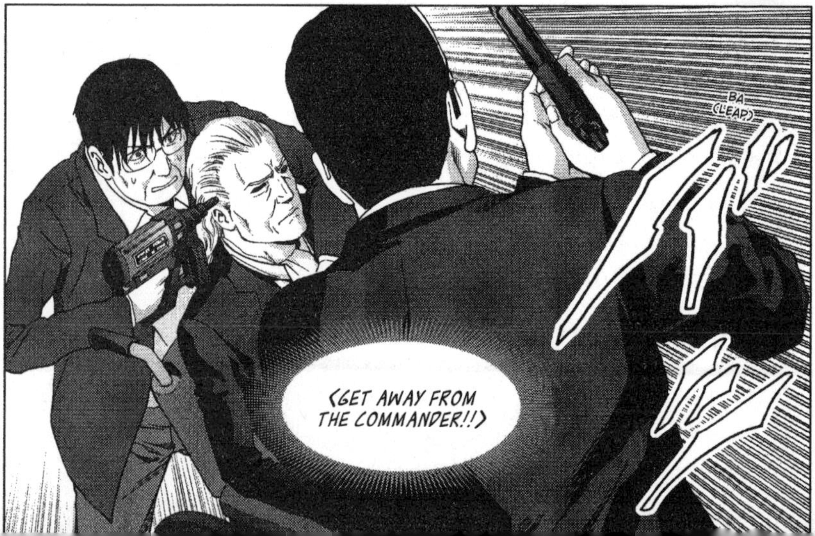
BA (LEAP)
〈GET AWAY FROM THE COMMANDER!!〉

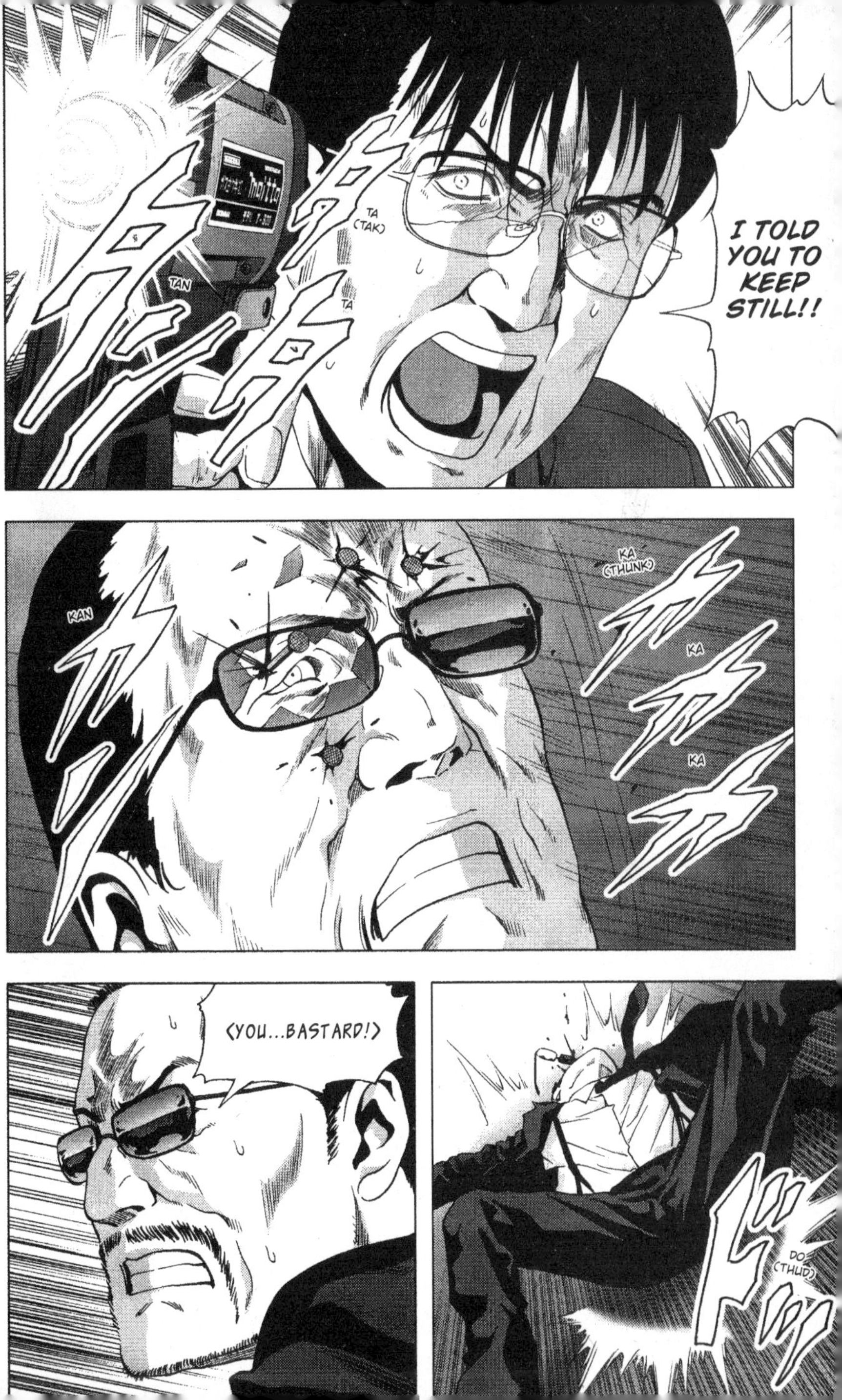
I TOLD YOU TO KEEP STILL!!
TA (TAK)
TA
TAN
KA (THUNK)
KA
KA
KAN
DO (THUD)
<YOU...BASTARD!>

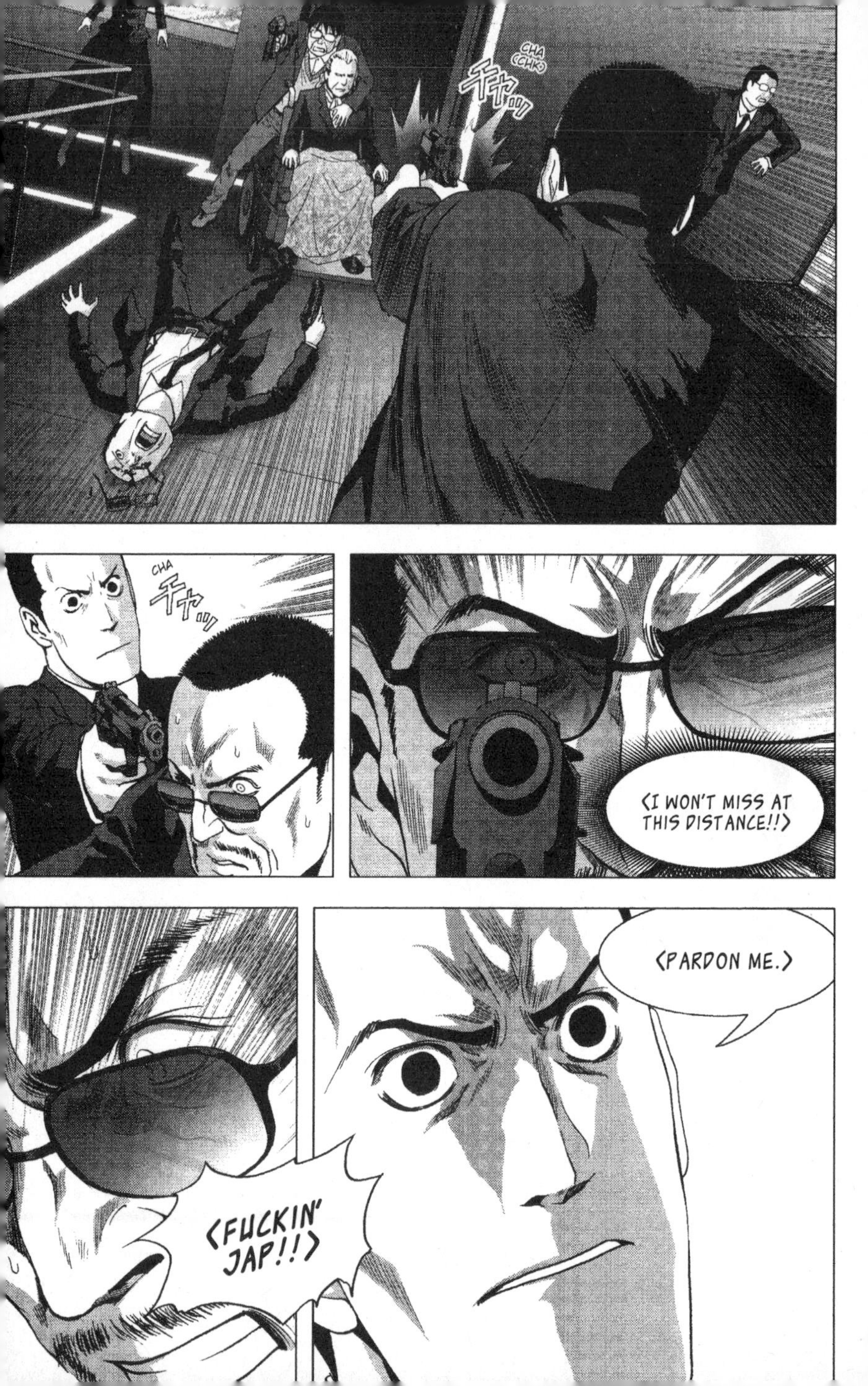
CHA
(CHK)
チャッ
⟨I WON'T MISS AT THIS DISTANCE!!⟩
CHA
チャッ
⟨PARDON ME.⟩
⟨FUCKIN' JAP!!⟩

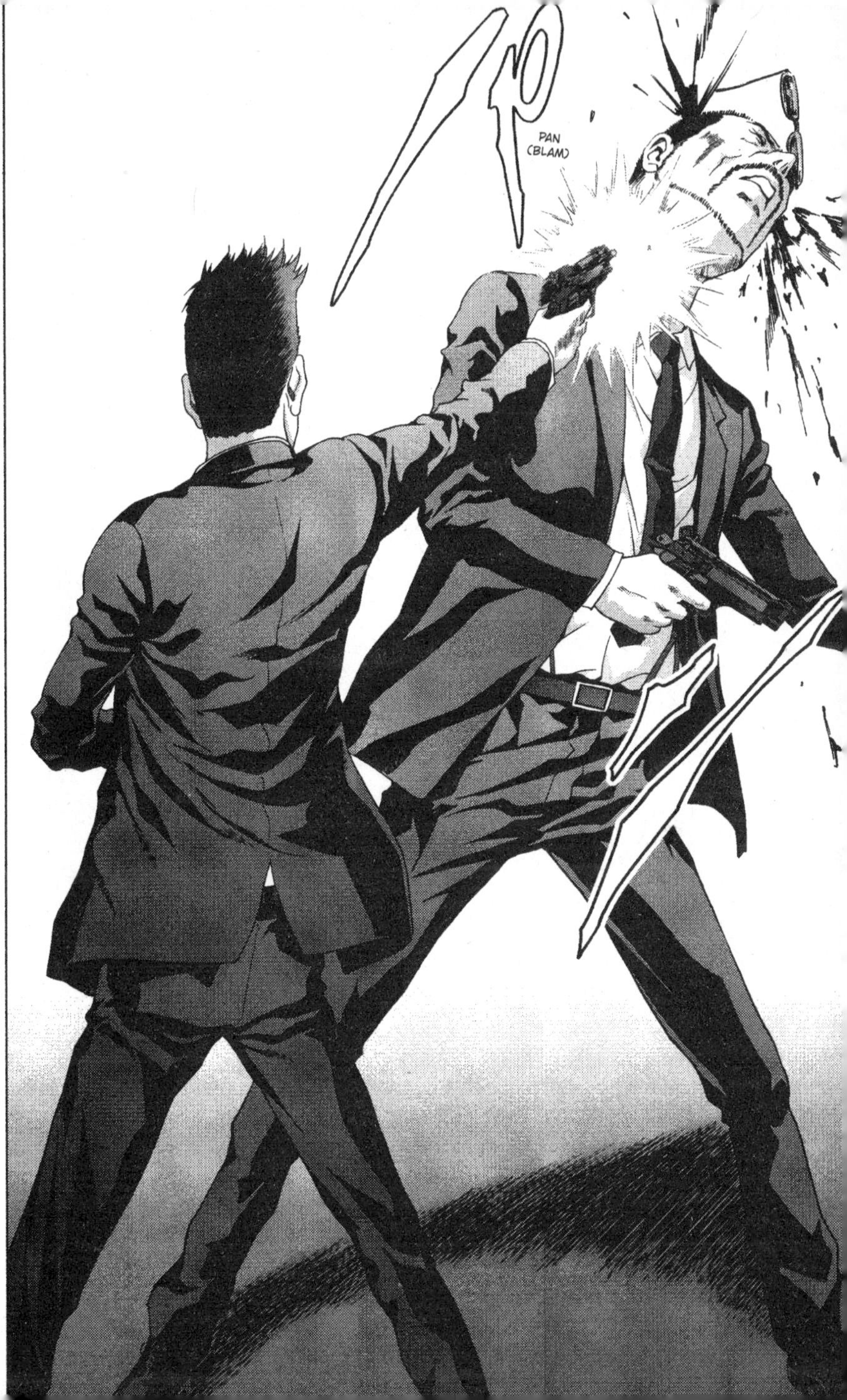
PAN
(BLAM)

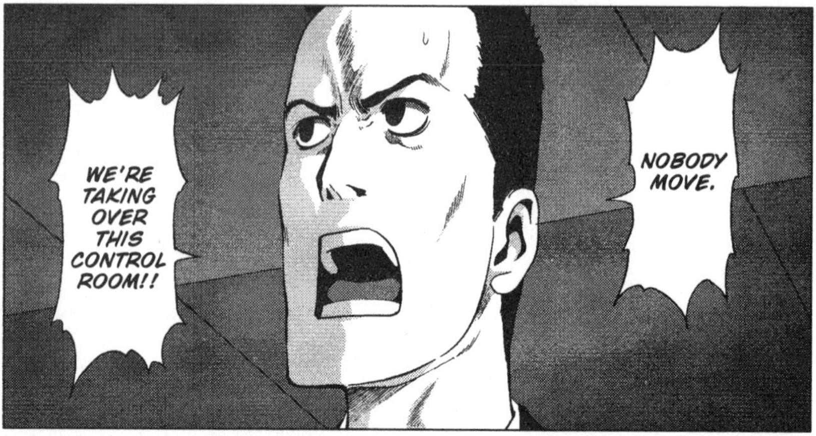
NOBODY MOVE.
WE'RE TAKING OVER THIS CONTROL ROOM!!

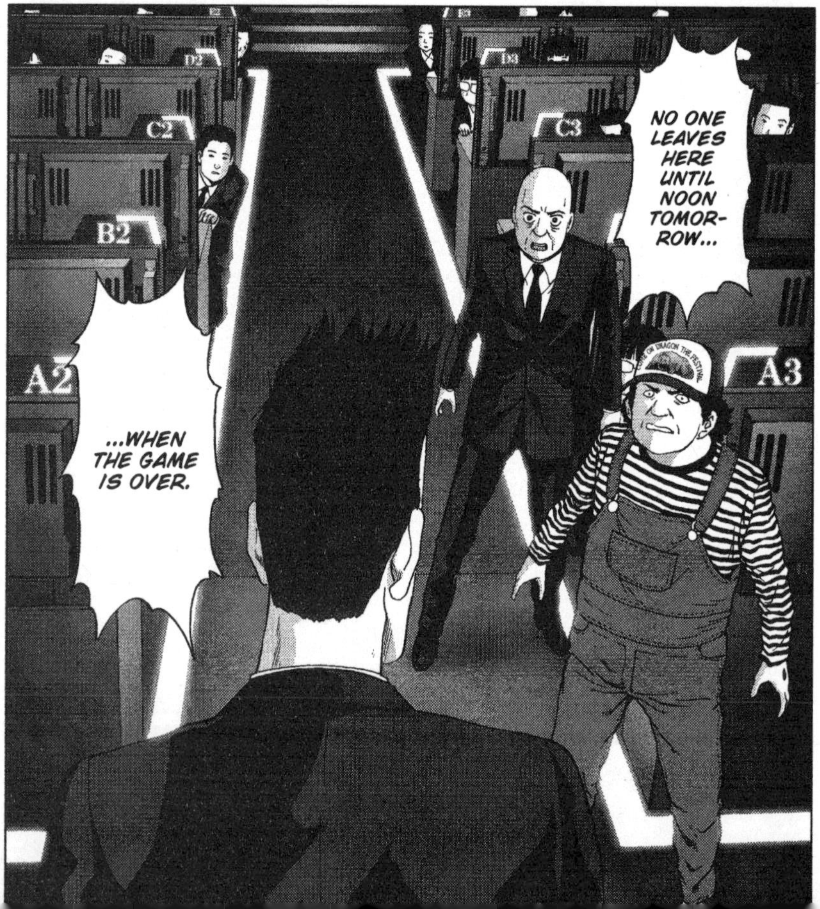
NO ONE LEAVES HERE UNTIL NOON TOMOR-ROW...
...WHEN THE GAME IS OVER.

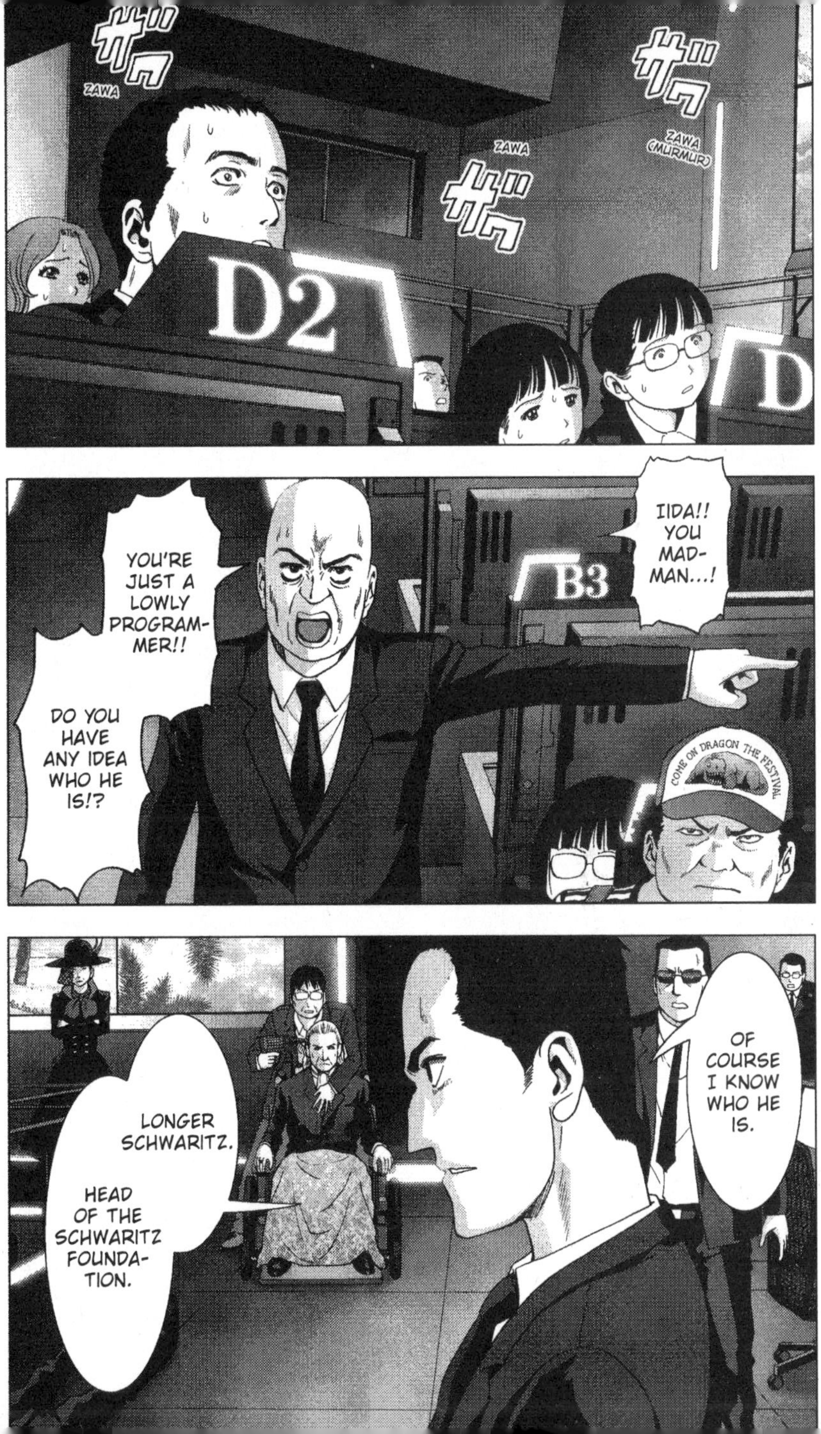
ザワ
ZAWA (MURMUR)
ザワ
ZAWA
ザワ
ZAWA
D2
D
IIDA!! YOU MAD-MAN...!
B3
YOU'RE JUST A LOWLY PROGRAM-MER!!
DO YOU HAVE ANY IDEA WHO HE IS!?
COME ON DRAGON THE FESTIVAL
OF COURSE I KNOW WHO HE IS.
LONGER SCHWARITZ.
HEAD OF THE SCHWARITZ FOUNDA-TION.

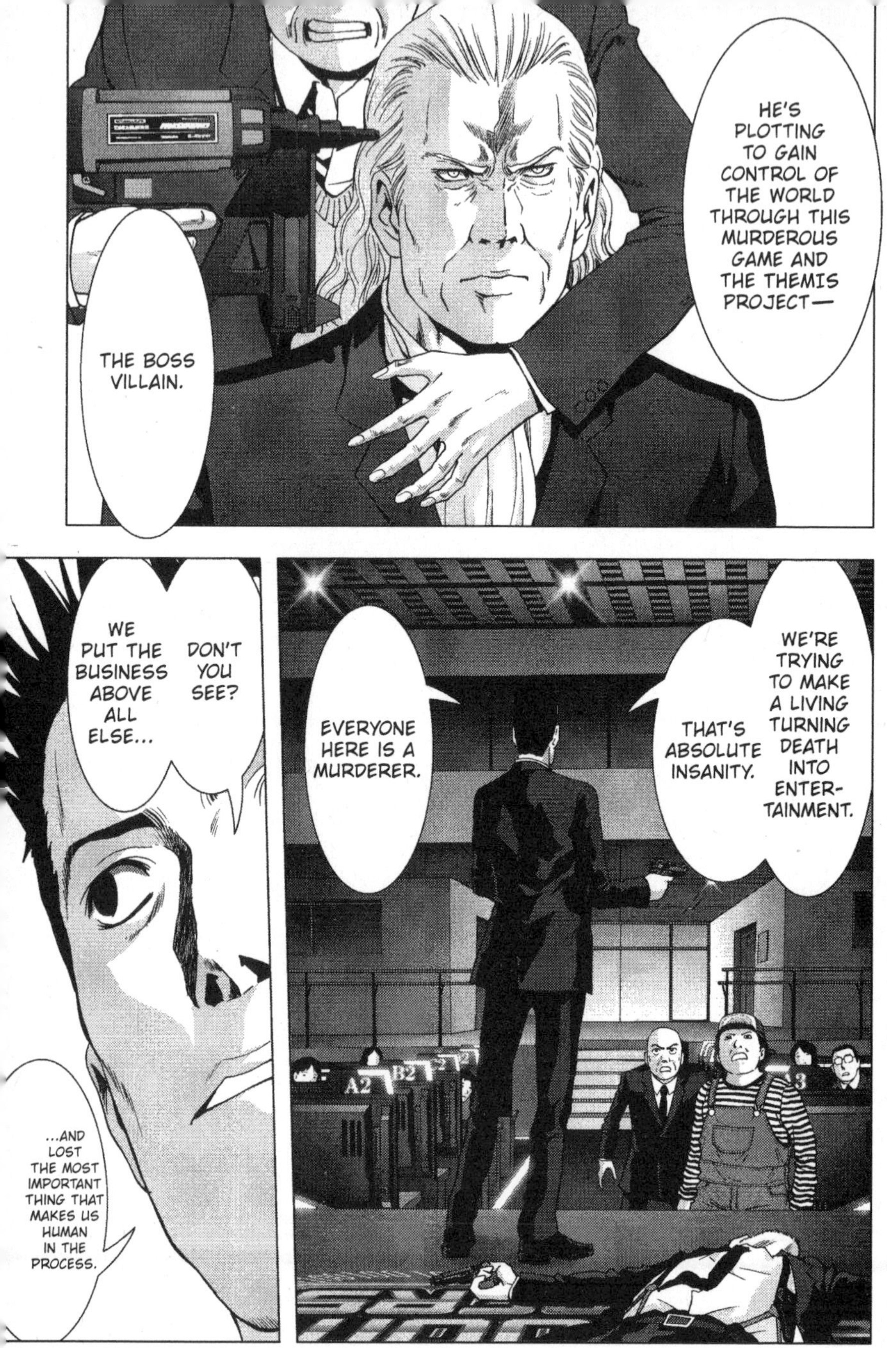
HE'S PLOTTING TO GAIN CONTROL OF THE WORLD THROUGH THIS MURDEROUS GAME AND THE THEMIS PROJECT—
THE BOSS VILLAIN.
WE'RE TRYING TO MAKE A LIVING TURNING DEATH INTO ENTERTAINMENT.
THAT'S ABSOLUTE INSANITY.
EVERYONE HERE IS A MURDERER.
DON'T YOU SEE?
WE PUT THE BUSINESS ABOVE ALL ELSE...
...AND LOST THE MOST IMPORTANT THING THAT MAKES US HUMAN IN THE PROCESS.

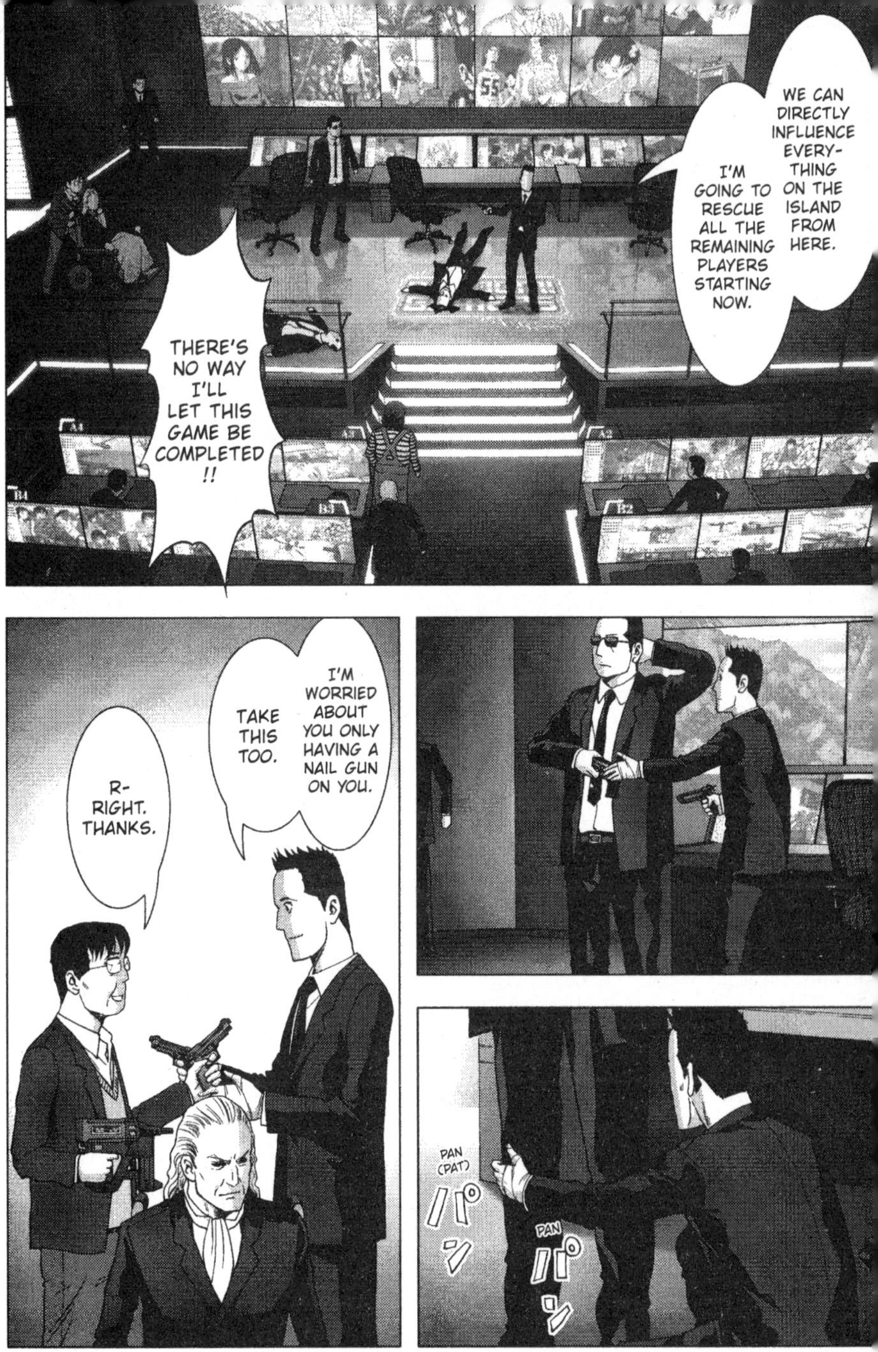
WE CAN DIRECTLY INFLUENCE EVERYTHING ON THE ISLAND FROM HERE.
I'M GOING TO RESCUE ALL THE REMAINING PLAYERS STARTING NOW.
THERE'S NO WAY I'LL LET THIS GAME BE COMPLETED !!
I'M WORRIED ABOUT YOU ONLY HAVING A NAIL GUN ON YOU.
TAKE THIS TOO.
R-RIGHT. THANKS.
PAN (PAT)
パン
PAN
パン

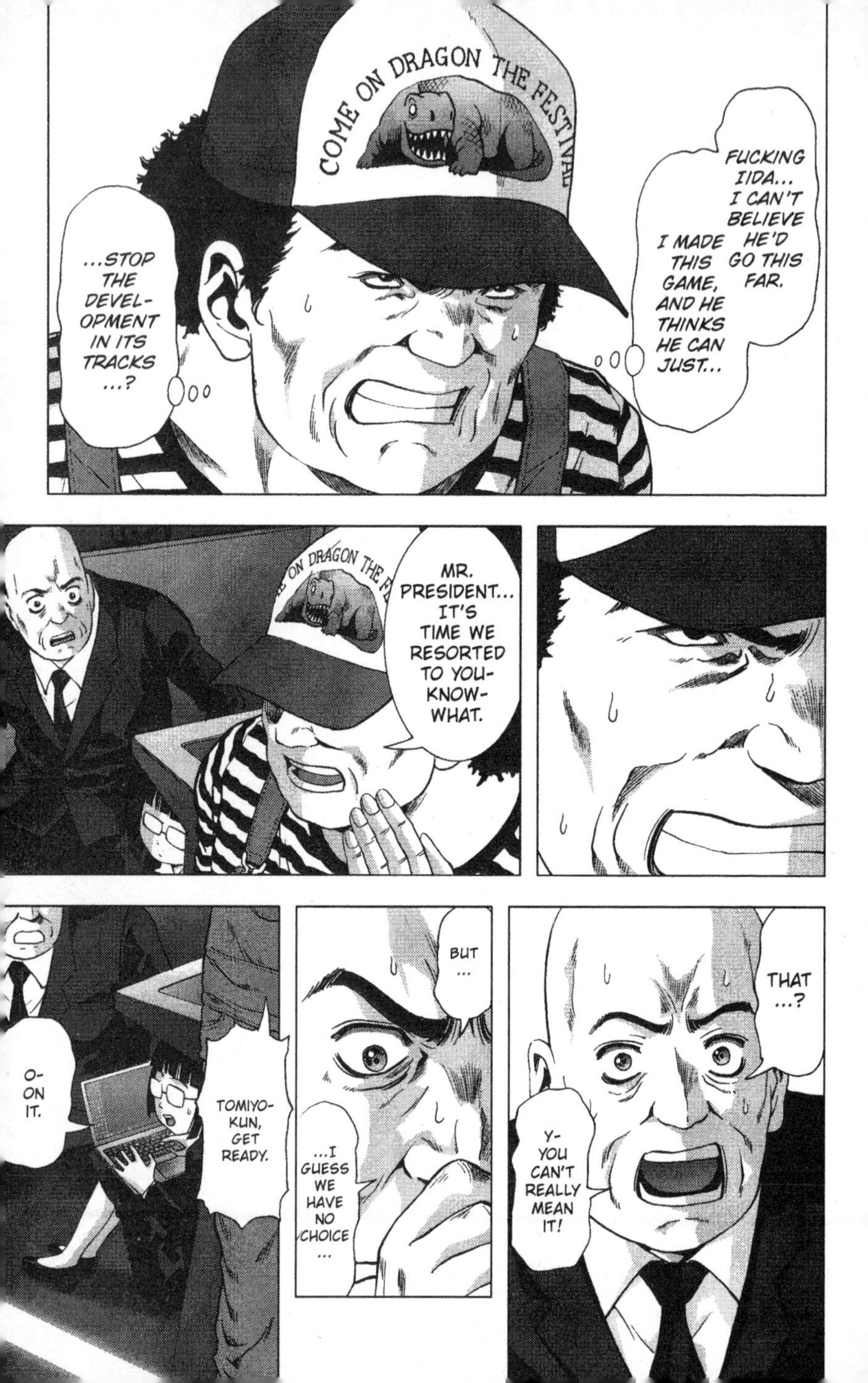
COME ON DRAGON THE FESTIVAL
FUCKING IIDA... I CAN'T BELIEVE HE'D GO THIS FAR.
I MADE THIS GAME, AND HE THINKS HE CAN JUST...
...STOP THE DEVEL-OPMENT IN ITS TRACKS...?
MR. PRESIDENT... IT'S TIME WE RESORTED TO YOU-KNOW-WHAT.
THAT...?
Y-YOU CAN'T REALLY MEAN IT!
BUT...
...I GUESS WE HAVE NO CHOICE...
TOMIYO-KUN, GET READY.
O-ON IT.

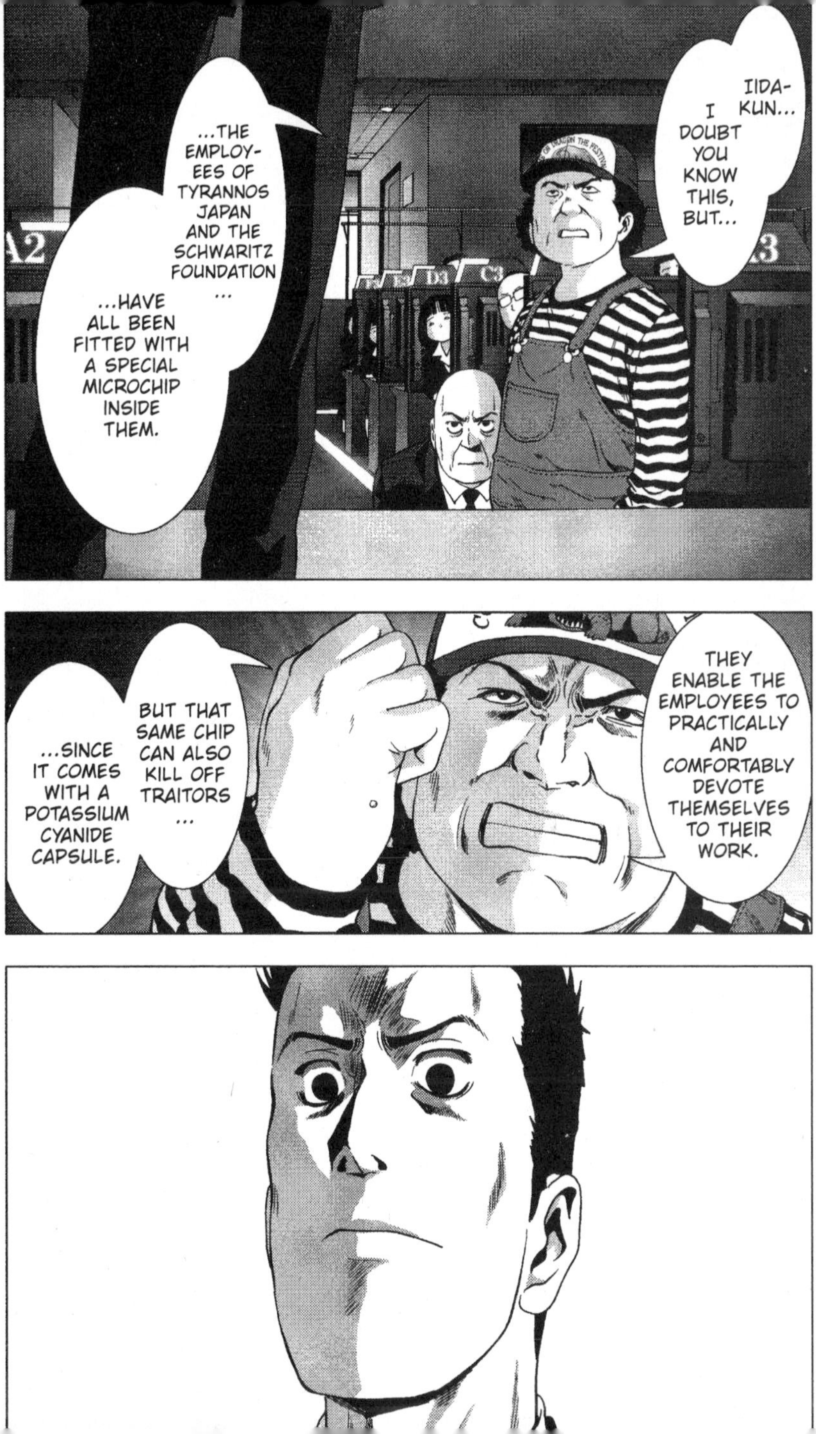
IIDA-KUN... I DOUBT YOU KNOW THIS, BUT...
...THE EMPLOYEES OF TYRANNOS JAPAN AND THE SCHWARITZ FOUNDATION...
...HAVE ALL BEEN FITTED WITH A SPECIAL MICROCHIP INSIDE THEM.
THEY ENABLE THE EMPLOYEES TO PRACTICALLY AND COMFORTABLY DEVOTE THEMSELVES TO THEIR WORK.
BUT THAT SAME CHIP CAN ALSO KILL OFF TRAITORS...
...SINCE IT COMES WITH A POTASSIUM CYANIDE CAPSULE.

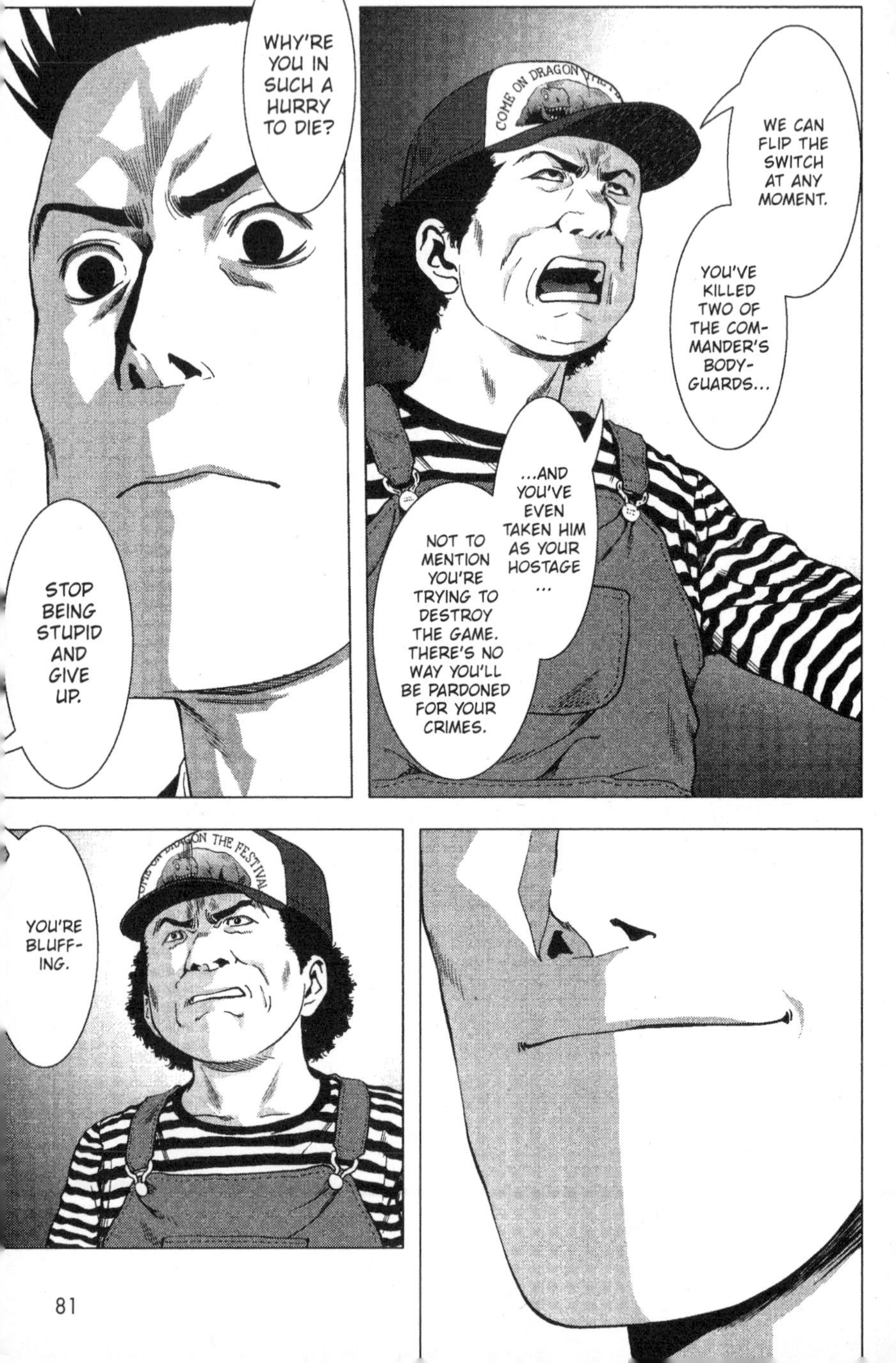
COME ON DRAGON
WE CAN FLIP THE SWITCH AT ANY MOMENT.
YOU'VE KILLED TWO OF THE COM-MANDER'S BODY-GUARDS...
...AND YOU'VE EVEN TAKEN HIM AS YOUR HOSTAGE ...
NOT TO MENTION YOU'RE TRYING TO DESTROY THE GAME. THERE'S NO WAY YOU'LL BE PARDONED FOR YOUR CRIMES.
WHY'RE YOU IN SUCH A HURRY TO DIE?
STOP BEING STUPID AND GIVE UP.
YOU'RE BLUFF-ING.

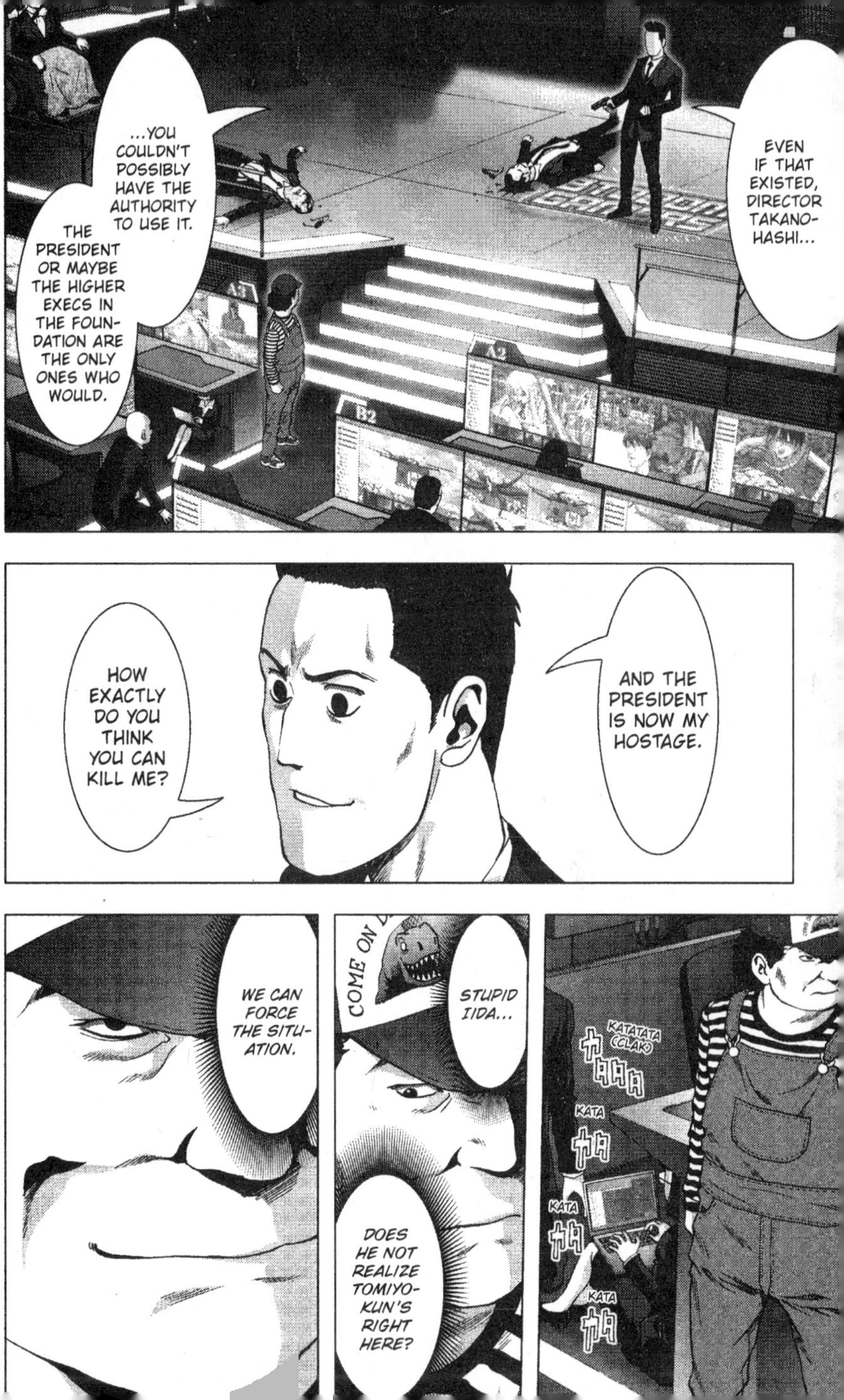
EVEN IF THAT EXISTED, DIRECTOR TAKANO-HASHI...
...YOU COULDN'T POSSIBLY HAVE THE AUTHORITY TO USE IT.
THE PRESIDENT OR MAYBE THE HIGHER EXECS IN THE FOUN-DATION ARE THE ONLY ONES WHO WOULD.
AND THE PRESIDENT IS NOW MY HOSTAGE.
HOW EXACTLY DO YOU THINK YOU CAN KILL ME?
KATATATA (CLAK)
KATA
KATA
KATA
COME ON
STUPID IIDA...
DOES HE NOT REALIZE TOMIYO-KUN'S RIGHT HERE?
WE CAN FORCE THE SITU-ATION.

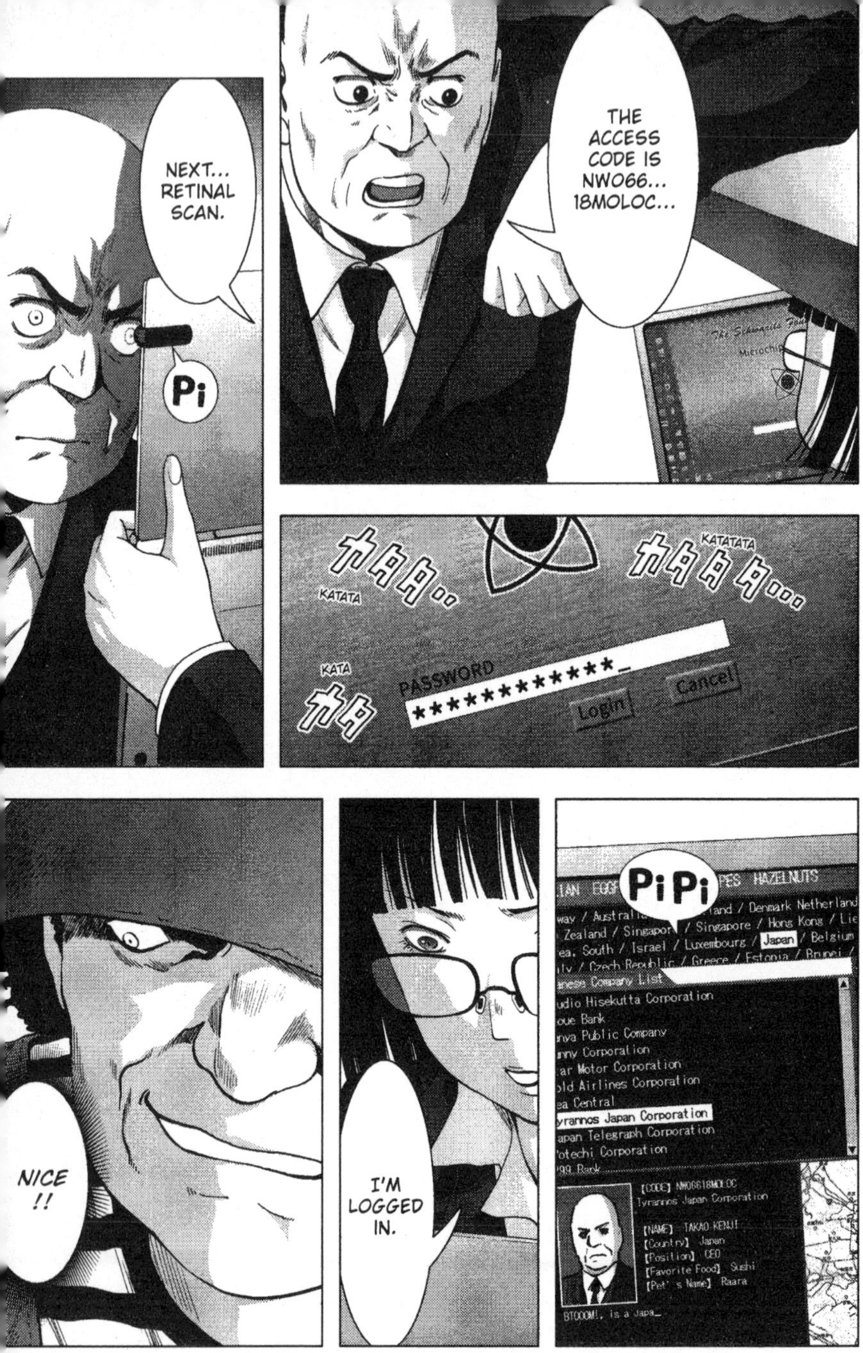
THE ACCESS CODE IS NW066... 18MOLOC...
カタタ。。
KATATA
カタタタ。。。
KATATATA
カタ
KATA
PASSWORD
************_
Login
Cancel
NEXT... RETINAL SCAN.
Pi
PiPi
HAZELNUTS
Japan
Tyrannos Japan Corporation
[CODE] NW0618MOLOC
Tyrannos Japan Corporation
[NAME] TAKAO KENJI
[Country] Japan
[Position] CEO
[Favorite Food] Sushi
[Pet's Name] Raara
BTOOOM!, is a Japa_
I'M LOGGED IN.
NICE !!

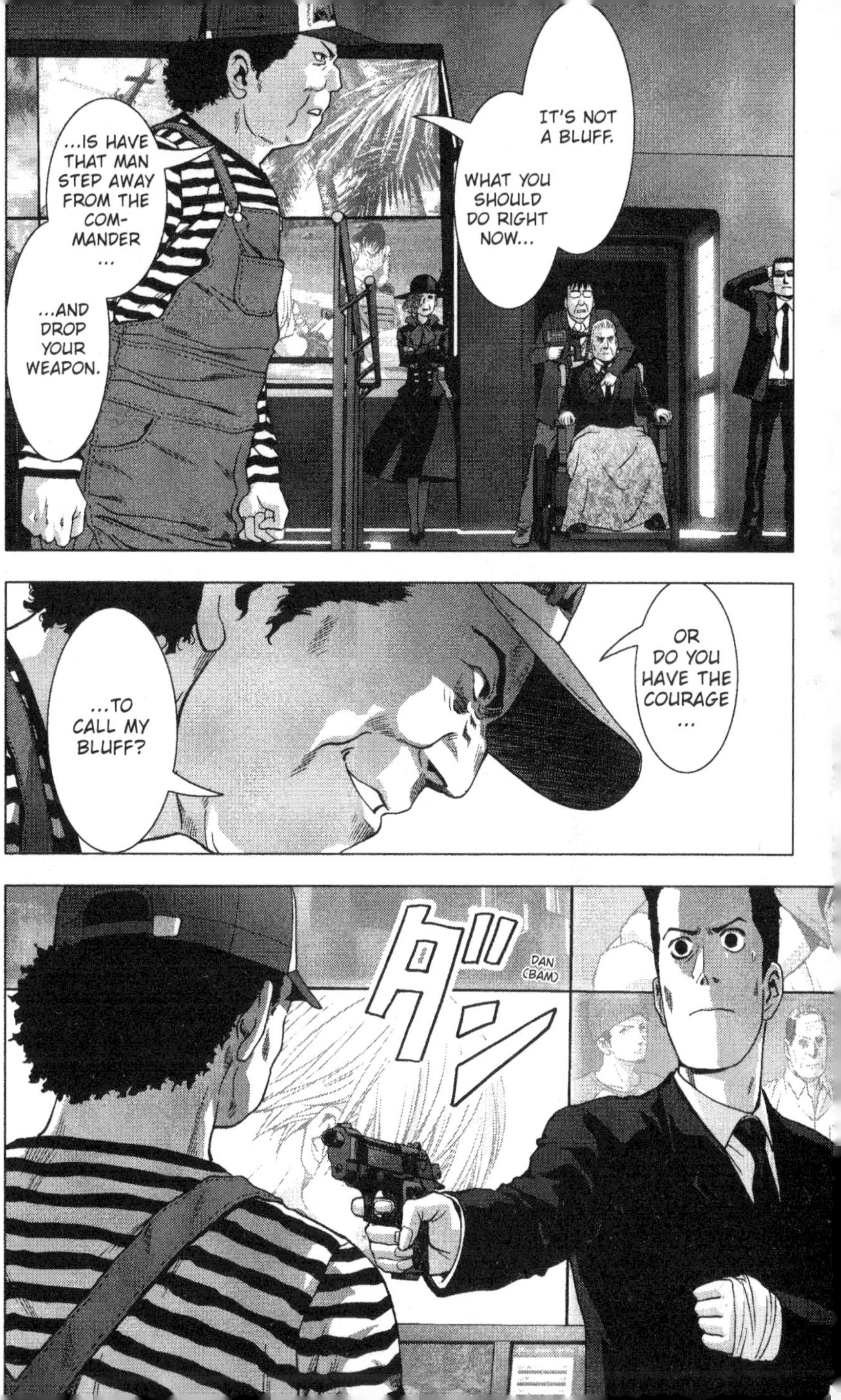
IT'S NOT A BLUFF.
WHAT YOU SHOULD DO RIGHT NOW...
...IS HAVE THAT MAN STEP AWAY FROM THE COM-MANDER ...
...AND DROP YOUR WEAPON.
OR DO YOU HAVE THE COURAGE ...
...TO CALL MY BLUFF?
ダン
DAN (BAM)

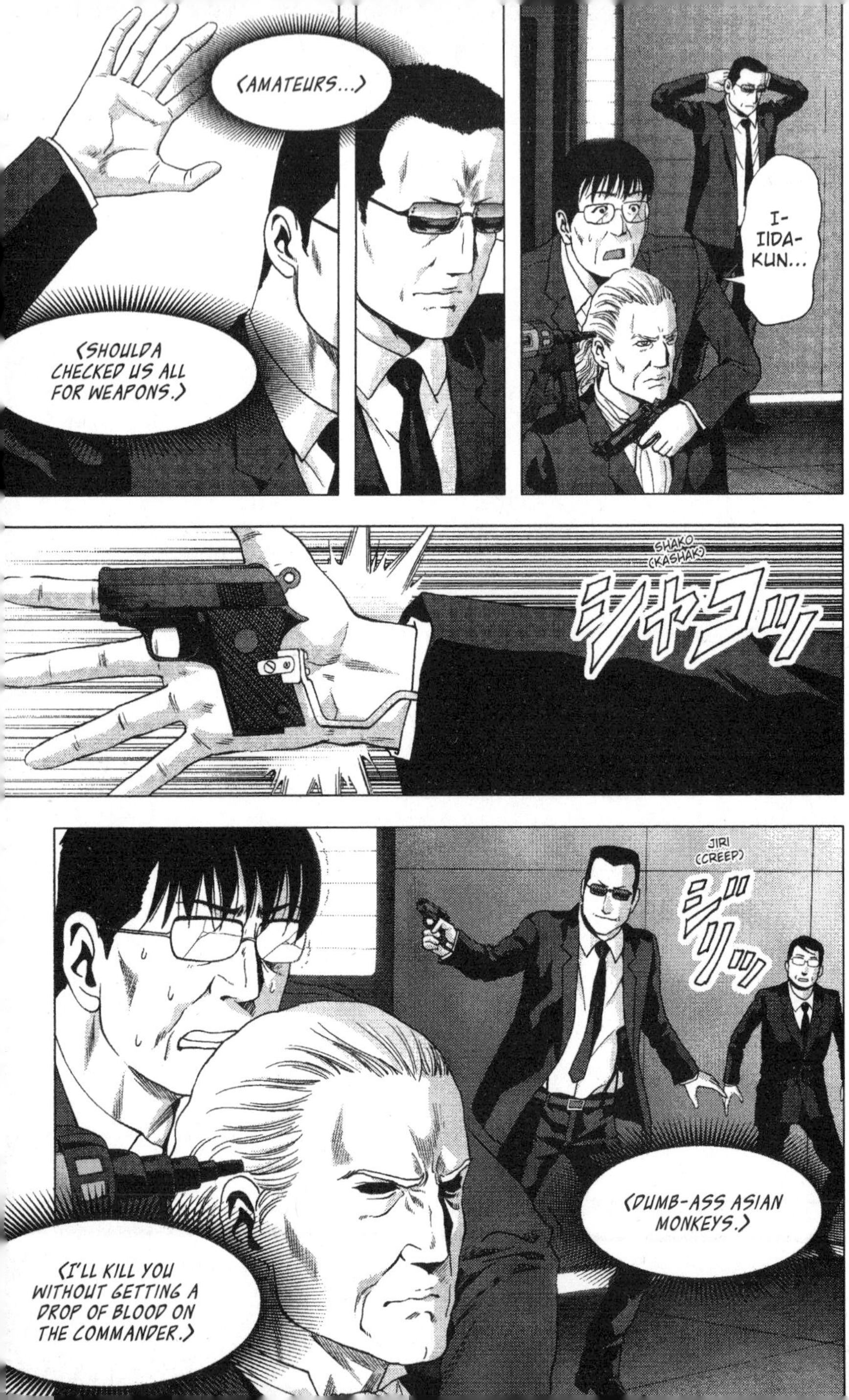
I- IIDA- KUN...
<AMATEURS...>
<SHOULDA CHECKED US ALL FOR WEAPONS.>
SHAKO (KASHAK)
シャコッ
JIRI (CREEP)
ジリッ
<DUMB-ASS ASIAN MONKEYS.>
<I'LL KILL YOU WITHOUT GETTING A DROP OF BLOOD ON THE COMMANDER.>

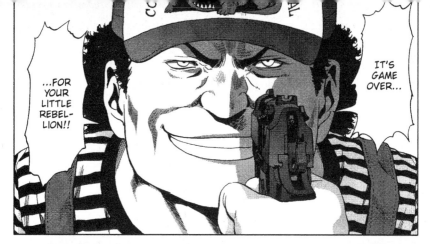

...FOR YOUR LITTLE REBELLION!!

IT'S GAME OVER...

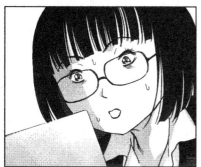

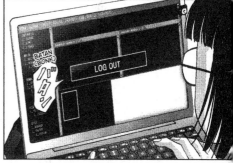

BATAN (BONK)

LOG OUT

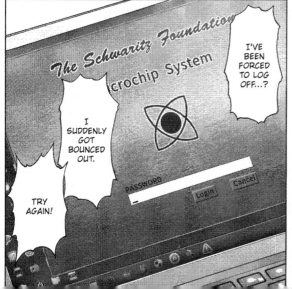

The Schwaritz Foundation

crochip System

I'VE BEEN FORCED TO LOG OFF...?

I SUDDENLY GOT BOUNCED OUT.

TRY AGAIN!

PASSWORD

Login   Cancel

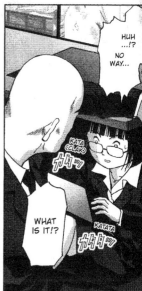

HUH ...!? NO WAY...

KATA (CLAK)

WHAT IS IT!?

KATATA

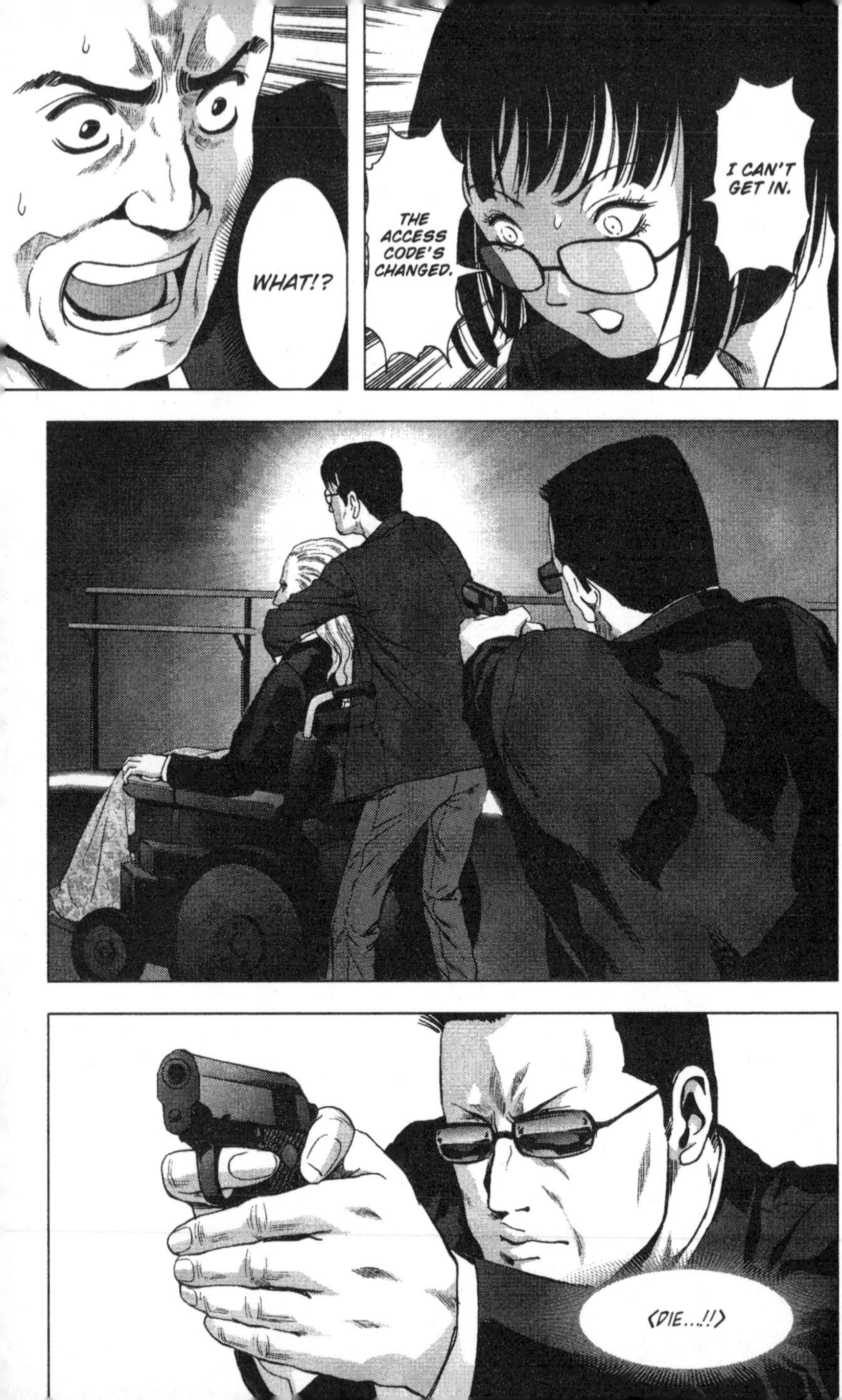
I CAN'T GET IN.
THE ACCESS CODE'S CHANGED.
WHAT!?
‹DIE...!!›

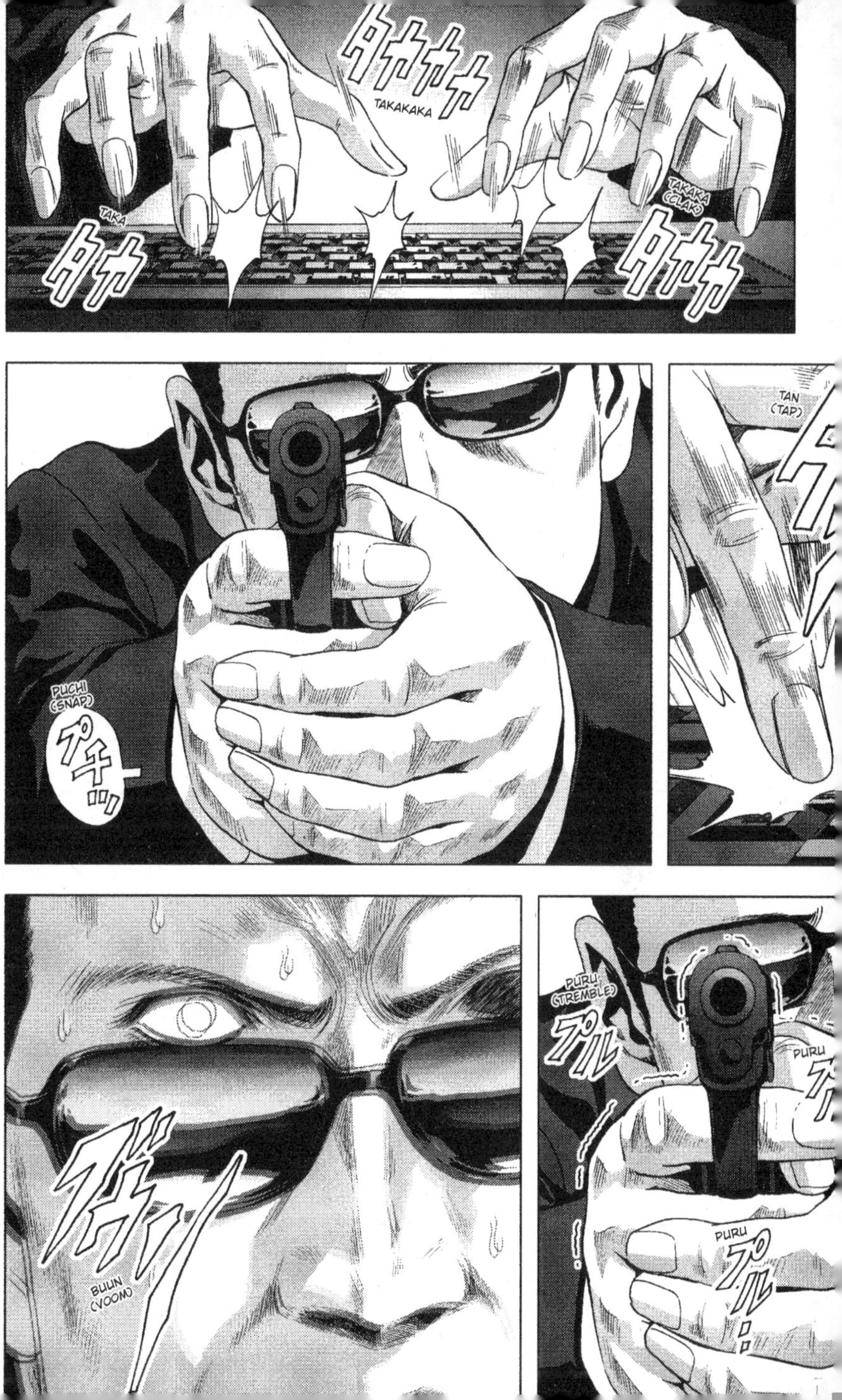
TAKAKA (CLAK)
TAKAKAKA
TAKA
TAN (TAP)
PUCHI (SNAP)
PURU (TREMBLE)
PURU
PURU
BUUN (VOOM)

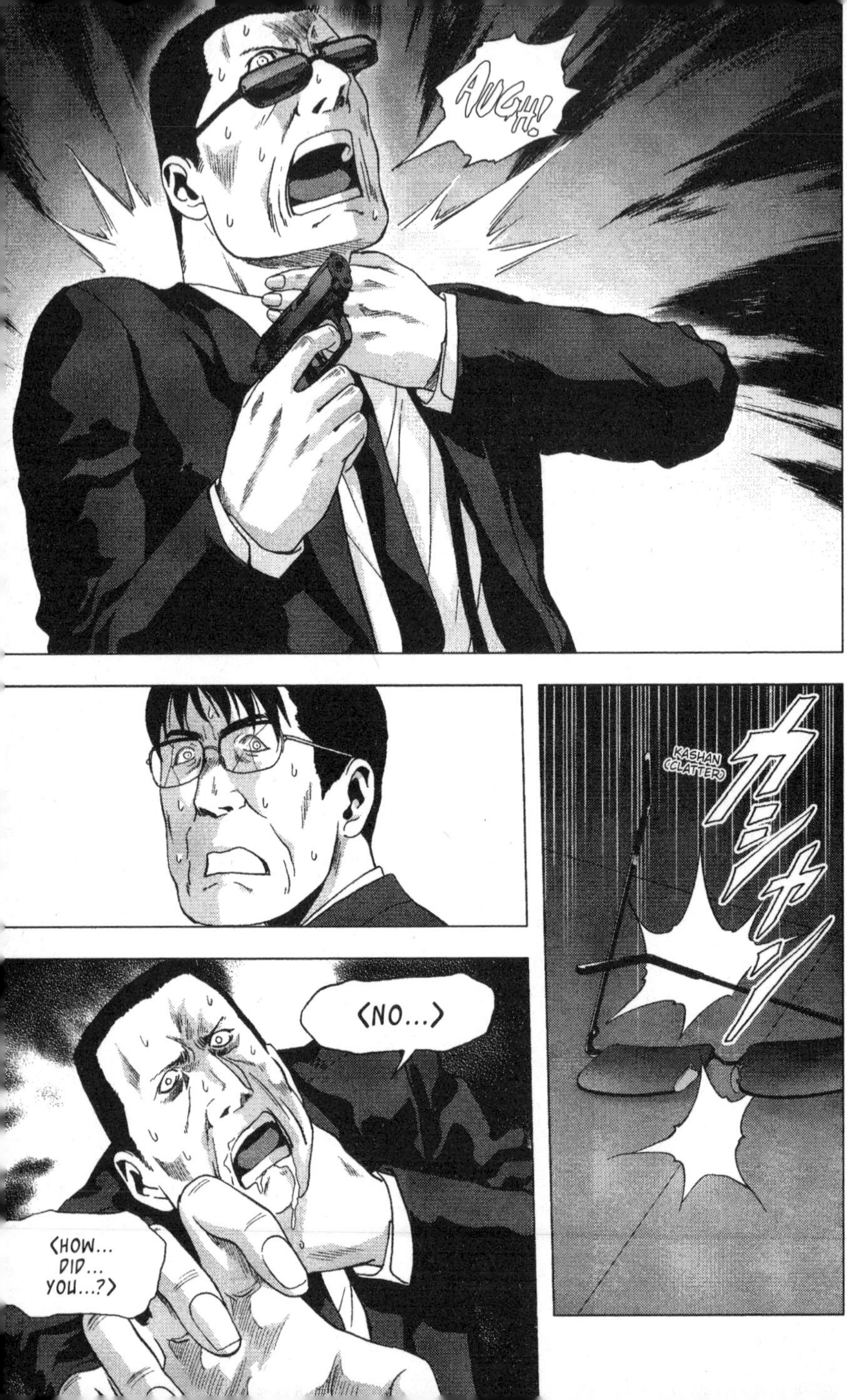
AUGH!
KASHAN (CLATTER)
カシャン
<NO...>
<HOW... DID... YOU...?>

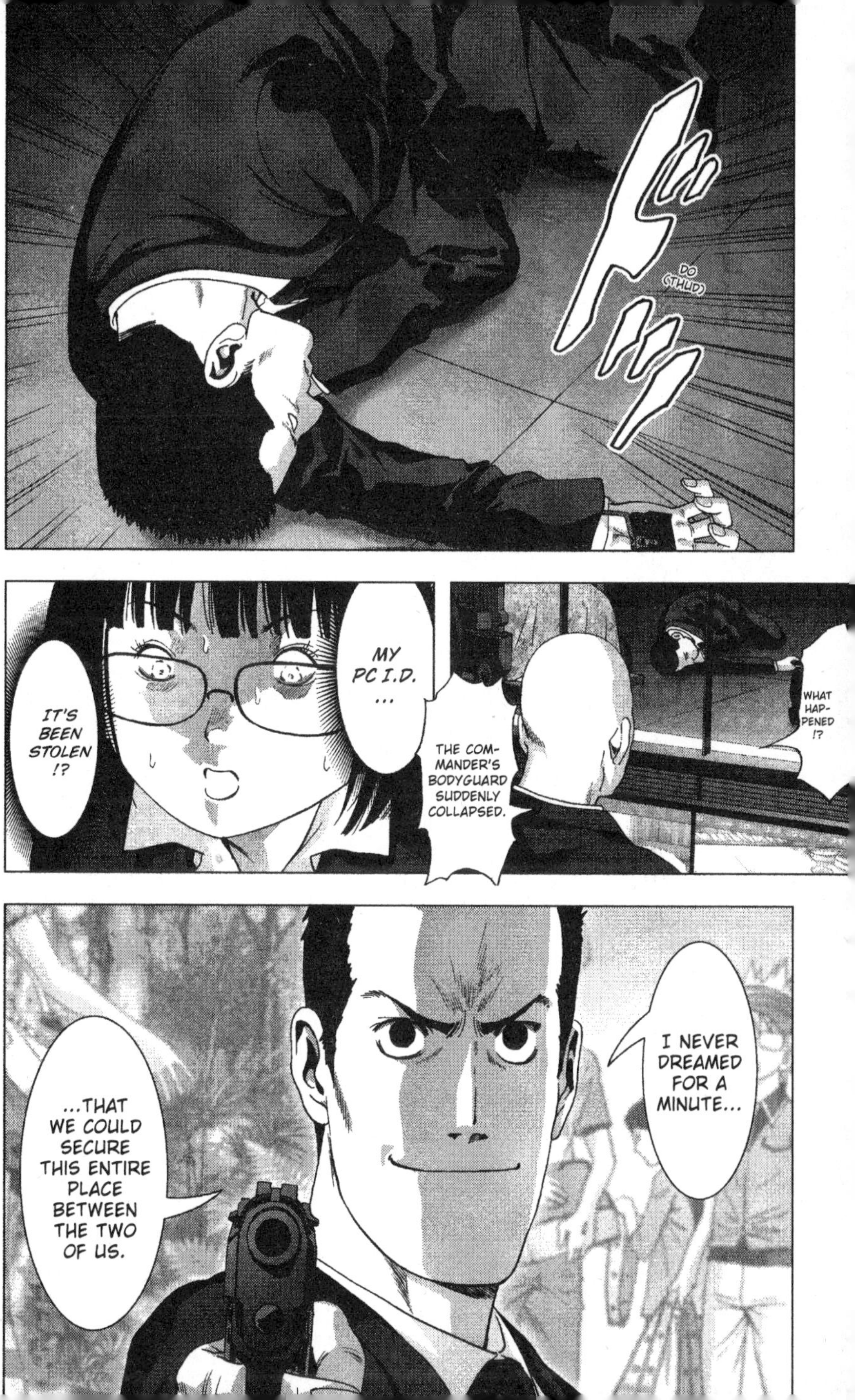
DO (THUD)
WHAT HAP-PENED !?
THE COM-MANDER'S BODYGUARD SUDDENLY COLLAPSED.
MY PC I.D. ...
IT'S BEEN STOLEN !?
I NEVER DREAMED FOR A MINUTE...
...THAT WE COULD SECURE THIS ENTIRE PLACE BETWEEN THE TWO OF US.

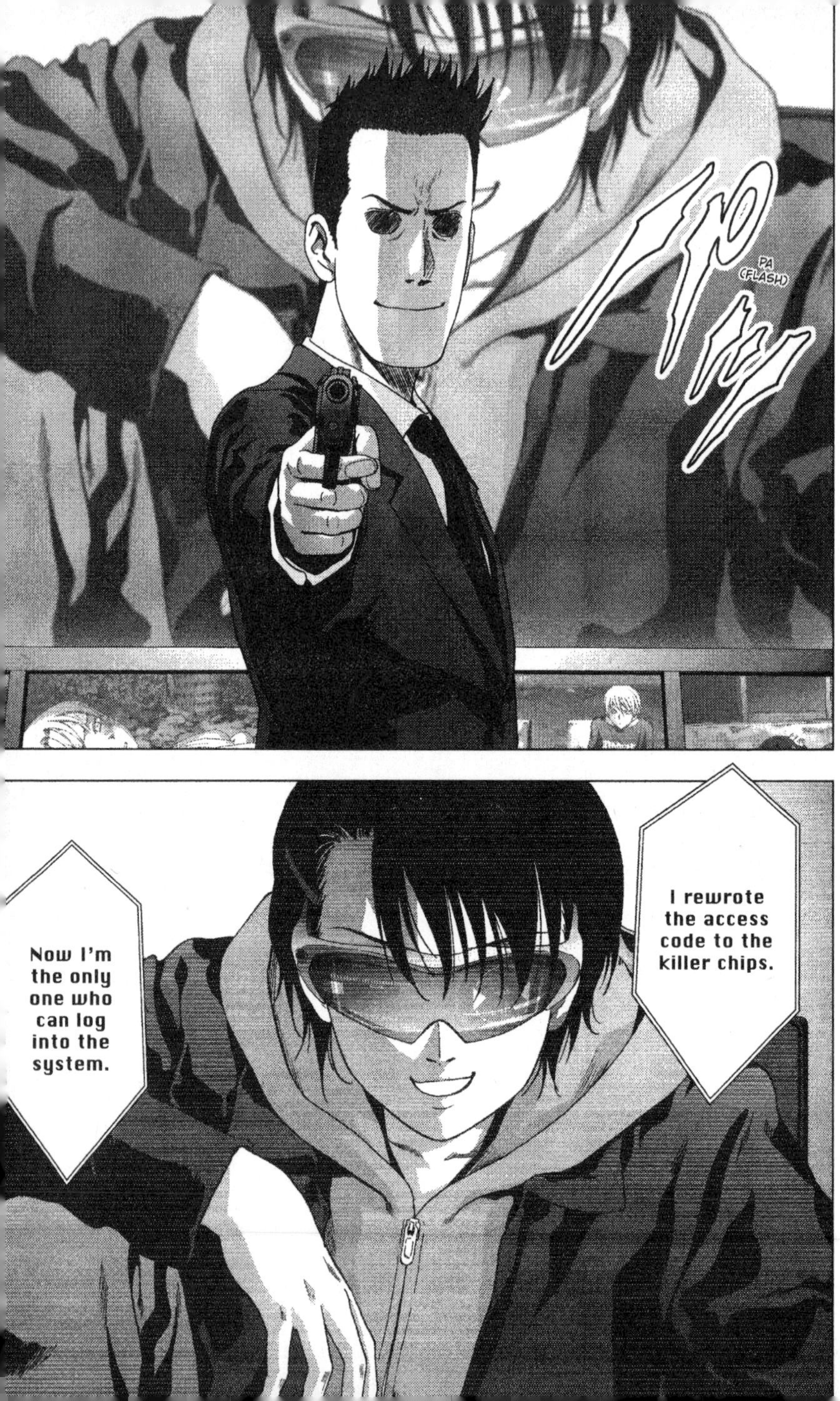
PA (FLASH)
I rewrote the access code to the killer chips.
Now I'm the only one who can log into the system.

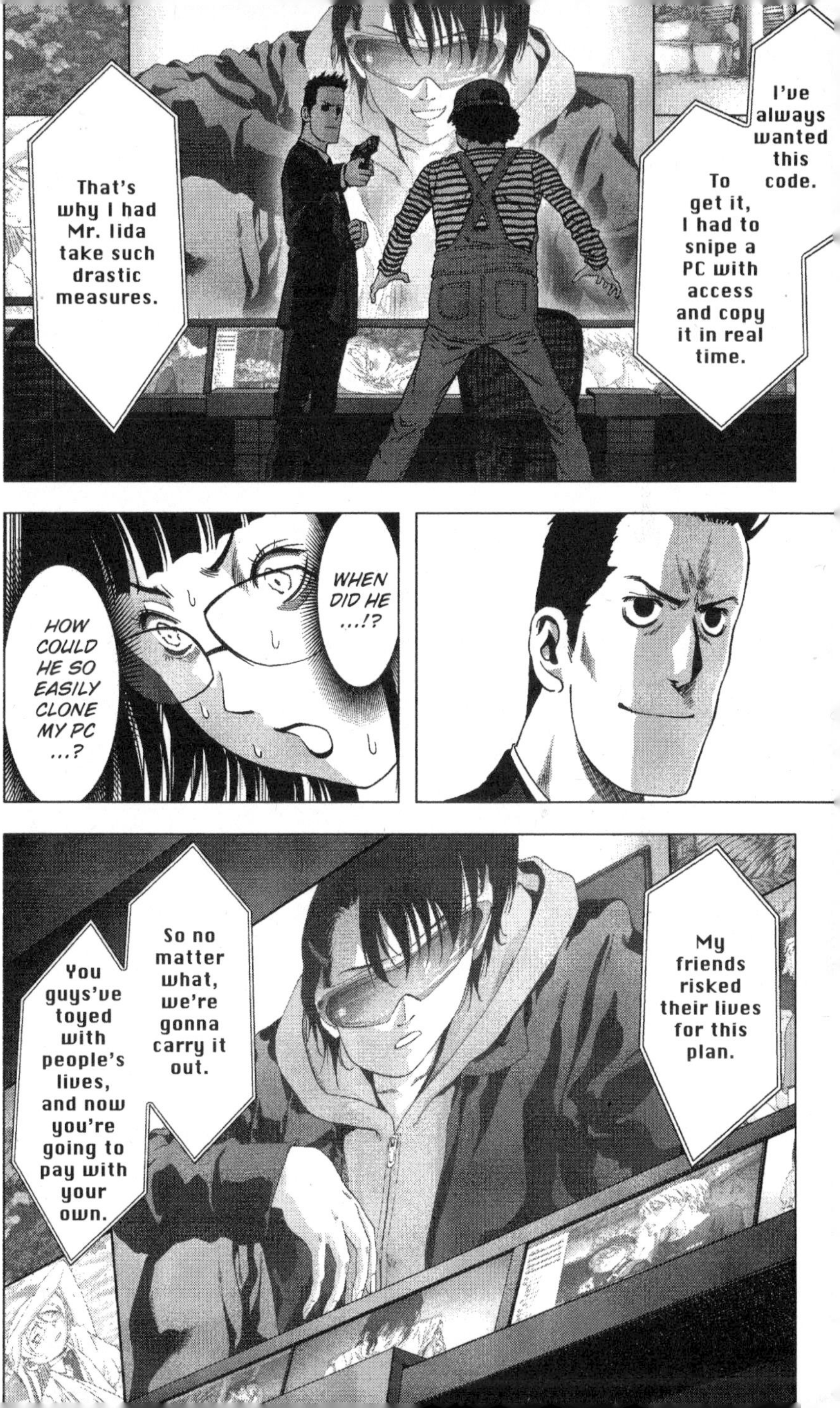
I've always wanted this code.
To get it, I had to snipe a PC with access and copy it in real time.
That's why I had Mr. Iida take such drastic measures.
WHEN DID HE ...!?
HOW COULD HE SO EASILY CLONE MY PC ...?
My friends risked their lives for this plan.
So no matter what, we're gonna carry it out.
You guys've toyed with people's lives, and now you're going to pay with your own.

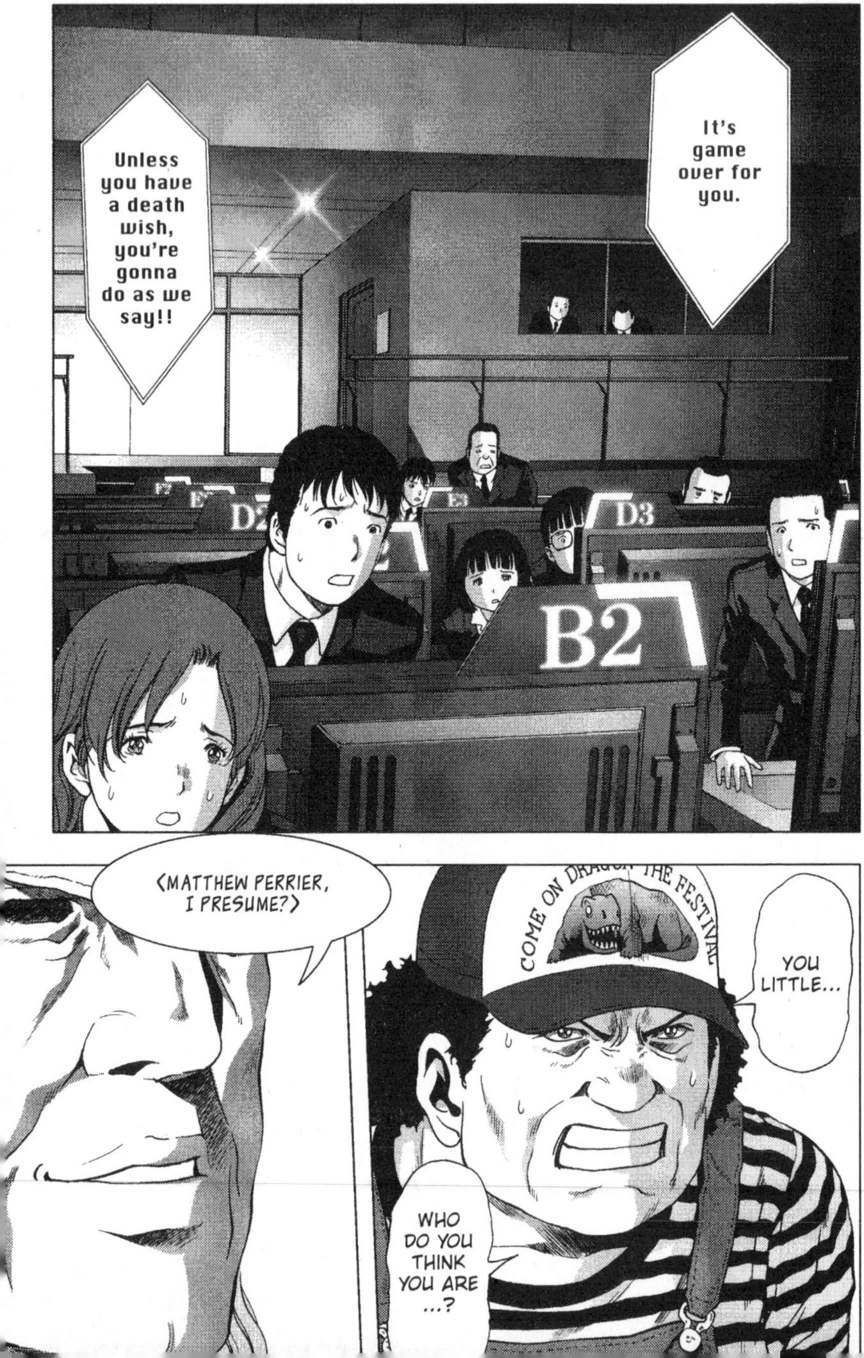
It's game over for you.
Unless you have a death wish, you're gonna do as we say!!
B2
D3
YOU LITTLE...
WHO DO YOU THINK YOU ARE ...?
〈MATTHEW PERRIER, I PRESUME?〉

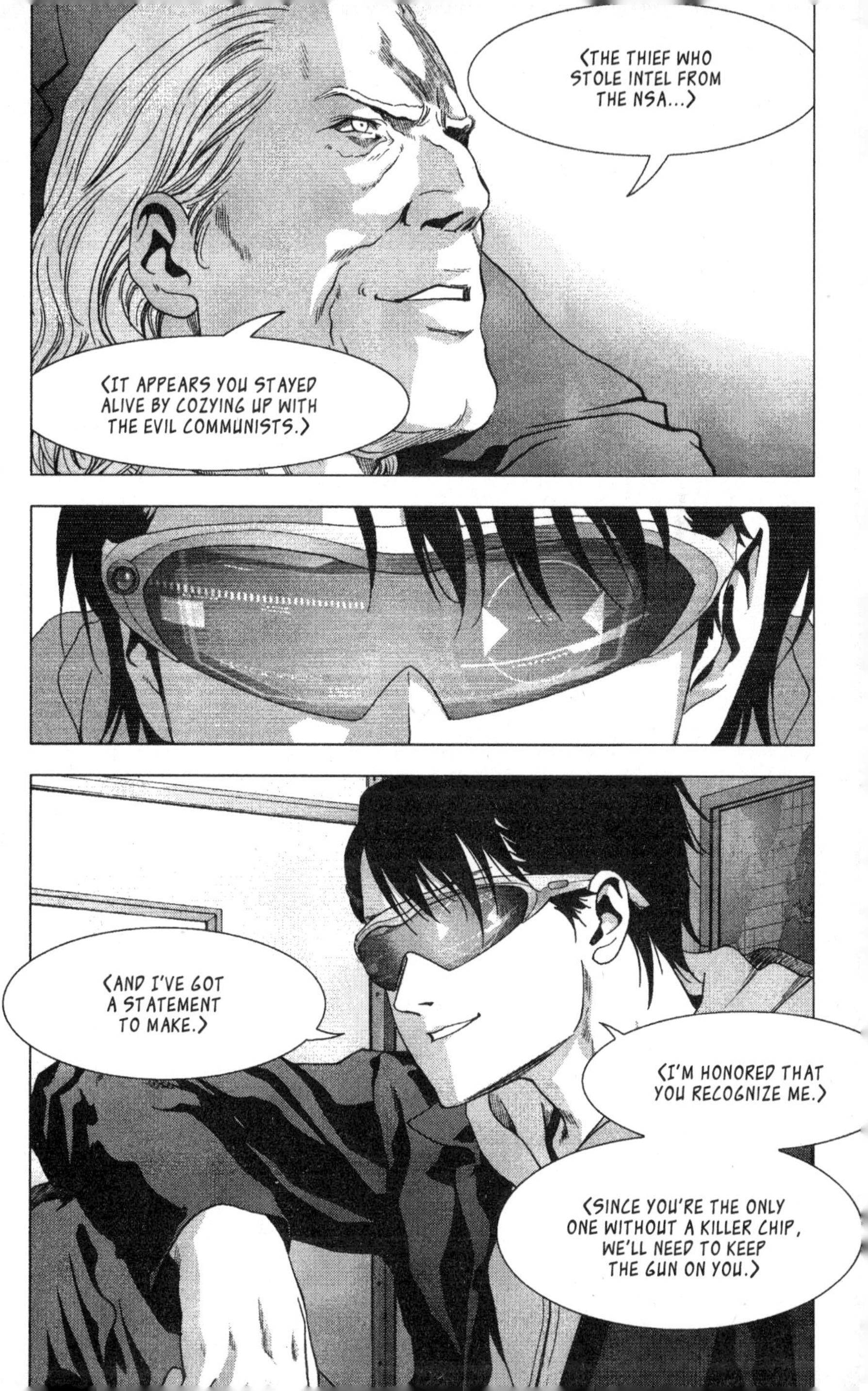
<THE THIEF WHO STOLE INTEL FROM THE NSA...>
<IT APPEARS YOU STAYED ALIVE BY COZYING UP WITH THE EVIL COMMUNISTS.>
<I'M HONORED THAT YOU RECOGNIZE ME.>
<SINCE YOU'RE THE ONLY ONE WITHOUT A KILLER CHIP, WE'LL NEED TO KEEP THE GUN ON YOU.>
<AND I'VE GOT A STATEMENT TO MAKE.>

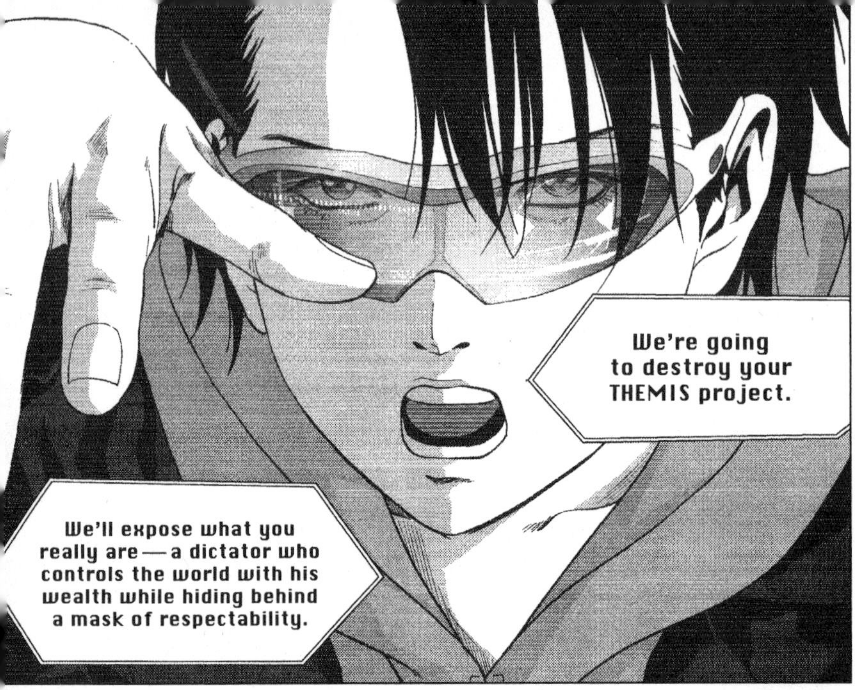
We're going to destroy your THEMIS project.
We'll expose what you really are — a dictator who controls the world with his wealth while hiding behind a mask of respectability.
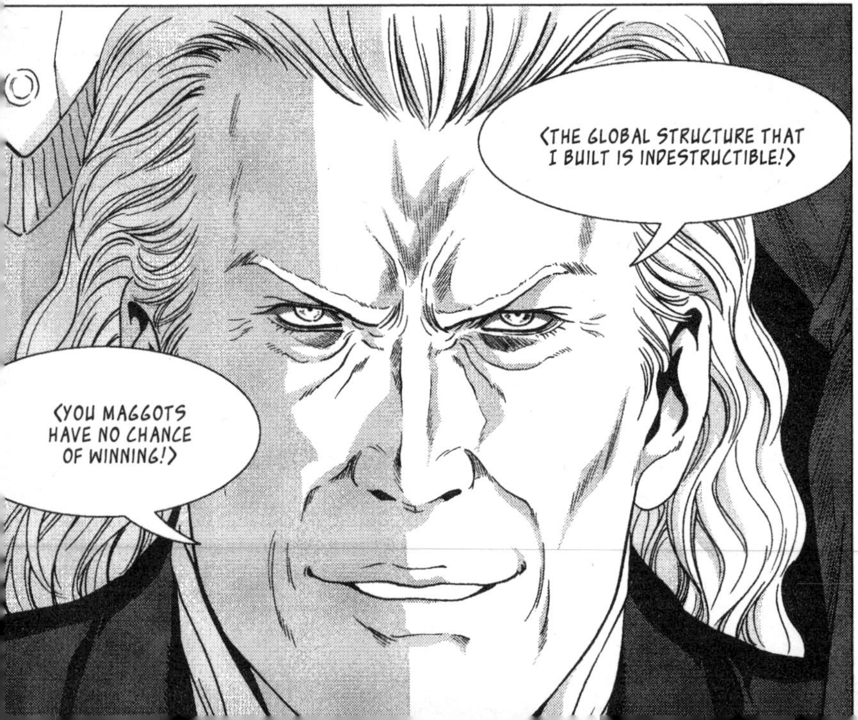
‹THE GLOBAL STRUCTURE THAT I BUILT IS INDESTRUCTIBLE!›
‹YOU MAGGOTS HAVE NO CHANCE OF WINNING!›

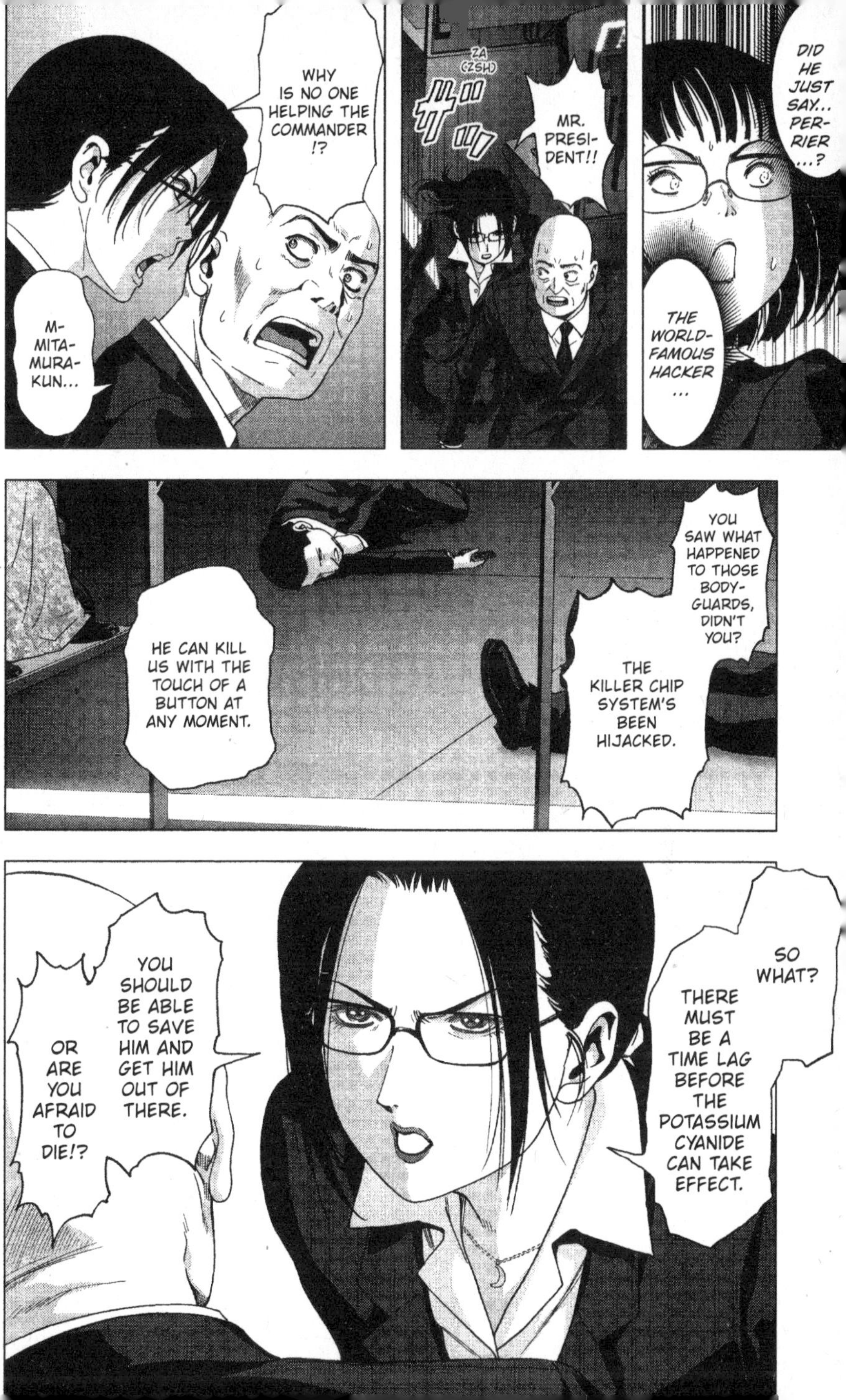
DID HE JUST SAY... PERRIER...?
THE WORLD-FAMOUS HACKER...
ZA CZSHD
MR. PRESIDENT!!
WHY IS NO ONE HELPING THE COMMANDER!?
M-MITAMURA-KUN...
YOU SAW WHAT HAPPENED TO THOSE BODYGUARDS, DIDN'T YOU?
THE KILLER CHIP SYSTEM'S BEEN HIJACKED.
HE CAN KILL US WITH THE TOUCH OF A BUTTON AT ANY MOMENT.
SO WHAT?
THERE MUST BE A TIME LAG BEFORE THE POTASSIUM CYANIDE CAN TAKE EFFECT.
YOU SHOULD BE ABLE TO SAVE HIM AND GET HIM OUT OF THERE.
OR ARE YOU AFRAID TO DIE!?

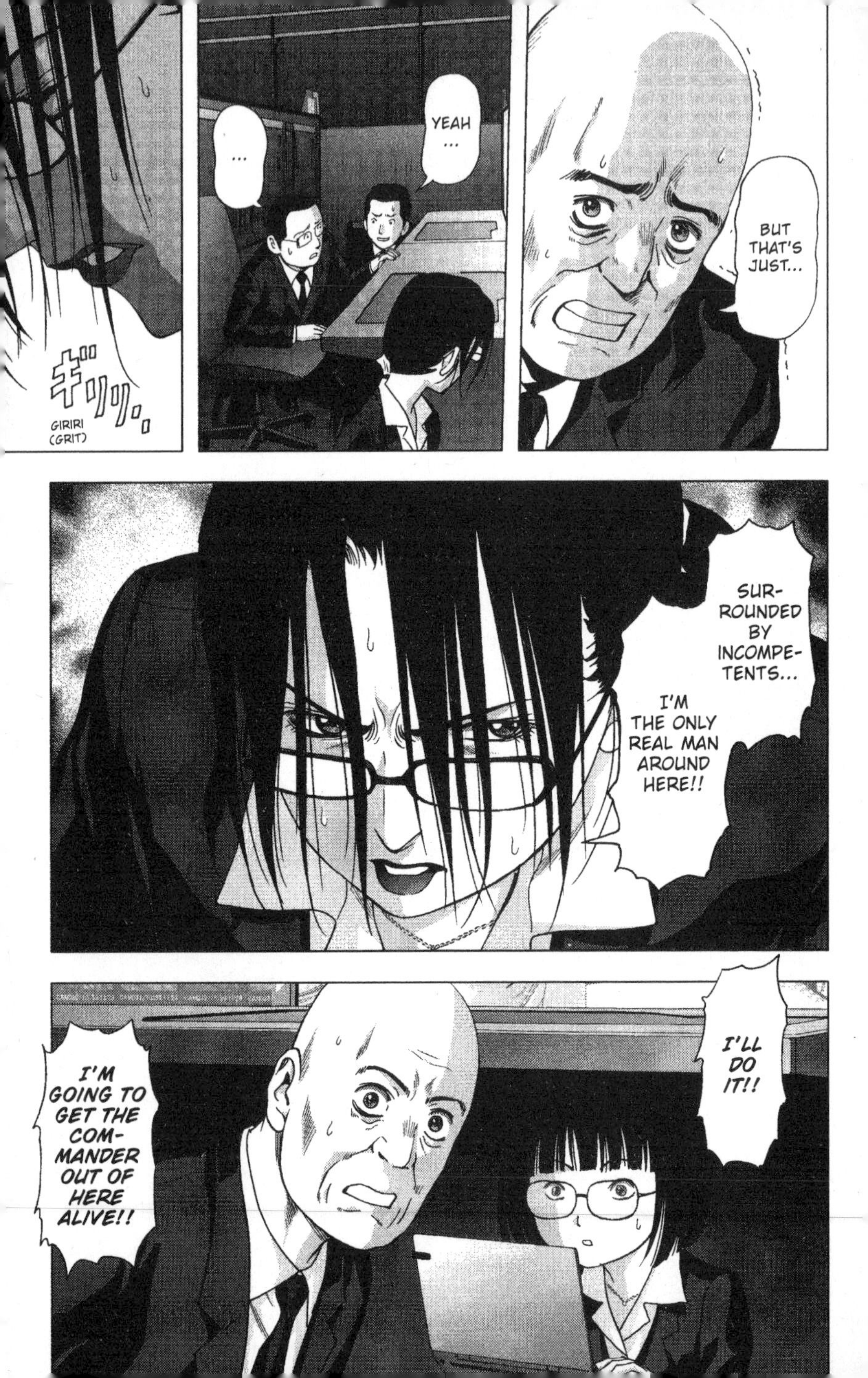
BUT THAT'S JUST...
YEAH ...
...
GIRIRI (GRIT)
SUR-ROUNDED BY INCOMPETE-TENTS...
I'M THE ONLY REAL MAN AROUND HERE!!
I'LL DO IT!!
I'M GOING TO GET THE COM-MANDER OUT OF HERE ALIVE!!

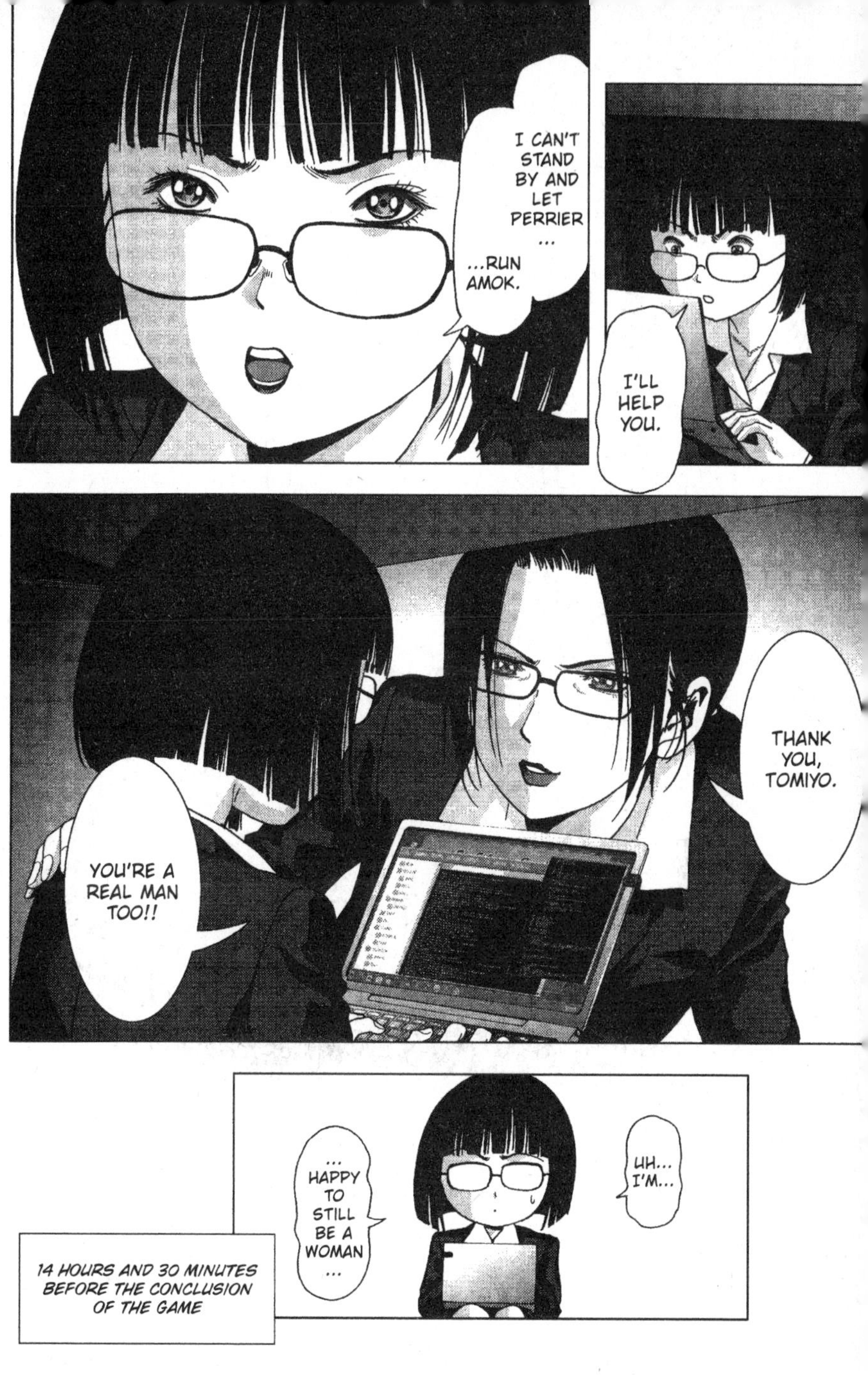
I'LL HELP YOU.
I CAN'T STAND BY AND LET PERRIER ...
...RUN AMOK.
THANK YOU, TOMIYO.
YOU'RE A REAL MAN TOO!!
UH... I'M...
... HAPPY TO STILL BE A WOMAN ...
14 HOURS AND 30 MINUTES BEFORE THE CONCLUSION OF THE GAME

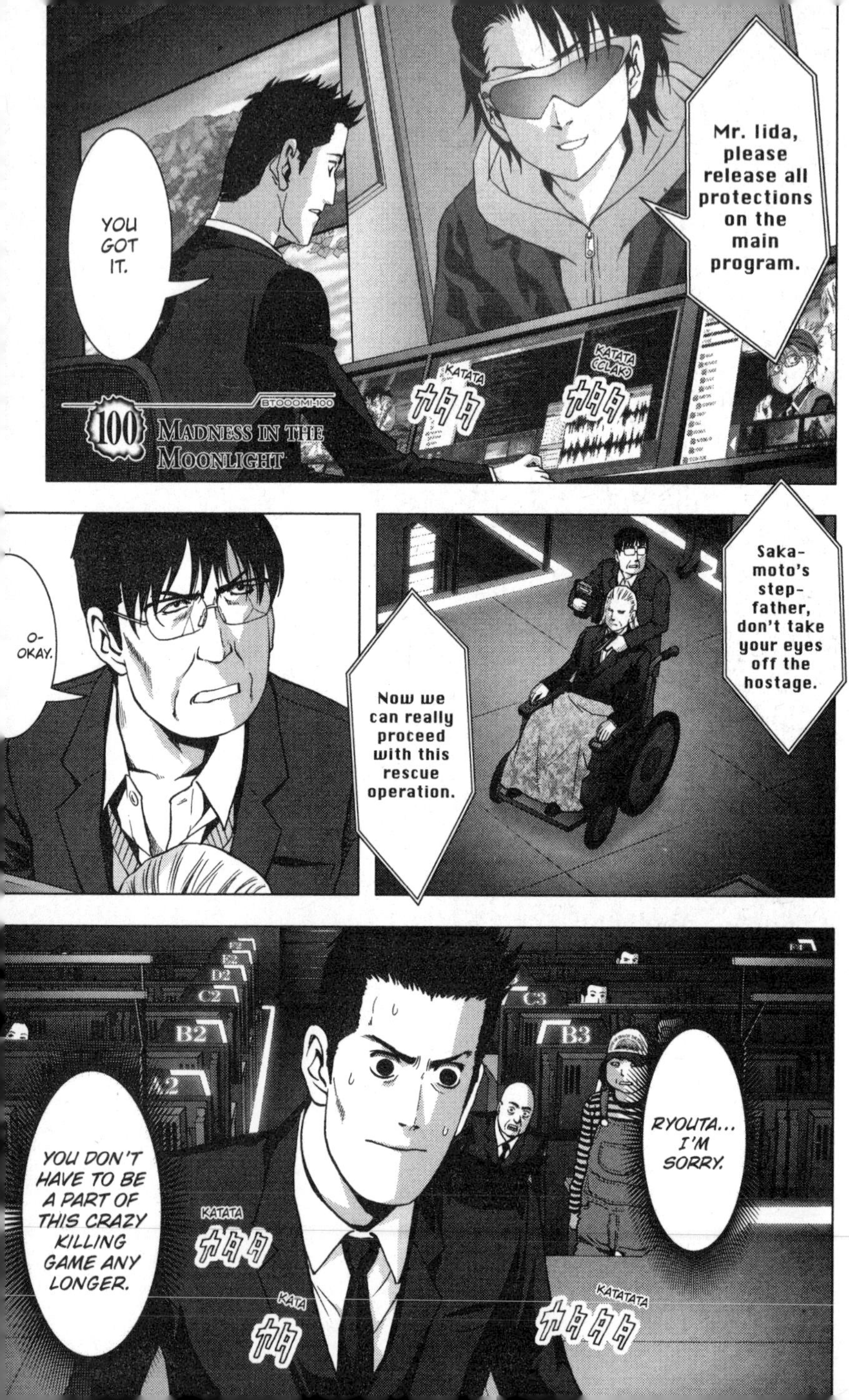
Mr. Iida, please release all protections on the main program.
YOU GOT IT.
KATATA (CLAK)
カタタ
KATATA
カタタ
BTOOOM!-100
100 MADNESS IN THE MOONLIGHT
Saka-moto's step-father, don't take your eyes off the hostage.
Now we can really proceed with this rescue operation.
O-OKAY.
RYOUTA... I'M SORRY.
YOU DON'T HAVE TO BE A PART OF THIS CRAZY KILLING GAME ANY LONGER.
KATATATA
カタタタ
KATA
カタ
KATATA
カタタ

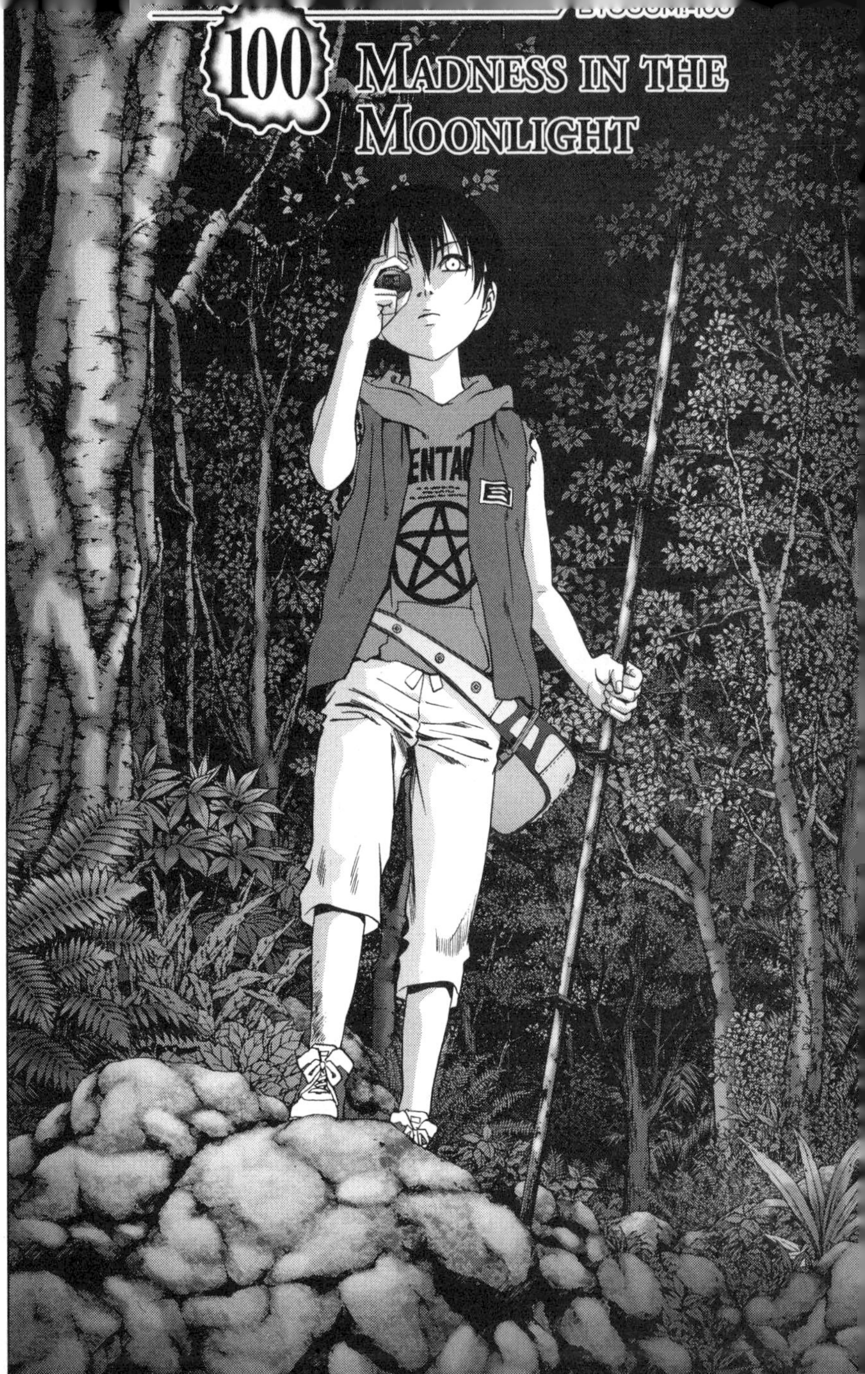
100
MADNESS IN THE MOONLIGHT

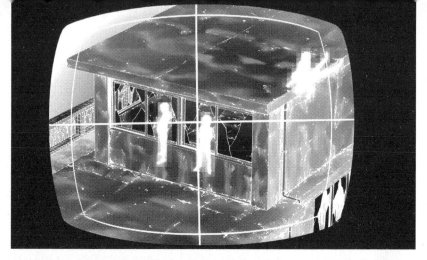

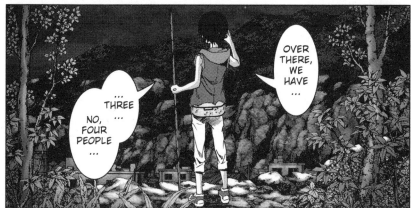

OVER THERE, WE HAVE ...

... THREE ... NO, FOUR PEOPLE ...

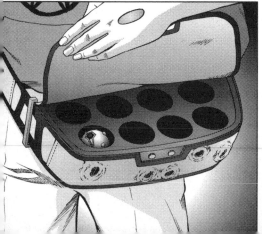

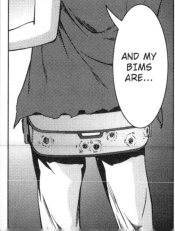

AND MY BIMS ARE...

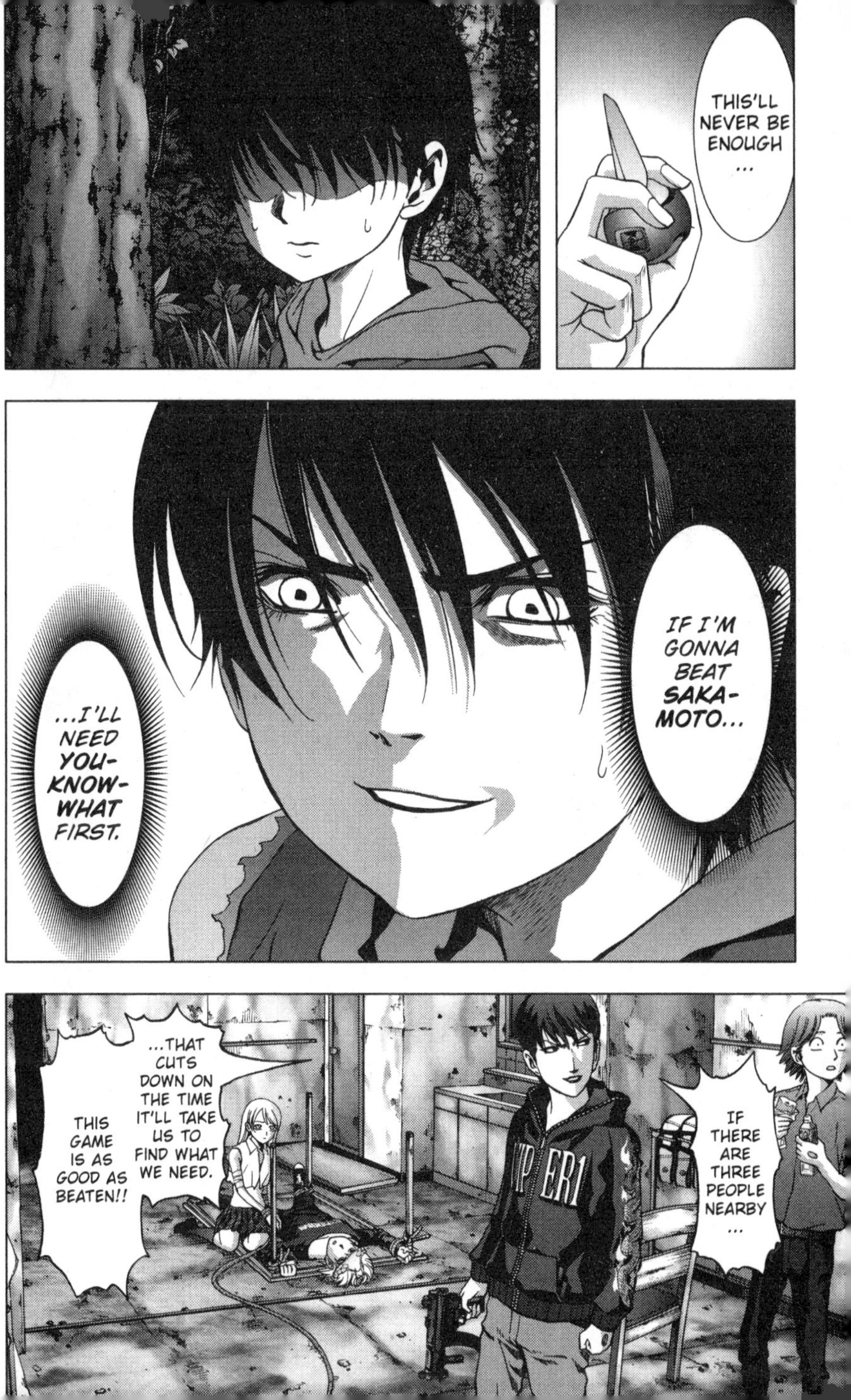
THIS'LL NEVER BE ENOUGH ...
IF I'M GONNA BEAT SAKAMOTO...
...I'LL NEED YOU-KNOW-WHAT FIRST.
IF THERE ARE THREE PEOPLE NEARBY ...
...THAT CUTS DOWN ON THE TIME IT'LL TAKE US TO FIND WHAT WE NEED.
THIS GAME IS AS GOOD AS BEATEN!!

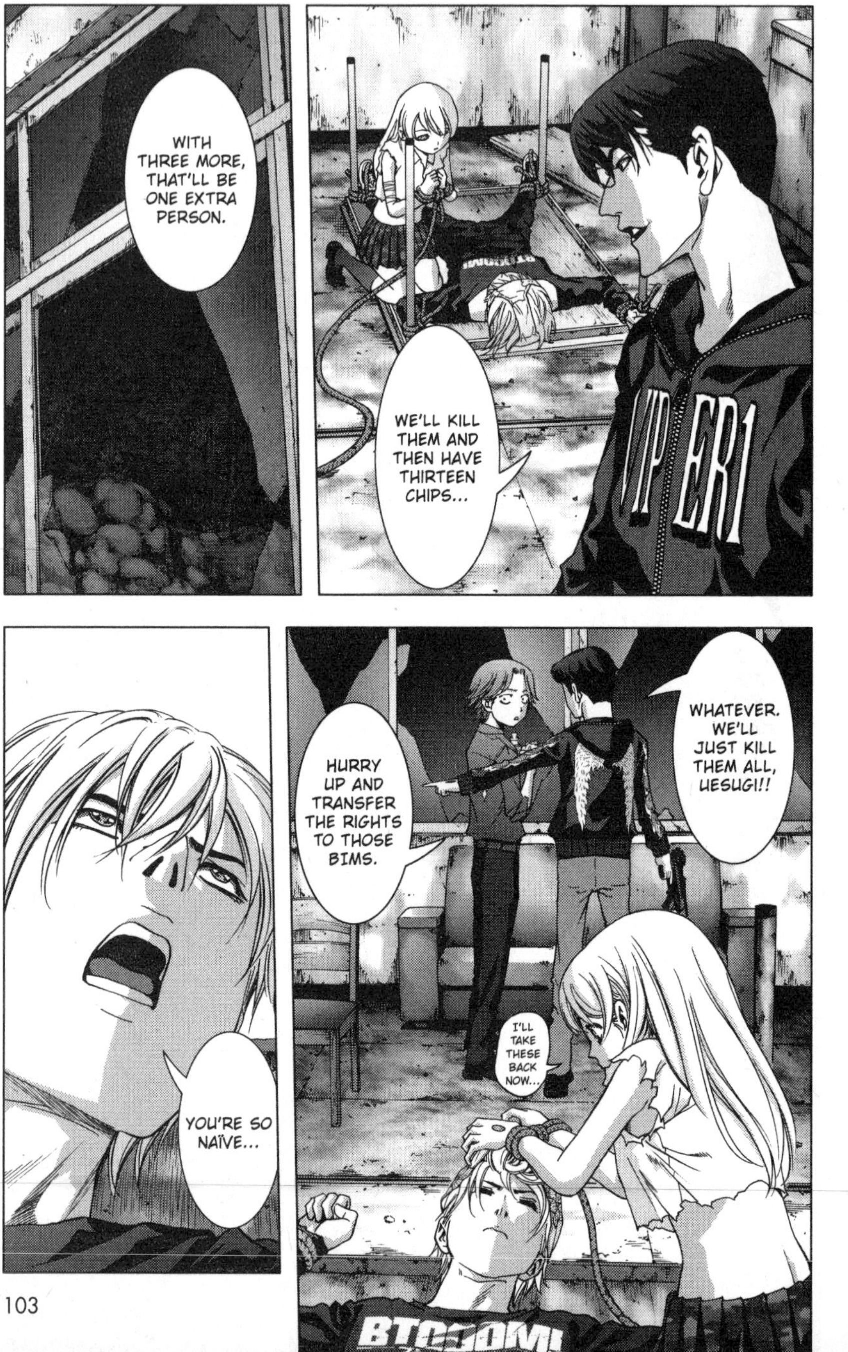
WE'LL KILL THEM AND THEN HAVE THIRTEEN CHIPS...
WITH THREE MORE, THAT'LL BE ONE EXTRA PERSON.
VIPER1
WHATEVER. WE'LL JUST KILL THEM ALL, UESUGI!!
HURRY UP AND TRANSFER THE RIGHTS TO THOSE BIMS.
I'LL TAKE THESE BACK NOW...
YOU'RE SO NAÏVE...

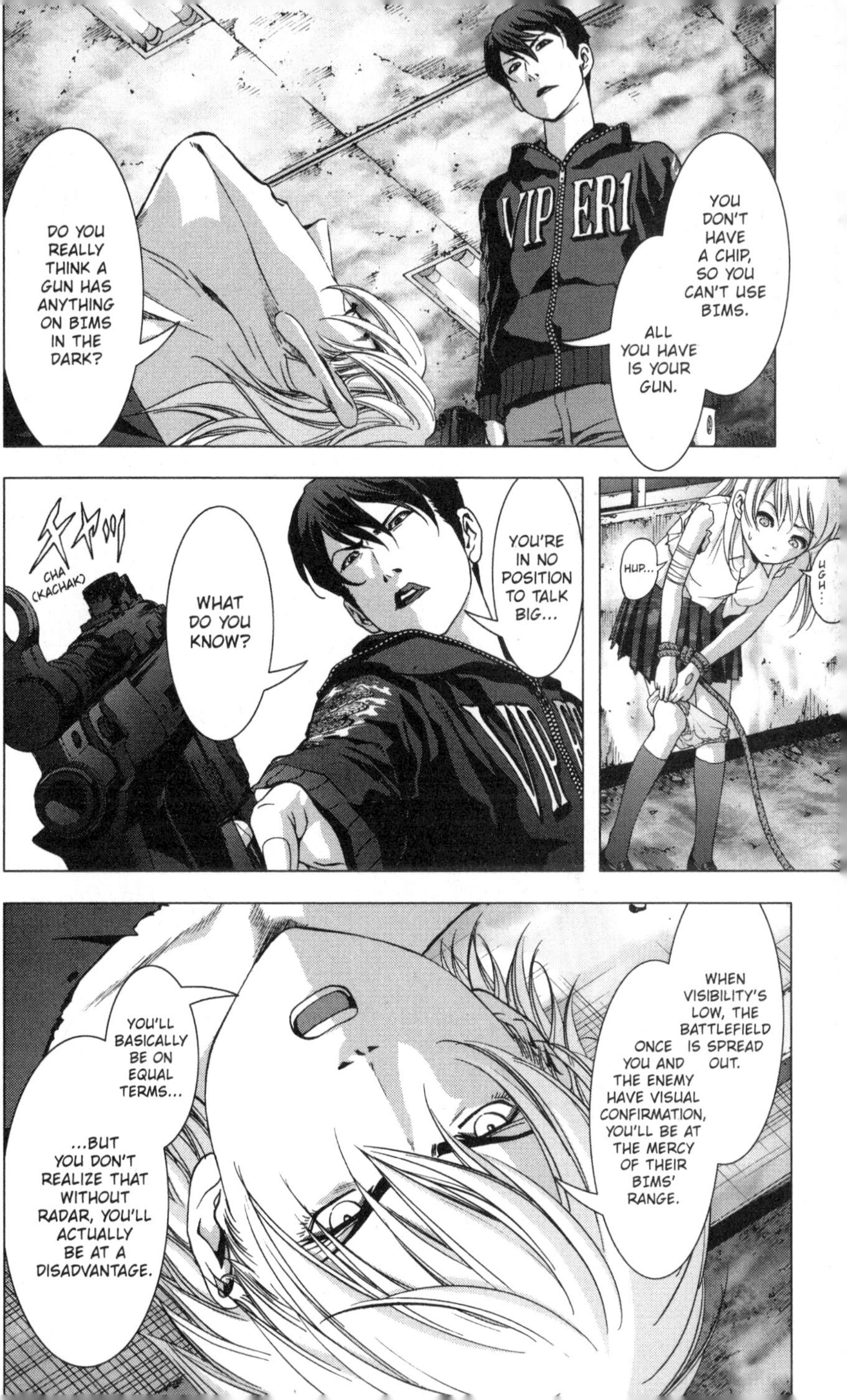
YOU DON'T HAVE A CHIP, SO YOU CAN'T USE BIMS.
ALL YOU HAVE IS YOUR GUN.
DO YOU REALLY THINK A GUN HAS ANYTHING ON BIMS IN THE DARK?
UGH...
HUP...
YOU'RE IN NO POSITION TO TALK BIG...
WHAT DO YOU KNOW?
CHA (KACHAK)
WHEN VISIBILITY'S LOW, THE BATTLEFIELD IS SPREAD OUT.
ONCE YOU AND THE ENEMY HAVE VISUAL CONFIRMATION, YOU'LL BE AT THE MERCY OF THEIR BIMS' RANGE.
YOU'LL BASICALLY BE ON EQUAL TERMS...
...BUT YOU DON'T REALIZE THAT WITHOUT RADAR, YOU'LL ACTUALLY BE AT A DISADVANTAGE.

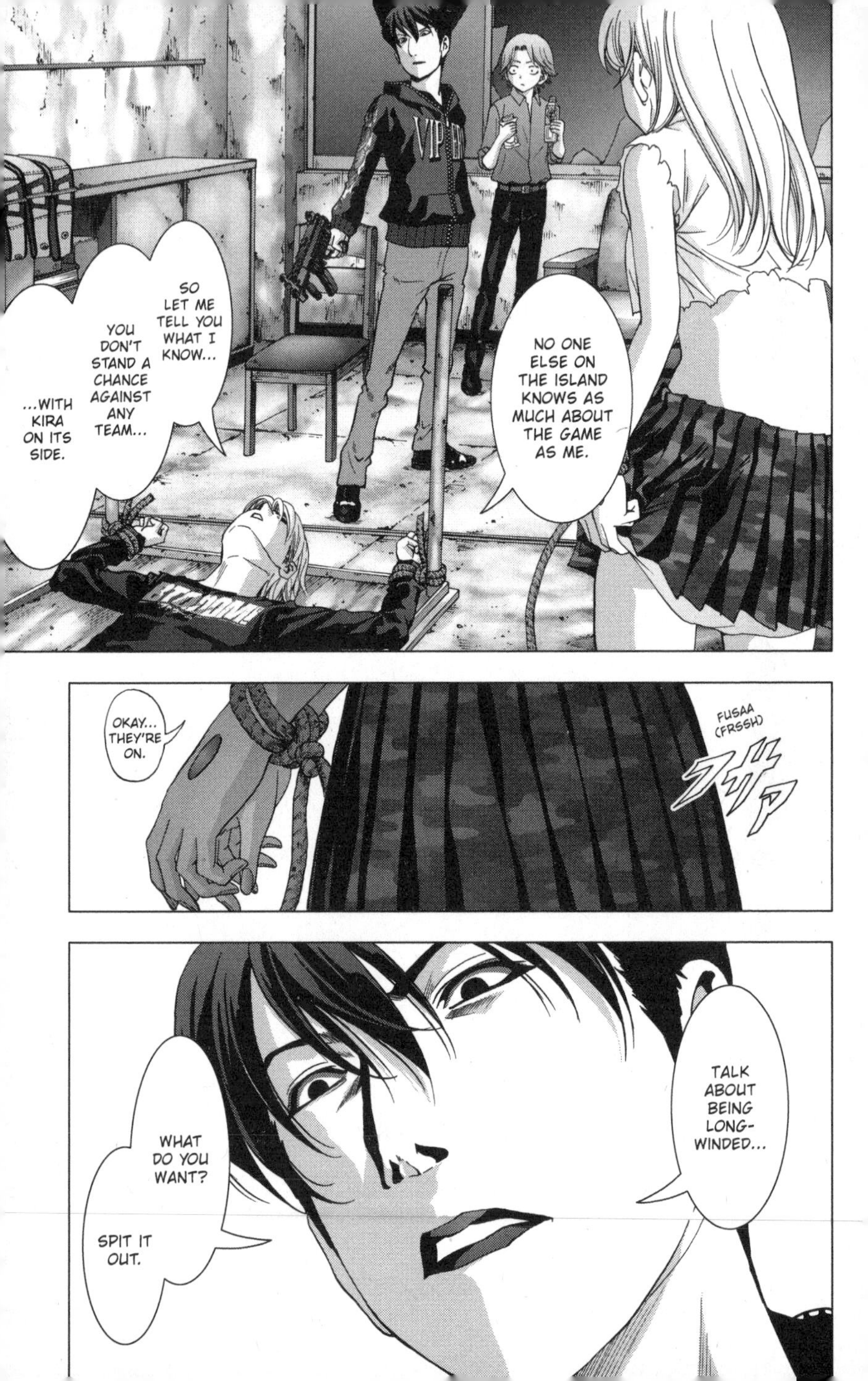
NO ONE ELSE ON THE ISLAND KNOWS AS MUCH ABOUT THE GAME AS ME.
SO LET ME TELL YOU WHAT I KNOW...
YOU DON'T STAND A CHANCE AGAINST ANY TEAM...
...WITH KIRA ON ITS SIDE.
フサァ
FUSAA (FRSSH)
OKAY... THEY'RE ON.
TALK ABOUT BEING LONG-WINDED...
WHAT DO YOU WANT?
SPIT IT OUT.

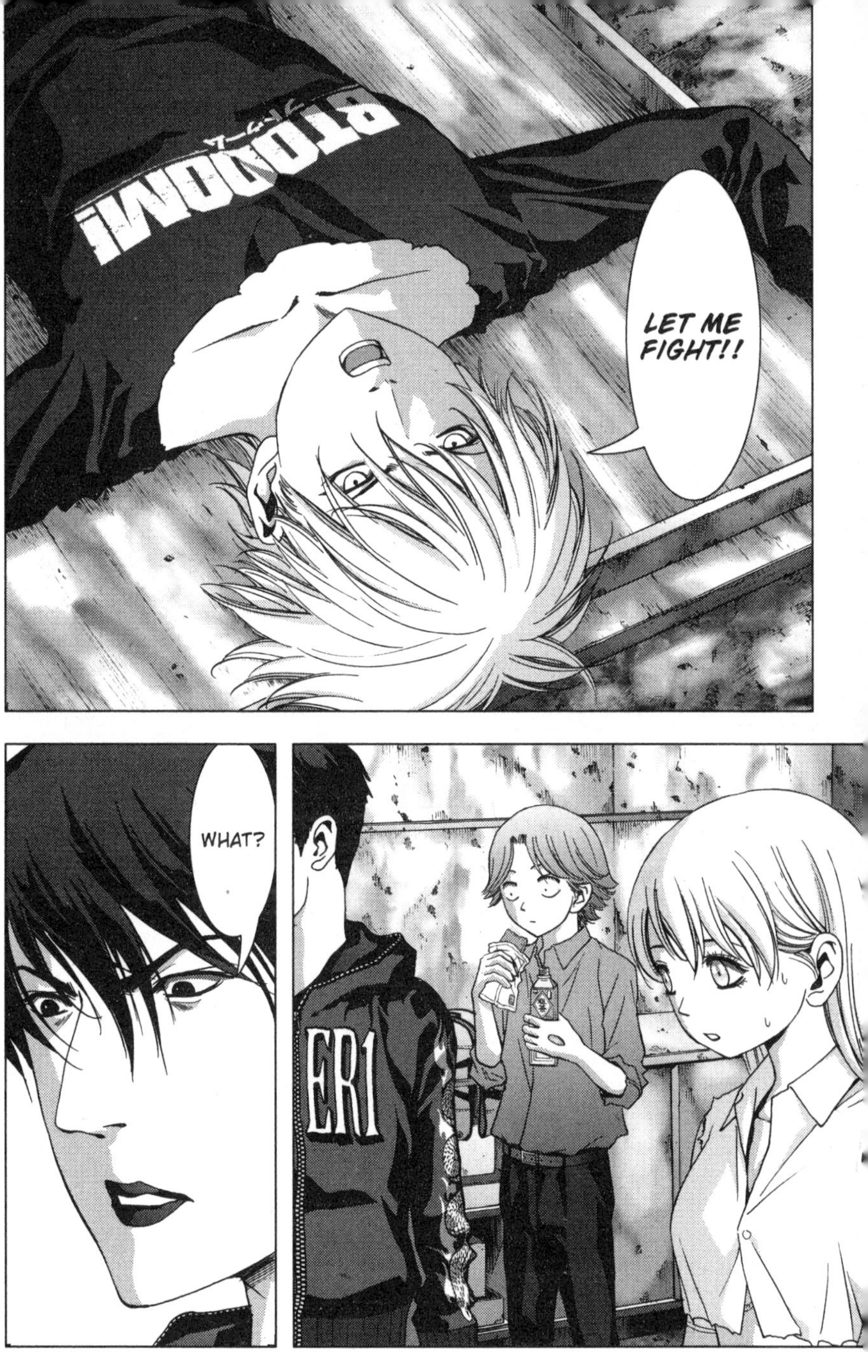
LET ME FIGHT!!
WHAT?

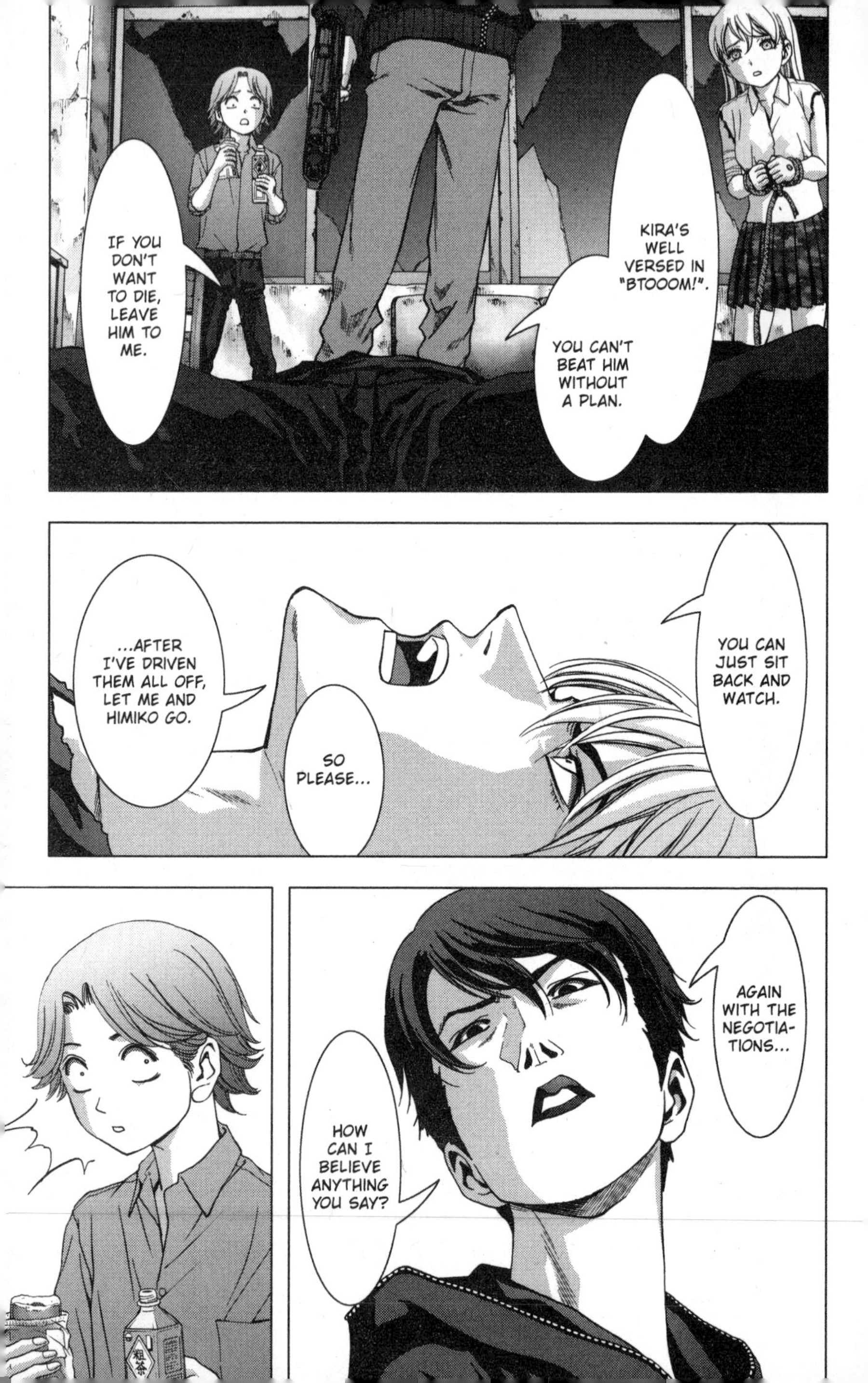
KIRA'S WELL VERSED IN "BTOOOM!".
YOU CAN'T BEAT HIM WITHOUT A PLAN.
IF YOU DON'T WANT TO DIE, LEAVE HIM TO ME.
YOU CAN JUST SIT BACK AND WATCH.
...AFTER I'VE DRIVEN THEM ALL OFF, LET ME AND HIMIKO GO.
SO PLEASE...
AGAIN WITH THE NEGOTIA-TIONS...
HOW CAN I BELIEVE ANYTHING YOU SAY?

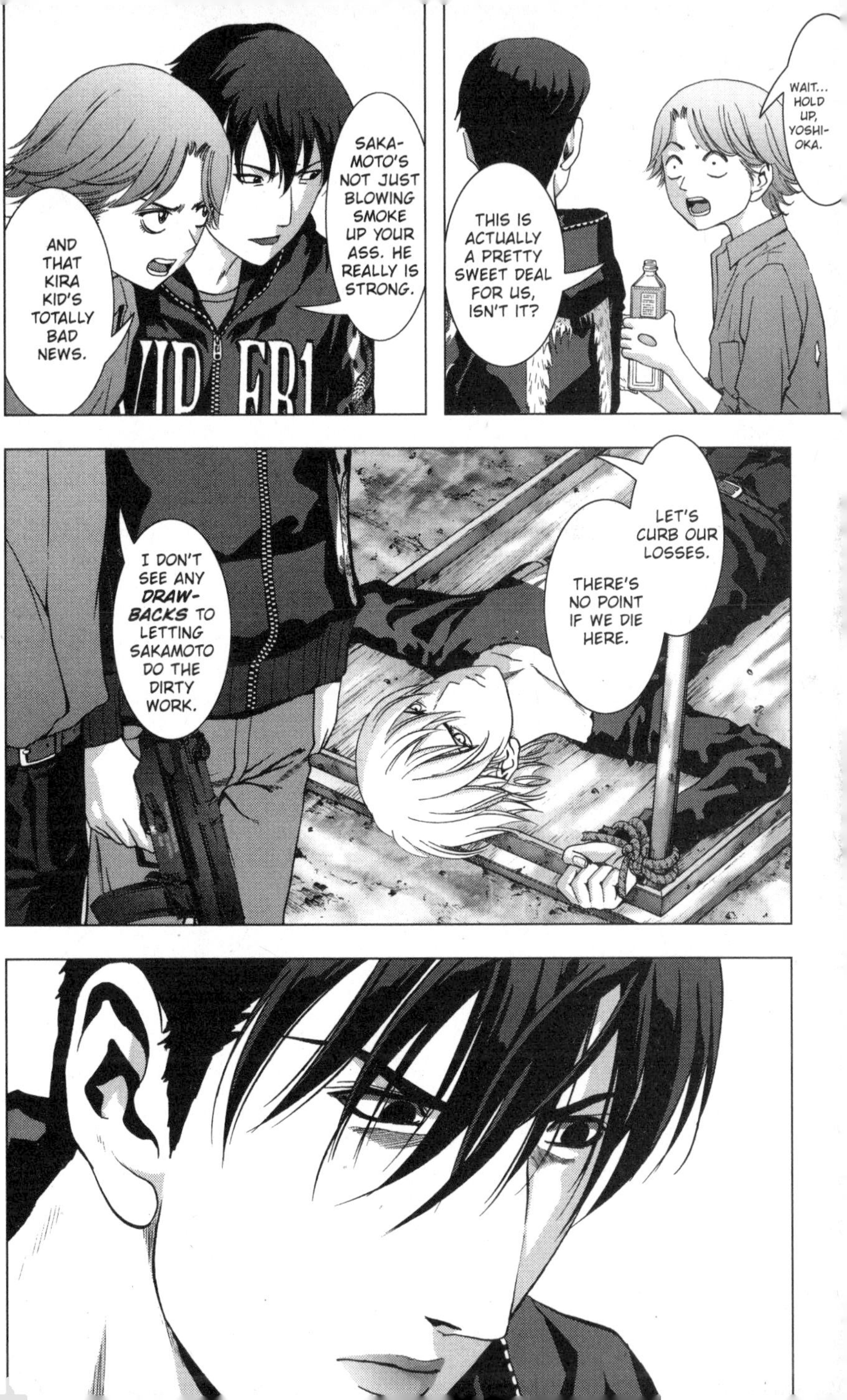
WAIT... HOLD UP, YOSHI-OKA.
THIS IS ACTUALLY A PRETTY SWEET DEAL FOR US, ISN'T IT?
SAKA-MOTO'S NOT JUST BLOWING SMOKE UP YOUR ASS. HE REALLY IS STRONG.
AND THAT KIRA KID'S TOTALLY BAD NEWS.
LET'S CURB OUR LOSSES.
THERE'S NO POINT IF WE DIE HERE.
I DON'T SEE ANY *DRAW-BACKS* TO LETTING SAKAMOTO DO THE DIRTY WORK.

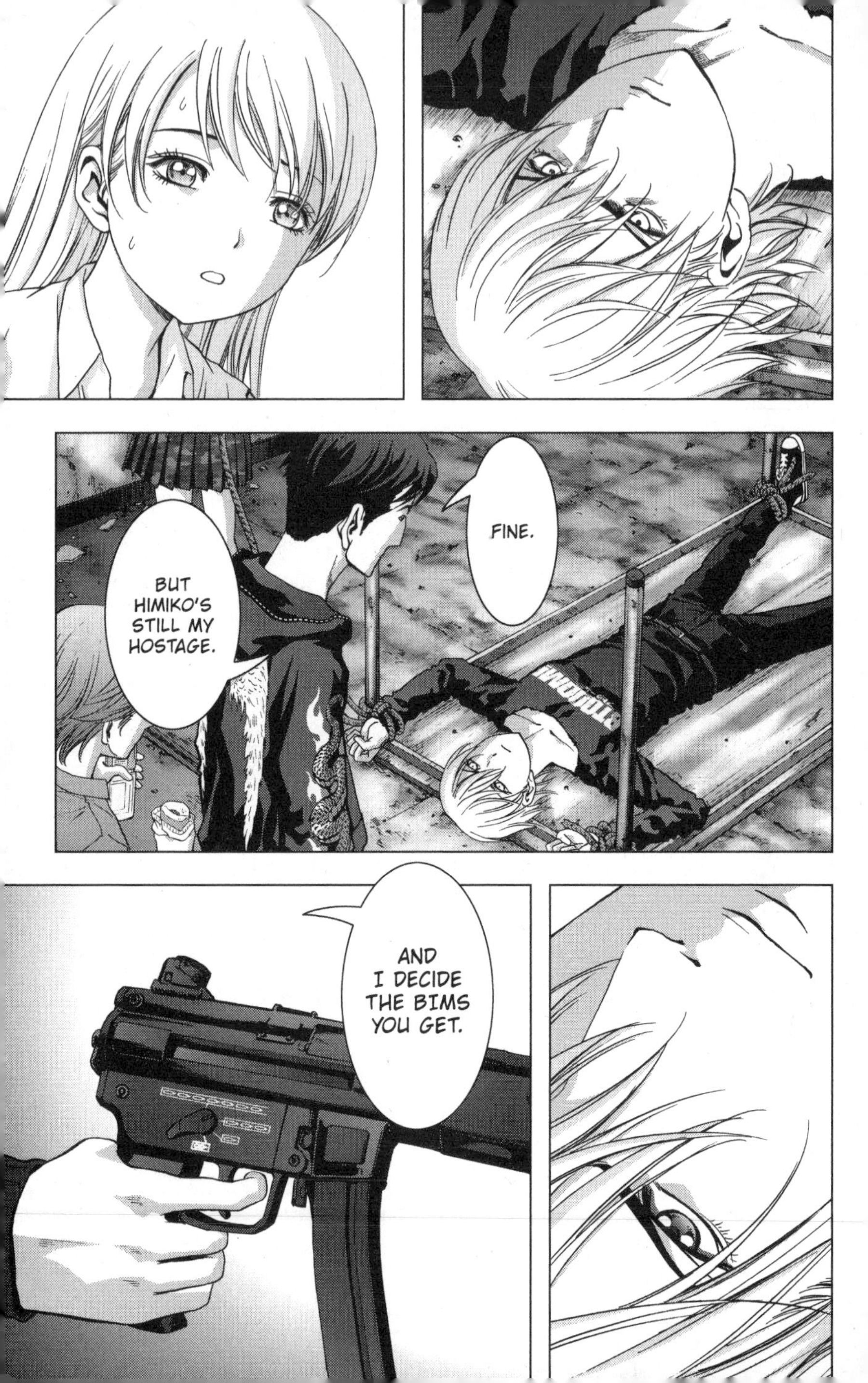
FINE.
BUT HIMIKO'S STILL MY HOSTAGE.
AND I DECIDE THE BIMS YOU GET.

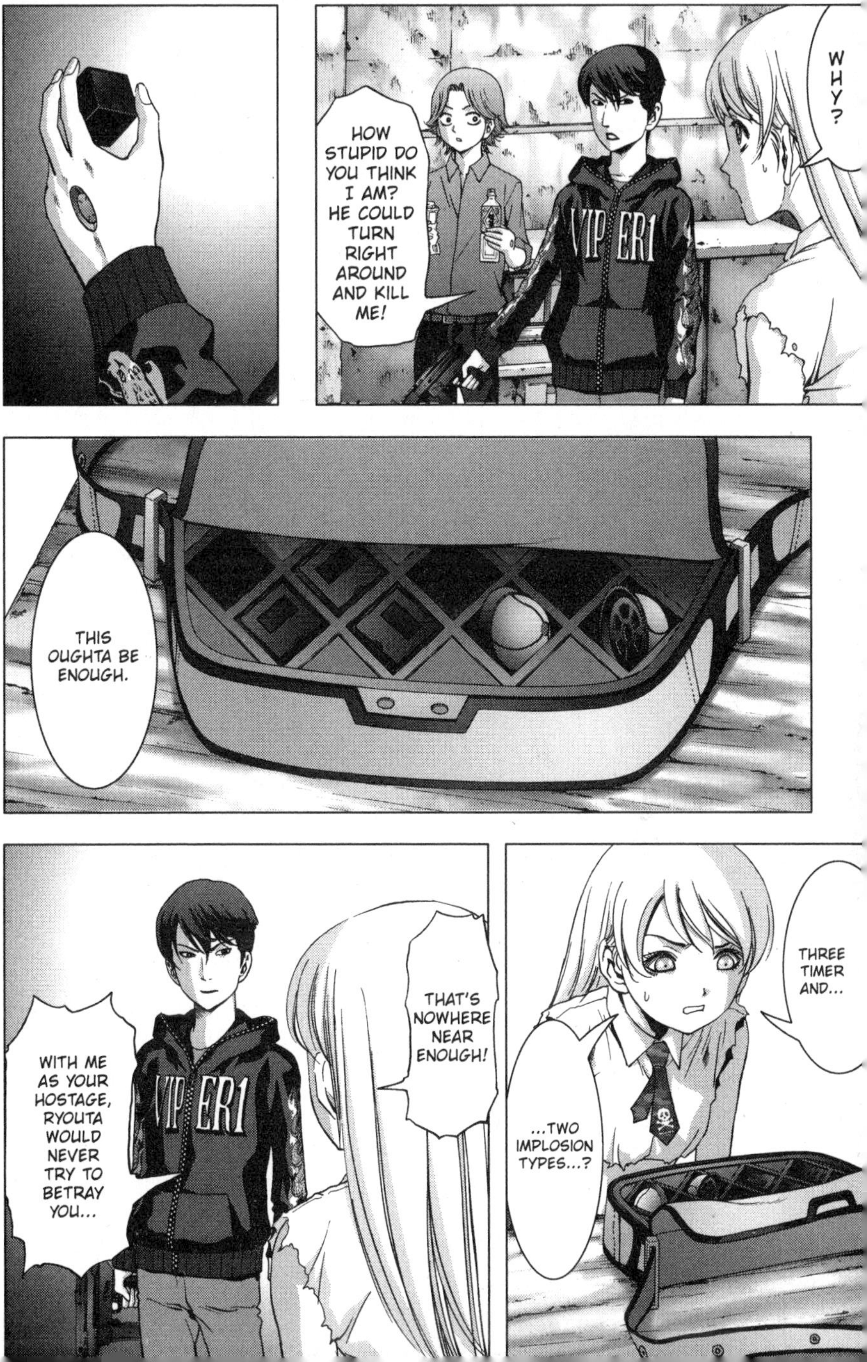
WHY?
HOW STUPID DO YOU THINK I AM? HE COULD TURN RIGHT AROUND AND KILL ME!
THIS OUGHTA BE ENOUGH.
THREE TIMER AND...
...TWO IMPLOSION TYPES...?
THAT'S NOWHERE NEAR ENOUGH!
WITH ME AS YOUR HOSTAGE, RYOUTA WOULD NEVER TRY TO BETRAY YOU...

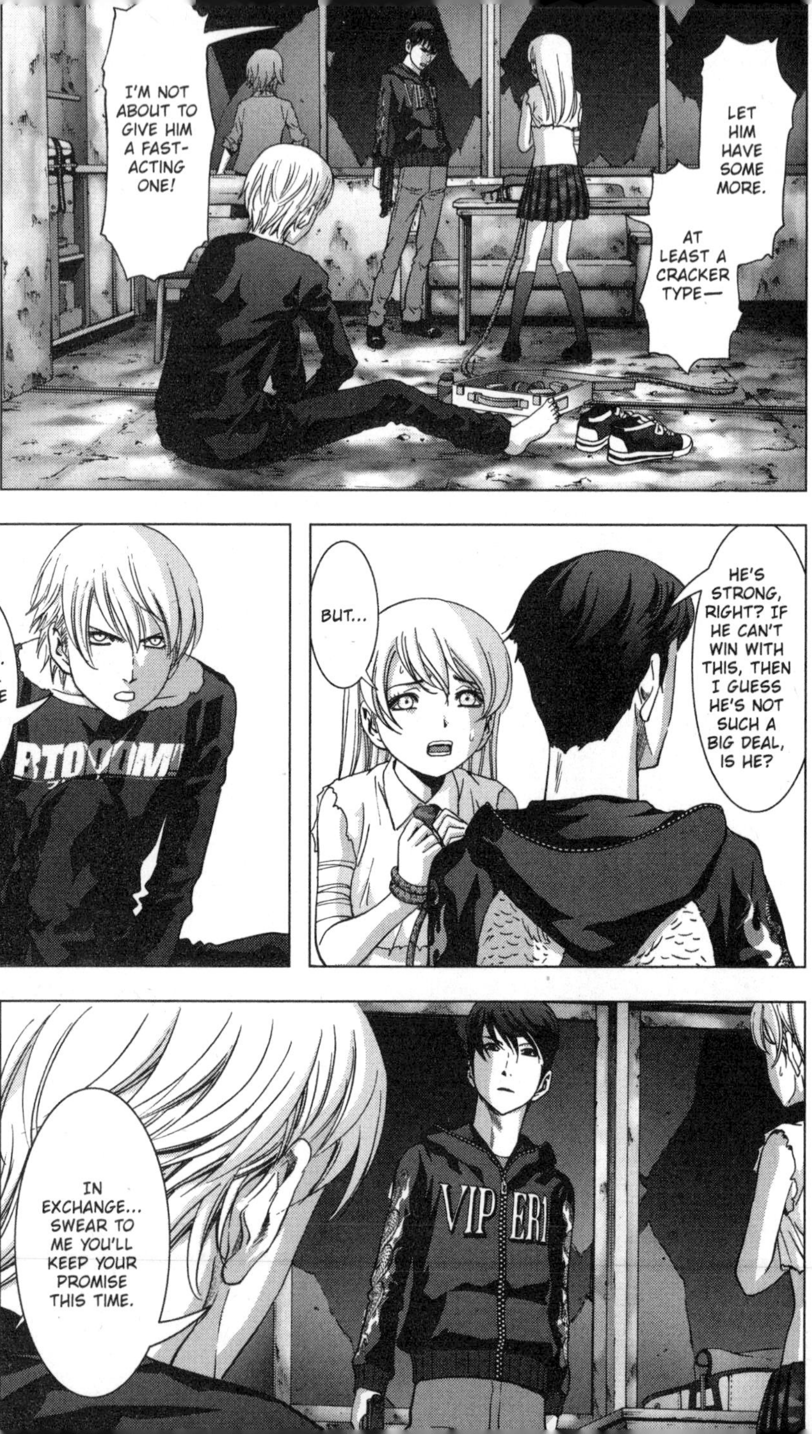
LET HIM HAVE SOME MORE.
AT LEAST A CRACKER TYPE—
I'M NOT ABOUT TO GIVE HIM A FAST-ACTING ONE!
HE'S STRONG, RIGHT? IF HE CAN'T WIN WITH THIS, THEN I GUESS HE'S NOT SUCH A BIG DEAL, IS HE?
BUT...
FINE. I'LL MAKE DO.
IN EXCHANGE... SWEAR TO ME YOU'LL KEEP YOUR PROMISE THIS TIME.

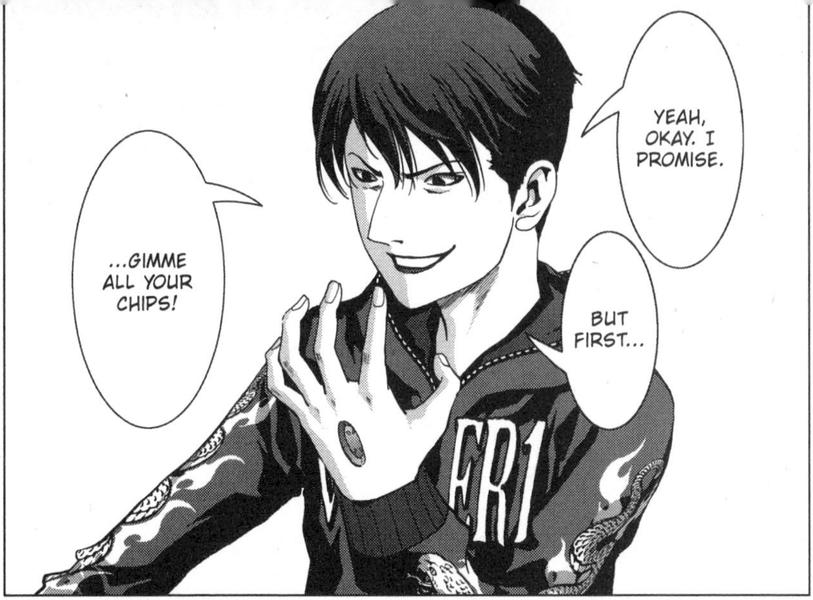
YEAH, OKAY. I PROMISE.
BUT FIRST...
...GIMME ALL YOUR CHIPS!

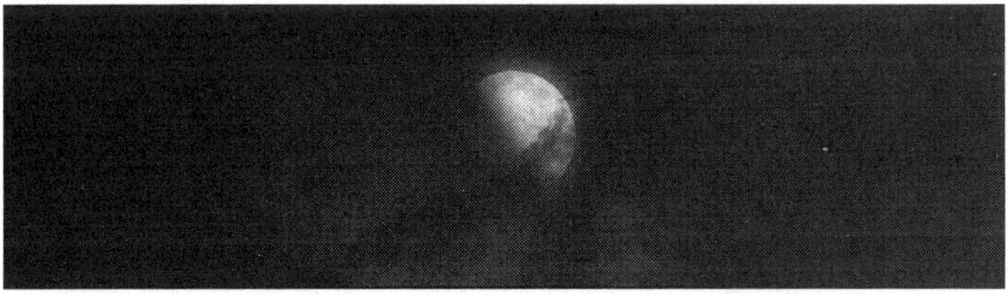

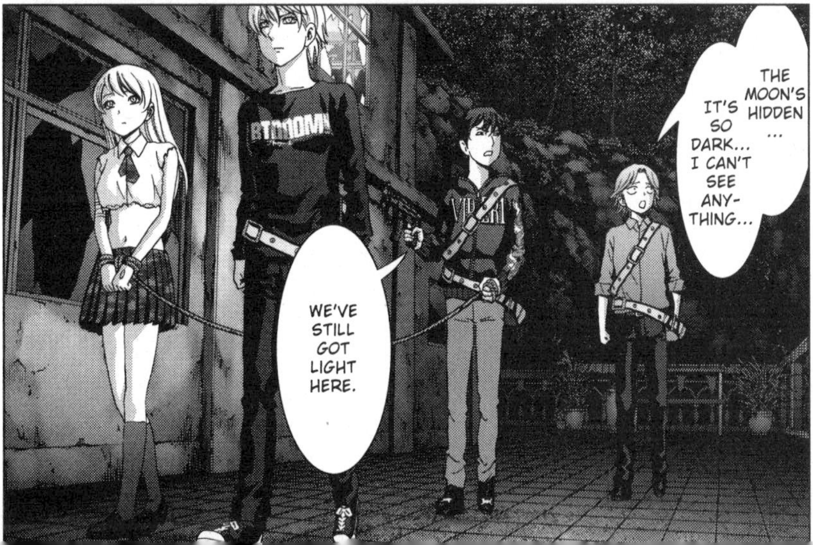
THE MOON'S HIDDEN...
IT'S SO DARK... I CAN'T SEE ANYTHING...
WE'VE STILL GOT LIGHT HERE.

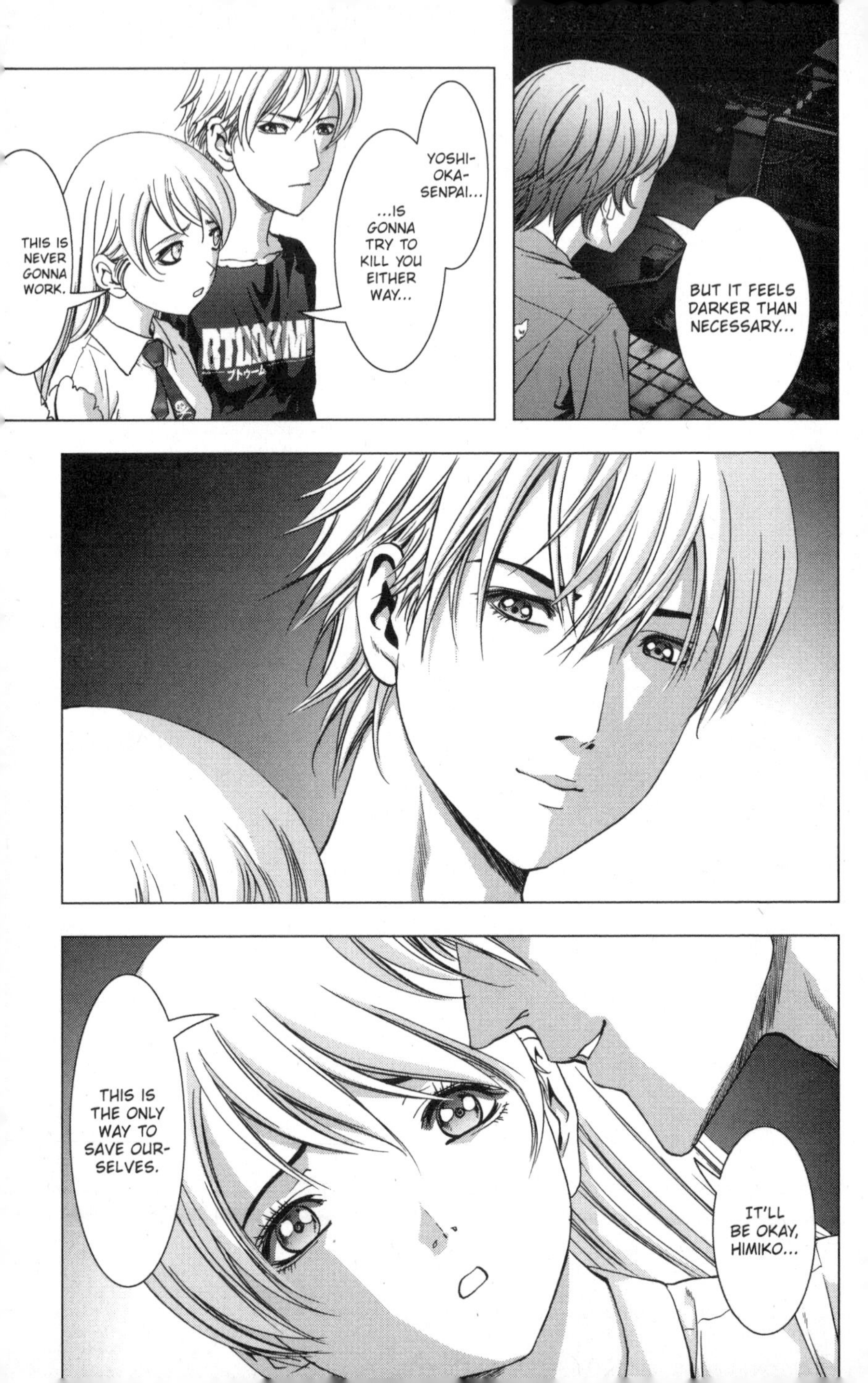
BUT IT FEELS DARKER THAN NECESSARY...
YOSHI-OKA-SENPAI...
...IS GONNA TRY TO KILL YOU EITHER WAY...
THIS IS NEVER GONNA WORK.
THIS IS THE ONLY WAY TO SAVE OUR-SELVES.
IT'LL BE OKAY, HIMIKO...

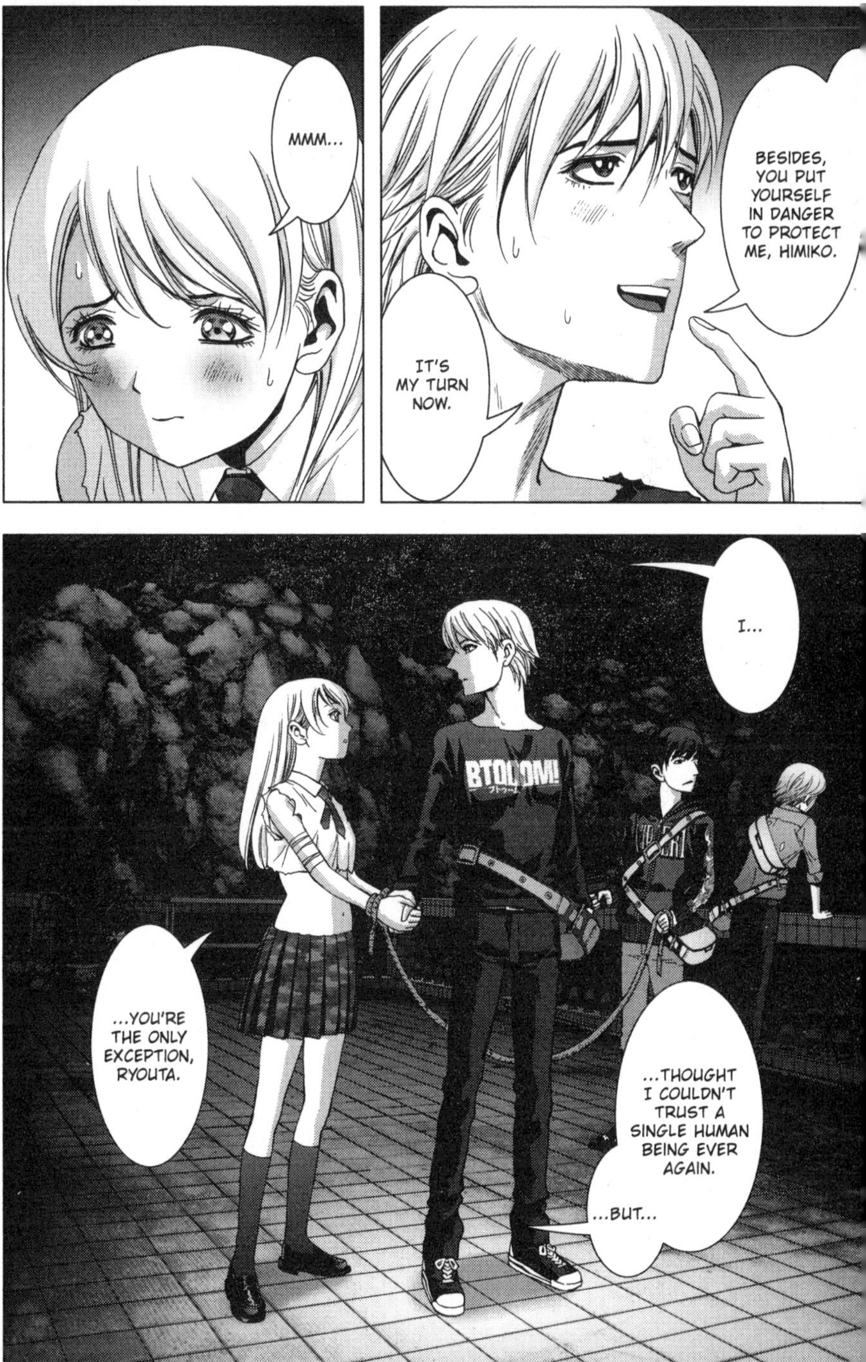
BESIDES, YOU PUT YOURSELF IN DANGER TO PROTECT ME, HIMIKO.
IT'S MY TURN NOW.
MMM...
I...
...THOUGHT I COULDN'T TRUST A SINGLE HUMAN BEING EVER AGAIN.
...BUT...
...YOU'RE THE ONLY EXCEPTION, RYOUTA.

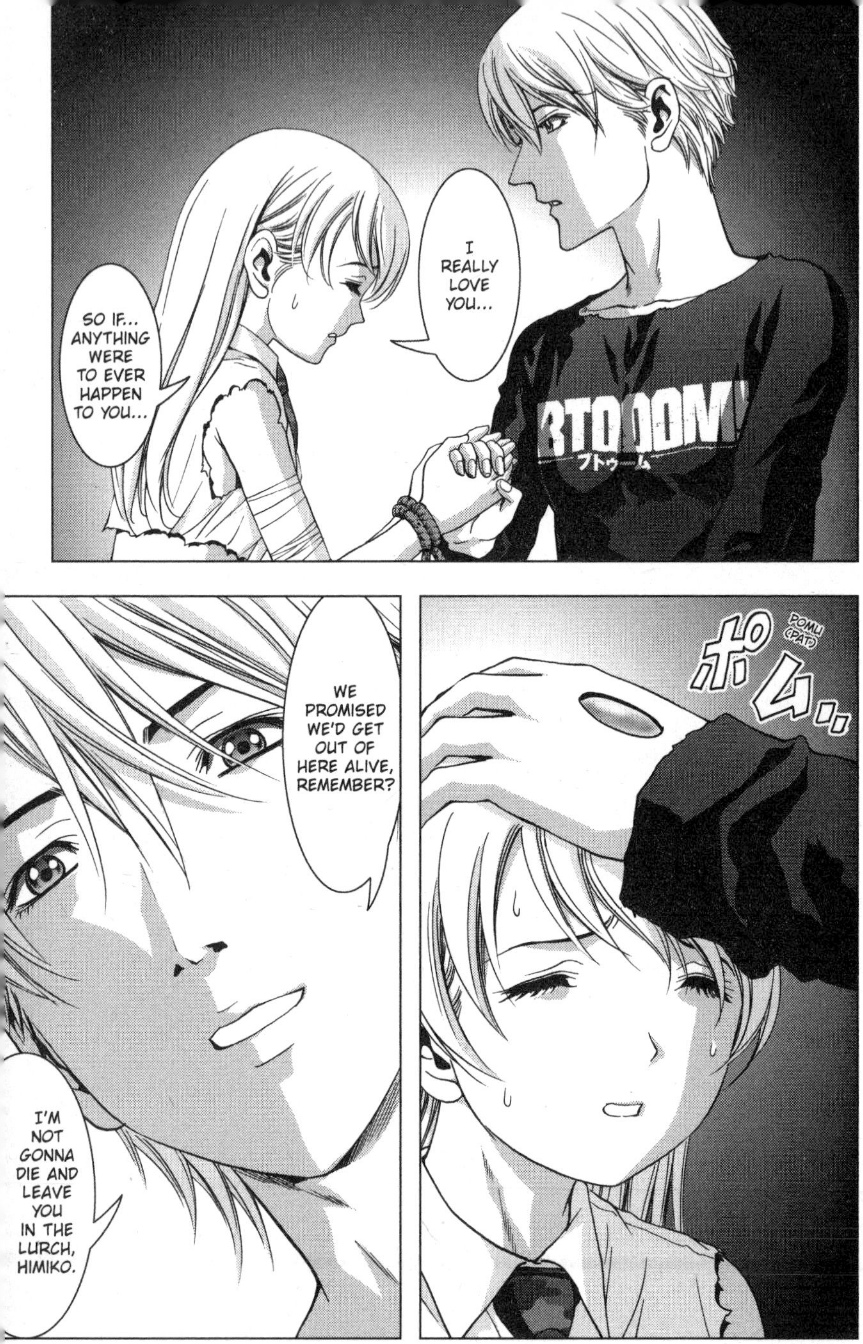
I REALLY LOVE YOU...
BTOOOM!
ブトゥーム
SO IF... ANYTHING WERE TO EVER HAPPEN TO YOU...
ポム..
POMU (PAT)
WE PROMISED WE'D GET OUT OF HERE ALIVE, REMEMBER?
I'M NOT GONNA DIE AND LEAVE YOU IN THE LURCH, HIMIKO.

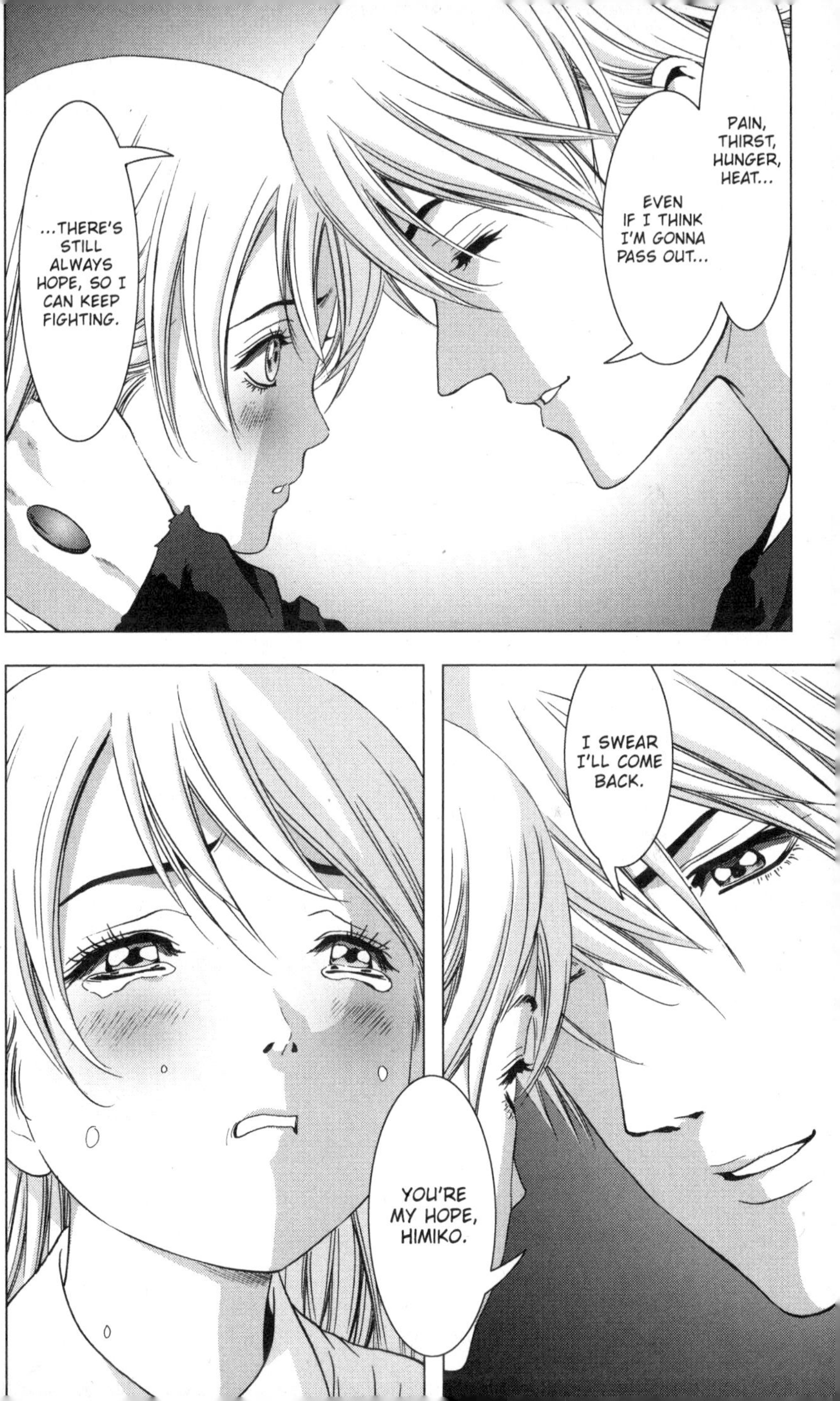
PAIN, THIRST, HUNGER, HEAT...
EVEN IF I THINK I'M GONNA PASS OUT...
...THERE'S STILL ALWAYS HOPE, SO I CAN KEEP FIGHTING.
I SWEAR I'LL COME BACK.
YOU'RE MY HOPE, HIMIKO.

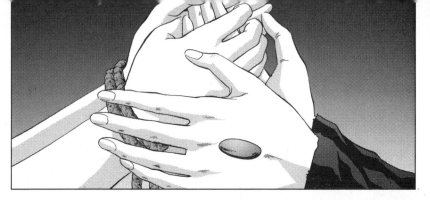

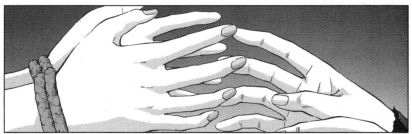

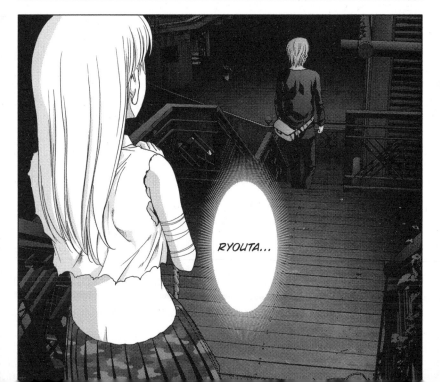

RYOUTA...

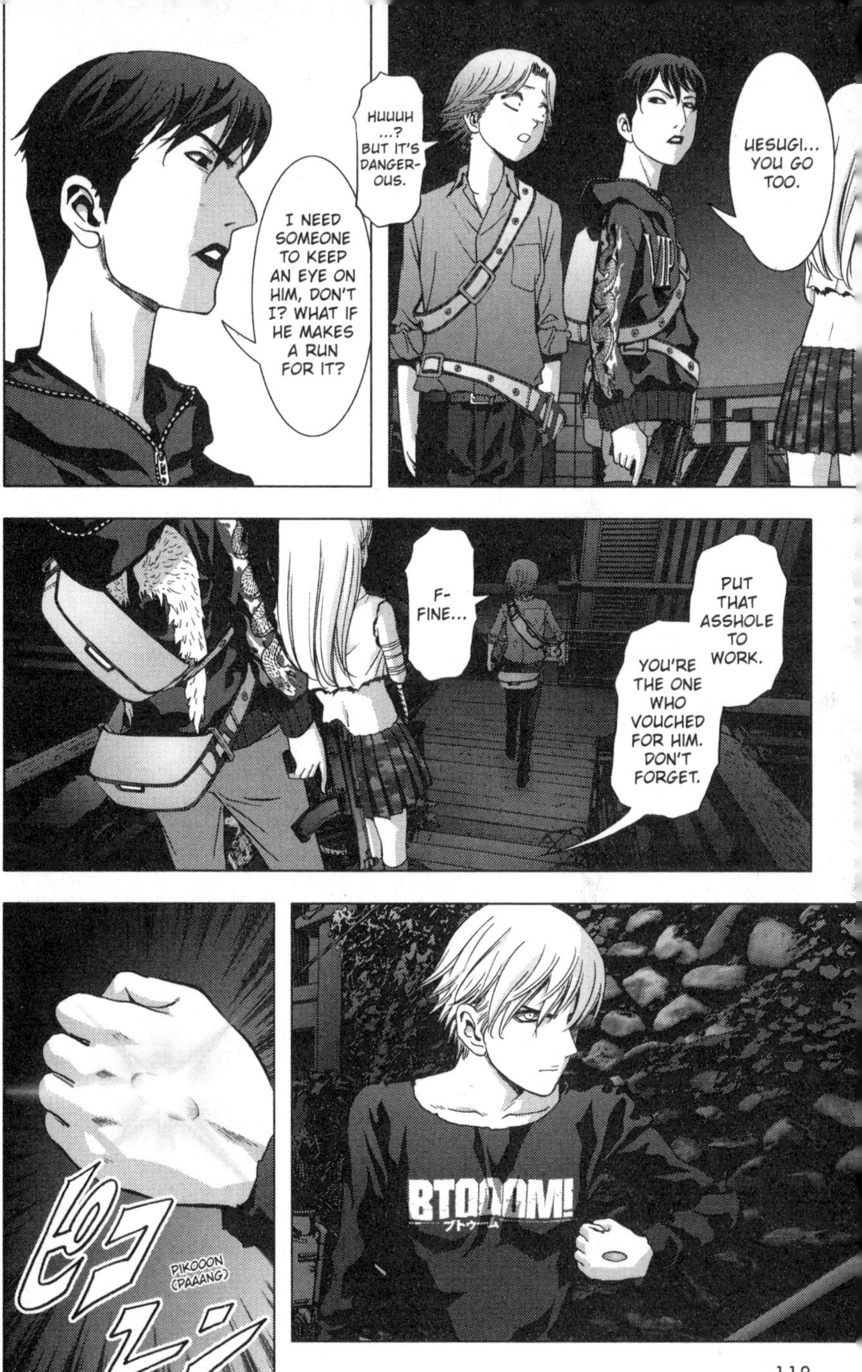
UESUGI... YOU GO TOO.
HUUUH ...? BUT IT'S DANGER-OUS.
I NEED SOMEONE TO KEEP AN EYE ON HIM, DON'T I? WHAT IF HE MAKES A RUN FOR IT?
PUT THAT ASSHOLE TO WORK.
YOU'RE THE ONE WHO VOUCHED FOR HIM. DON'T FORGET.
F- FINE...
BTOOOM!
PIKOOON (PAAANG)

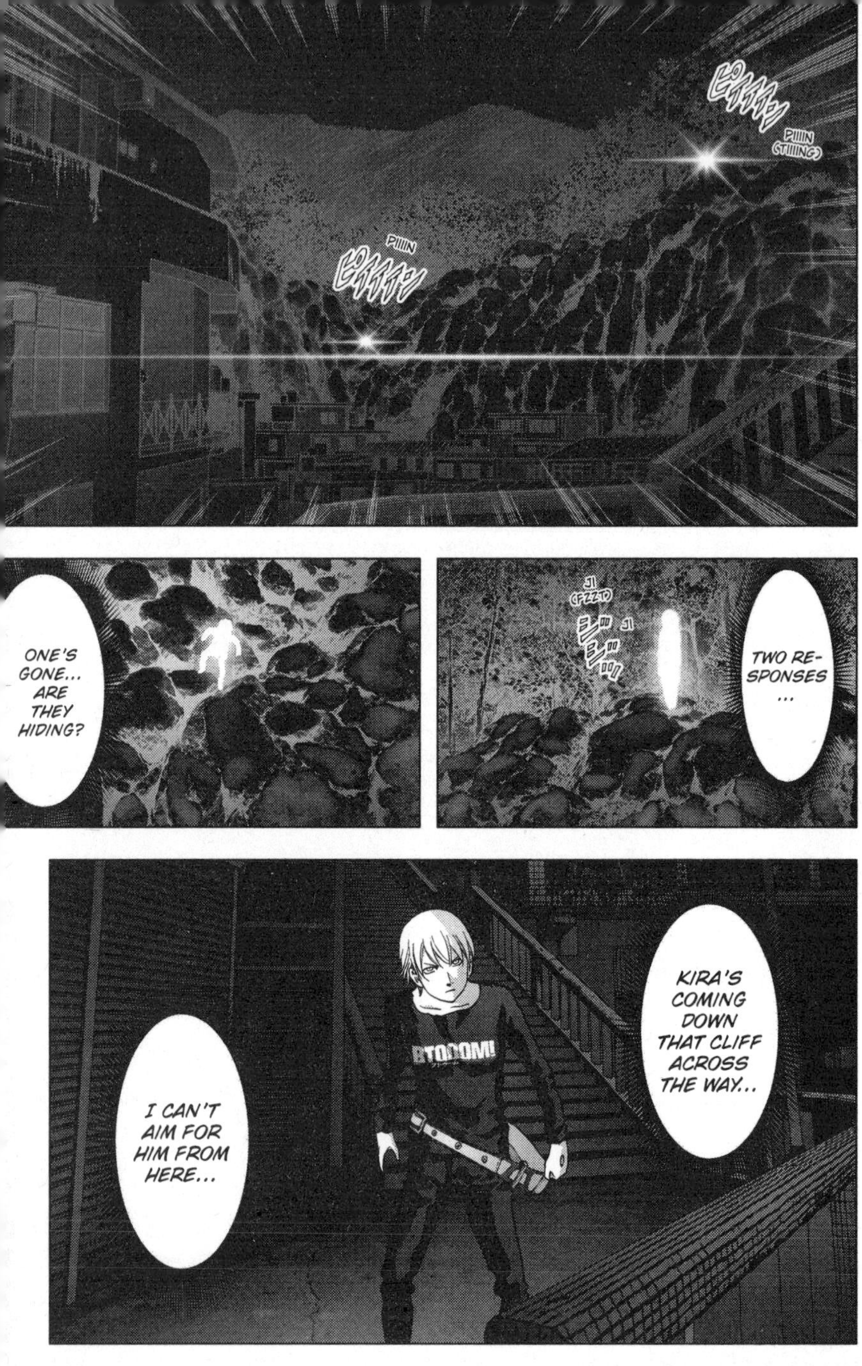
PIIIN (TIIIING)
PIIIN
JI (FZZT)
JI
TWO RE-SPONSES...
ONE'S GONE... ARE THEY HIDING?
KIRA'S COMING DOWN THAT CLIFF ACROSS THE WAY...
I CAN'T AIM FOR HIM FROM HERE...
BTOOOM!

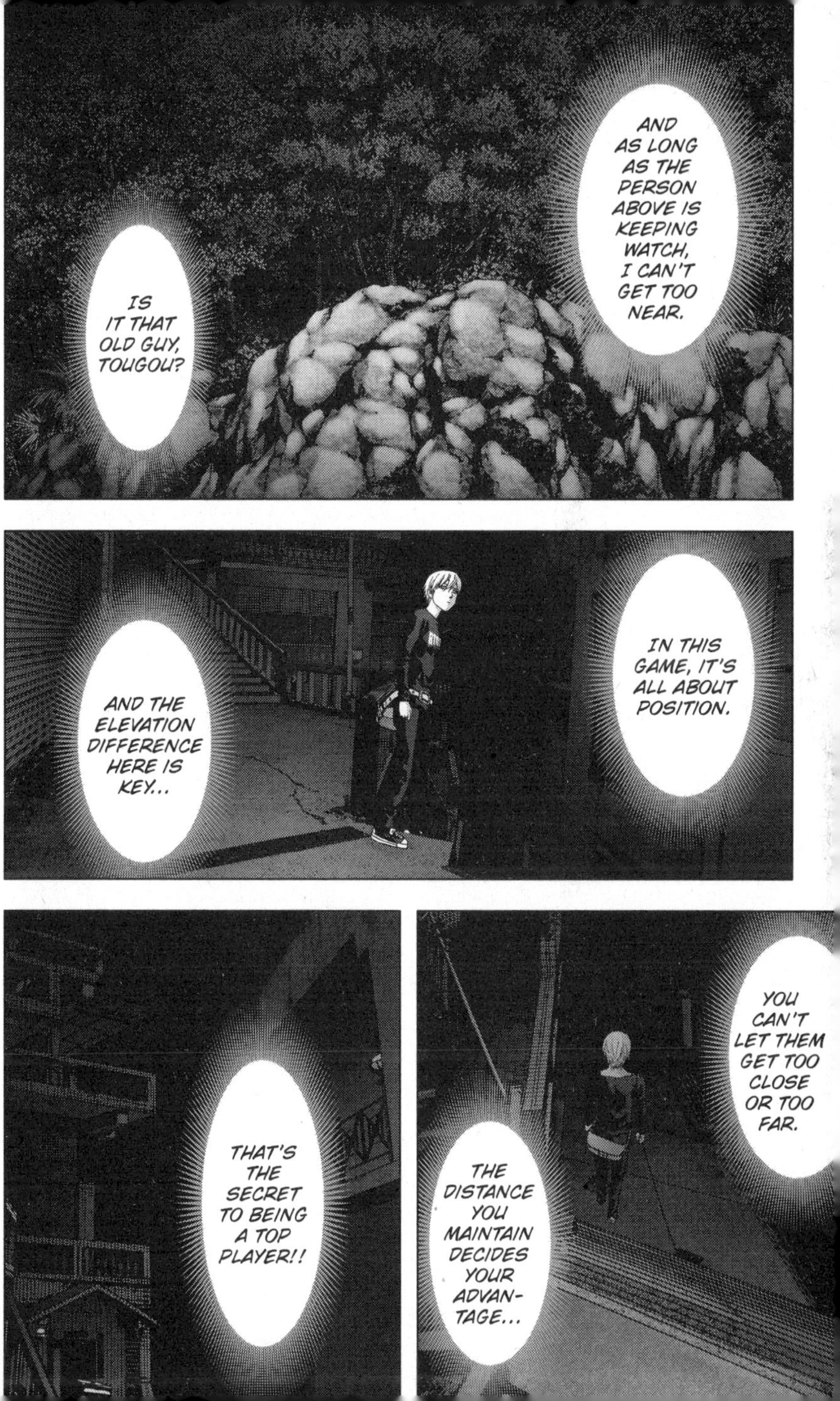
AND AS LONG AS THE PERSON ABOVE IS KEEPING WATCH, I CAN'T GET TOO NEAR.
IS IT THAT OLD GUY, TOUGOU?
IN THIS GAME, IT'S ALL ABOUT POSITION.
AND THE ELEVATION DIFFERENCE HERE IS KEY...
YOU CAN'T LET THEM GET TOO CLOSE OR TOO FAR.
THE DISTANCE YOU MAINTAIN DECIDES YOUR ADVAN-TAGE...
THAT'S THE SECRET TO BEING A TOP PLAYER!!

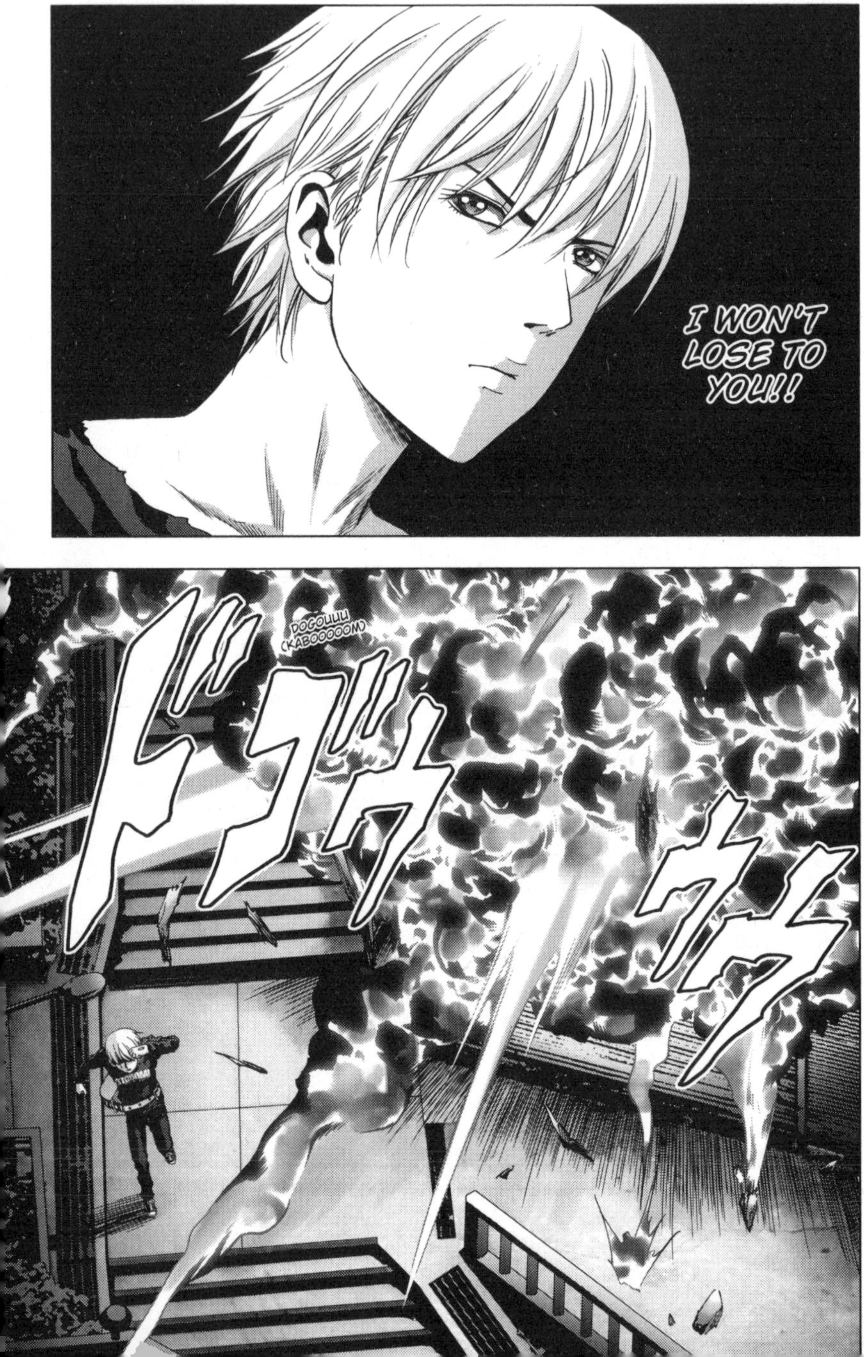
I WON'T LOSE TO YOU!!
ドゴウウウ
DOGOUUU (KABOOOOOM)

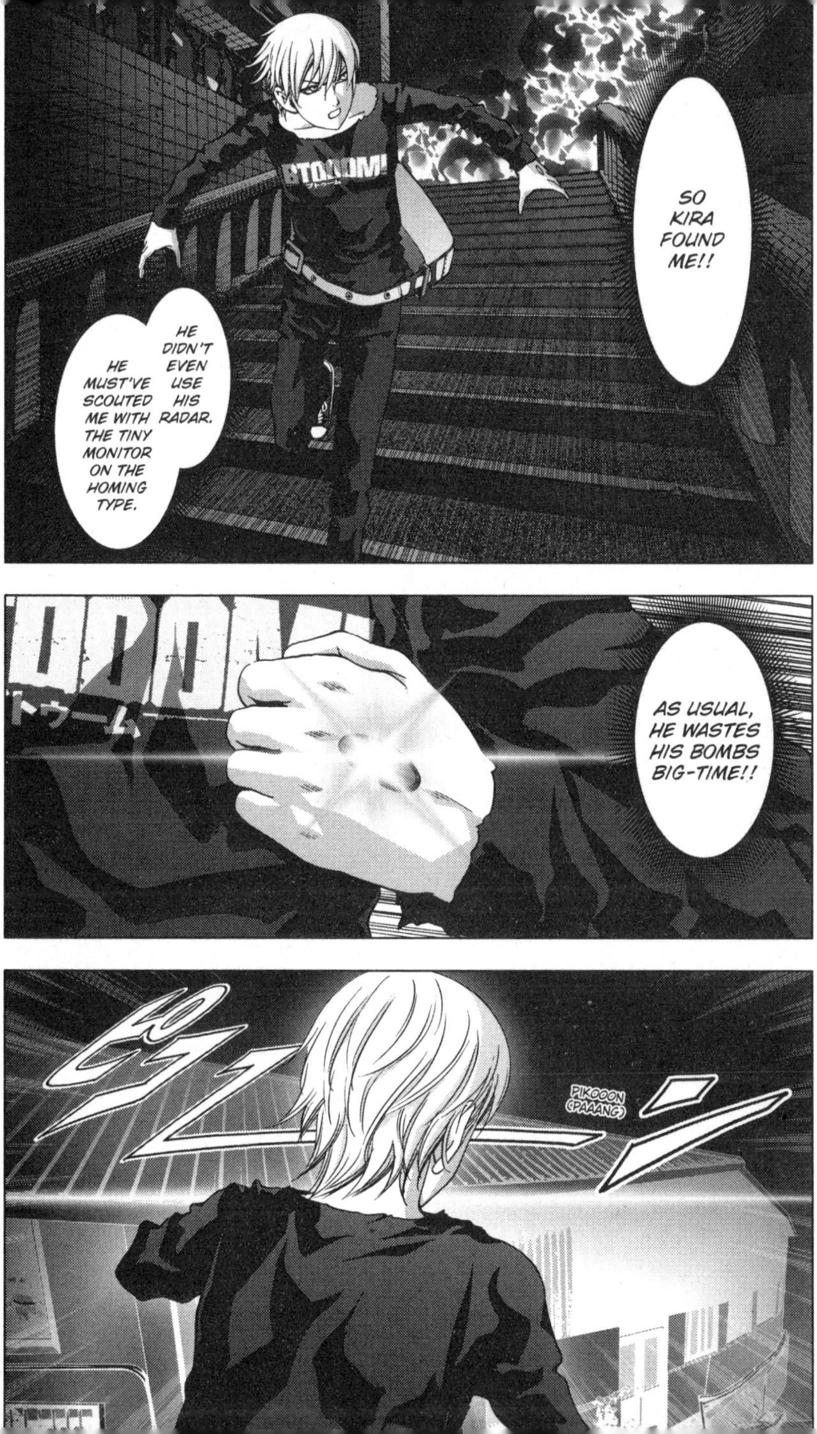
SO KIRA FOUND ME!!
HE DIDN'T EVEN USE HIS RADAR.
HE MUST'VE SCOUTED ME WITH THE TINY MONITOR ON THE HOMING TYPE.
AS USUAL, HE WASTES HIS BOMBS BIG-TIME!!
PIKOOON (PAAANG)

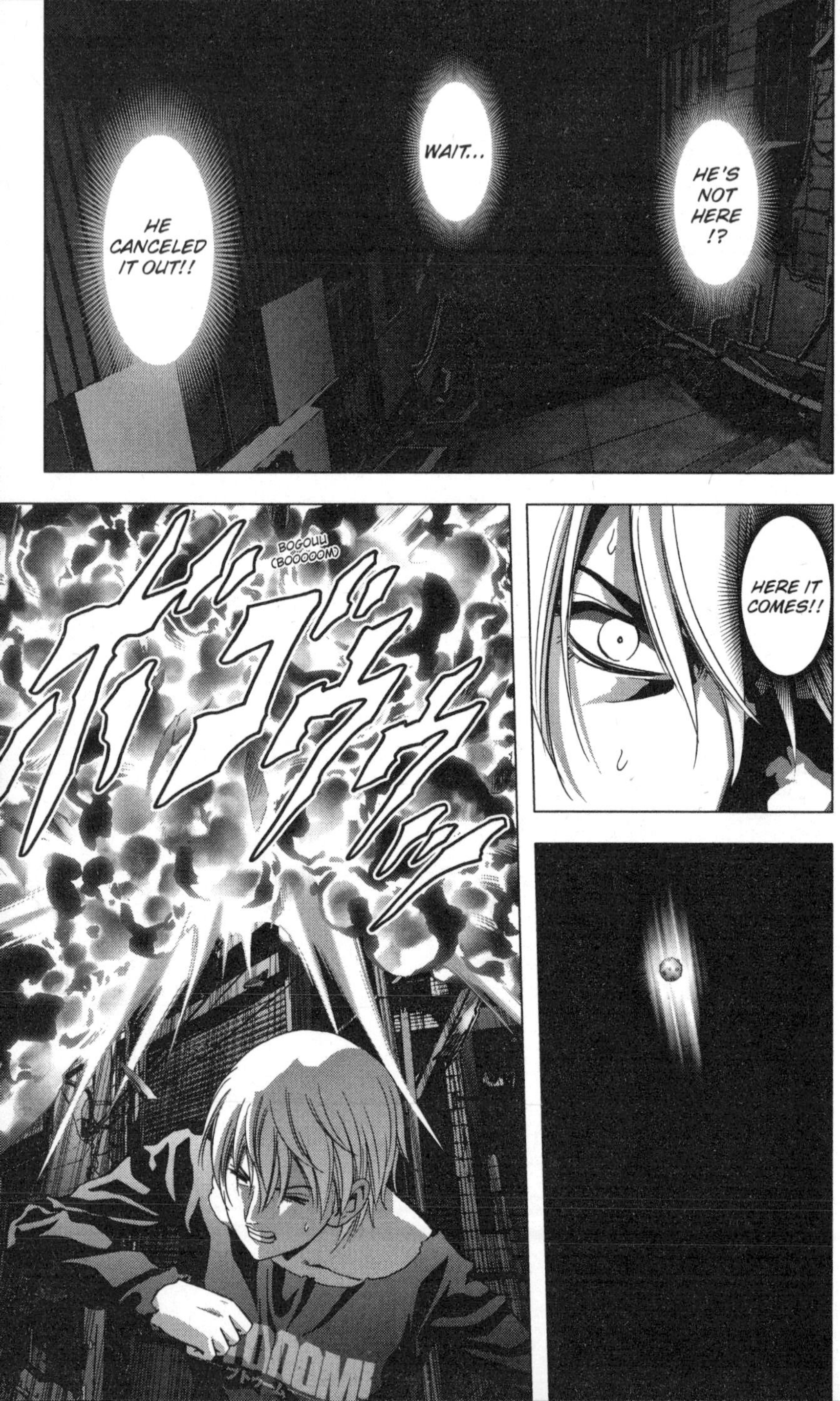
HE'S NOT HERE !?
WAIT...
HE CANCELED IT OUT!!
HERE IT COMES!!
BOGOUU (BOOOOOM)

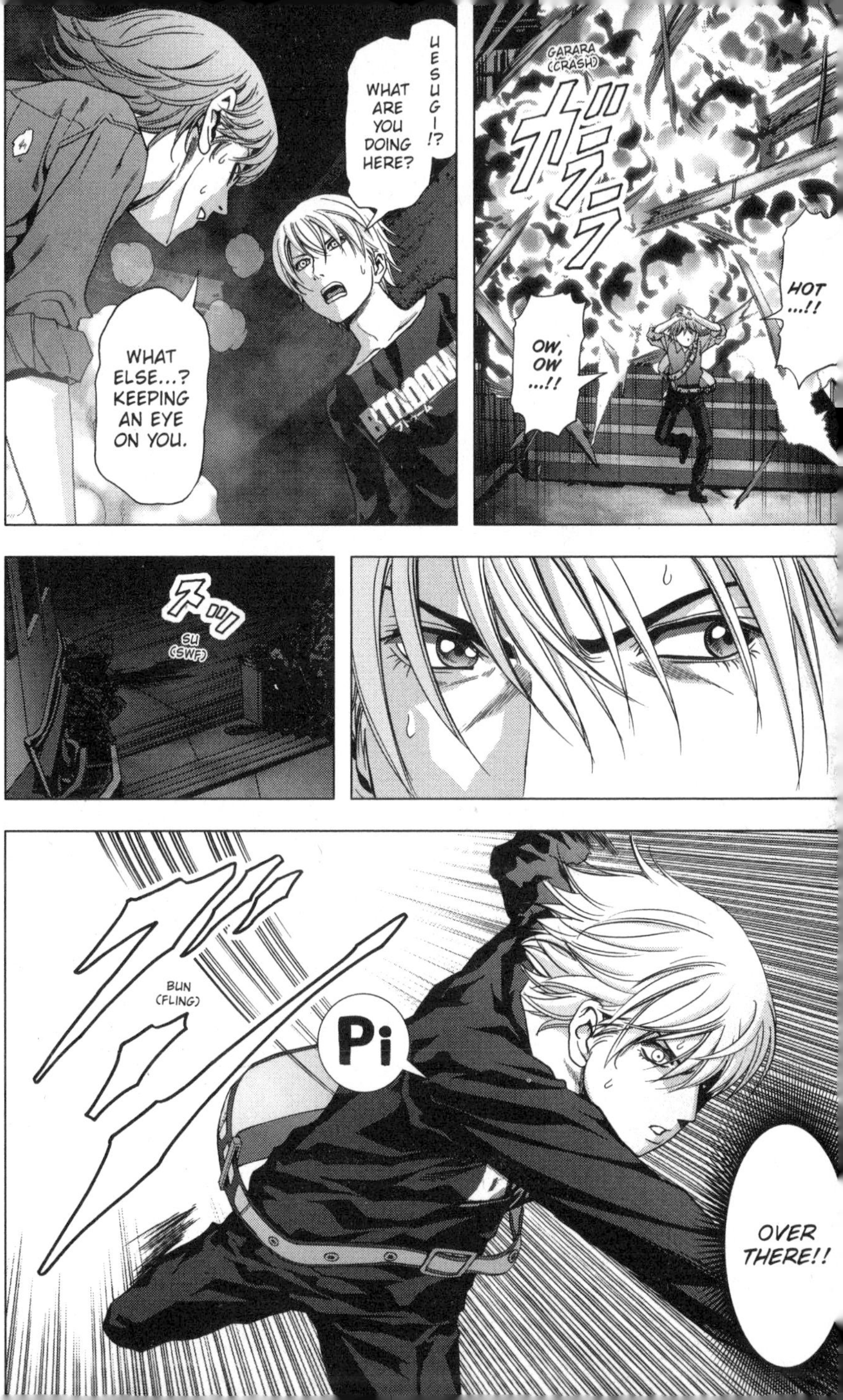
GARARA (CRASH)
HOT ...!!
OW, OW ...!!
UESUGI!?
WHAT ARE YOU DOING HERE?
WHAT ELSE...? KEEPING AN EYE ON YOU.
SU (SWF)
BUN (FLING)
Pi
OVER THERE!!

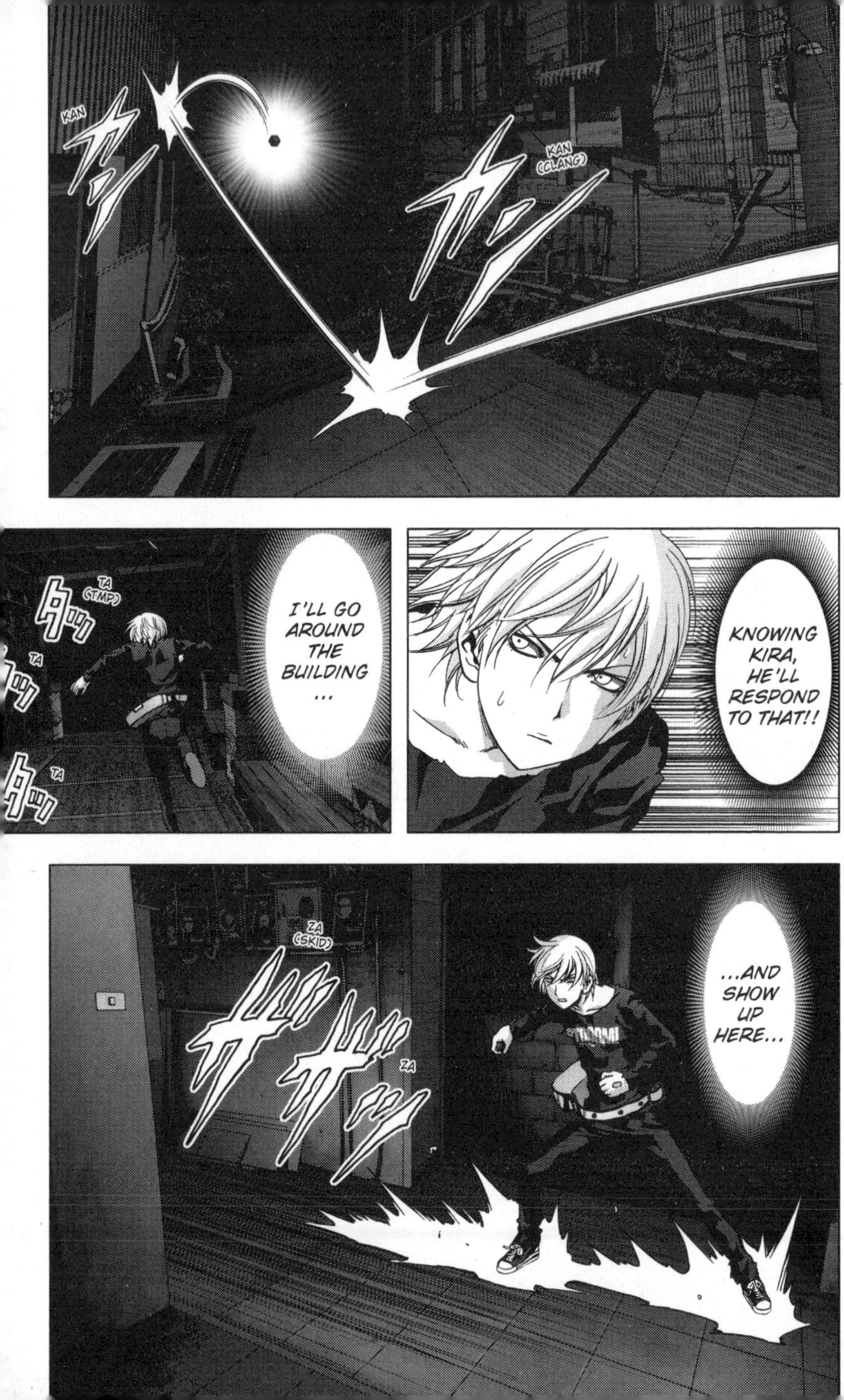
KAN (CLANG)
KAN
KNOWING KIRA, HE'LL RESPOND TO THAT!!
I'LL GO AROUND THE BUILDING...
TA (TMP)
TA
TA
...AND SHOW UP HERE...
ZA (SKID)
ZA

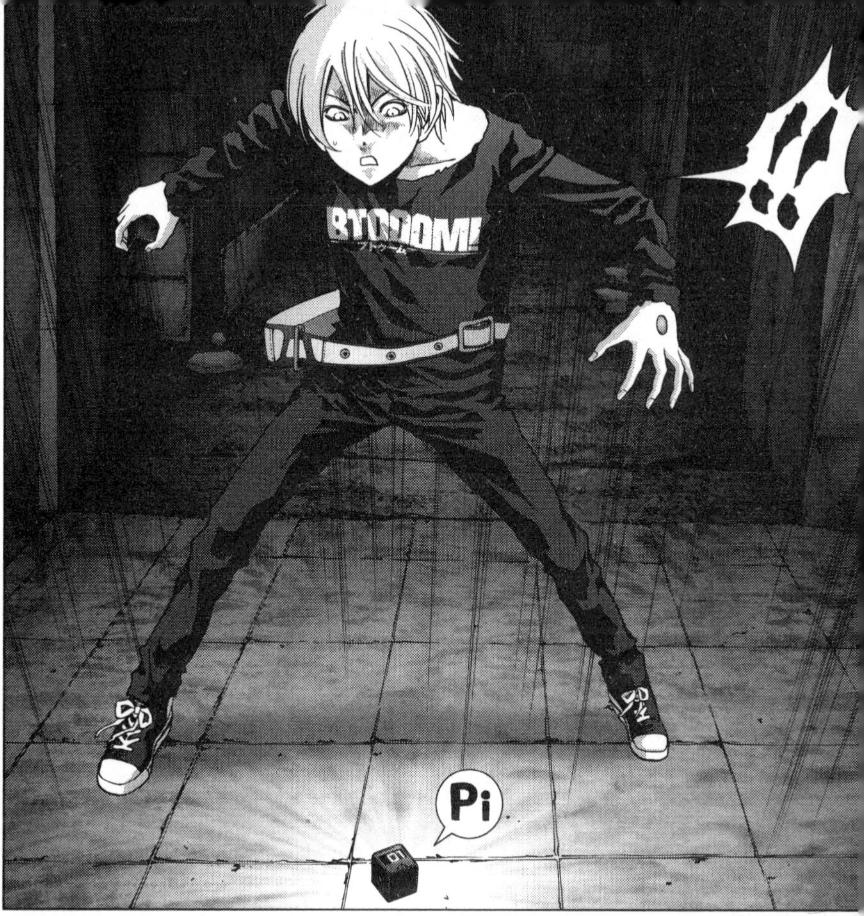
!!
Pi

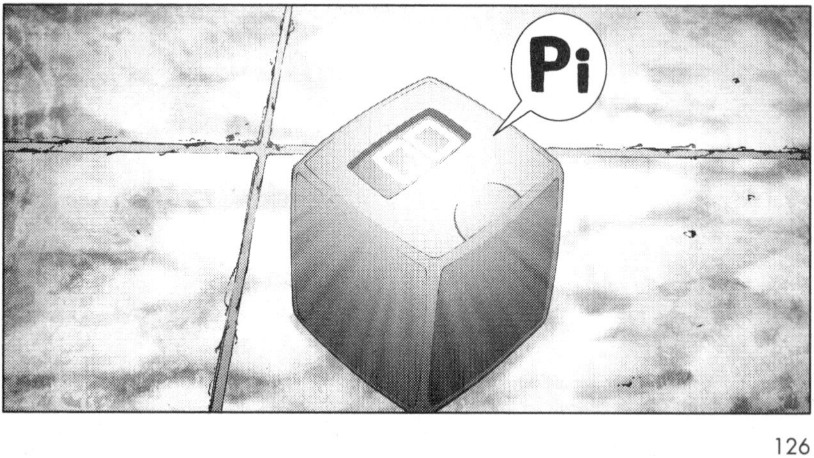
Pi

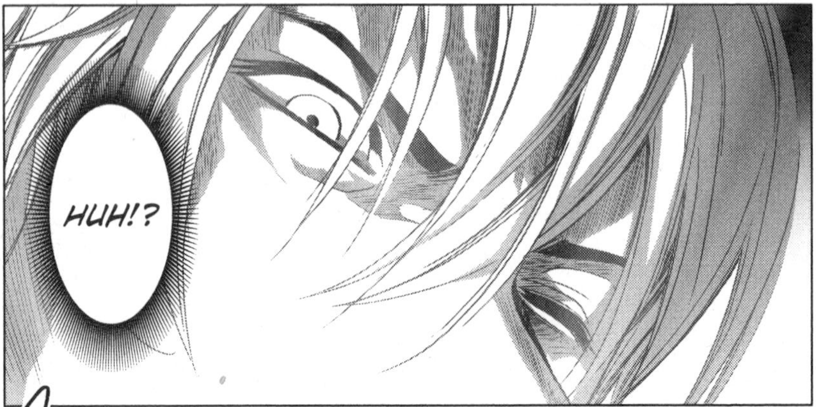
HUH!?
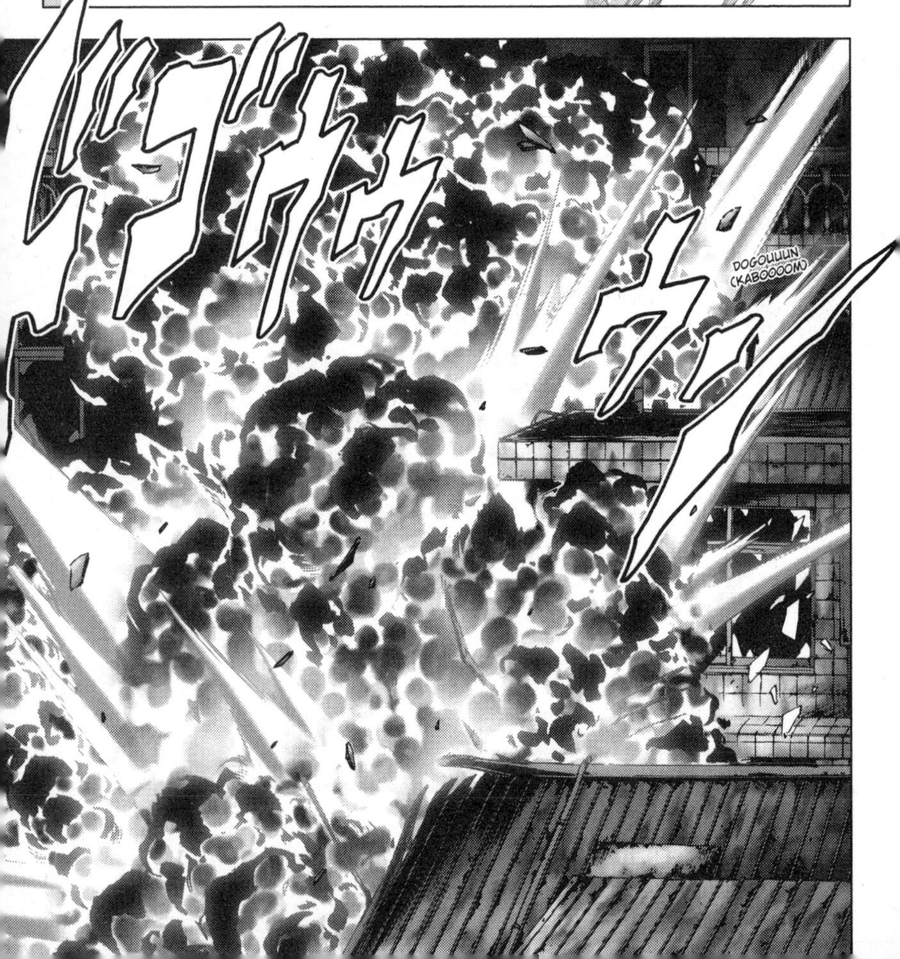
DOGOUUUN
(KABOOOOM)

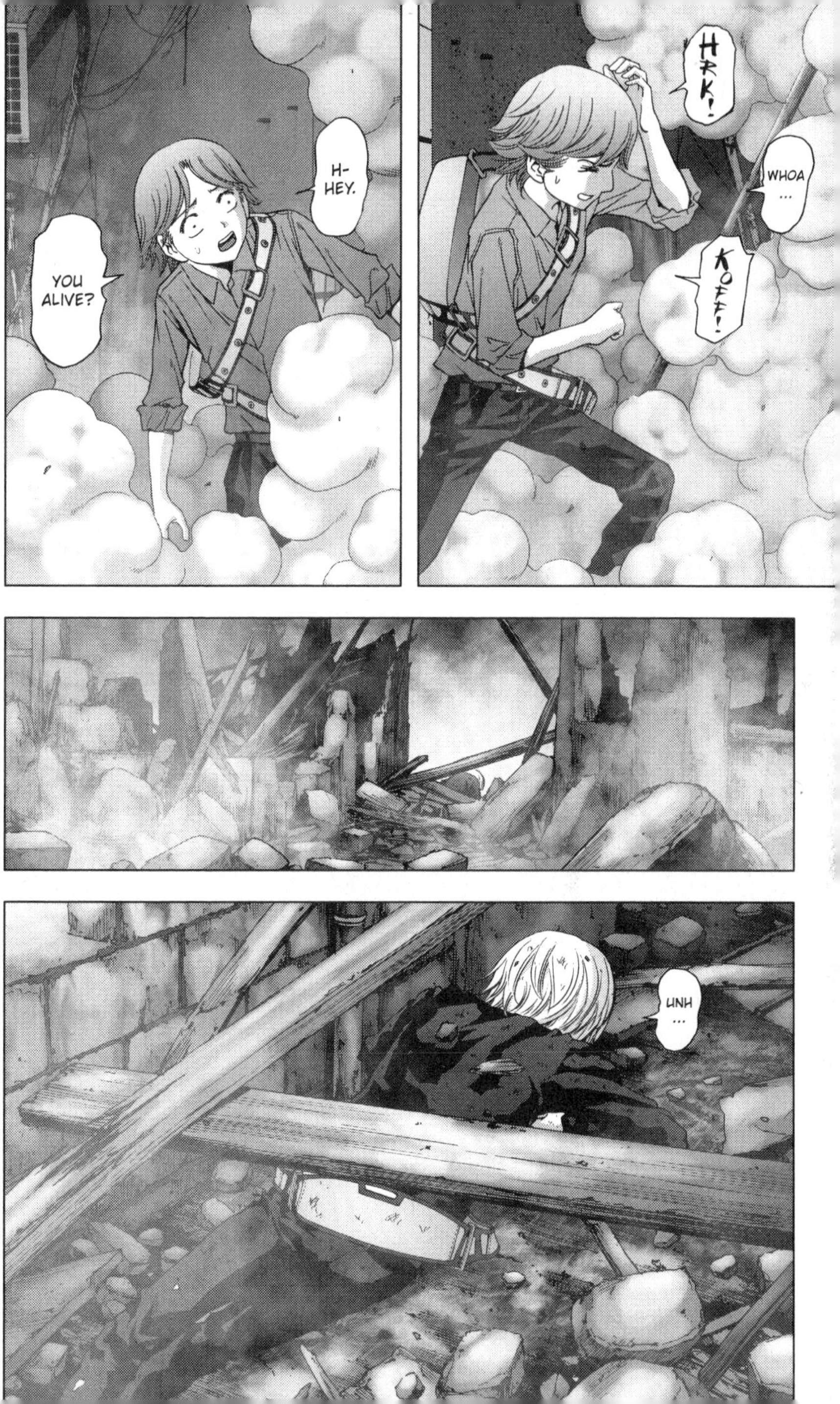
HRK!
WHOA ...
KOFF!
H- HEY.
YOU ALIVE?
UNH ...

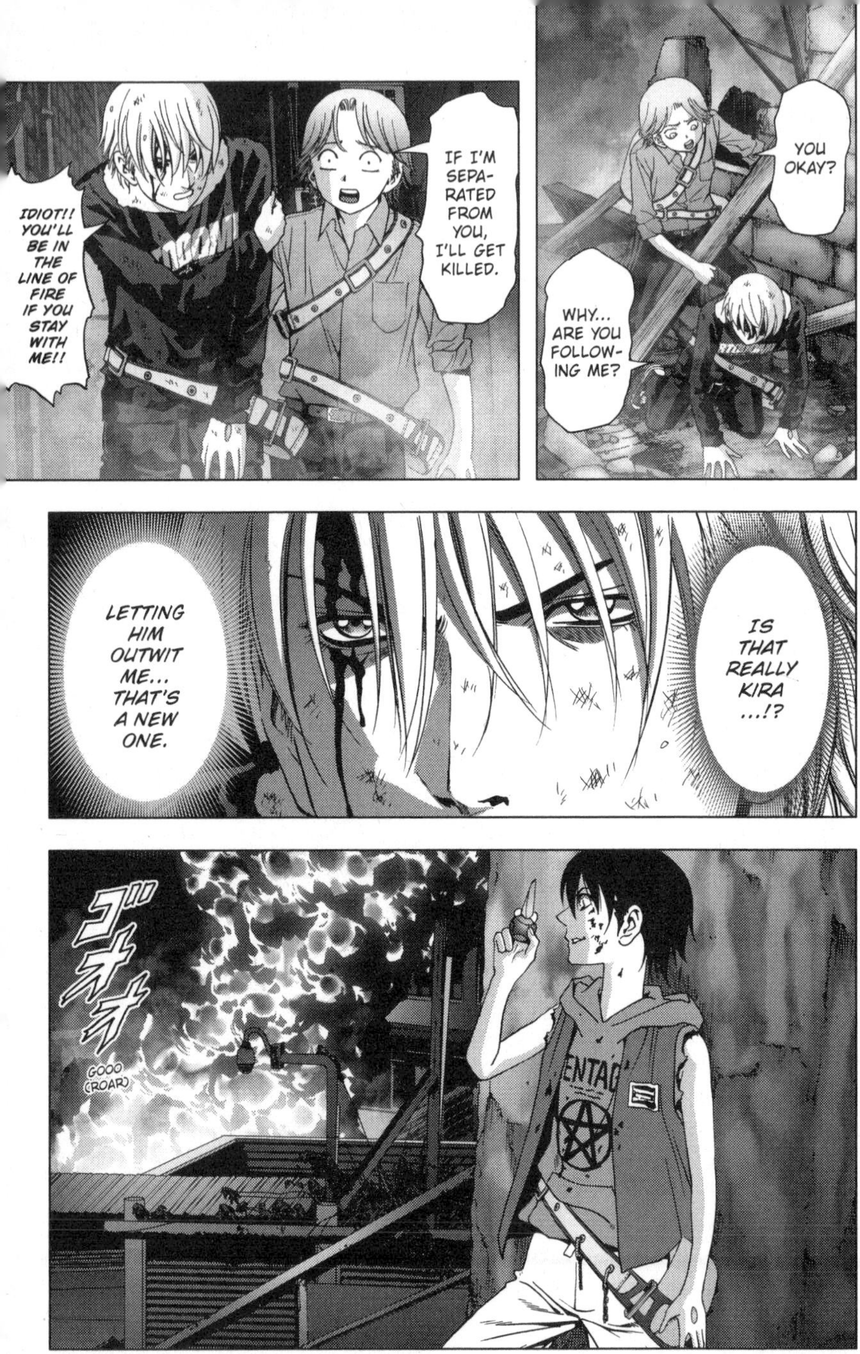
YOU OKAY?
WHY... ARE YOU FOLLOW-ING ME?
IF I'M SEPA-RATED FROM YOU, I'LL GET KILLED.
IDIOT!! YOU'LL BE IN THE LINE OF FIRE IF YOU STAY WITH ME!!
IS THAT REALLY KIRA ...!?
LETTING HIM OUTWIT ME... THAT'S A NEW ONE.
ゴオオ
GOOO (ROAR)

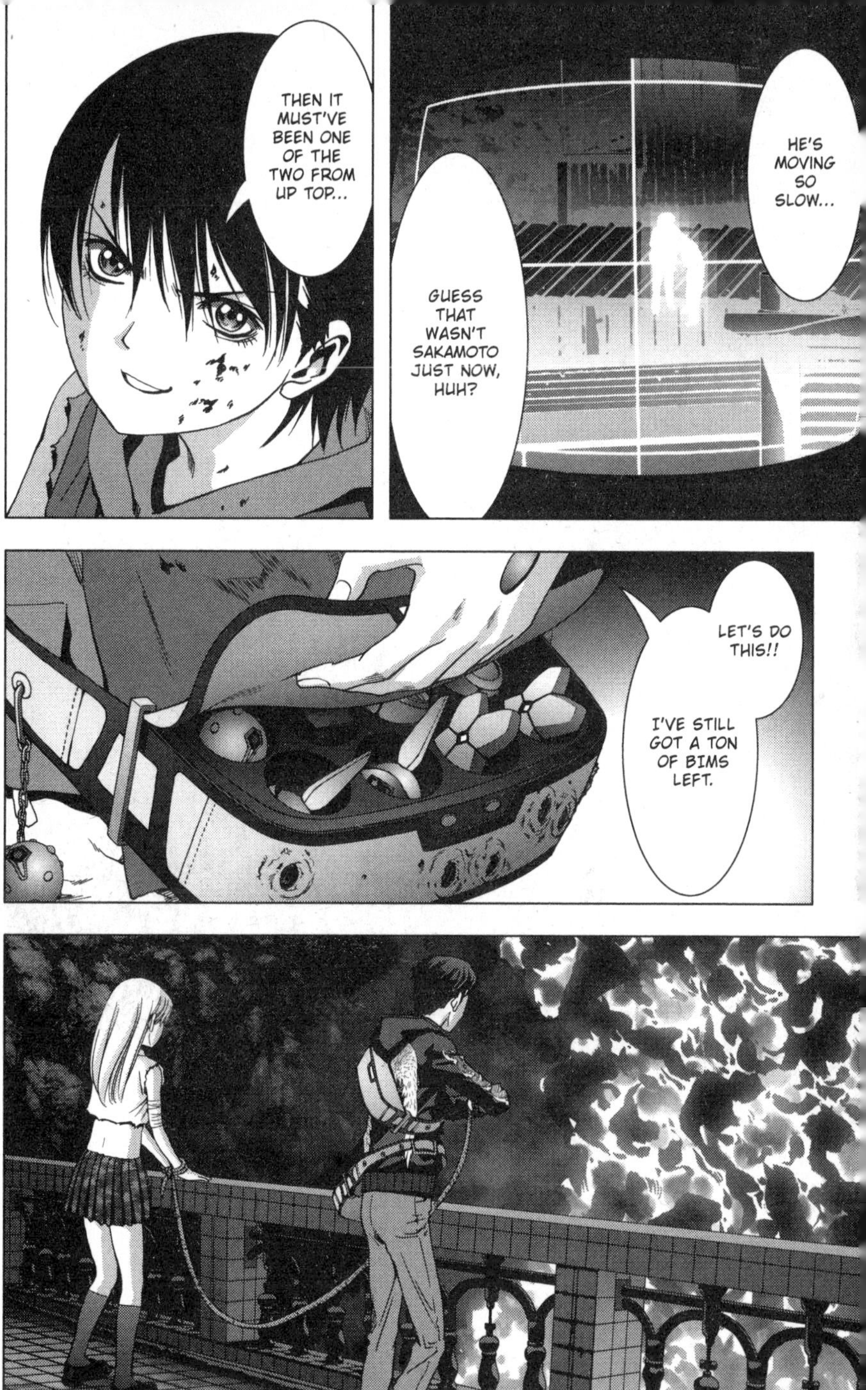
HE'S MOVING SO SLOW...
GUESS THAT WASN'T SAKAMOTO JUST NOW, HUH?
THEN IT MUST'VE BEEN ONE OF THE TWO FROM UP TOP...
LET'S DO THIS!!
I'VE STILL GOT A TON OF BIMS LEFT.

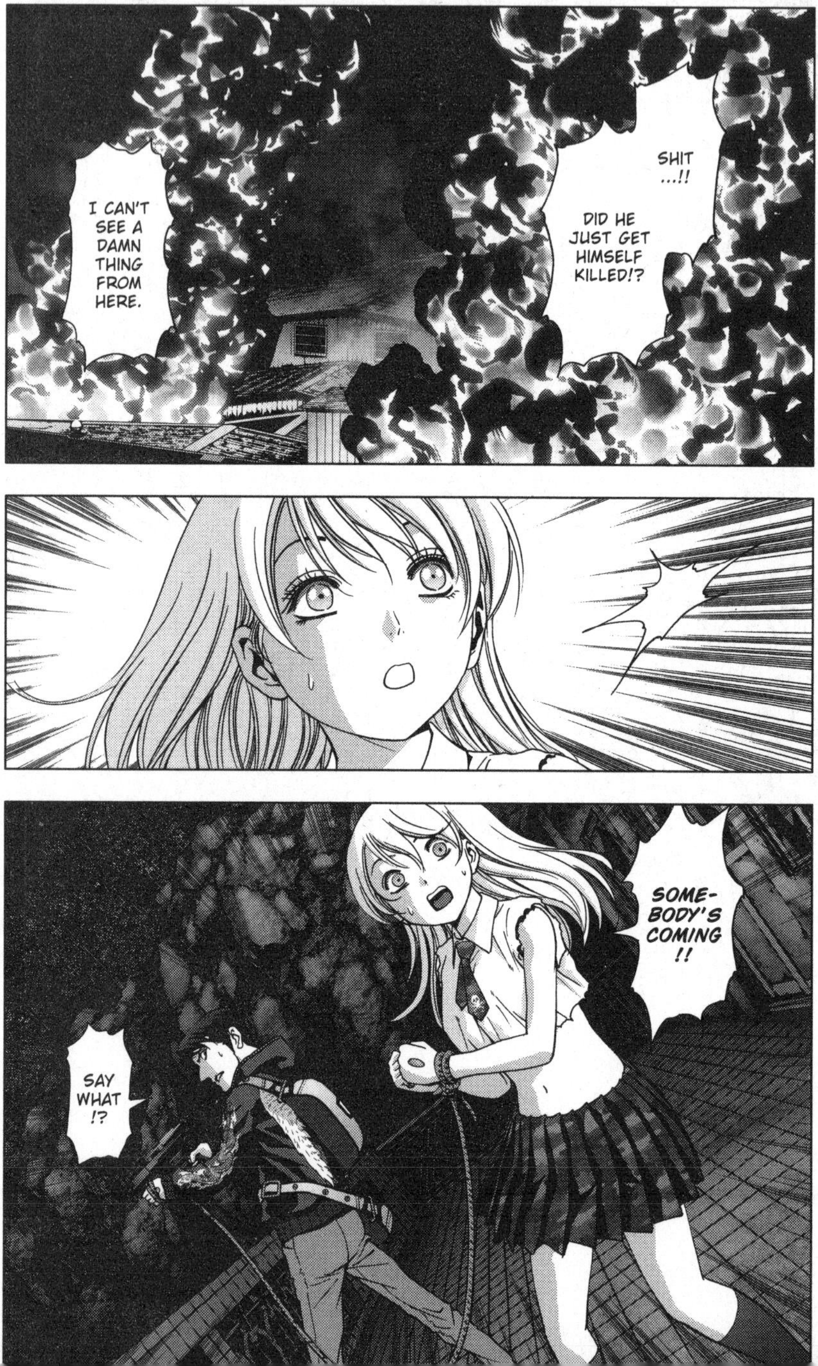
SHIT ...!!
DID HE JUST GET HIMSELF KILLED!?
I CAN'T SEE A DAMN THING FROM HERE.
SOME-BODY'S COMING !!
SAY WHAT !?

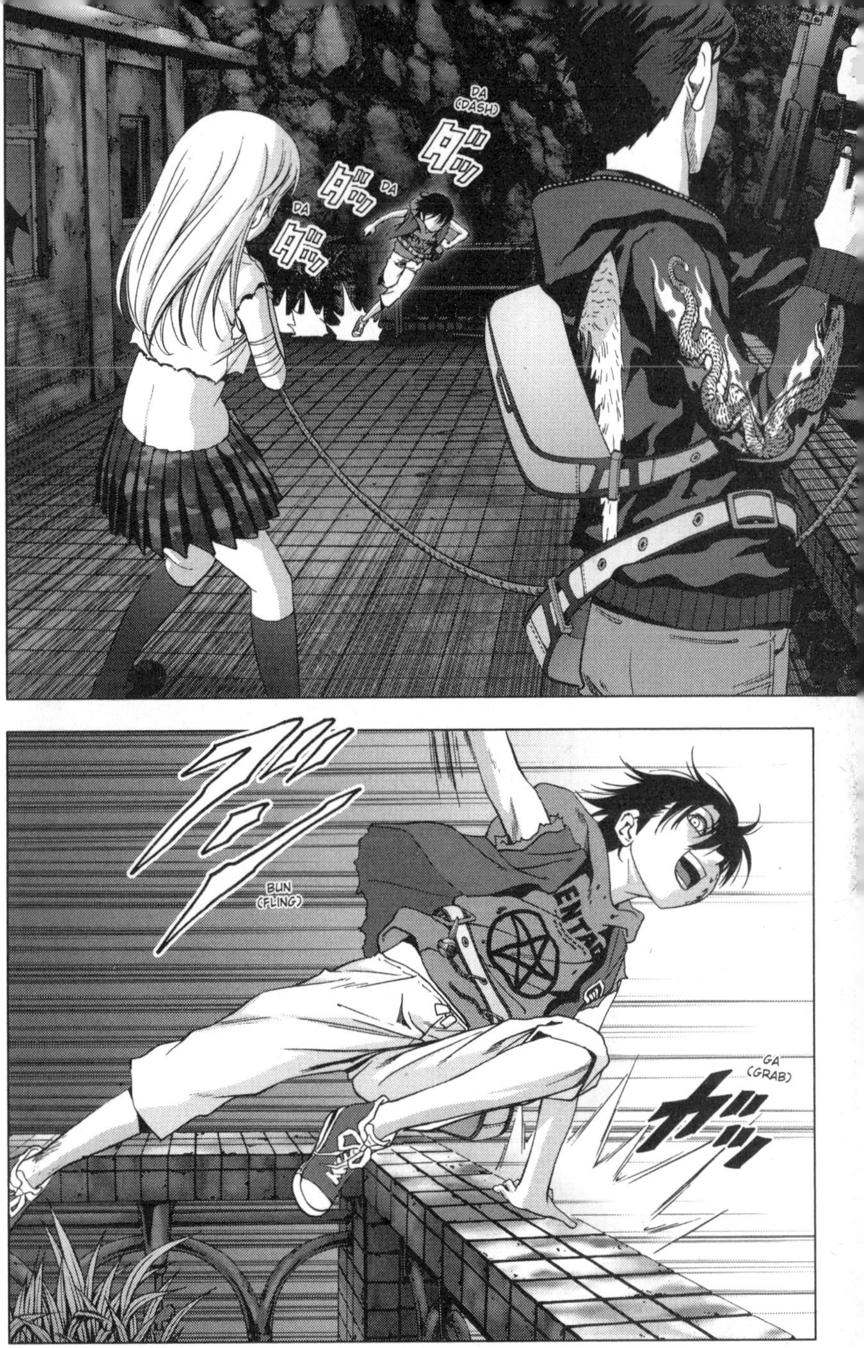
DA (DASH)
DA
DA
BUN (FLING)
GA (GRAB)

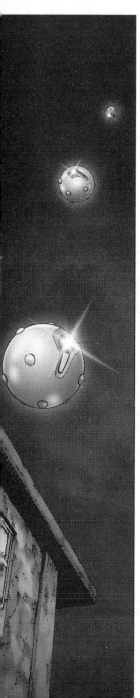
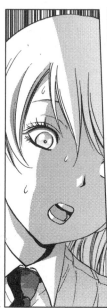
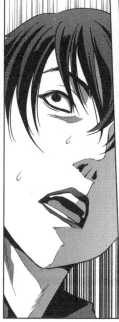
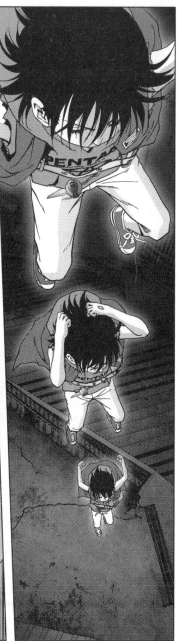

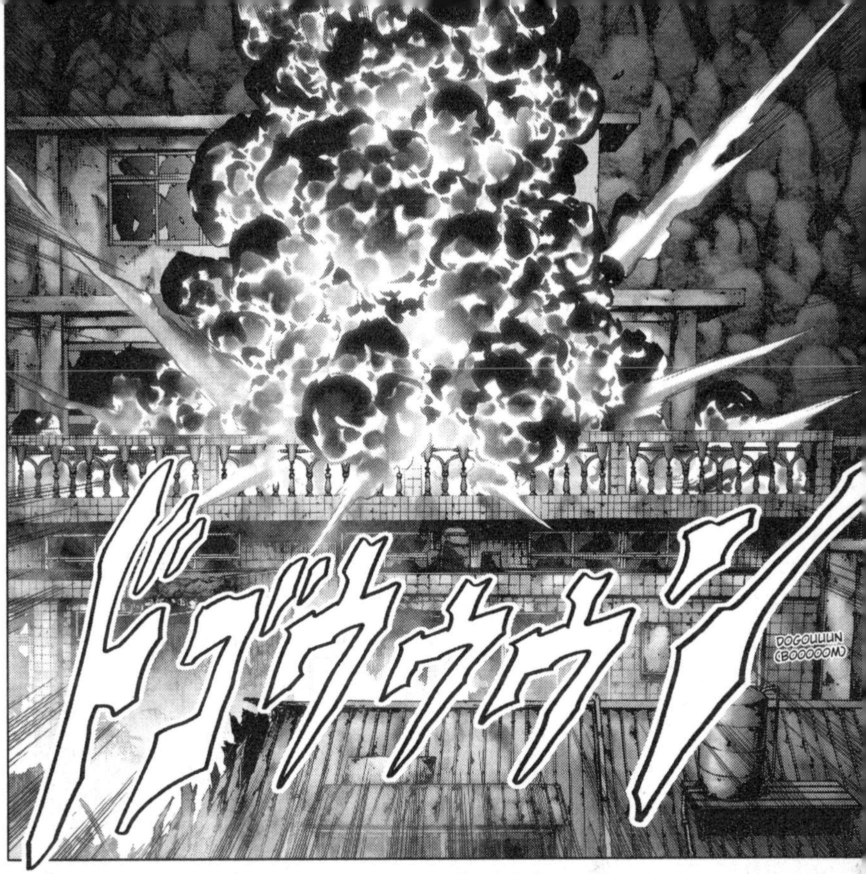
ドゴウウウン
DOGOUUUN
(BOOOOOM)
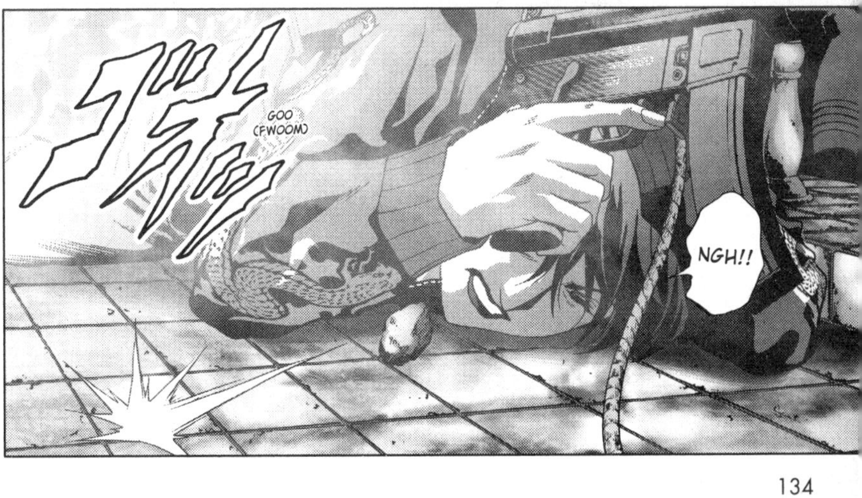
ゴォッ
GOO
(FWOOM)
NGH!!

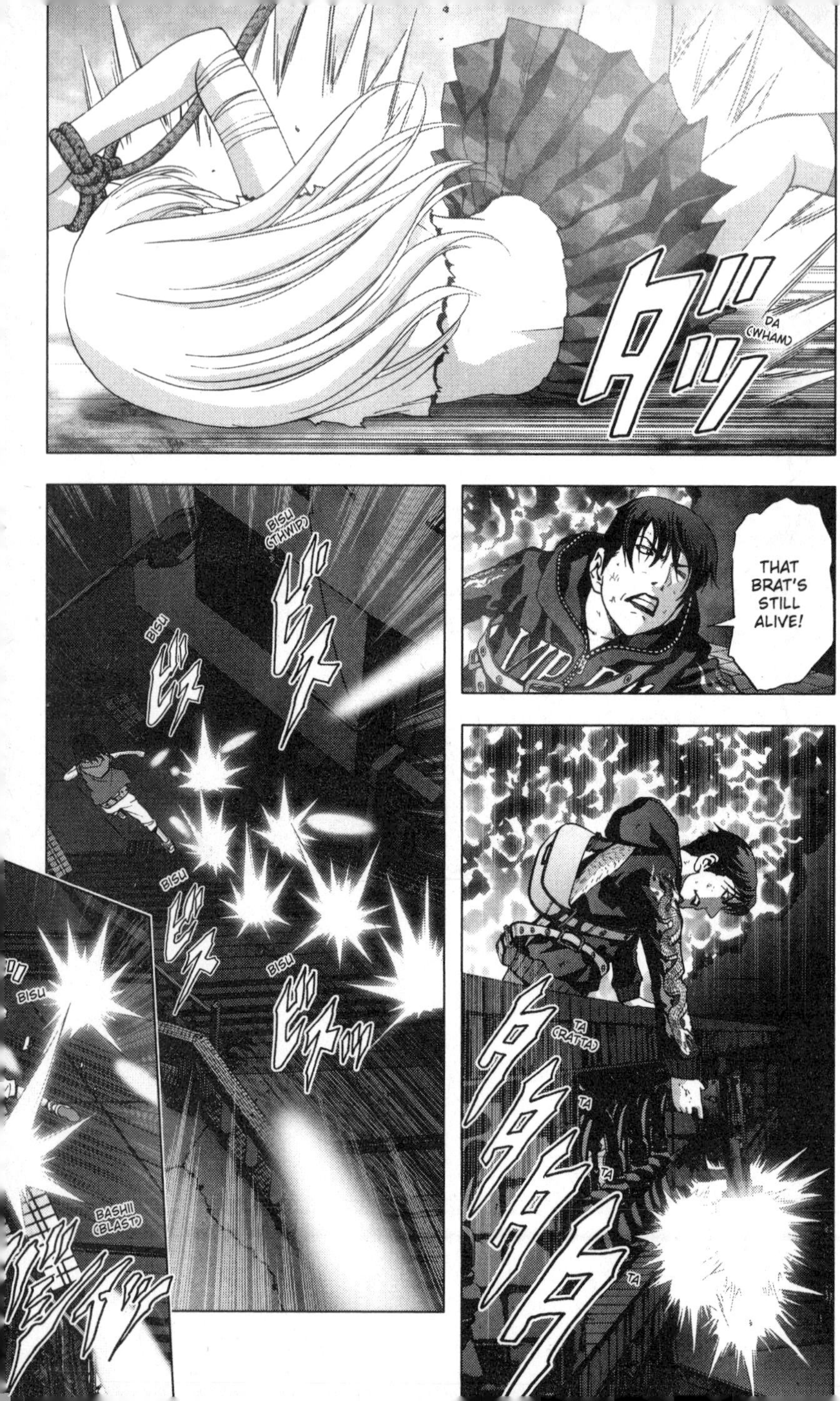
DA (WHAM)
THAT BRAT'S STILL ALIVE!
TA (RATTA)
TA
TA
TA
BISU (THWIP)
BISU
BISU
BISU
BISU
BASHII (BLAST)

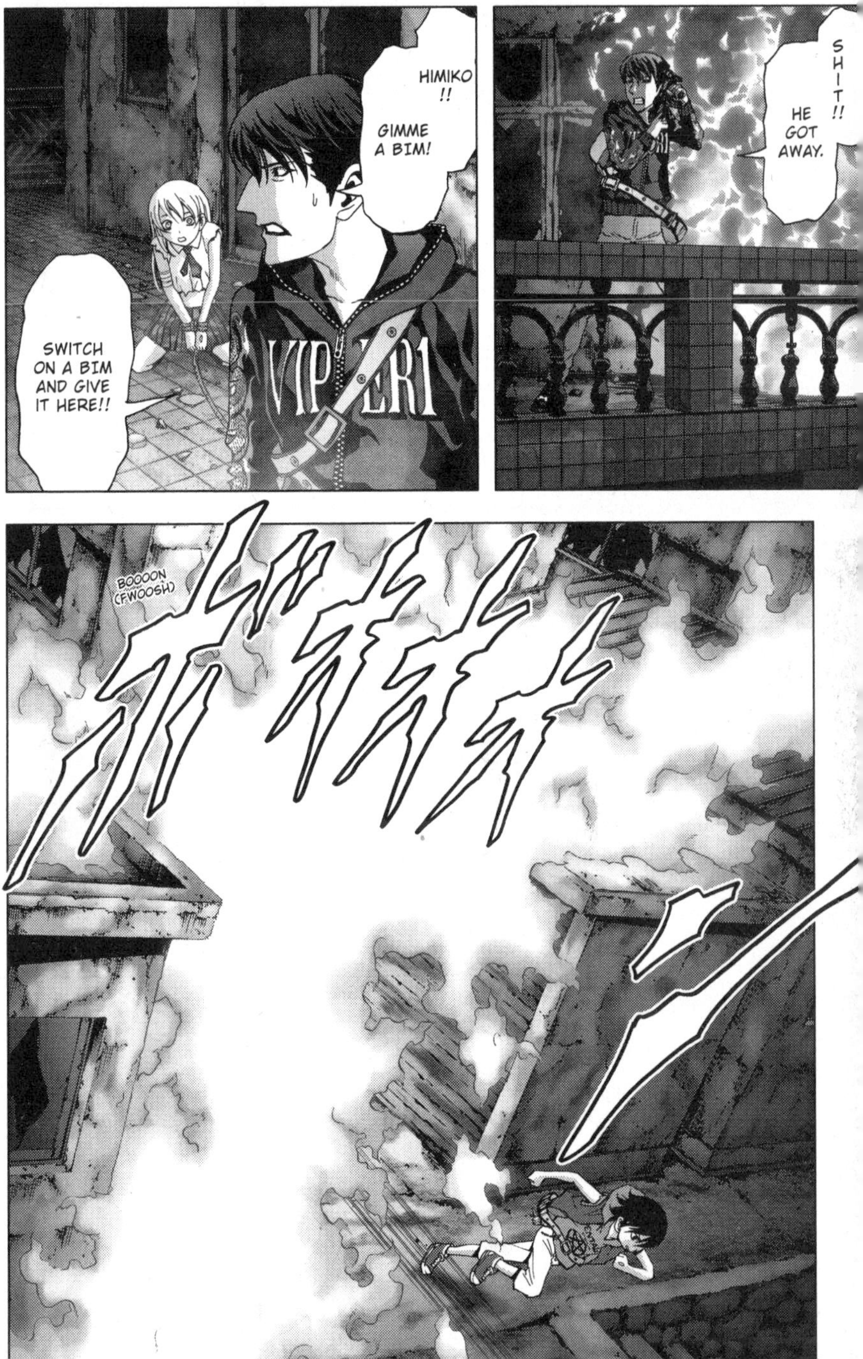
SHIT!!
HE GOT AWAY.
HIMIKO!!
GIMME A BIM!
SWITCH ON A BIM AND GIVE IT HERE!!
VIPER1
BOOOON (FWOOSH)

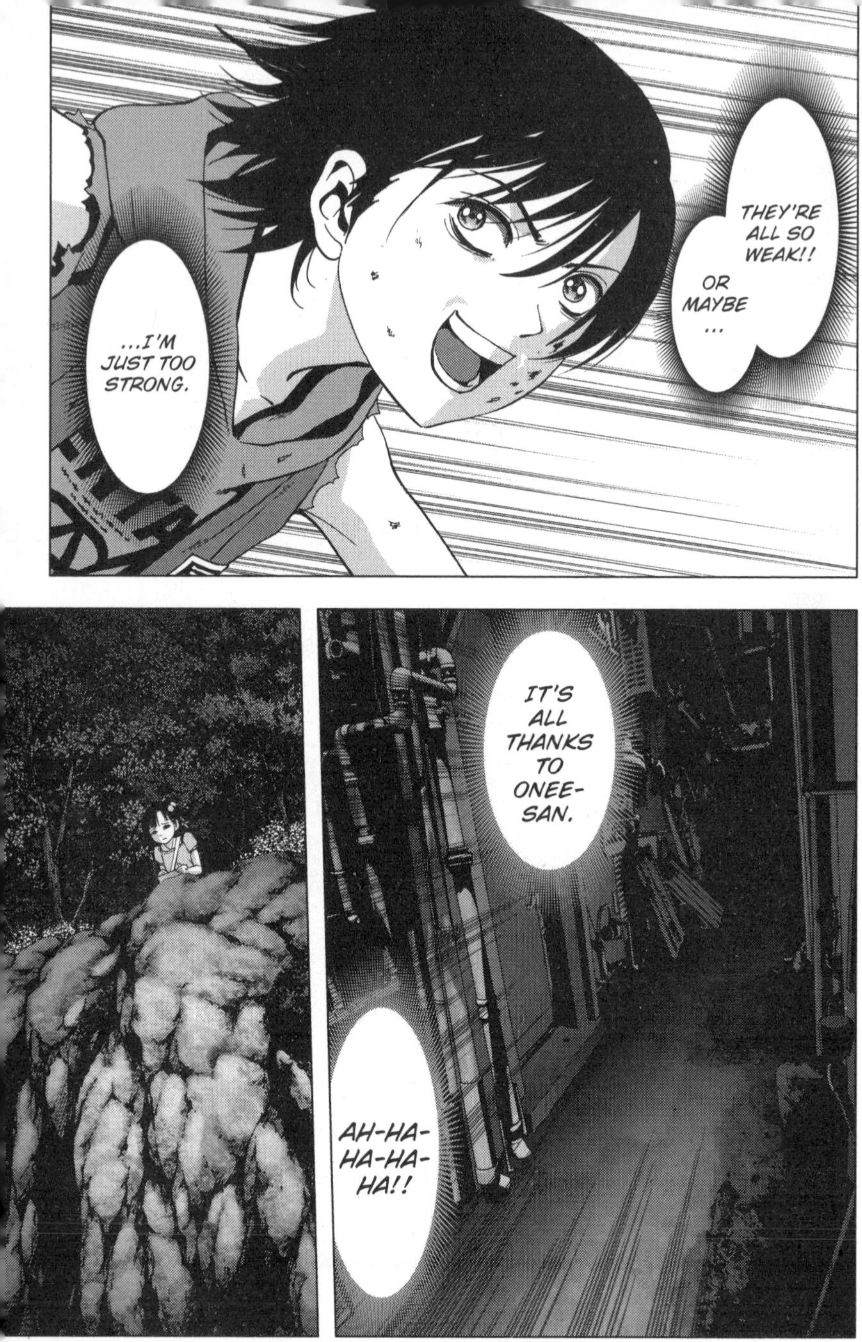
THEY'RE ALL SO WEAK!!
OR MAYBE ...
...I'M JUST TOO STRONG.
IT'S ALL THANKS TO ONEE-SAN.
AH-HA-HA-HA-HA!!

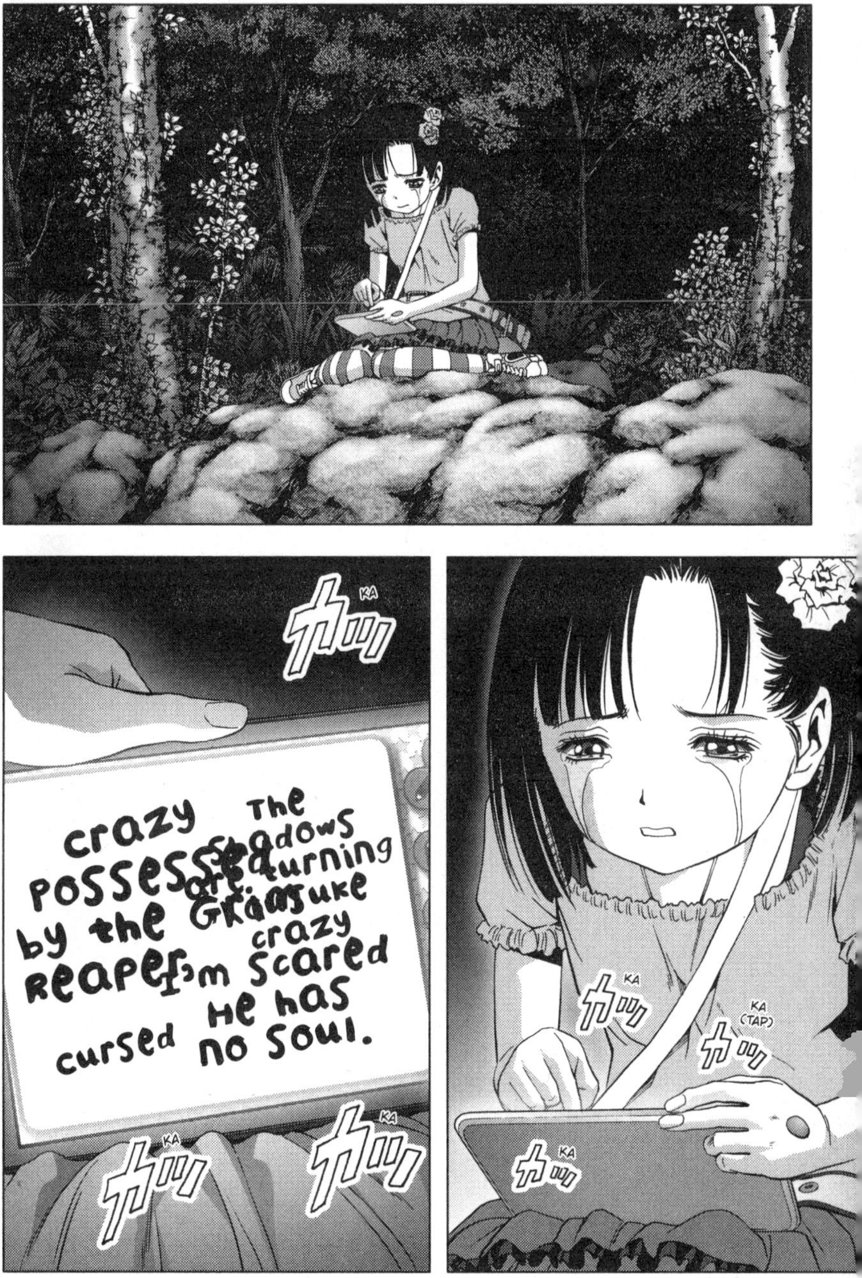
KA
KA (TAP)
KA
KA
crazy The
shadows
possessed are turning
by the
crazy
reaper I'm scared
He has
cursed no soul.
KA
KA

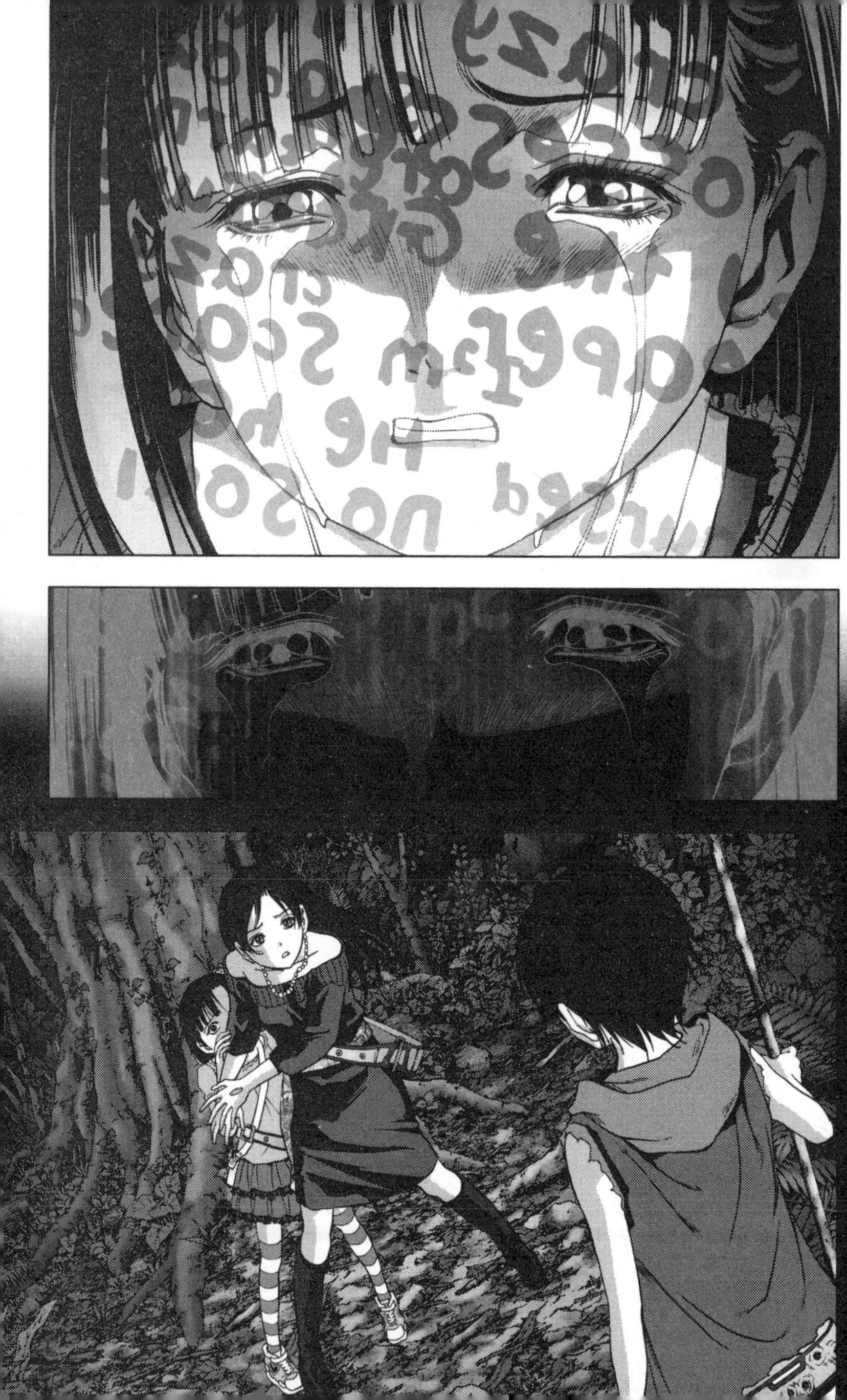

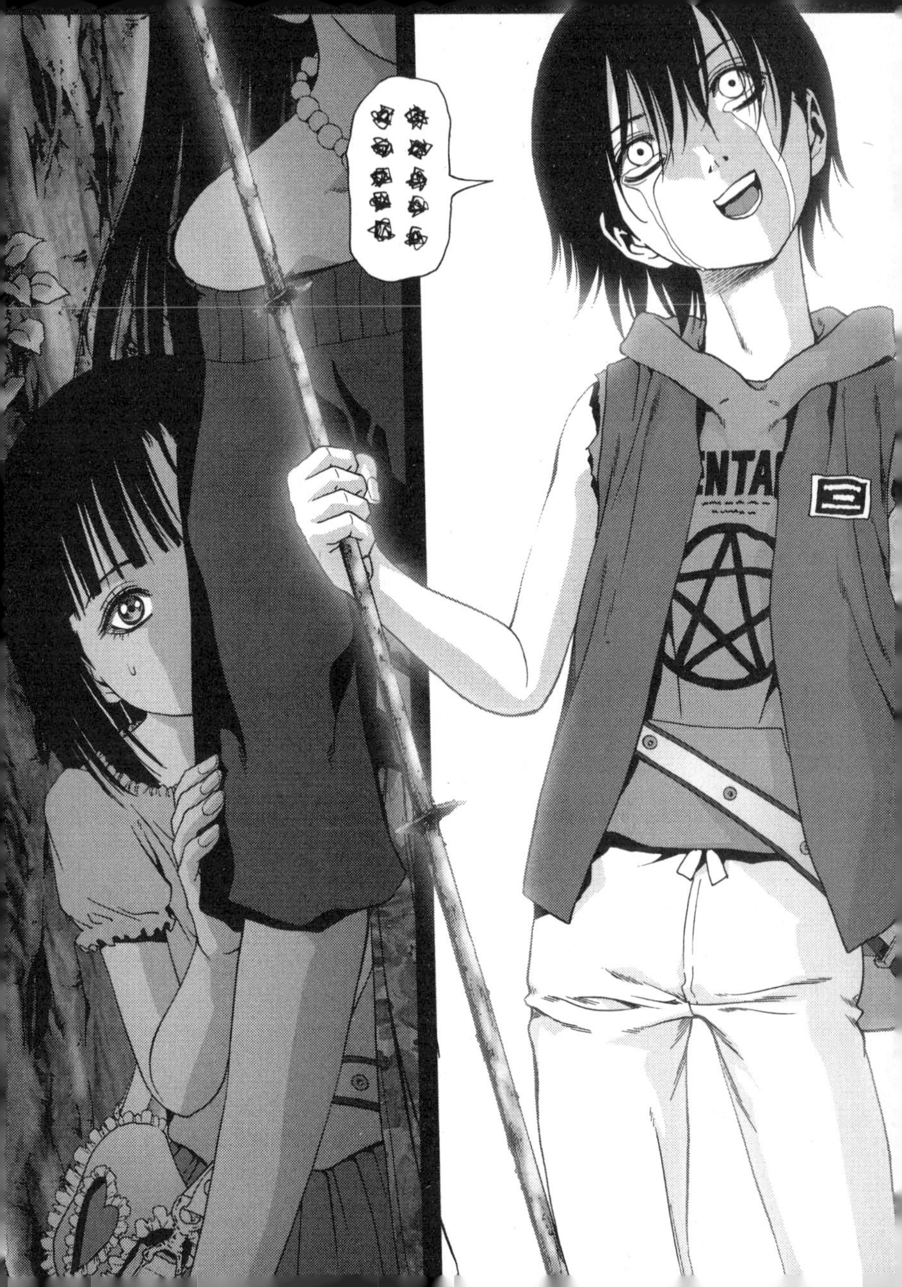

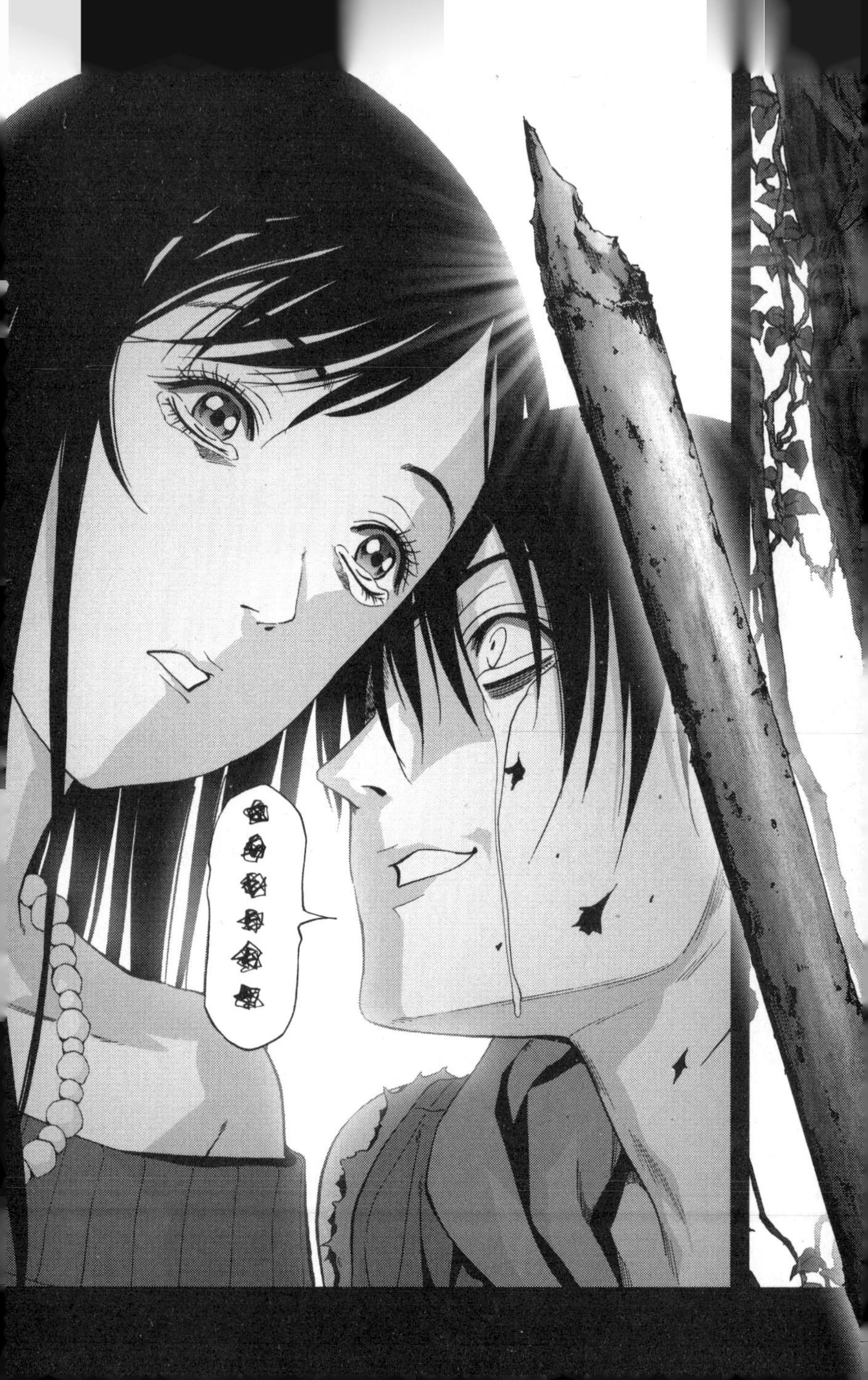

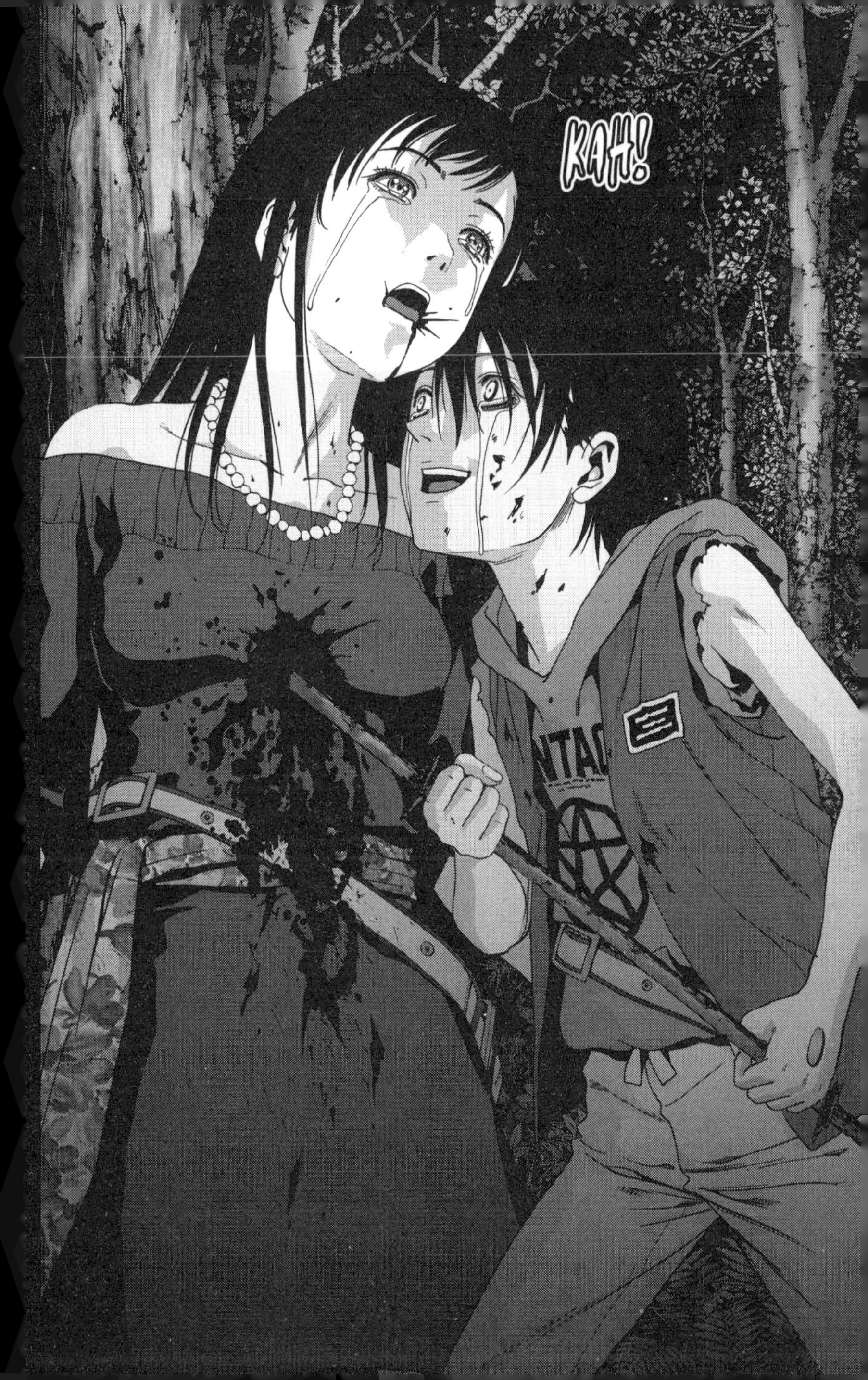
KAH!

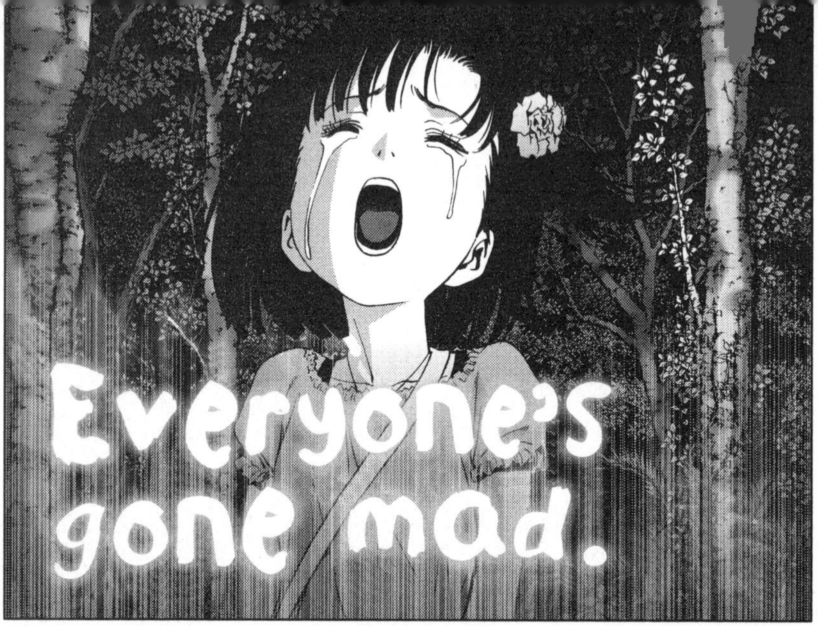
Everyone's gone mad.
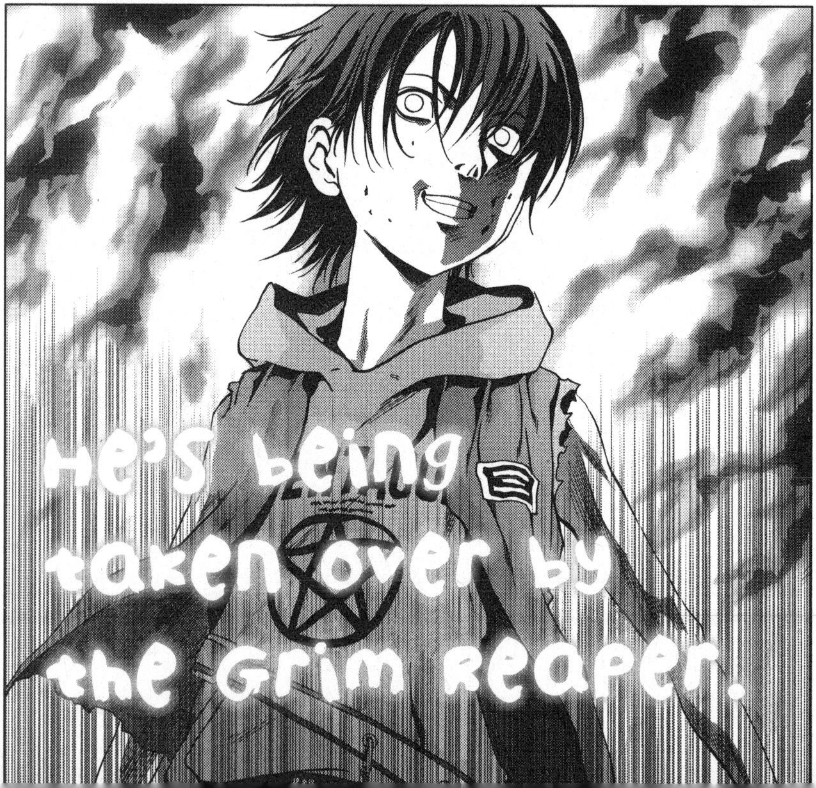
He's being taken over by the Grim Reaper.

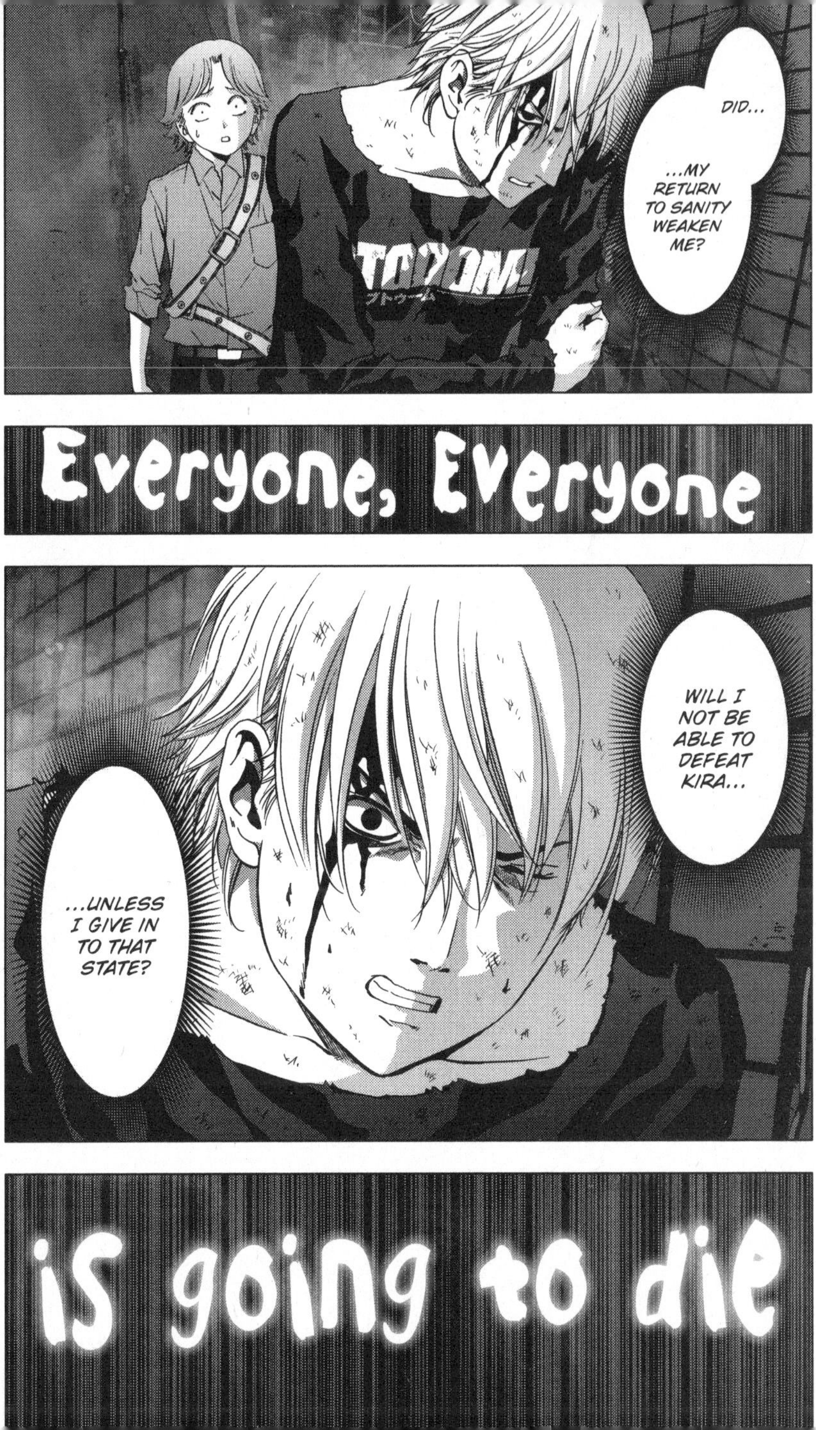
DID...
...MY RETURN TO SANITY WEAKEN ME?
Everyone, Everyone
WILL I NOT BE ABLE TO DEFEAT KIRA...
...UNLESS I GIVE IN TO THAT STATE?
is going to die

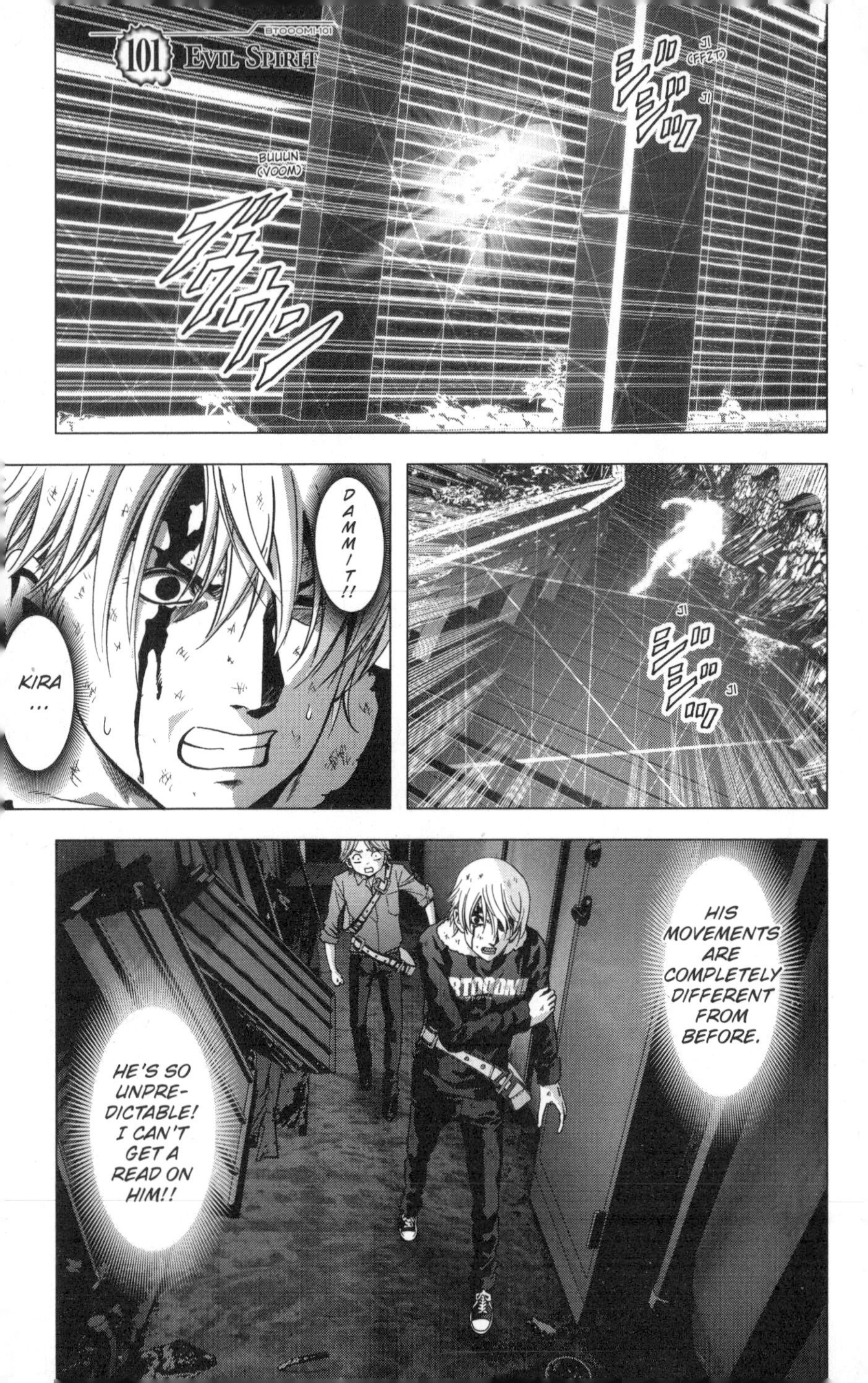
BTOOOM!101
101 EVIL SPIRIT
JI (FFZT) JI
BUUUN (VOOM)
JI JI
DAMMIT!!
KIRA ...
HIS MOVEMENTS ARE COMPLETELY DIFFERENT FROM BEFORE.
HE'S SO UNPRE-DICTABLE! I CAN'T GET A READ ON HIM!!

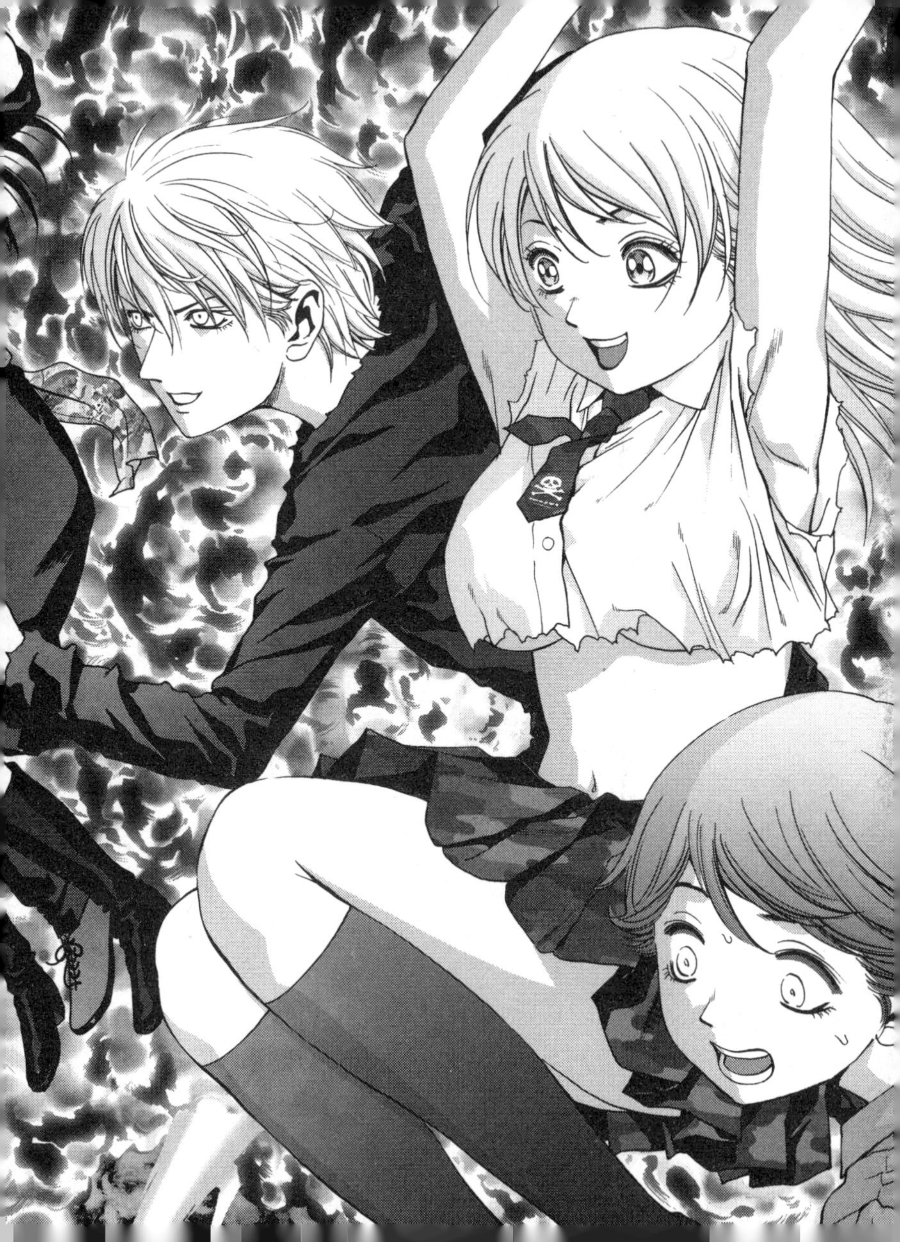

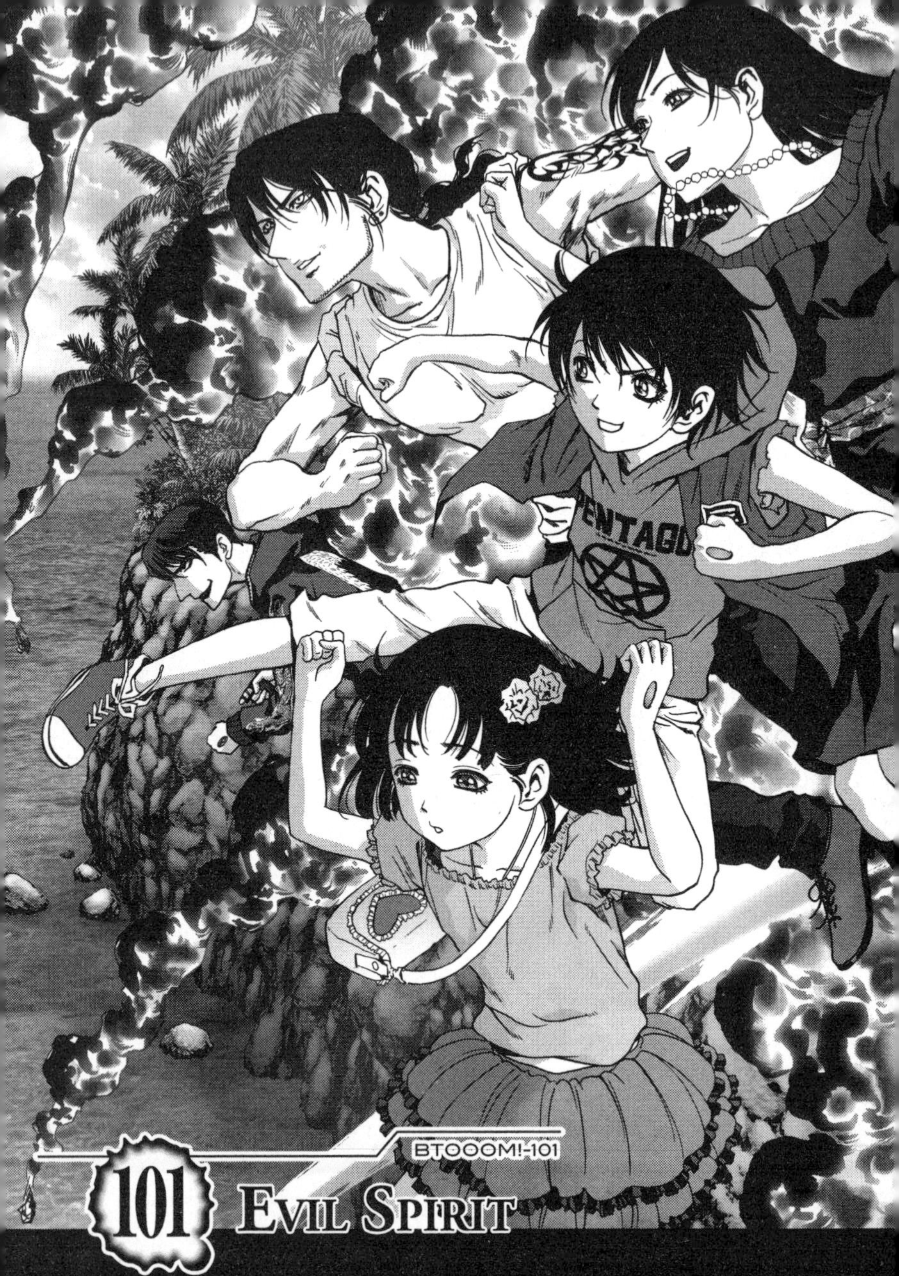
BTOOOM!-101
101
EVIL SPIRIT

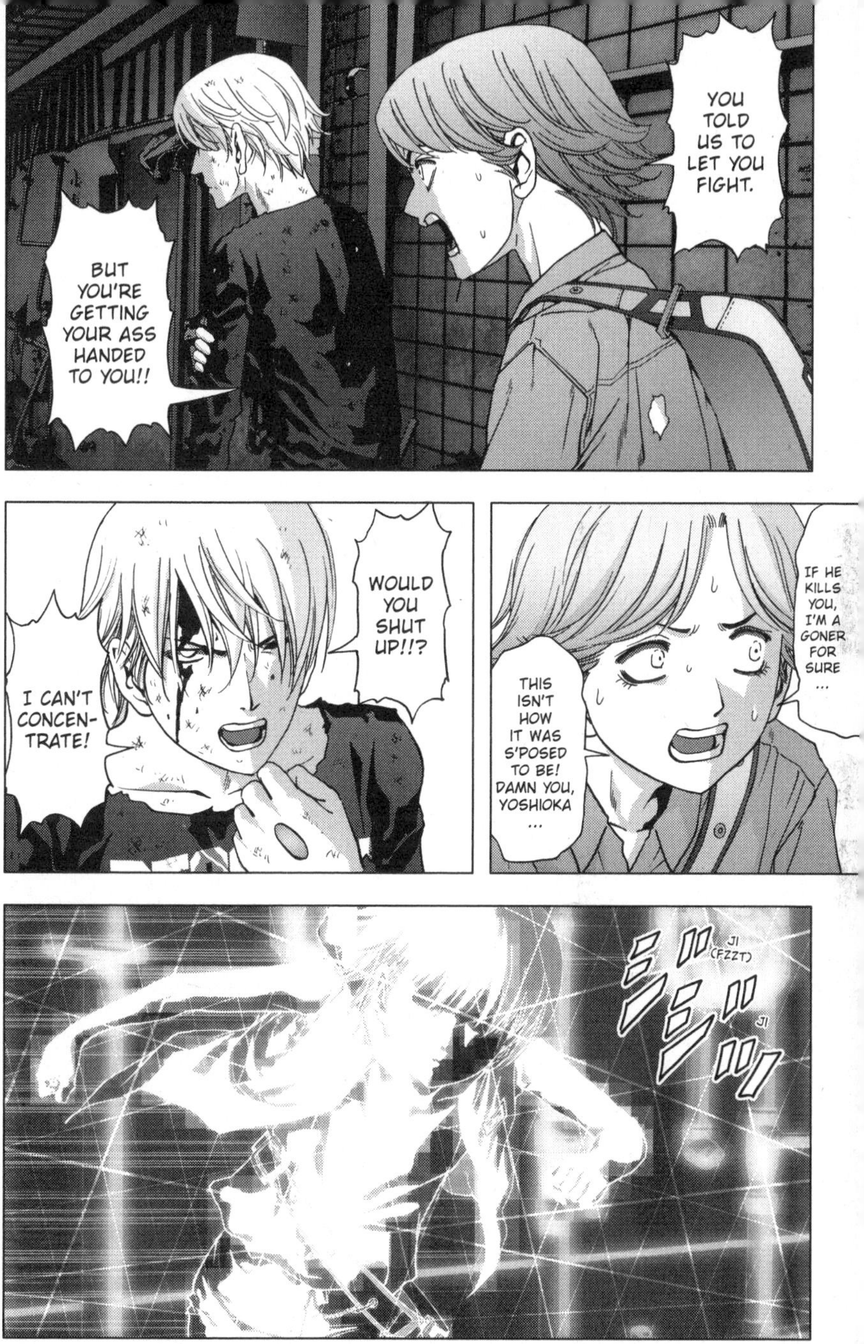
YOU TOLD US TO LET YOU FIGHT.
BUT YOU'RE GETTING YOUR ASS HANDED TO YOU!!
IF HE KILLS YOU, I'M A GONER FOR SURE ...
THIS ISN'T HOW IT WAS S'POSED TO BE! DAMN YOU, YOSHIOKA ...
WOULD YOU SHUT UP!!?
I CAN'T CONCENTRATE!
JI (FZZT)
JI

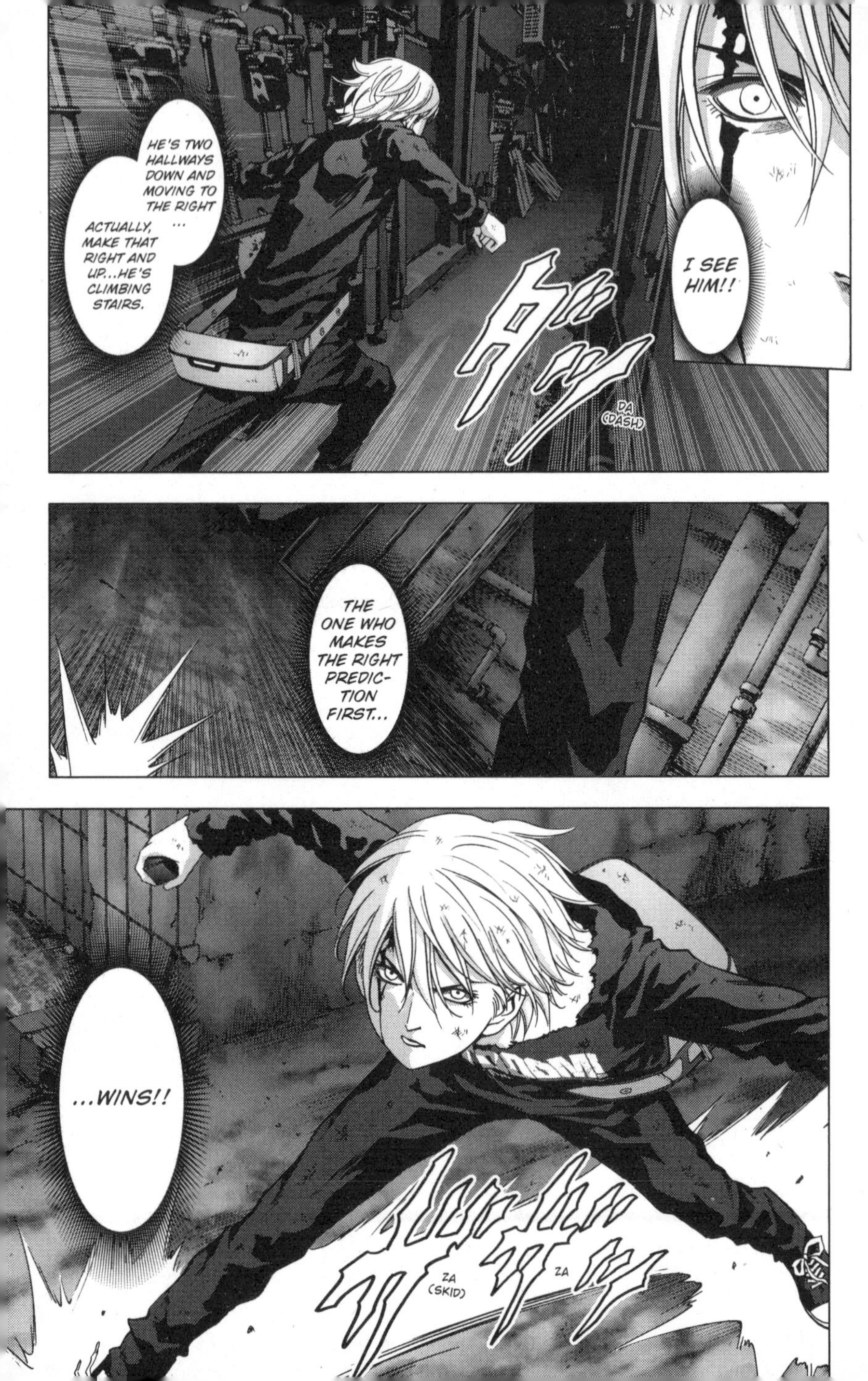
I SEE HIM!!
DA (DASH)
HE'S TWO HALLWAYS DOWN AND MOVING TO THE RIGHT ... ACTUALLY, MAKE THAT RIGHT AND UP...HE'S CLIMBING STAIRS.
THE ONE WHO MAKES THE RIGHT PREDICTION FIRST...
...WINS!!
ZA
ZA (SKID)

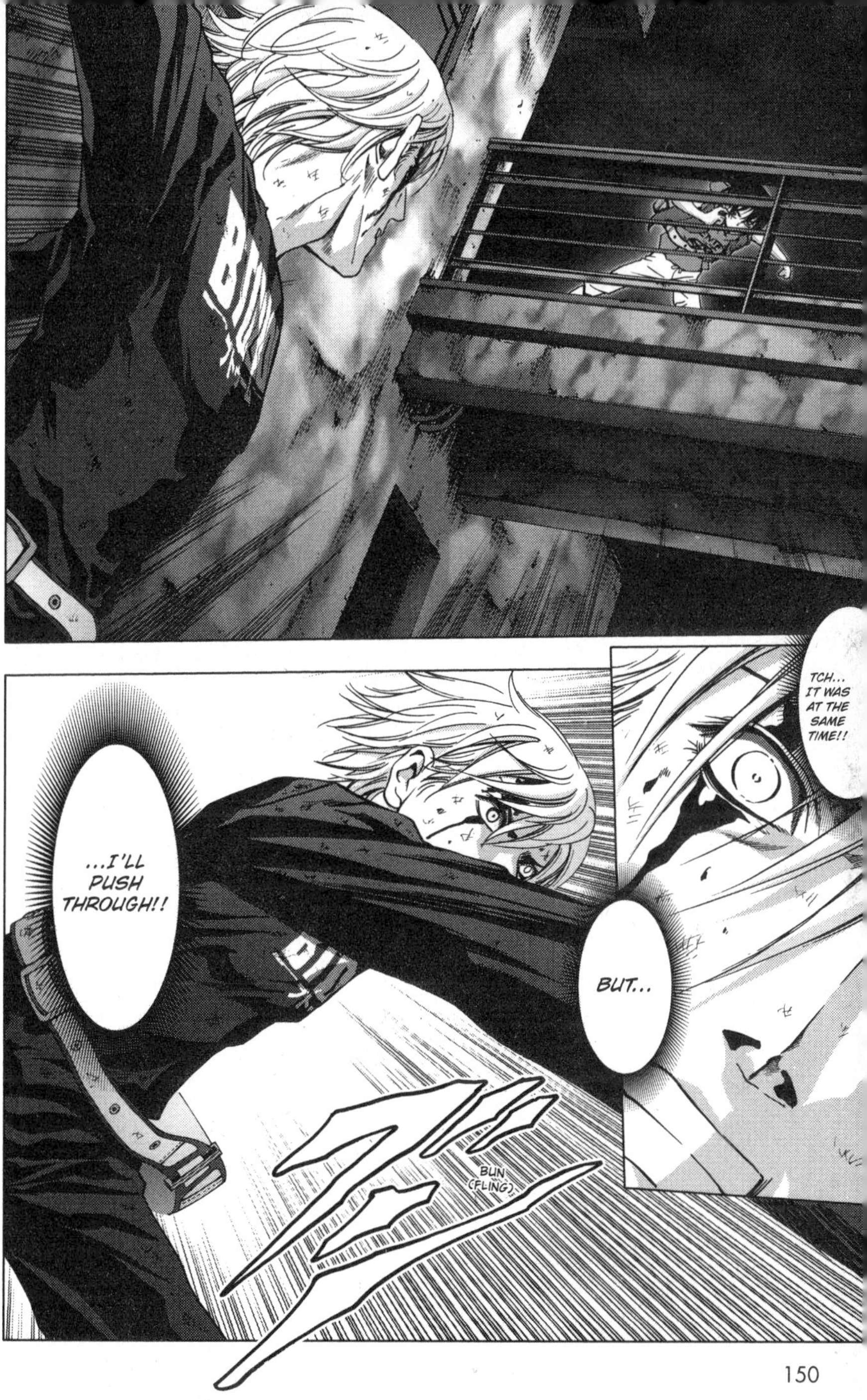
TCH... IT WAS AT THE SAME TIME!!
BUT...
...I'LL PUSH THROUGH!!
BUN (FLING)

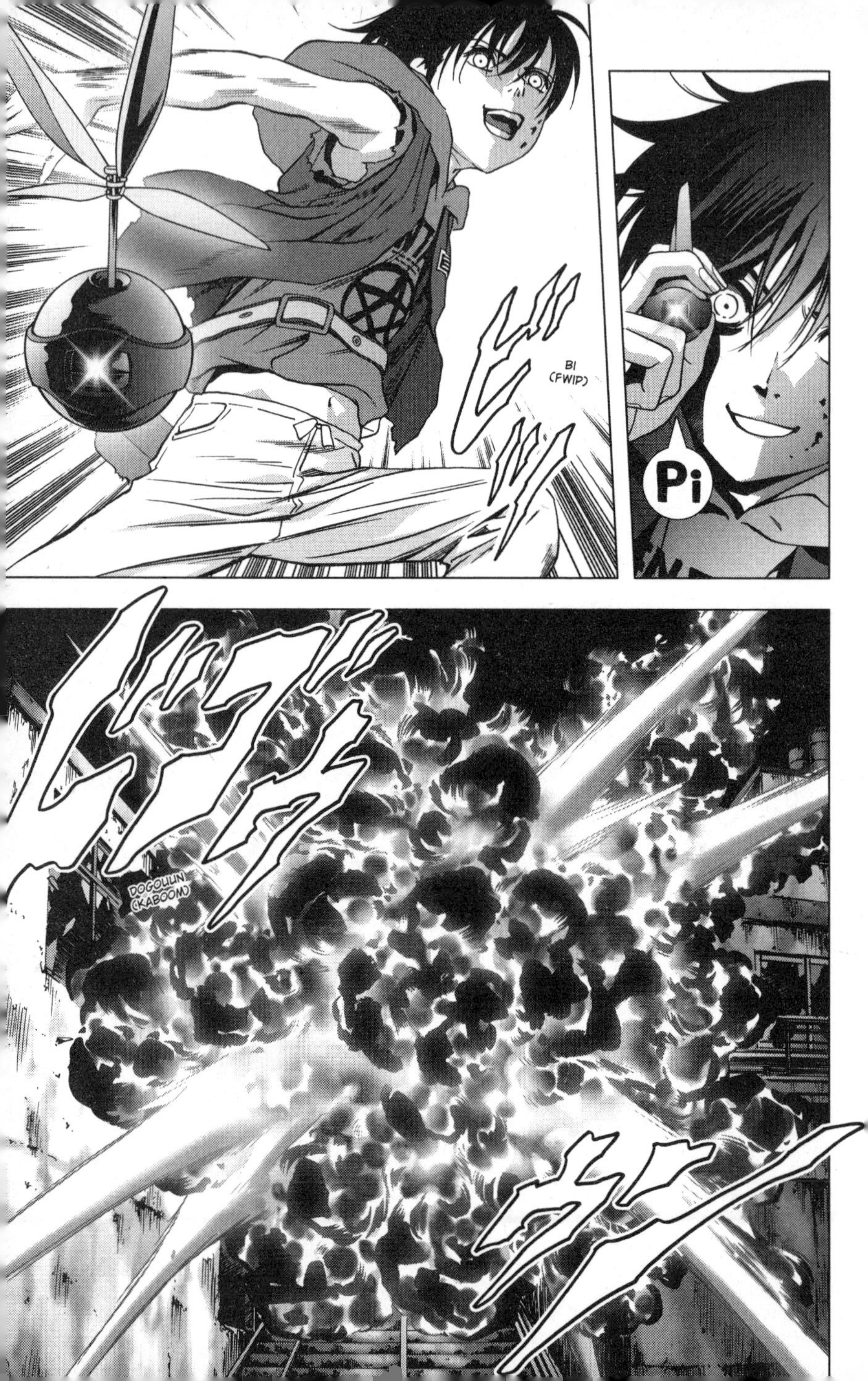
Pi
BI (FWIP)
DOGOUUN (KABOOM)

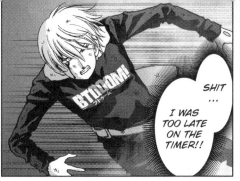

SHIT
...

I WAS TOO LATE ON THE TIMER!!

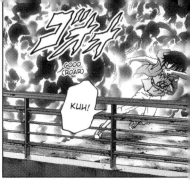

GOOO (ROAR)

KUH!

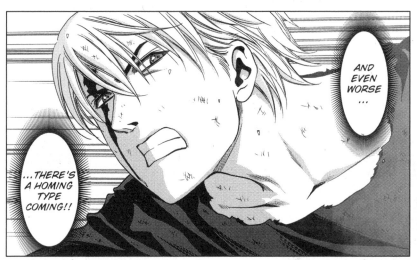

AND EVEN WORSE ...

...THERE'S A HOMING TYPE COMING!!

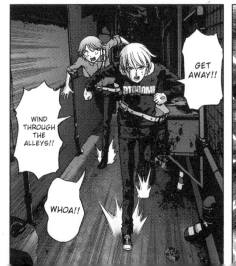

GET AWAY!!

WIND THROUGH THE ALLEYS!!

WHOA!!

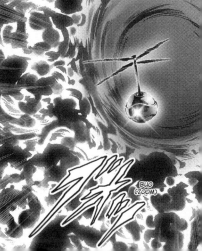

BUO (ZOOM)

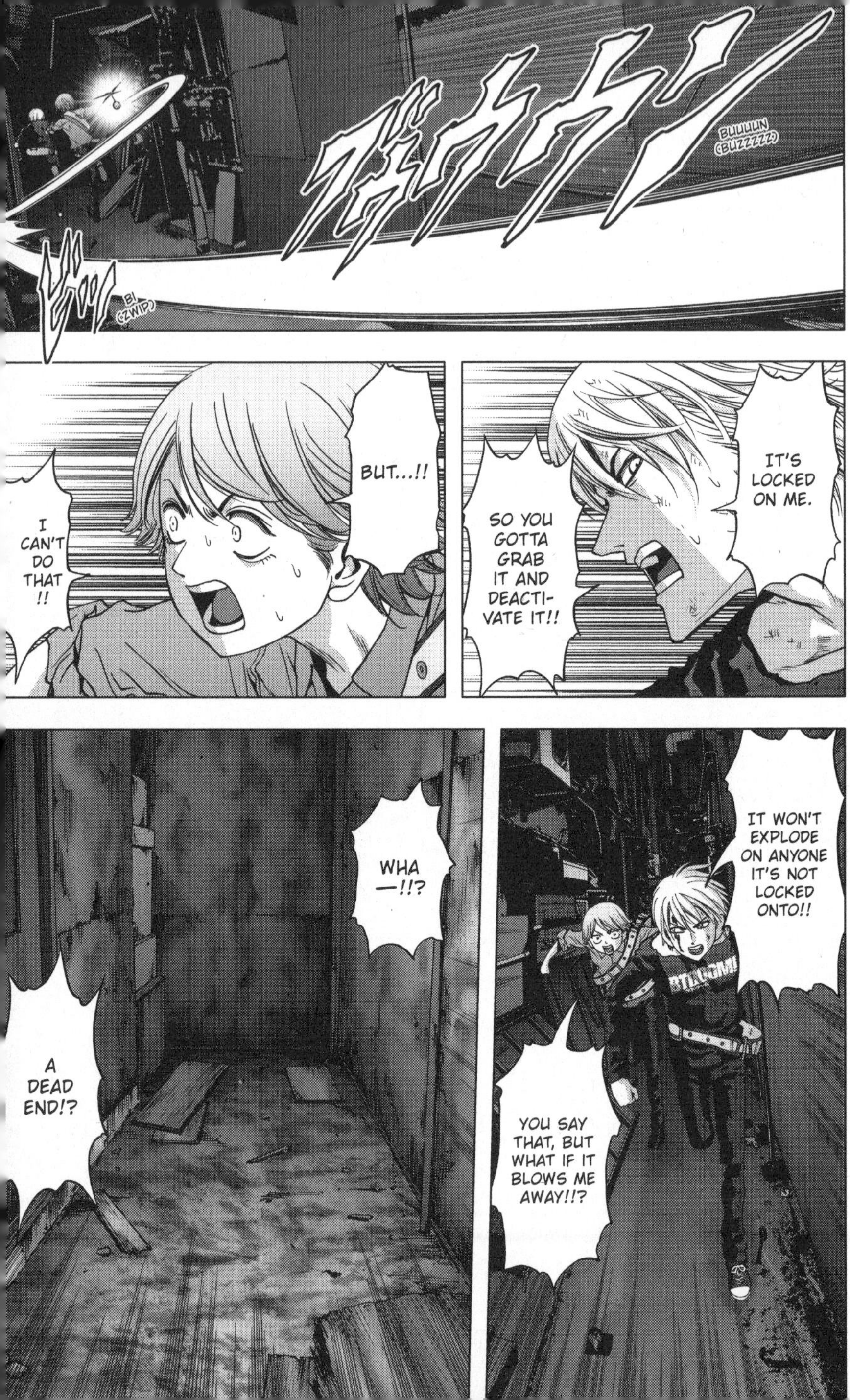
BUUUUN (BUZZZZZ)
BI (ZWIP)
IT'S LOCKED ON ME.
SO YOU GOTTA GRAB IT AND DEACTI- VATE IT!!
BUT...!!
I CAN'T DO THAT!!
IT WON'T EXPLODE ON ANYONE IT'S NOT LOCKED ONTO!!
YOU SAY THAT, BUT WHAT IF IT BLOWS ME AWAY!!?
WHA —!!?
A DEAD END!?

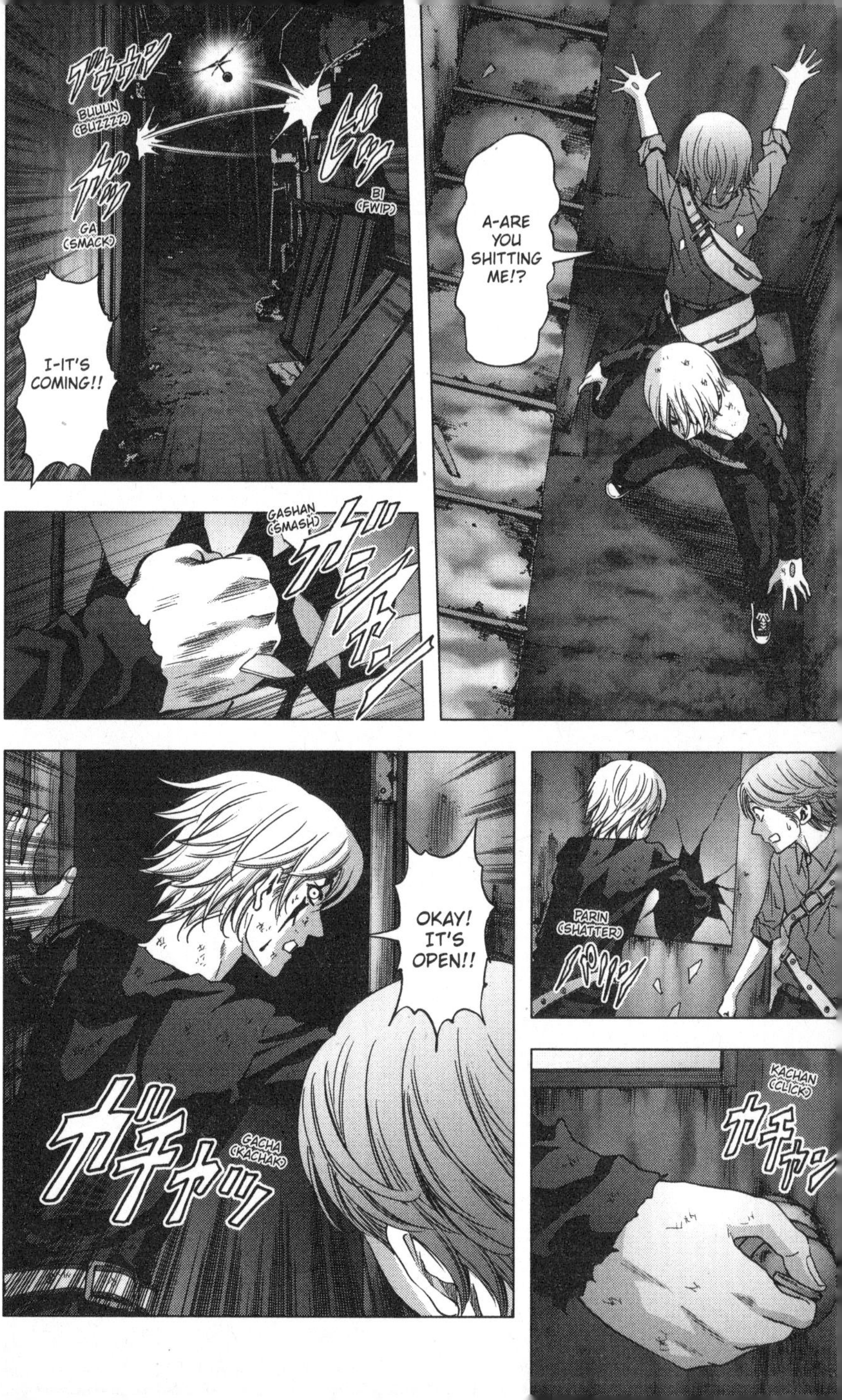
A-ARE YOU SHITTING ME!?
BUUUN (BUZZZZZ)
BI (FWIP)
GA (SMACK)
I-IT'S COMING!!
GASHAN (SMASH)
PARIN (SHATTER)
KACHAN (CLICK)
OKAY! IT'S OPEN!!
GACHA (KACHAK)

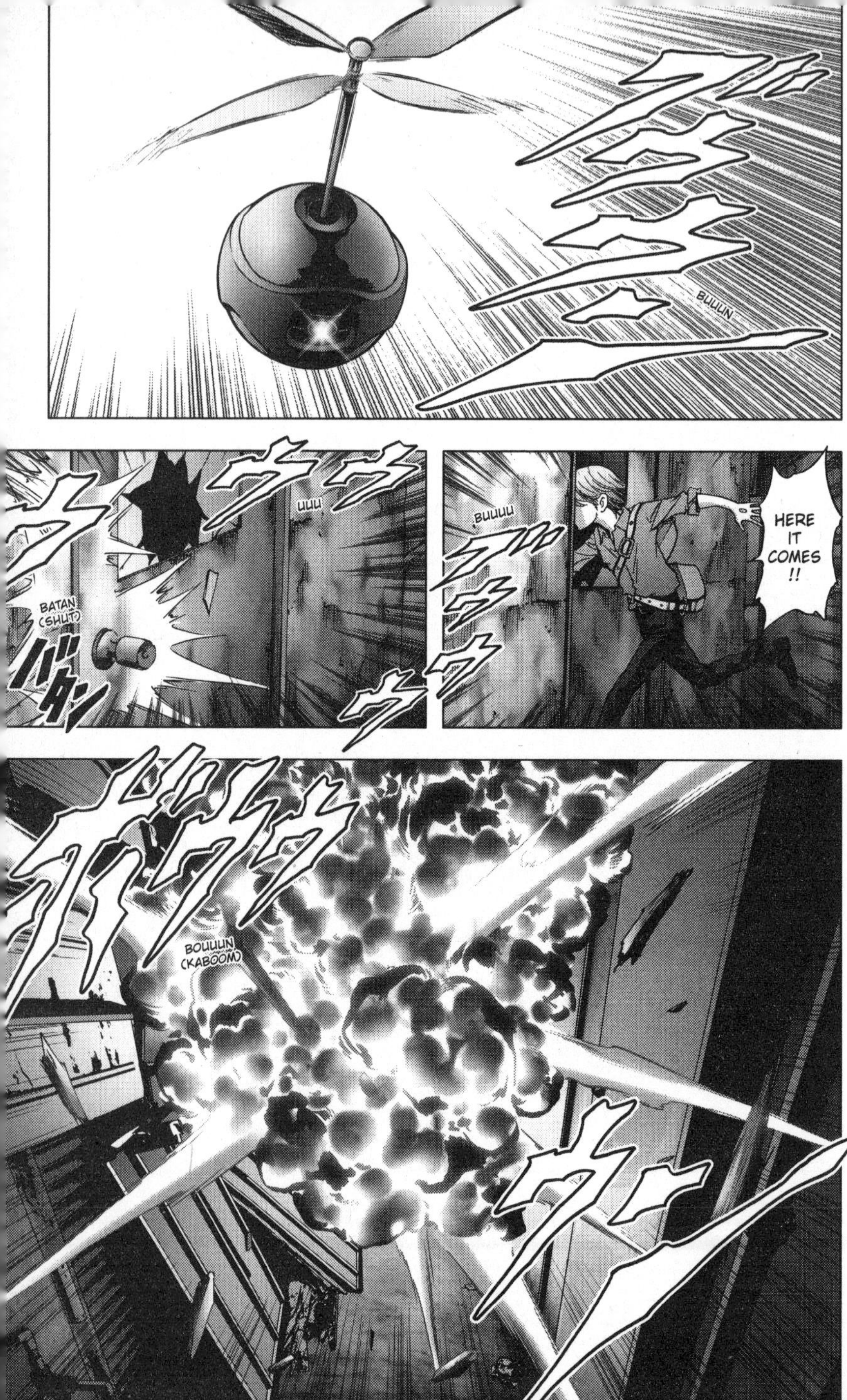
BUUUN
HERE IT COMES!!
BUUUU
UUU
BATAN (SHUT)
BOUUUN (KABOOM)

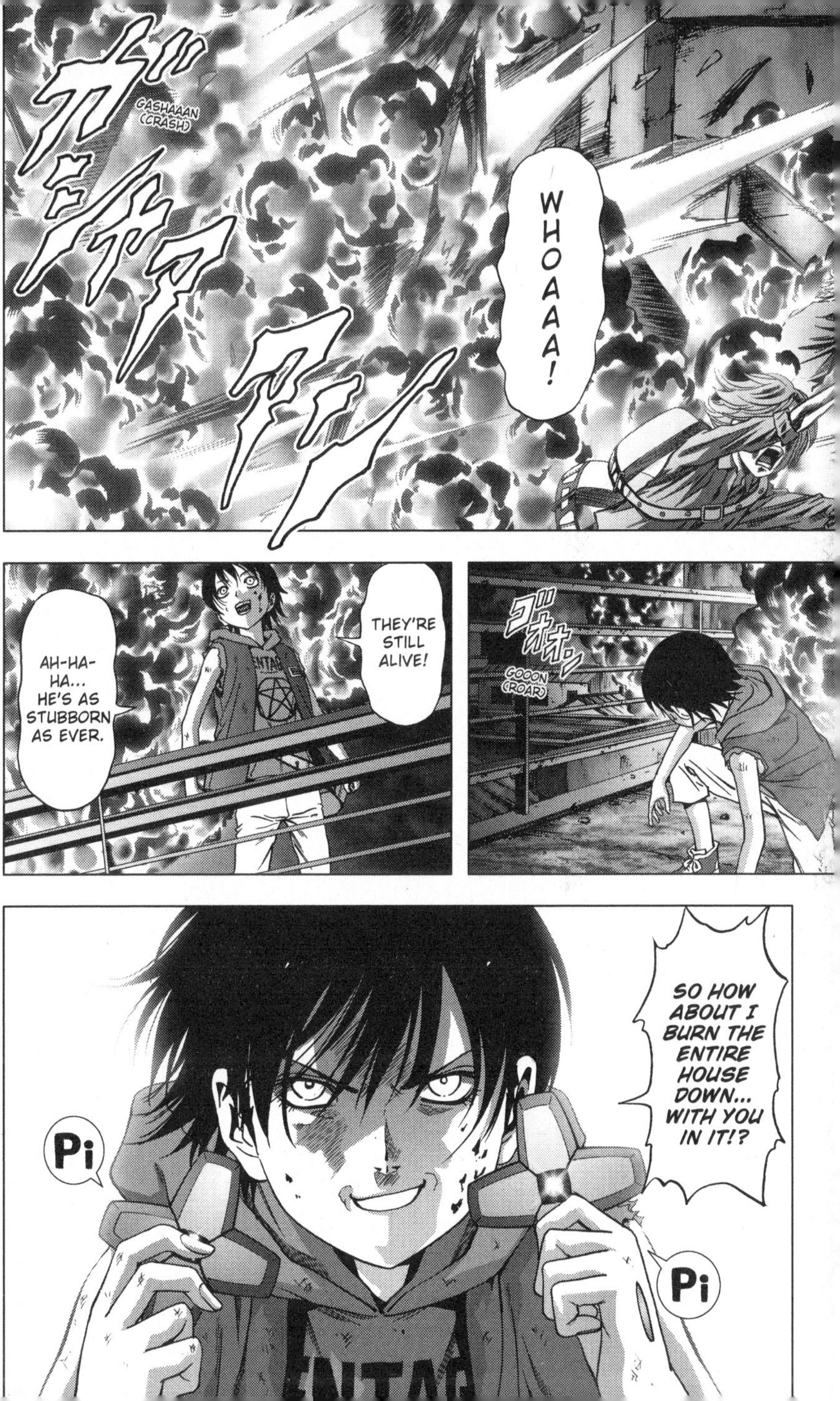
GASHAAAN (CRASH)
WHOAAA!
GOOON (ROAR)
THEY'RE STILL ALIVE!
AH-HA-HA... HE'S AS STUBBORN AS EVER.
SO HOW ABOUT I BURN THE ENTIRE HOUSE DOWN... WITH YOU IN IT!?
Pi
Pi

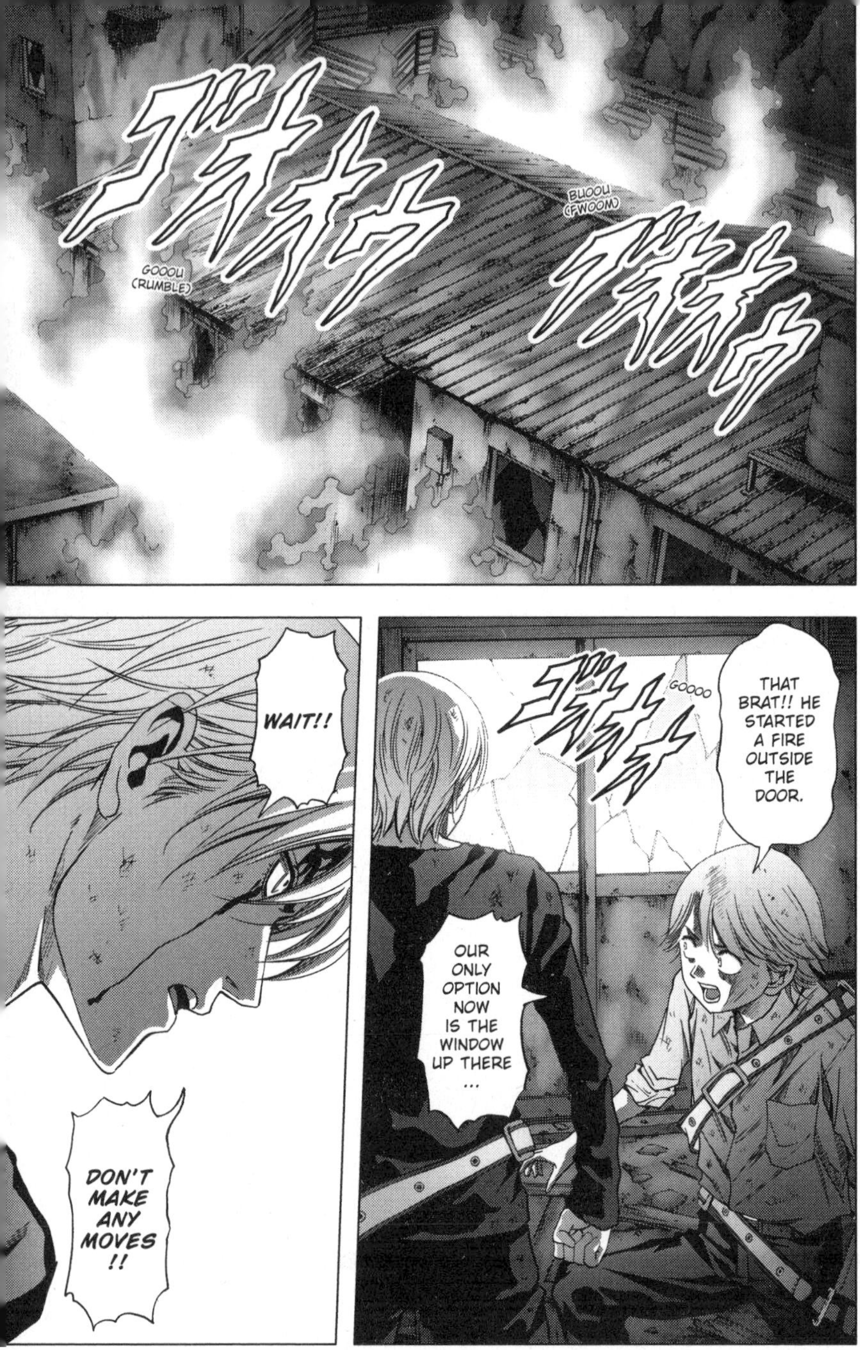
BUOOU (FWOOM)
GOOOU (RUMBLE)
THAT BRAT!! HE STARTED A FIRE OUTSIDE THE DOOR.
GOOOO
OUR ONLY OPTION NOW IS THE WINDOW UP THERE ...
WAIT!!
DON'T MAKE ANY MOVES !!

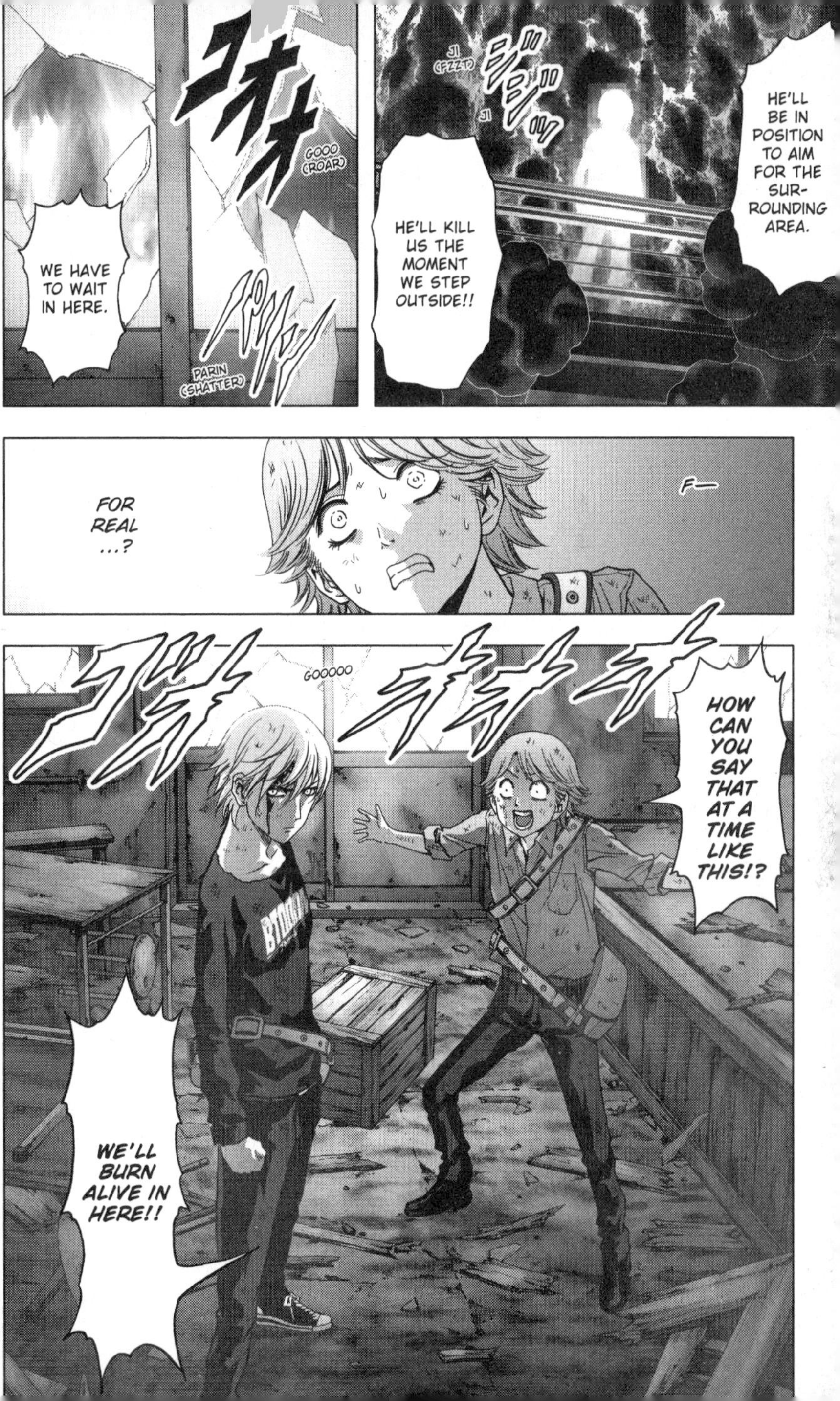
JI (FZZT)
JI
HE'LL BE IN POSITION TO AIM FOR THE SUR-ROUNDING AREA.
HE'LL KILL US THE MOMENT WE STEP OUTSIDE!!
GOOO (ROAR)
WE HAVE TO WAIT IN HERE.
PARIN (SHATTER)
F—
FOR REAL ...?
GOOOOO
HOW CAN YOU SAY THAT AT A TIME LIKE THIS!?
WE'LL BURN ALIVE IN HERE!!

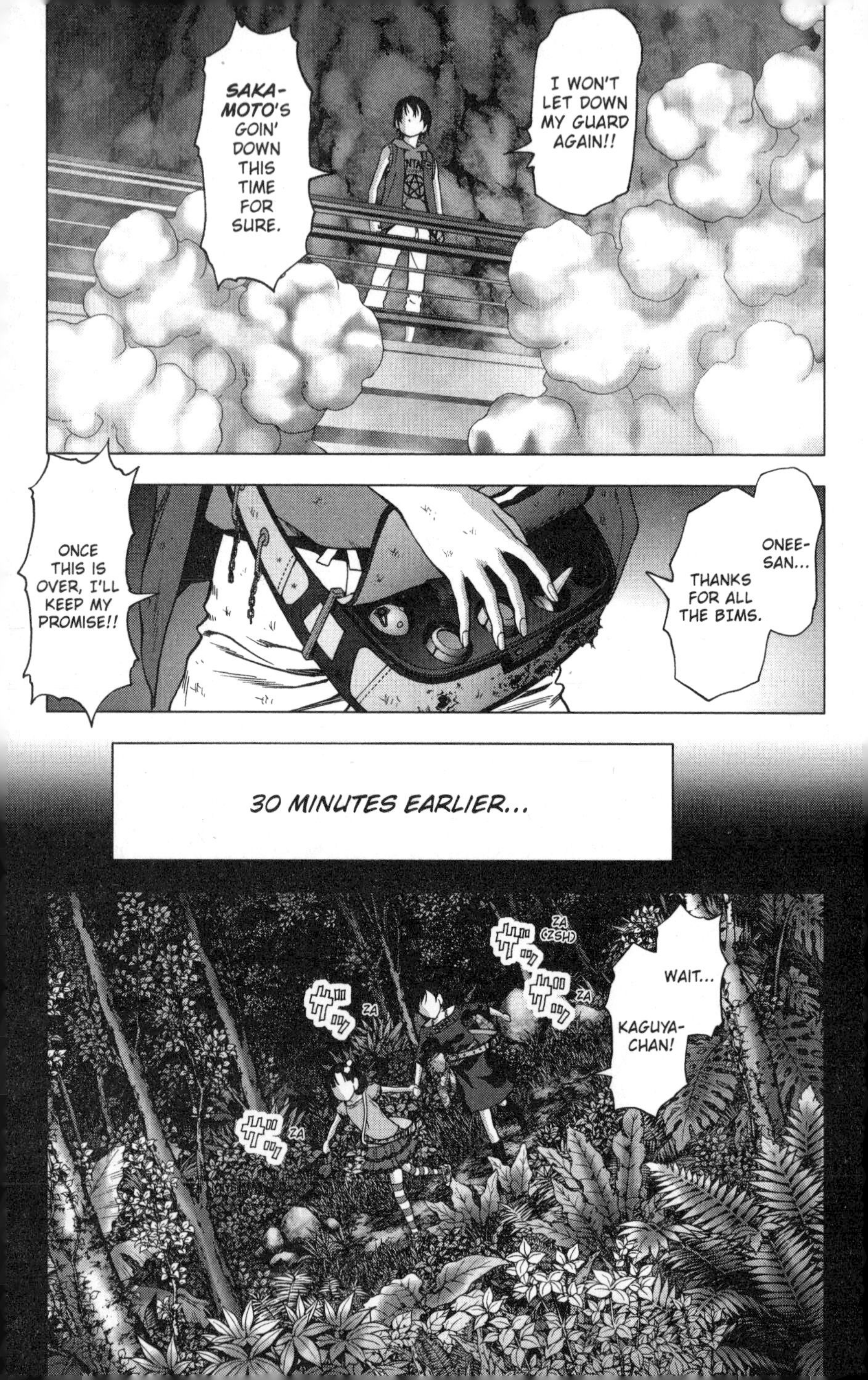
I WON'T LET DOWN MY GUARD AGAIN!!
SAKAMOTO'S GOIN' DOWN THIS TIME FOR SURE.
ONEE-SAN... THANKS FOR ALL THE BIMS.
ONCE THIS IS OVER, I'LL KEEP MY PROMISE!!
30 MINUTES EARLIER...
WAIT... KAGUYA-CHAN!
ZA (ZSH)
ZA
ZA
ZA

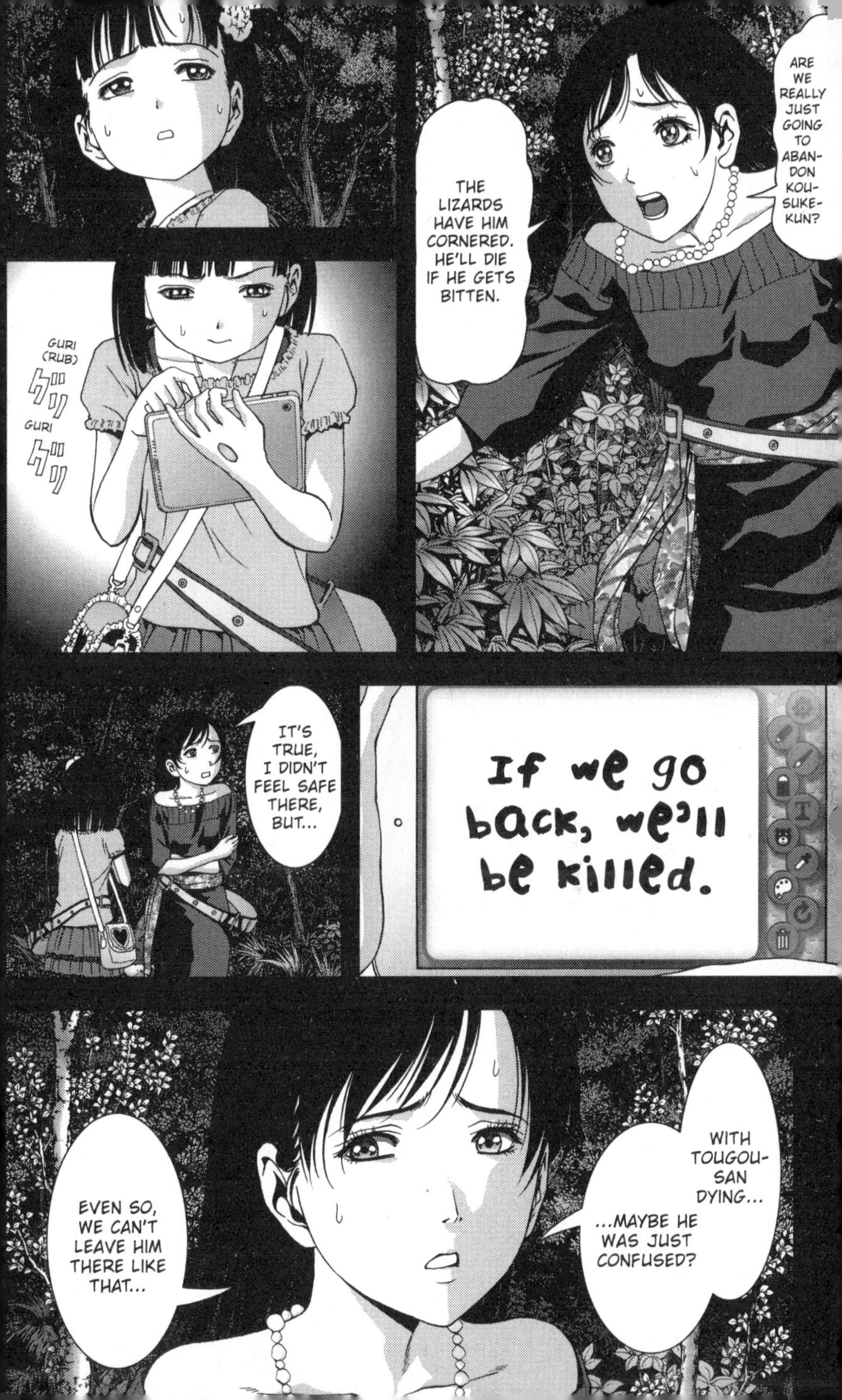
ARE WE REALLY JUST GOING TO ABANDON KOUSUKE-KUN?
THE LIZARDS HAVE HIM CORNERED. HE'LL DIE IF HE GETS BITTEN.
GURI (RUB)
GURI
If we go back, we'll be killed.
IT'S TRUE, I DIDN'T FEEL SAFE THERE, BUT...
WITH TOUGOU-SAN DYING...
...MAYBE HE WAS JUST CONFUSED?
EVEN SO, WE CAN'T LEAVE HIM THERE LIKE THAT...

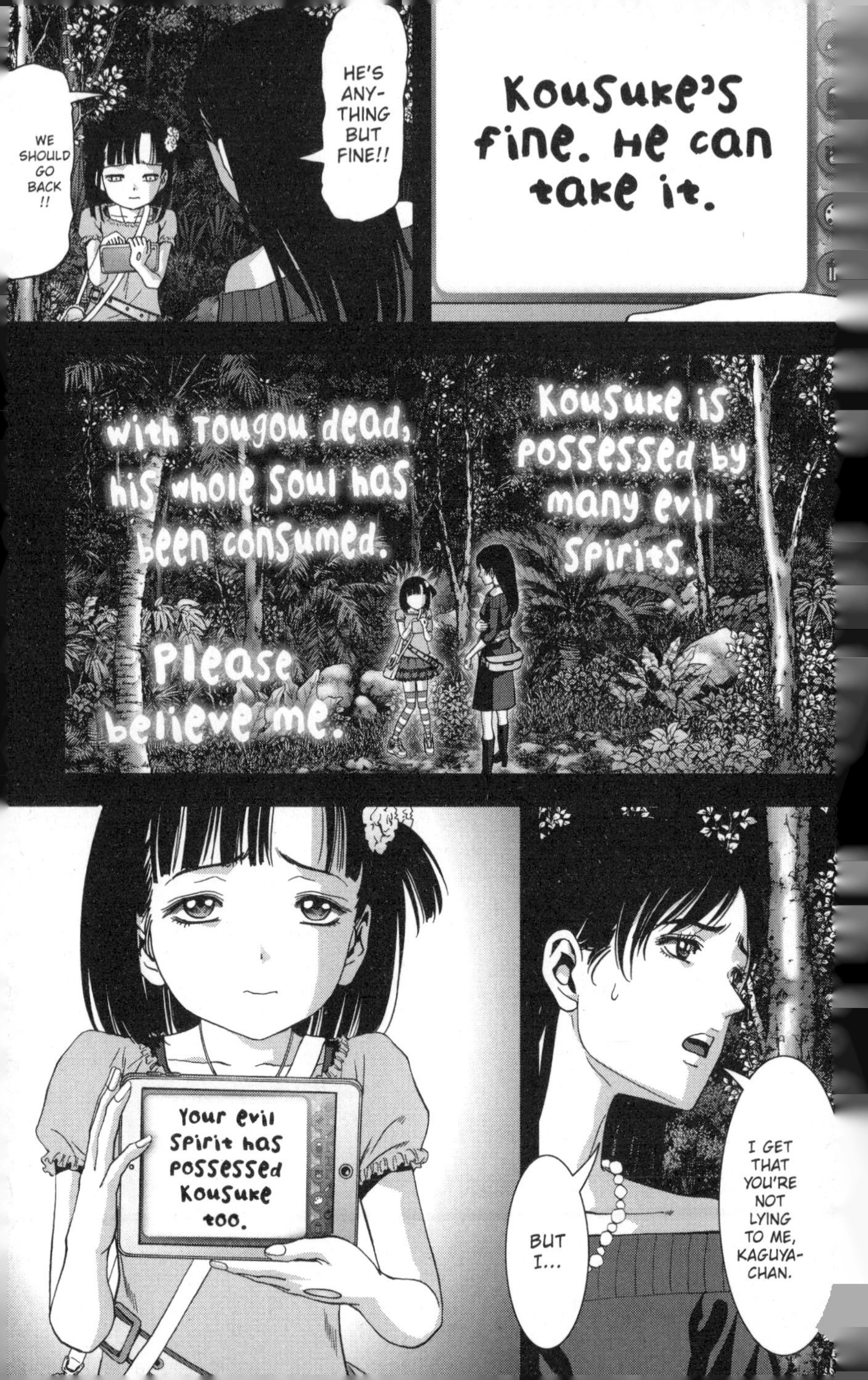
Kousuke's fine. He can take it.
HE'S ANYTHING BUT FINE!!
WE SHOULD GO BACK!!
Kousuke is possessed by many evil spirits.
With Tougou dead, his whole soul has been consumed.
Please believe me.
I GET THAT YOU'RE NOT LYING TO ME, KAGUYA-CHAN.
BUT I...
Your evil spirit has possessed Kousuke too.

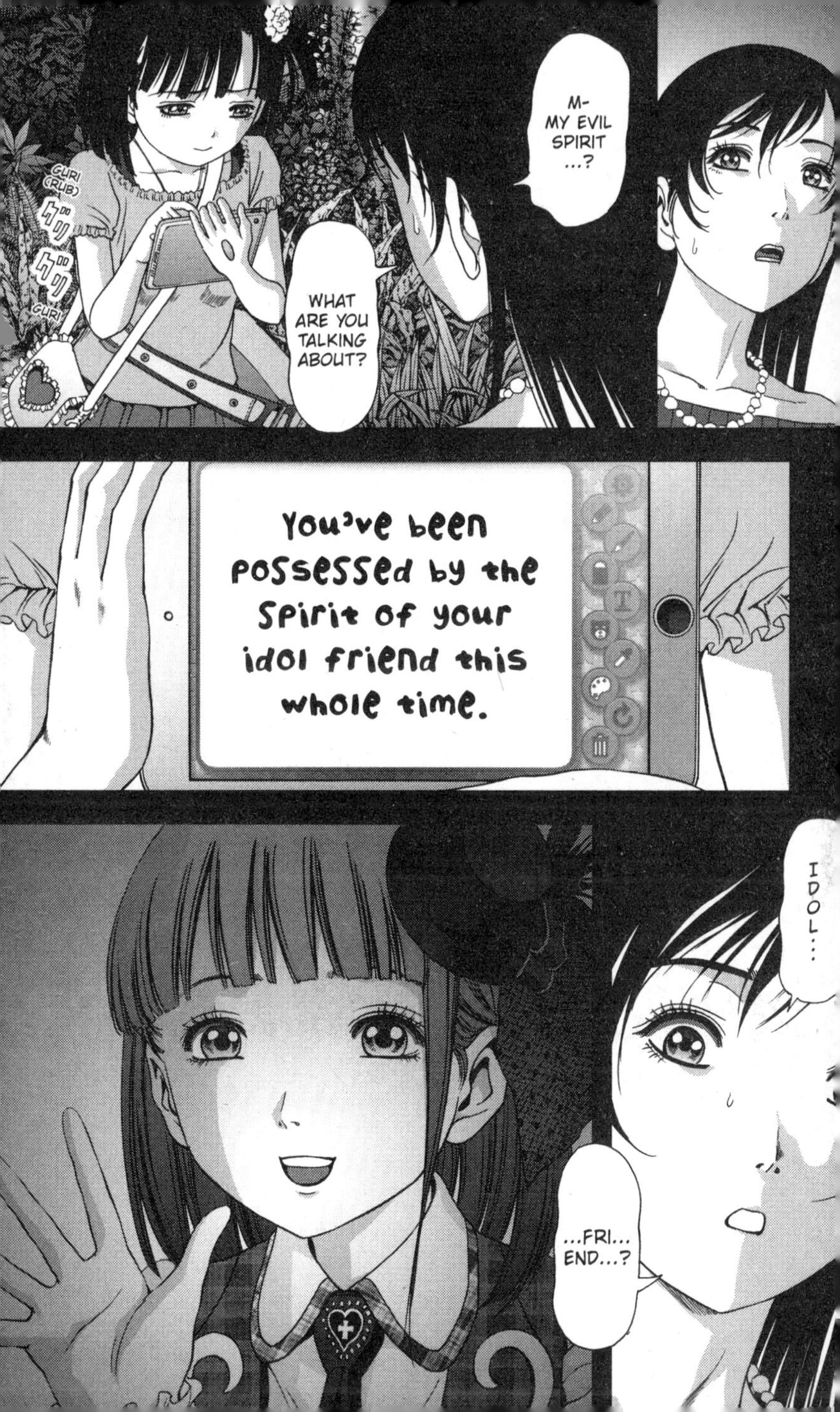
M- MY EVIL SPIRIT ...?
WHAT ARE YOU TALKING ABOUT?
GURI (RUB)
グリ
グリ
GURI
You've been possessed by the spirit of your idol friend this whole time.
IDOL...
...FRI... END...?

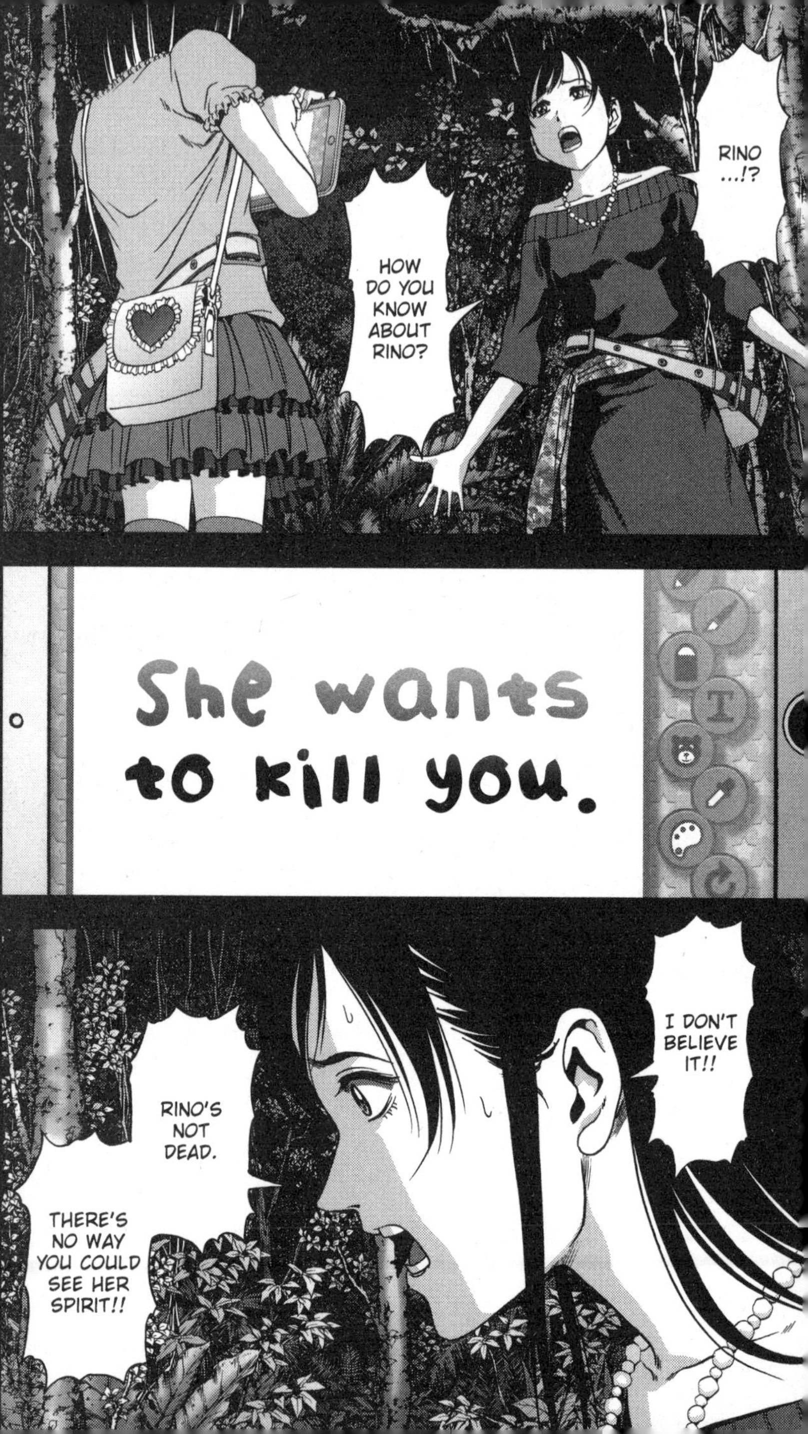
RINO ...!?
HOW DO YOU KNOW ABOUT RINO?
She wants to kill you.
I DON'T BELIEVE IT!!
RINO'S NOT DEAD.
THERE'S NO WAY YOU COULD SEE HER SPIRIT!!

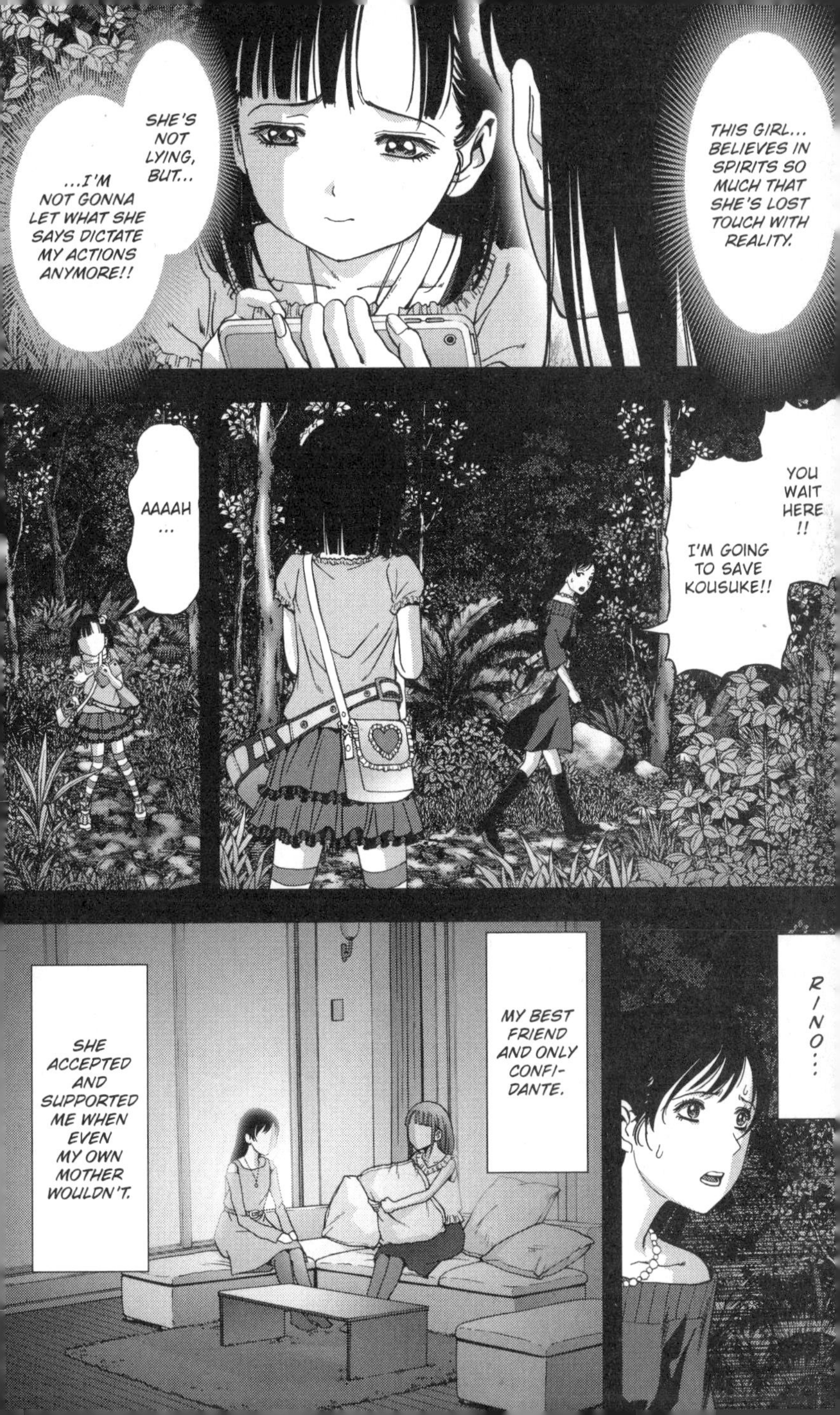
THIS GIRL... BELIEVES IN SPIRITS SO MUCH THAT SHE'S LOST TOUCH WITH REALITY.
SHE'S NOT LYING, BUT...
...I'M NOT GONNA LET WHAT SHE SAYS DICTATE MY ACTIONS ANYMORE!!
YOU WAIT HERE!!
I'M GOING TO SAVE KOUSUKE!!
AAAAH...
RINO...
MY BEST FRIEND AND ONLY CONFIDANTE.
SHE ACCEPTED AND SUPPORTED ME WHEN EVEN MY OWN MOTHER WOULDN'T.

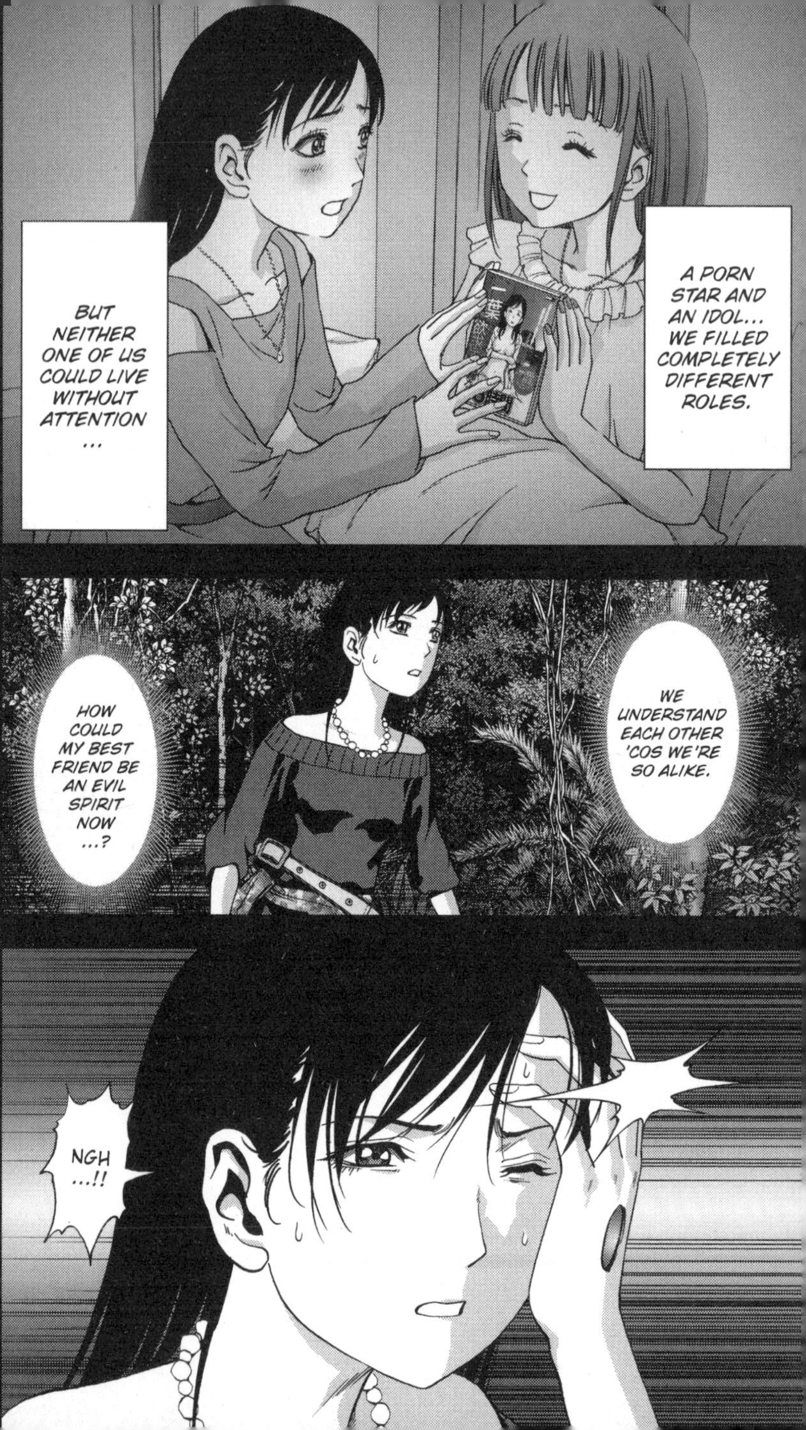
A PORN STAR AND AN IDOL... WE FILLED COMPLETELY DIFFERENT ROLES.
BUT NEITHER ONE OF US COULD LIVE WITHOUT ATTENTION...
WE UNDERSTAND EACH OTHER 'COS WE'RE SO ALIKE.
HOW COULD MY BEST FRIEND BE AN EVIL SPIRIT NOW...?
NGH...!!

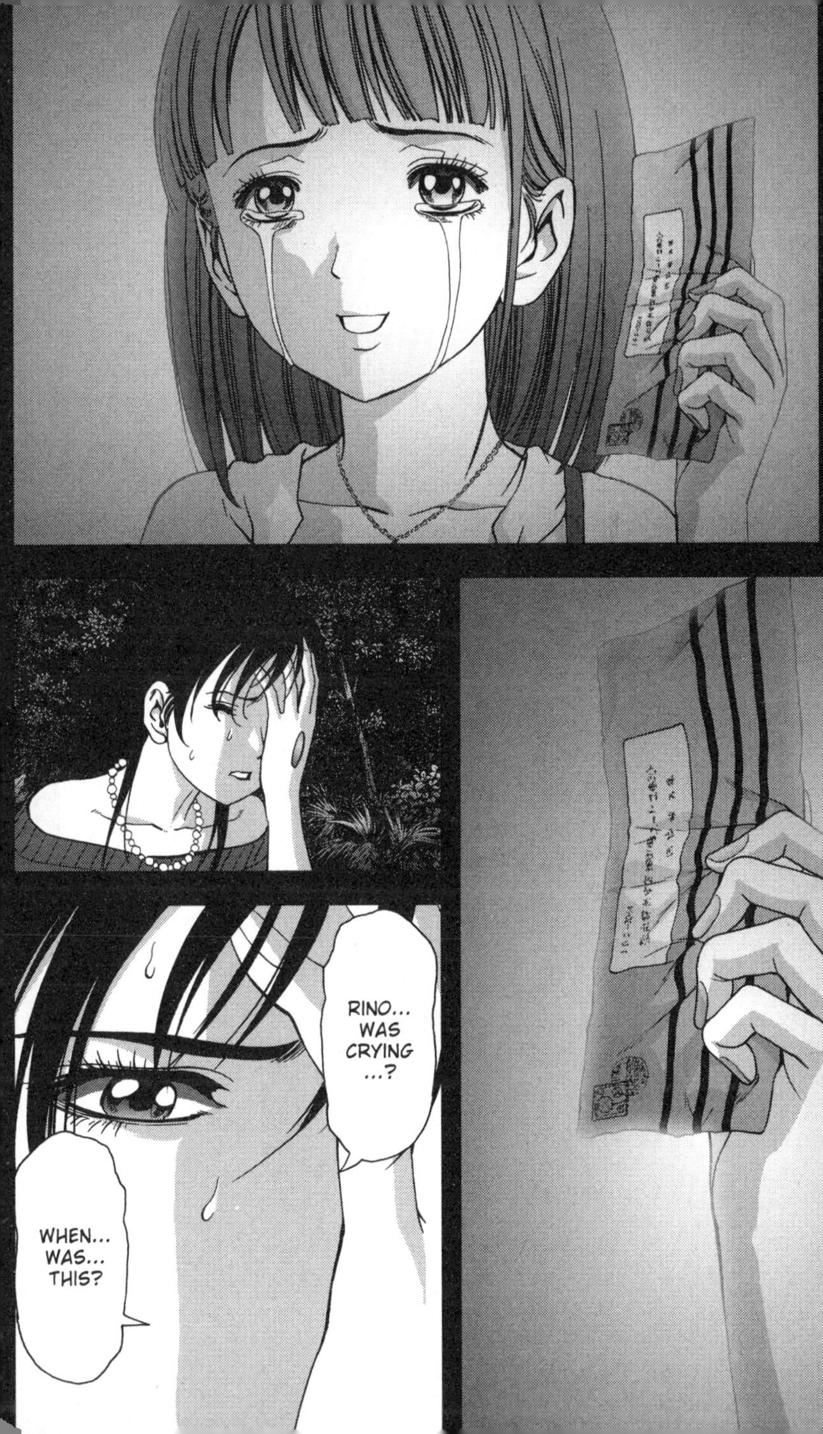
RINO... WAS CRYING ...?
WHEN... WAS... THIS?

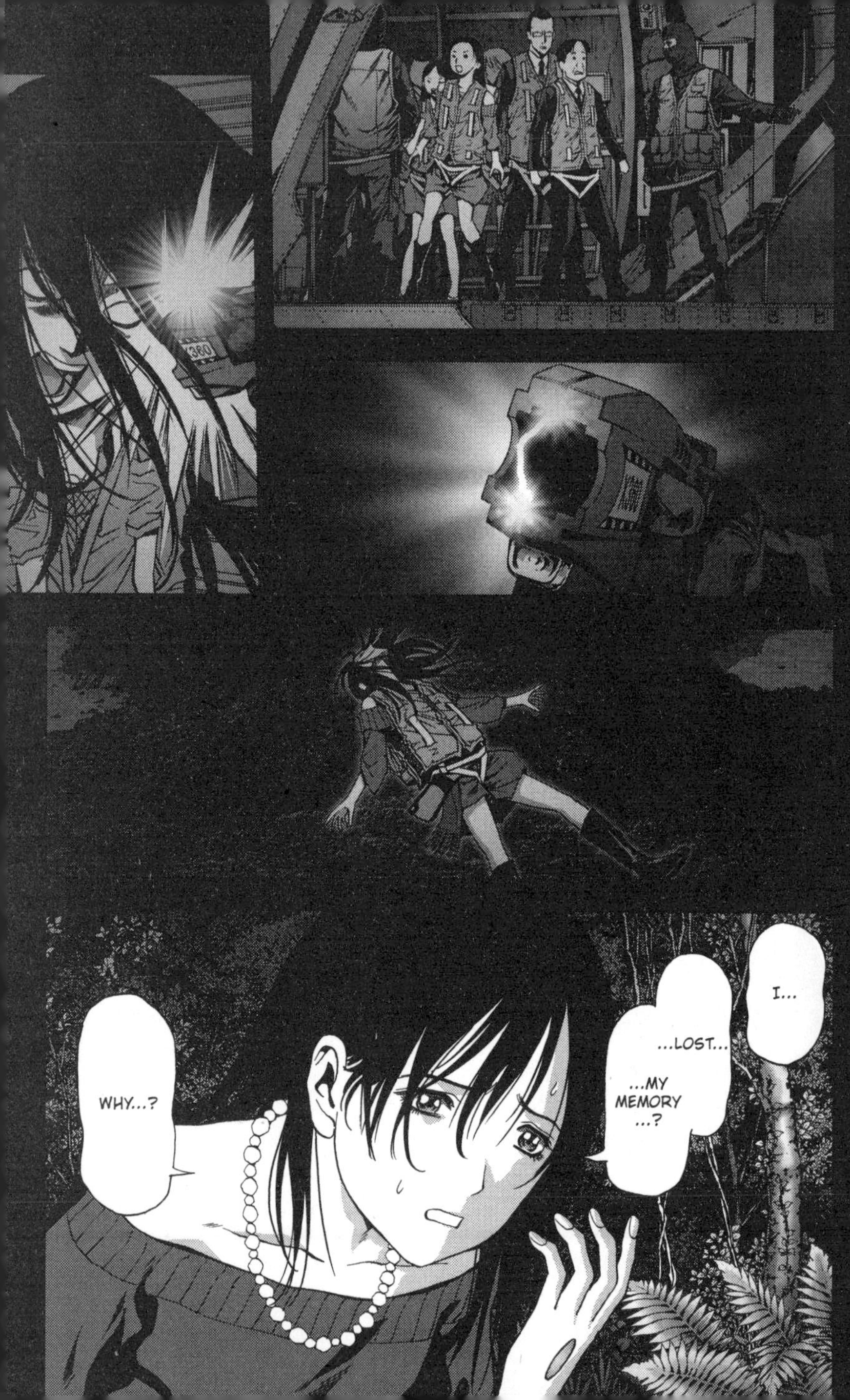
I...
...LOST... ...MY MEMORY ...?
WHY...?

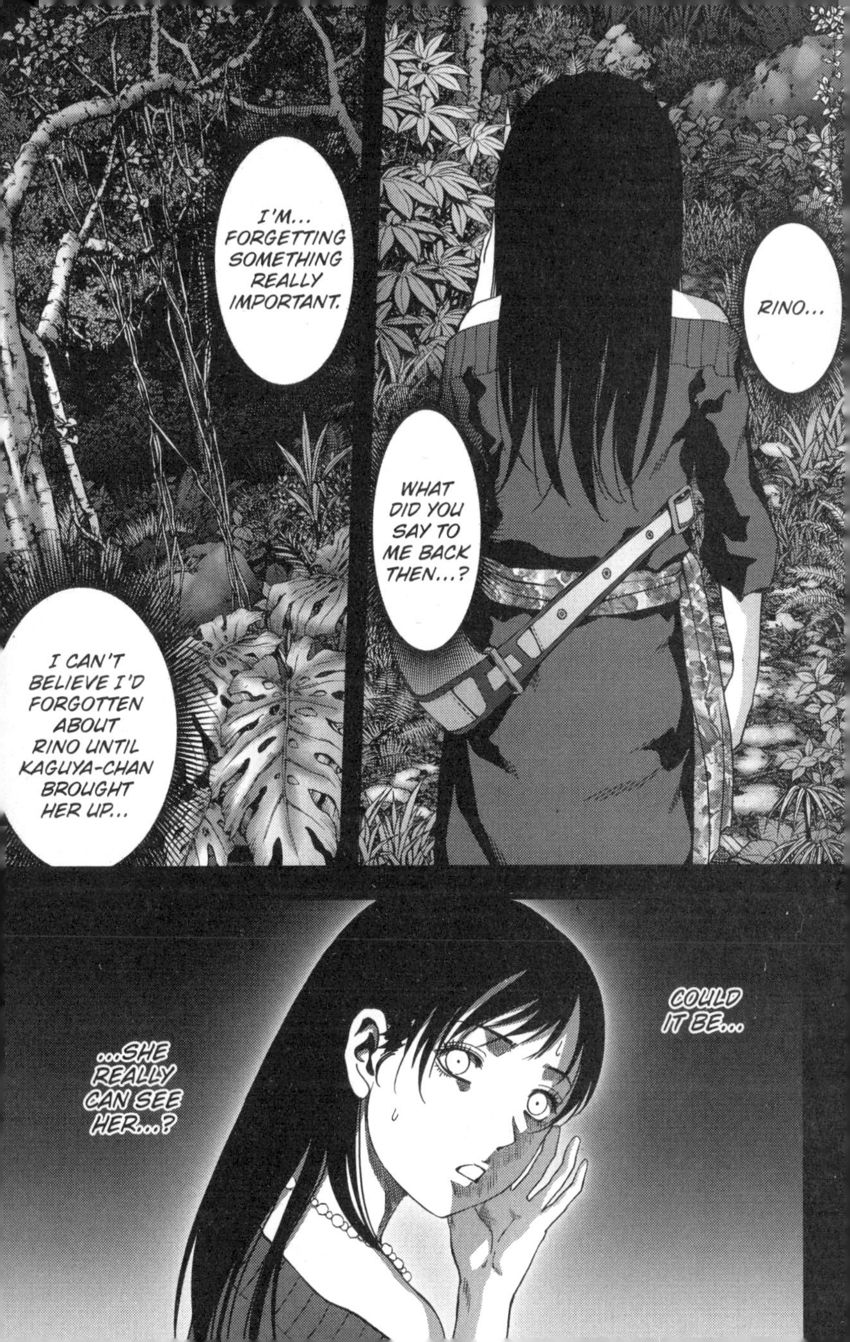
RINO...
WHAT DID YOU SAY TO ME BACK THEN...?
I'M... FORGETTING SOMETHING REALLY IMPORTANT.
I CAN'T BELIEVE I'D FORGOTTEN ABOUT RINO UNTIL KAGUYA-CHAN BROUGHT HER UP...
COULD IT BE...
...SHE REALLY CAN SEE HER...?

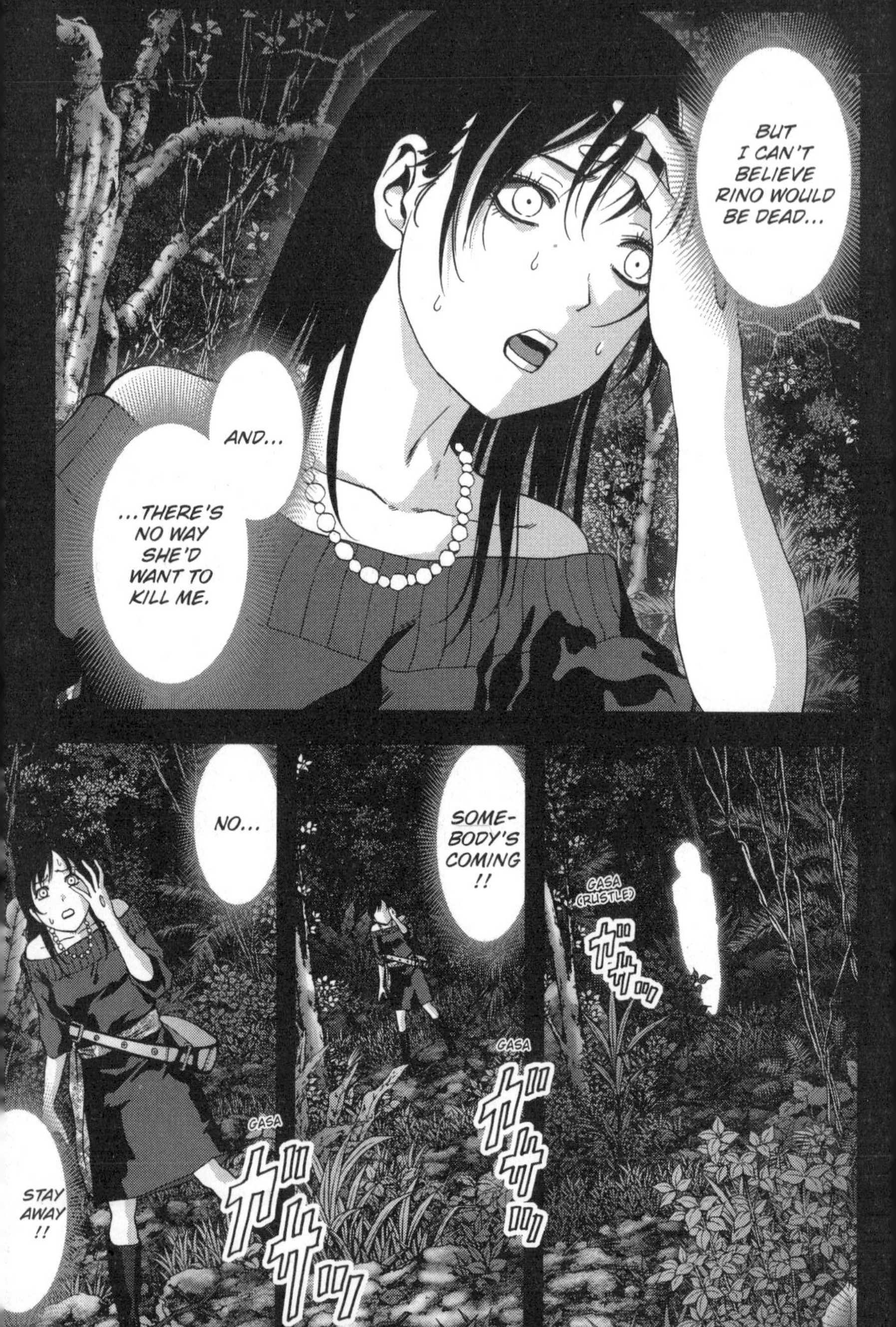
BUT I CAN'T BELIEVE RINO WOULD BE DEAD...
AND...
...THERE'S NO WAY SHE'D WANT TO KILL ME.
GASA (RUSTLE)
SOME-BODY'S COMING !!
GASA
NO...
GASA
STAY AWAY !!

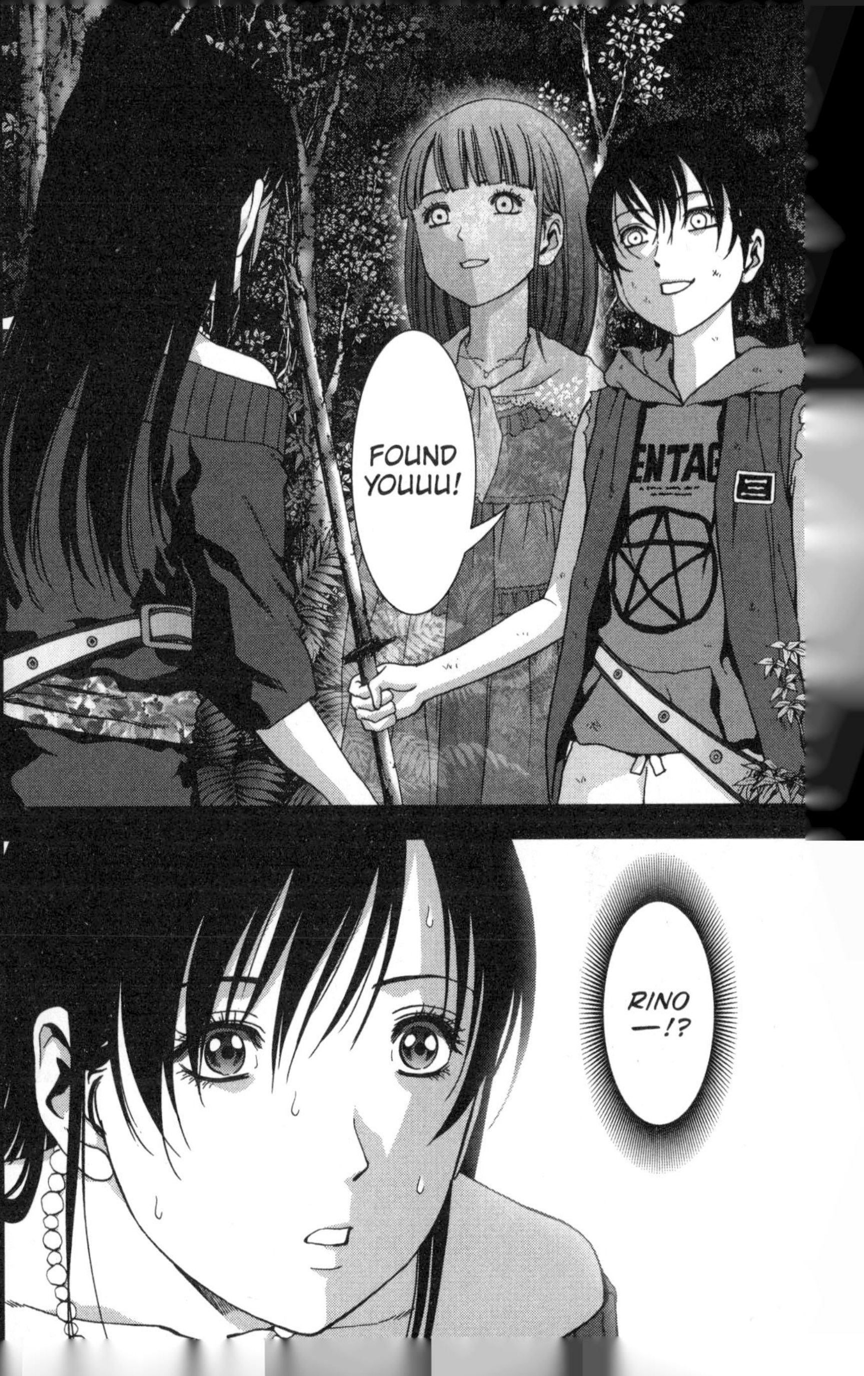
FOUND YOUUU!
RINO —!?

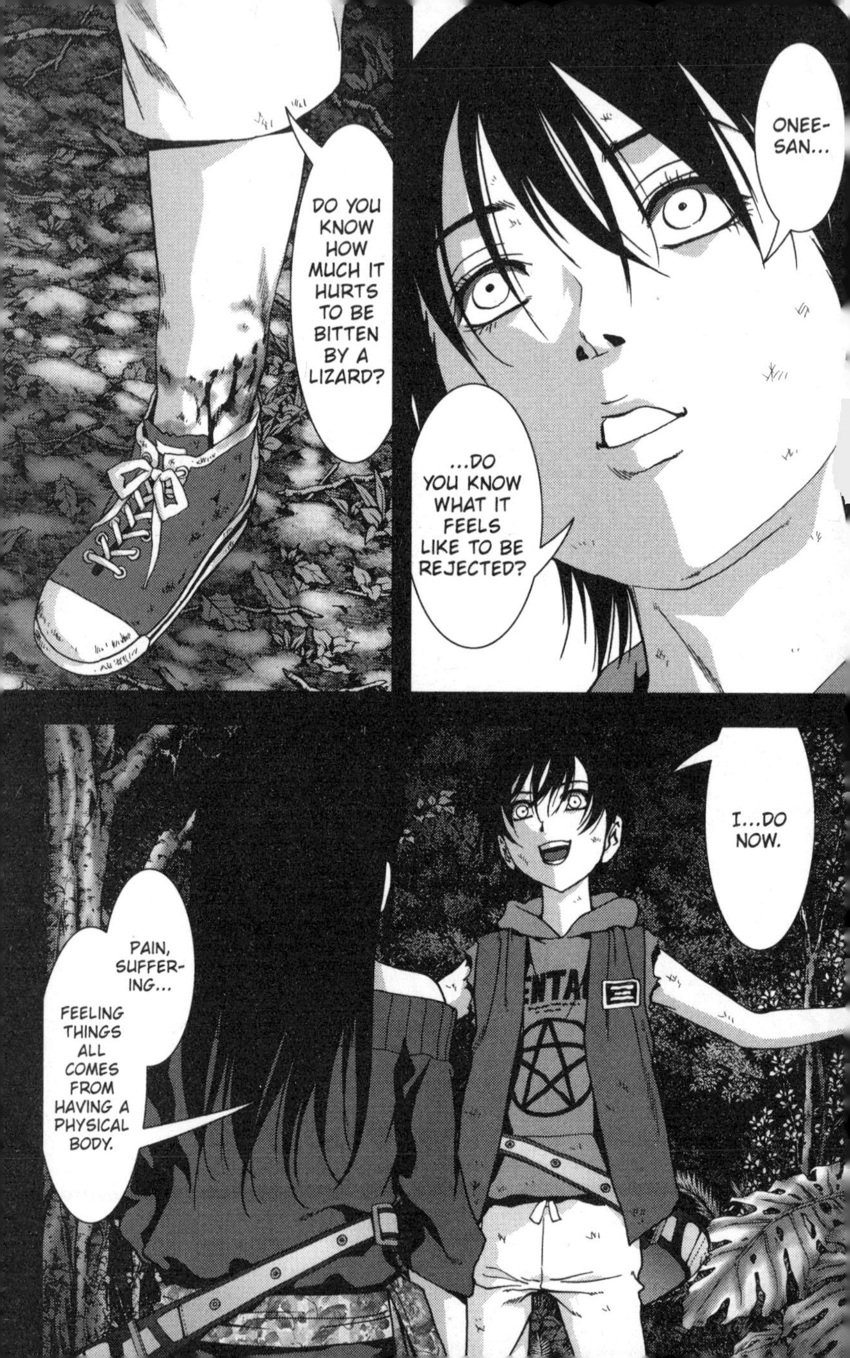
ONEE-SAN...
...DO YOU KNOW WHAT IT FEELS LIKE TO BE REJECTED?
DO YOU KNOW HOW MUCH IT HURTS TO BE BITTEN BY A LIZARD?
I...DO NOW.
PAIN, SUFFERING...
FEELING THINGS ALL COMES FROM HAVING A PHYSICAL BODY.

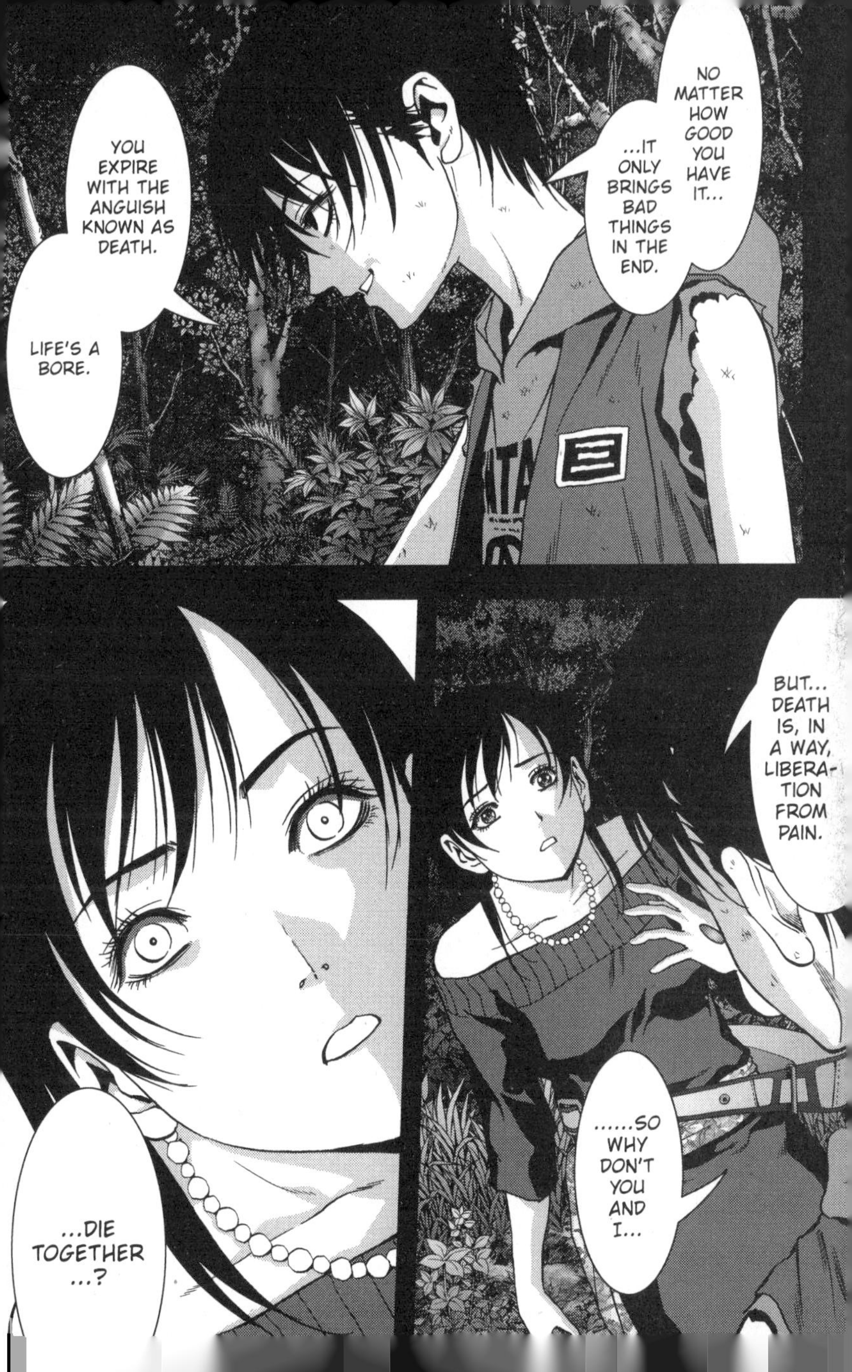
NO MATTER HOW GOOD YOU HAVE IT...
...IT ONLY BRINGS BAD THINGS IN THE END.
YOU EXPIRE WITH THE ANGUISH KNOWN AS DEATH.
LIFE'S A BORE.
BUT... DEATH IS, IN A WAY, LIBERA-TION FROM PAIN.
......SO WHY DON'T YOU AND I...
...DIE TOGETHER ...?

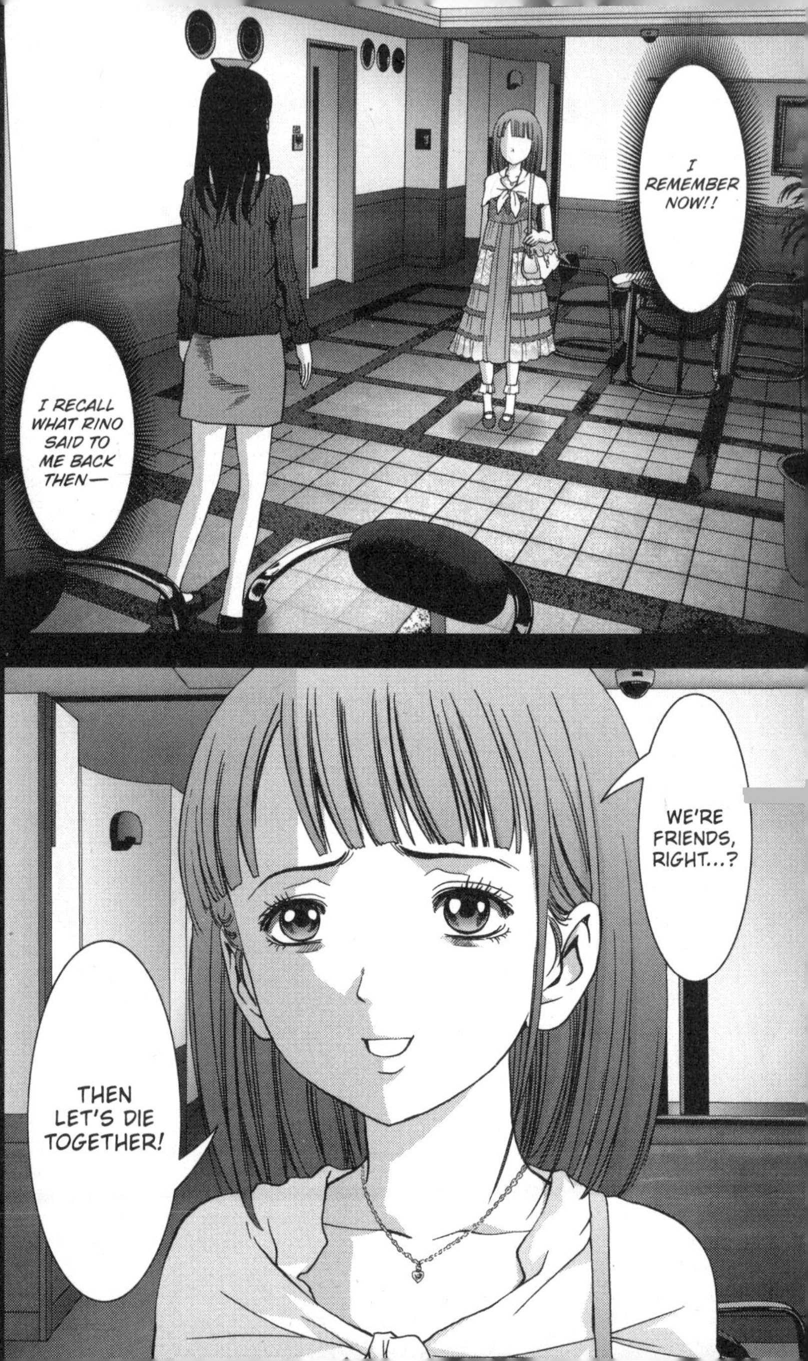
I REMEMBER NOW!!
I RECALL WHAT RINO SAID TO ME BACK THEN—
WE'RE FRIENDS, RIGHT...?
THEN LET'S DIE TOGETHER!

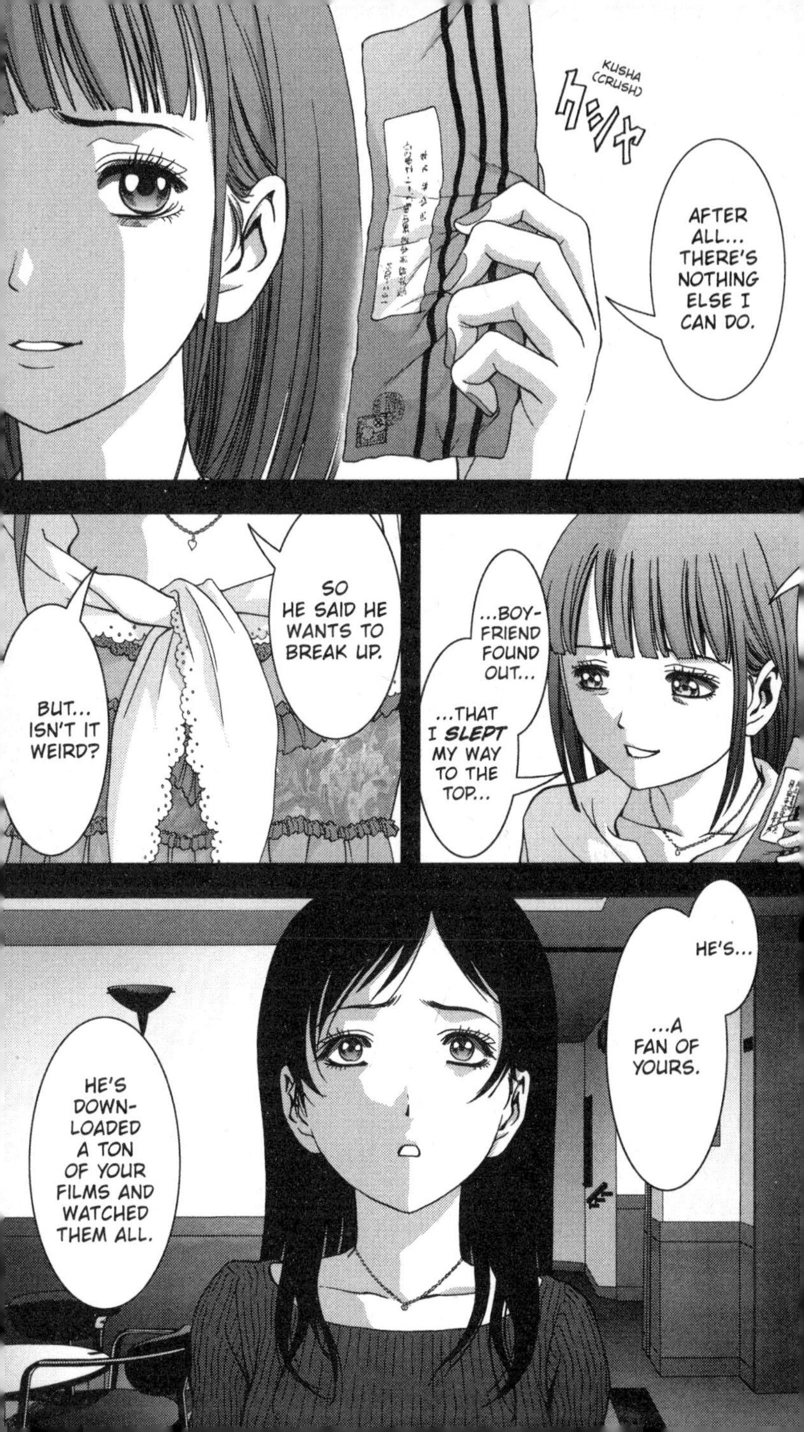
クシャ
KUSHA (CRUSH)
AFTER ALL... THERE'S NOTHING ELSE I CAN DO.
...BOY-FRIEND FOUND OUT...
...THAT I SLEPT MY WAY TO THE TOP...
SO HE SAID HE WANTS TO BREAK UP.
BUT... ISN'T IT WEIRD?
HE'S...
...A FAN OF YOURS.
HE'S DOWN-LOADED A TON OF YOUR FILMS AND WATCHED THEM ALL.

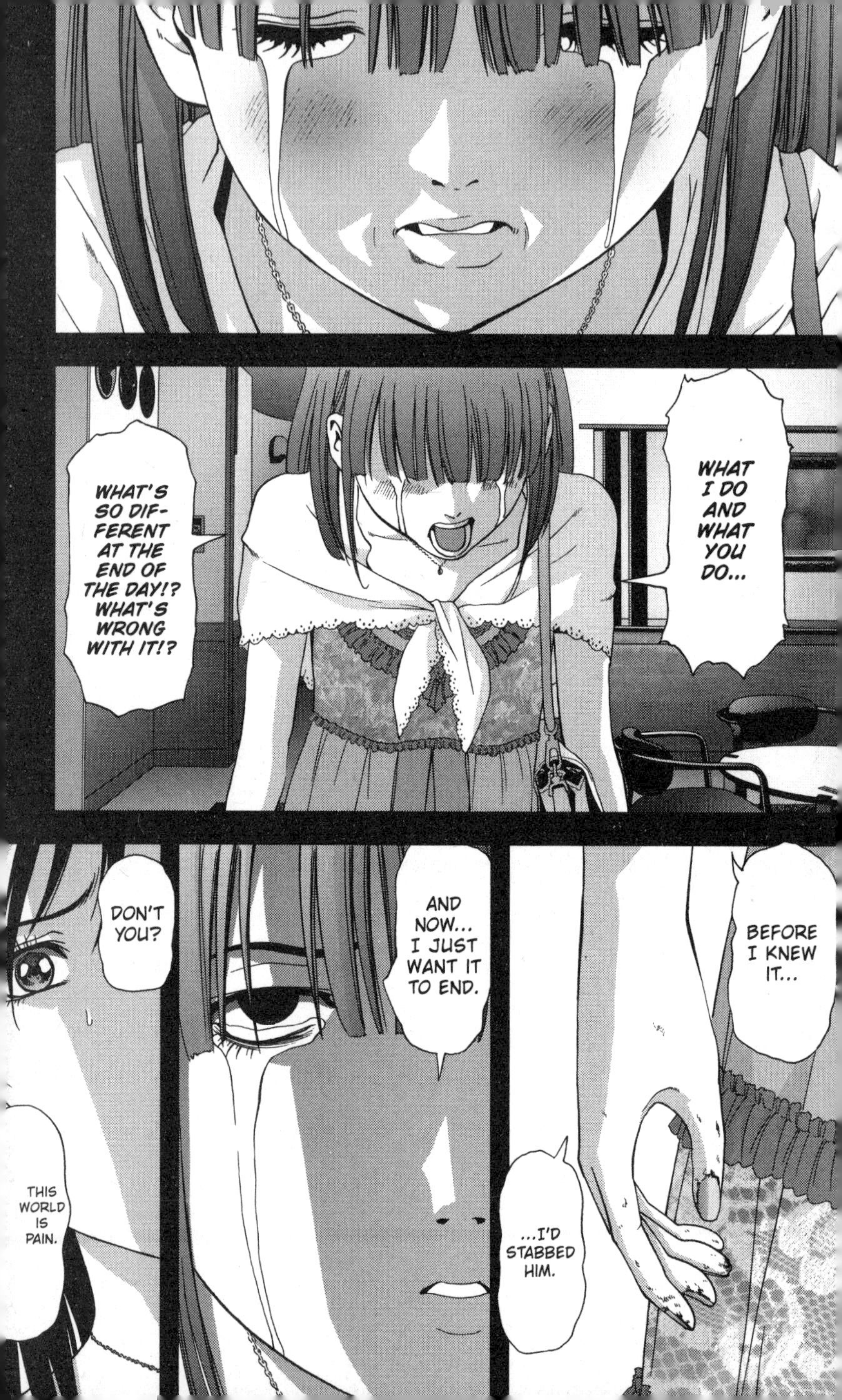
WHAT I DO AND WHAT YOU DO...
WHAT'S SO DIFFERENT AT THE END OF THE DAY!? WHAT'S WRONG WITH IT!?
BEFORE I KNEW IT...
...I'D STABBED HIM.
AND NOW... I JUST WANT IT TO END.
DON'T YOU?
THIS WORLD IS PAIN.

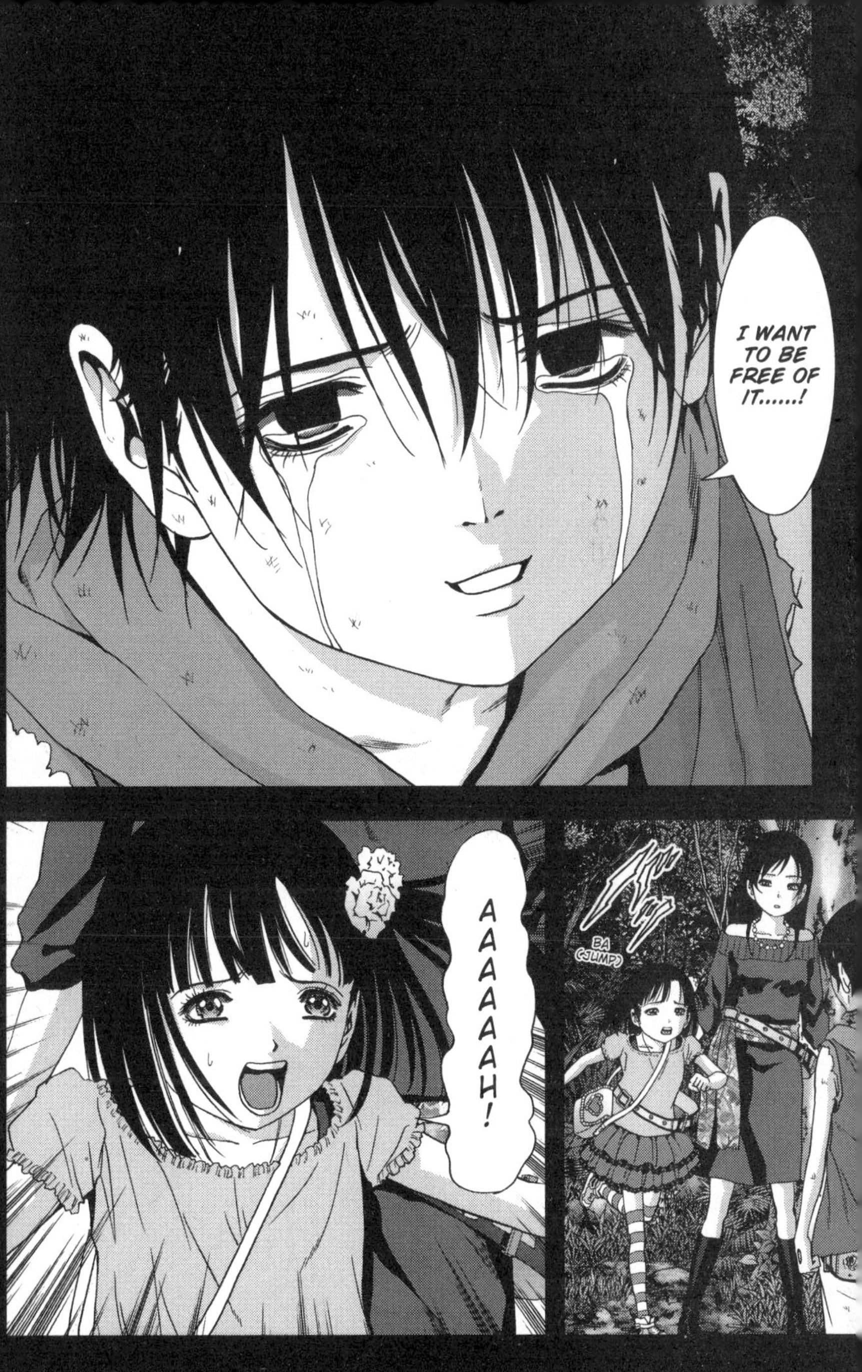
I WANT TO BE FREE OF IT......!
BA (JUMP)
AAAAAAAH!

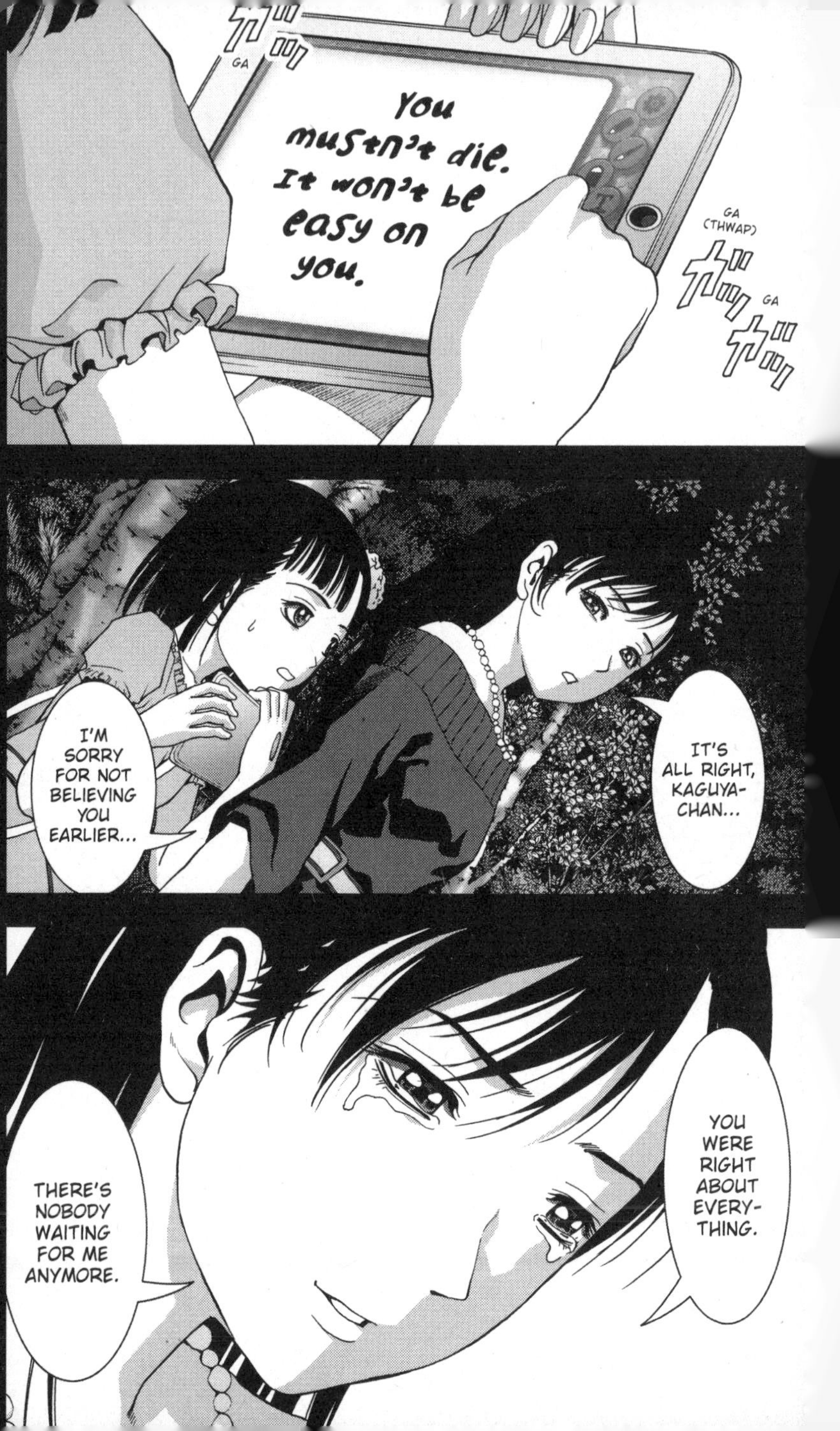
GA (THWAP)
GA
GA
You mustn't die. It won't be easy on you.
IT'S ALL RIGHT, KAGUYA-CHAN...
I'M SORRY FOR NOT BELIEVING YOU EARLIER...
YOU WERE RIGHT ABOUT EVERYTHING.
THERE'S NOBODY WAITING FOR ME ANYMORE.

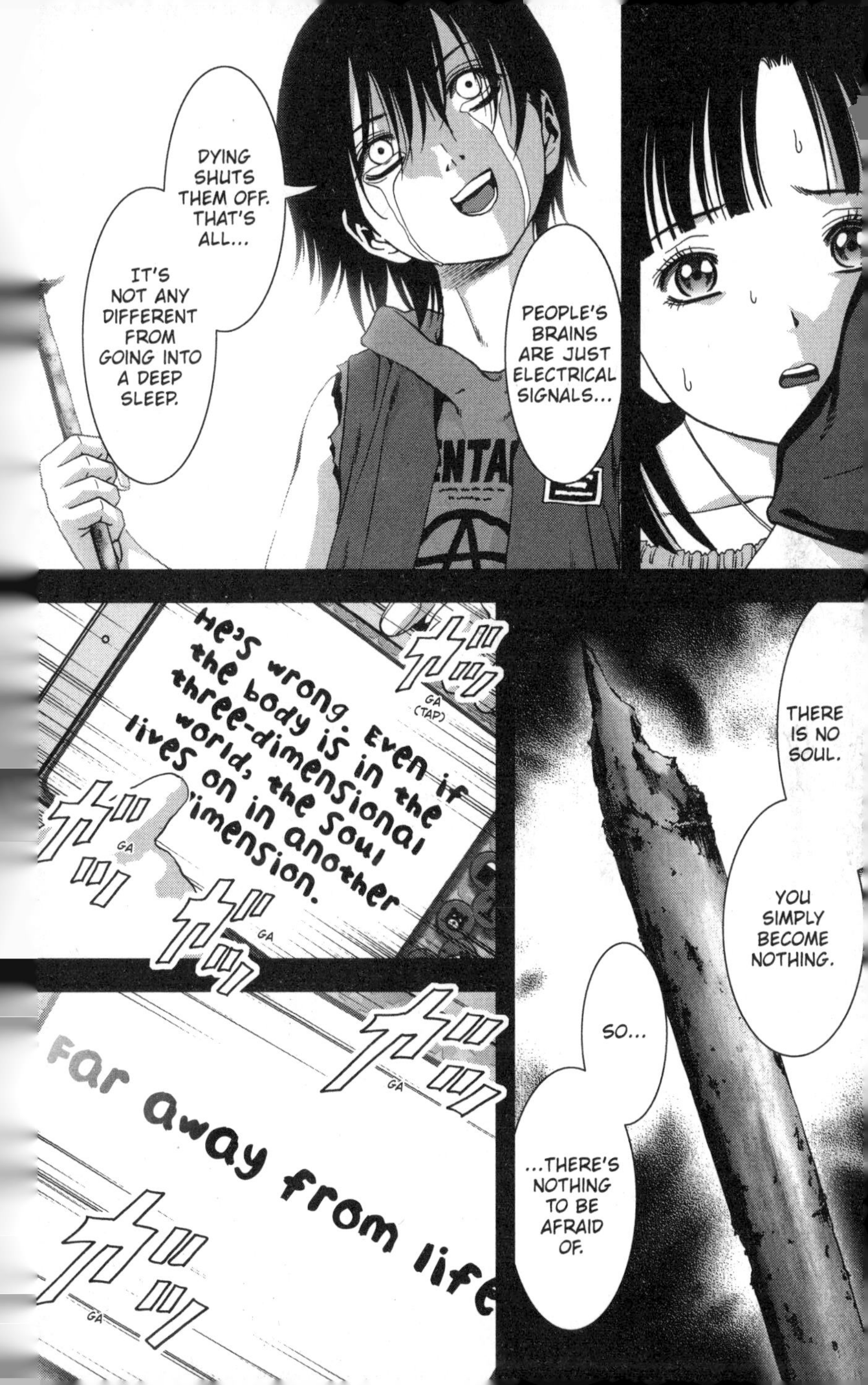
PEOPLE'S BRAINS ARE JUST ELECTRICAL SIGNALS...
DYING SHUTS THEM OFF. THAT'S ALL...
IT'S NOT ANY DIFFERENT FROM GOING INTO A DEEP SLEEP.
THERE IS NO SOUL.
YOU SIMPLY BECOME NOTHING.
SO...
...THERE'S NOTHING TO BE AFRAID OF.
GA (TAP)
He's wrong. Even if the body is in the three-dimensional world, the soul lives on in another dimension.
GA
GA
GA
Far away from life
GA

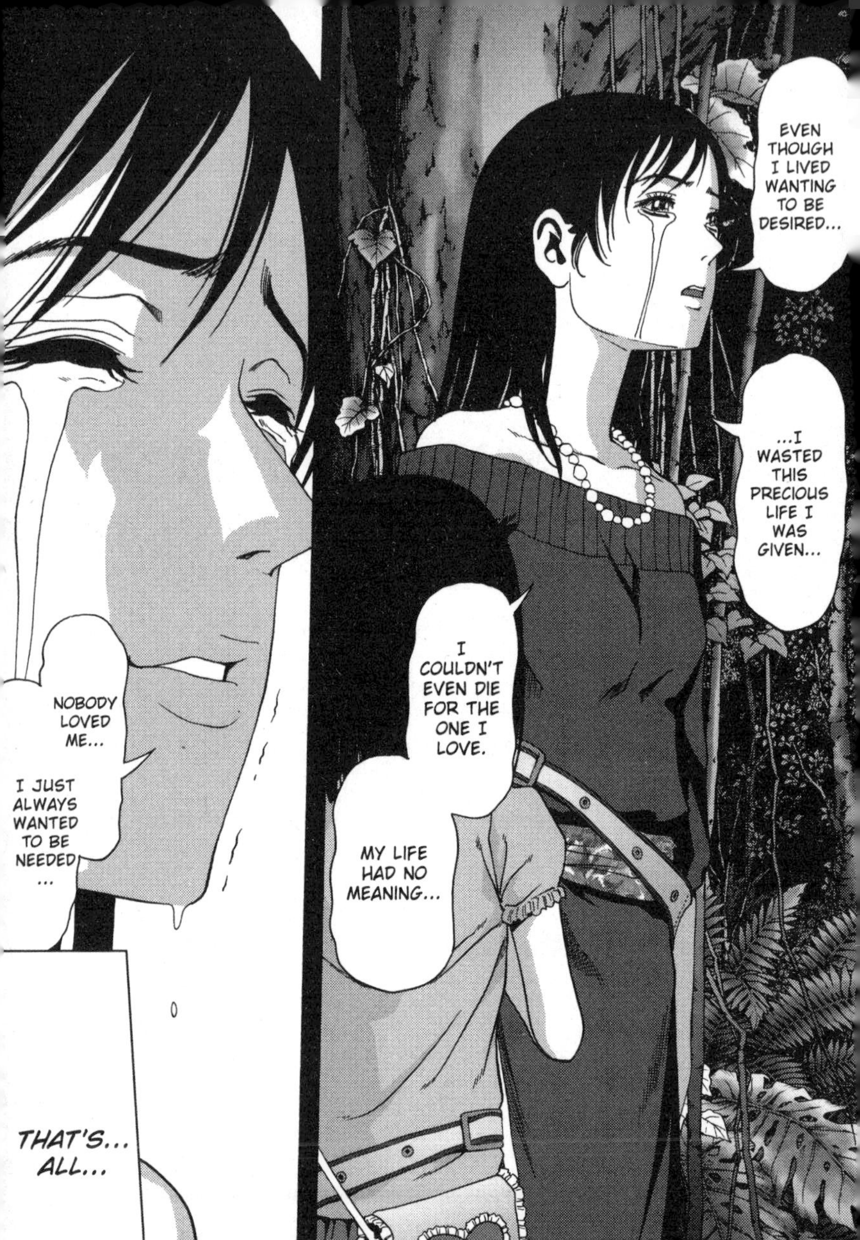
EVEN THOUGH I LIVED WANTING TO BE DESIRED...
...I WASTED THIS PRECIOUS LIFE I WAS GIVEN...
I COULDN'T EVEN DIE FOR THE ONE I LOVE.
MY LIFE HAD NO MEANING...
NOBODY LOVED ME...
I JUST ALWAYS WANTED TO BE NEEDED...
THAT'S... ALL...

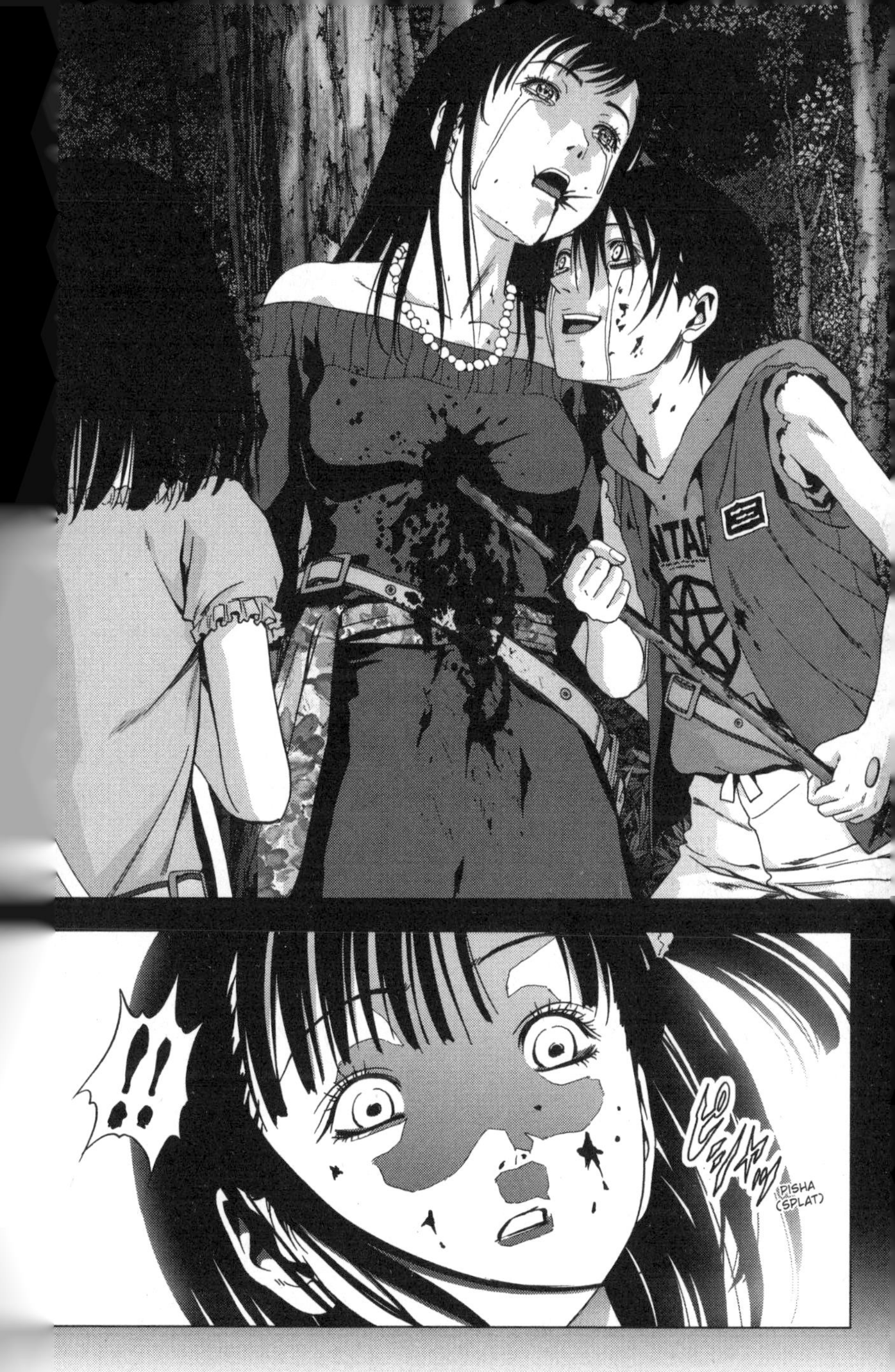
!!
PISHA
(SPLAT)

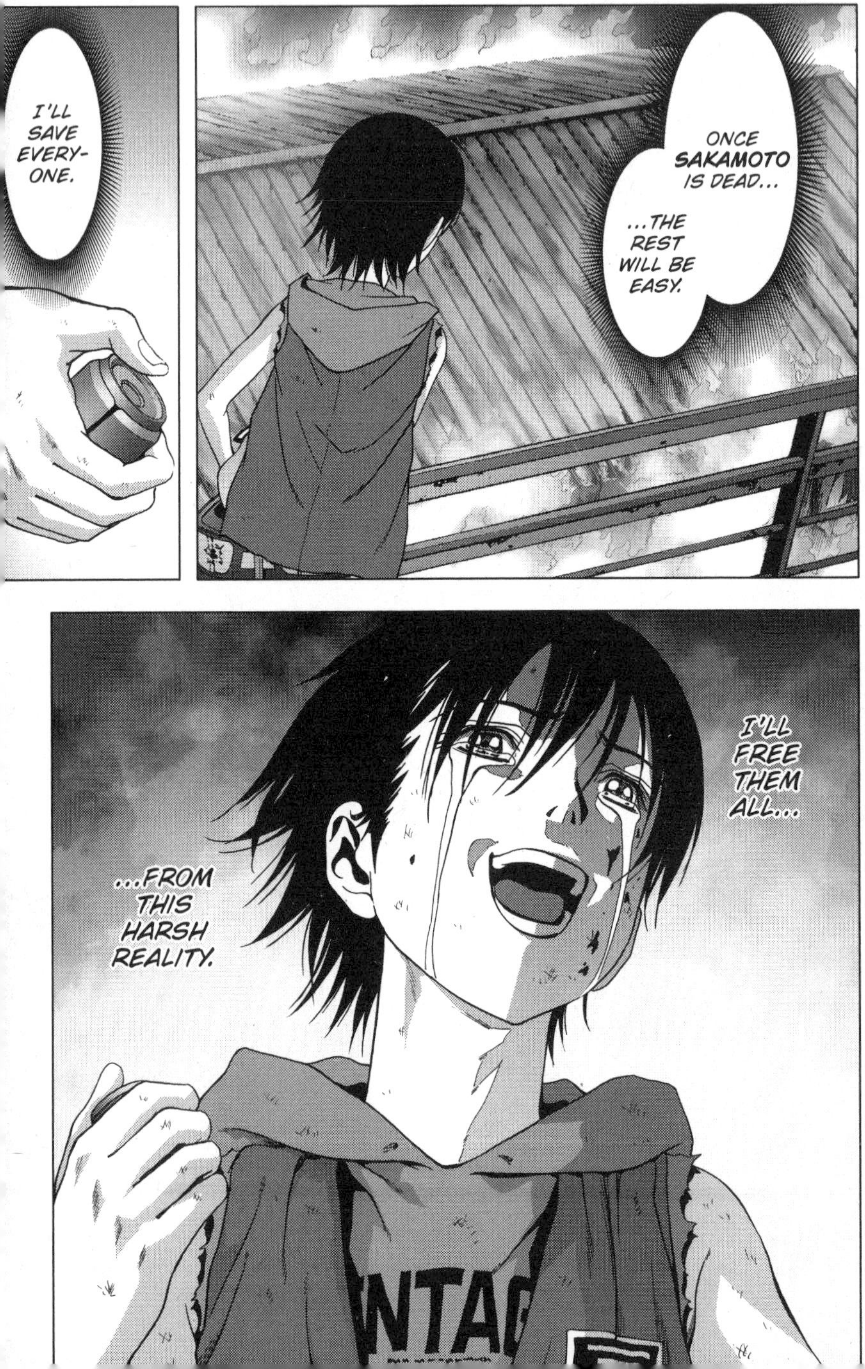
ONCE SAKAMOTO IS DEAD...
...THE REST WILL BE EASY.
I'LL SAVE EVERY-ONE.
I'LL FREE THEM ALL...
...FROM THIS HARSH REALITY.

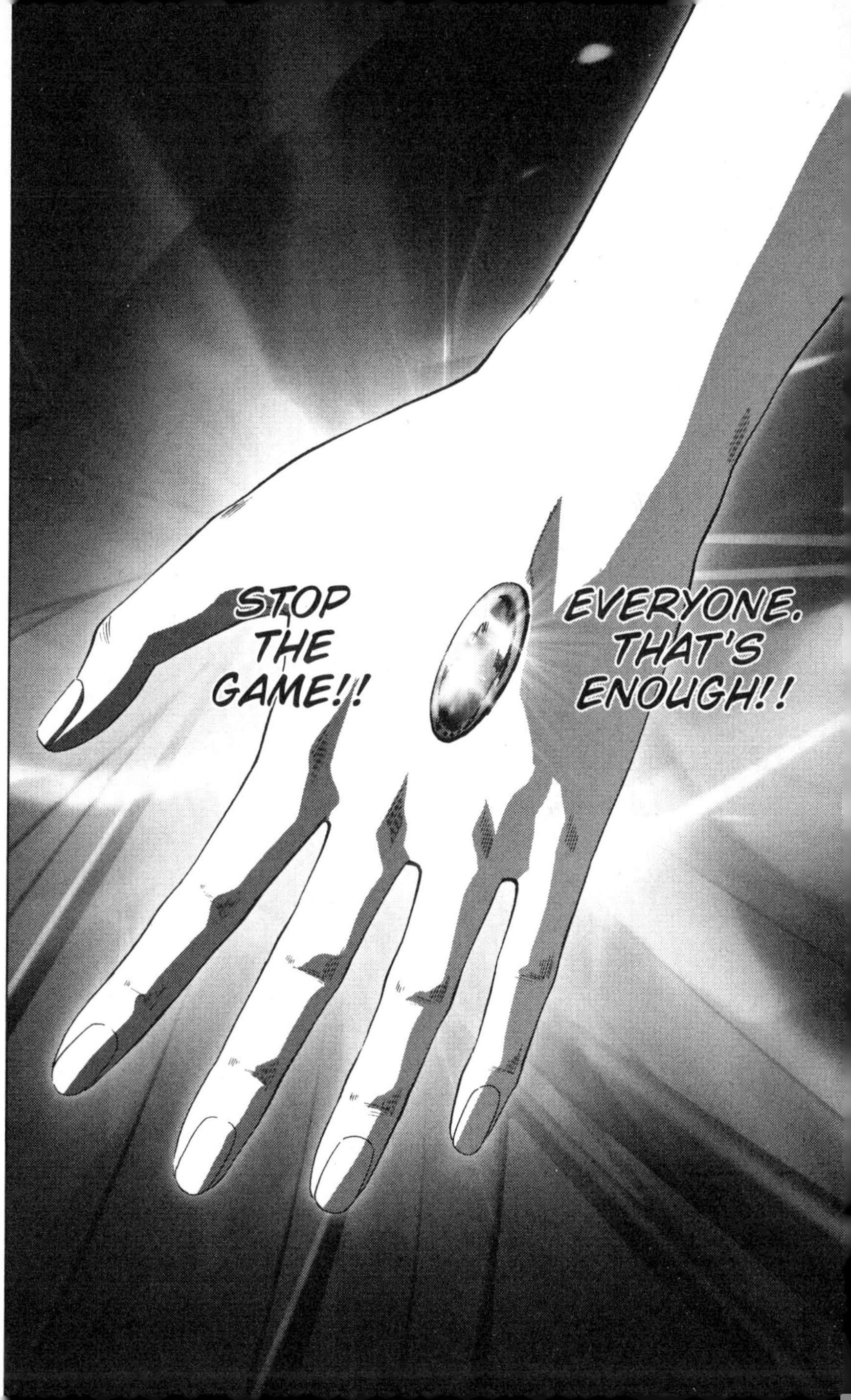
EVERYONE. THAT'S ENOUGH!!
STOP THE GAME!!

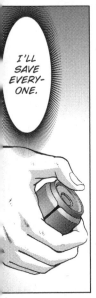

I'LL SAVE EVERY- ONE.

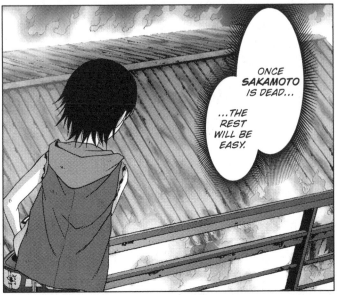

ONCE **SAKAMOTO** IS DEAD...

...THE REST WILL BE EASY.

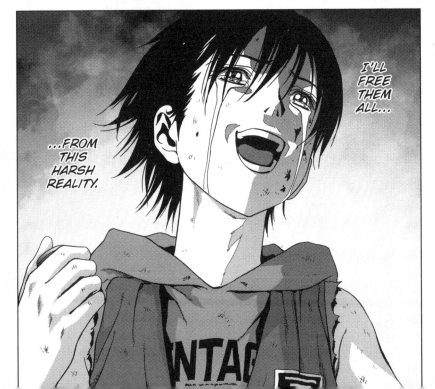

I'LL FREE THEM ALL...

...FROM THIS HARSH REALITY.

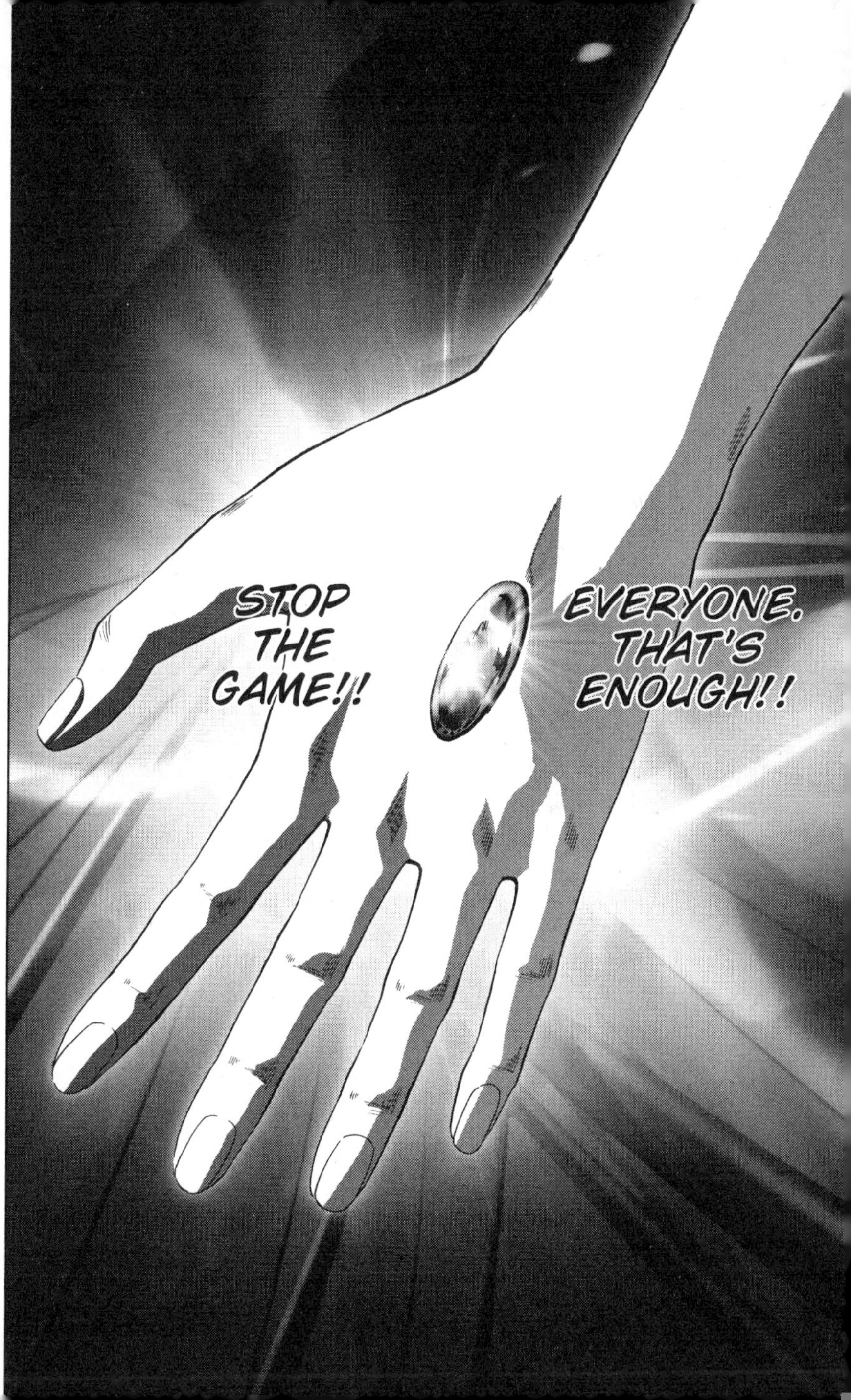
EVERYONE. THAT'S ENOUGH!!
STOP THE GAME!!

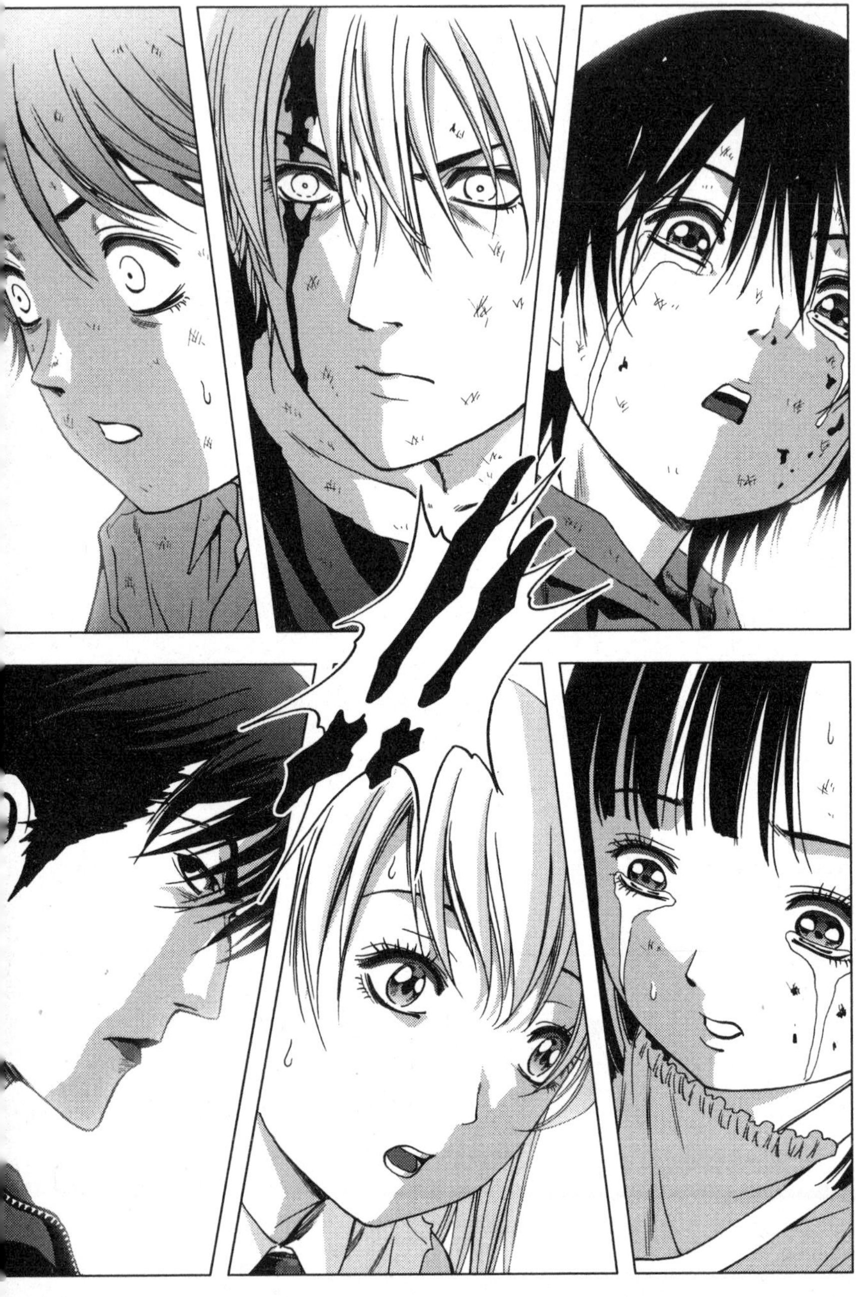

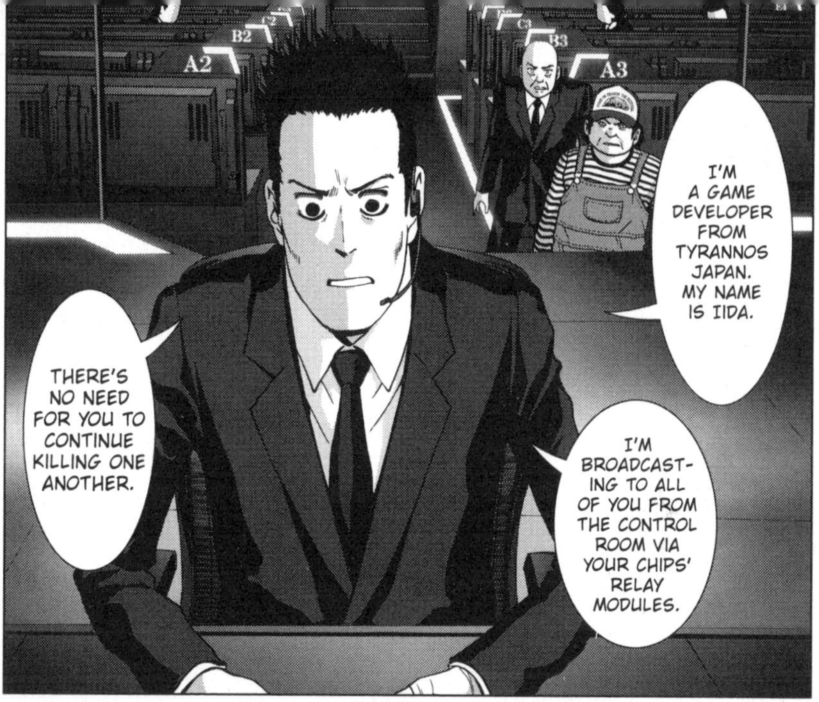
I'M A GAME DEVELOPER FROM TYRANNOS JAPAN. MY NAME IS IIDA.
I'M BROADCAST-ING TO ALL OF YOU FROM THE CONTROL ROOM VIA YOUR CHIPS' RELAY MODULES.
THERE'S NO NEED FOR YOU TO CONTINUE KILLING ONE ANOTHER.

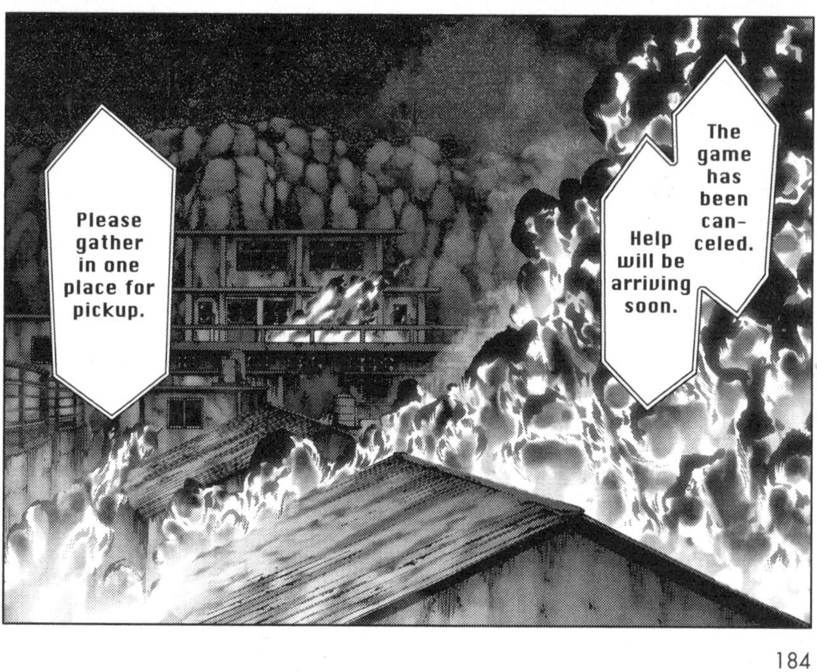
The game has been can-celed.
Help will be arriving soon.
Please gather in one place for pickup.

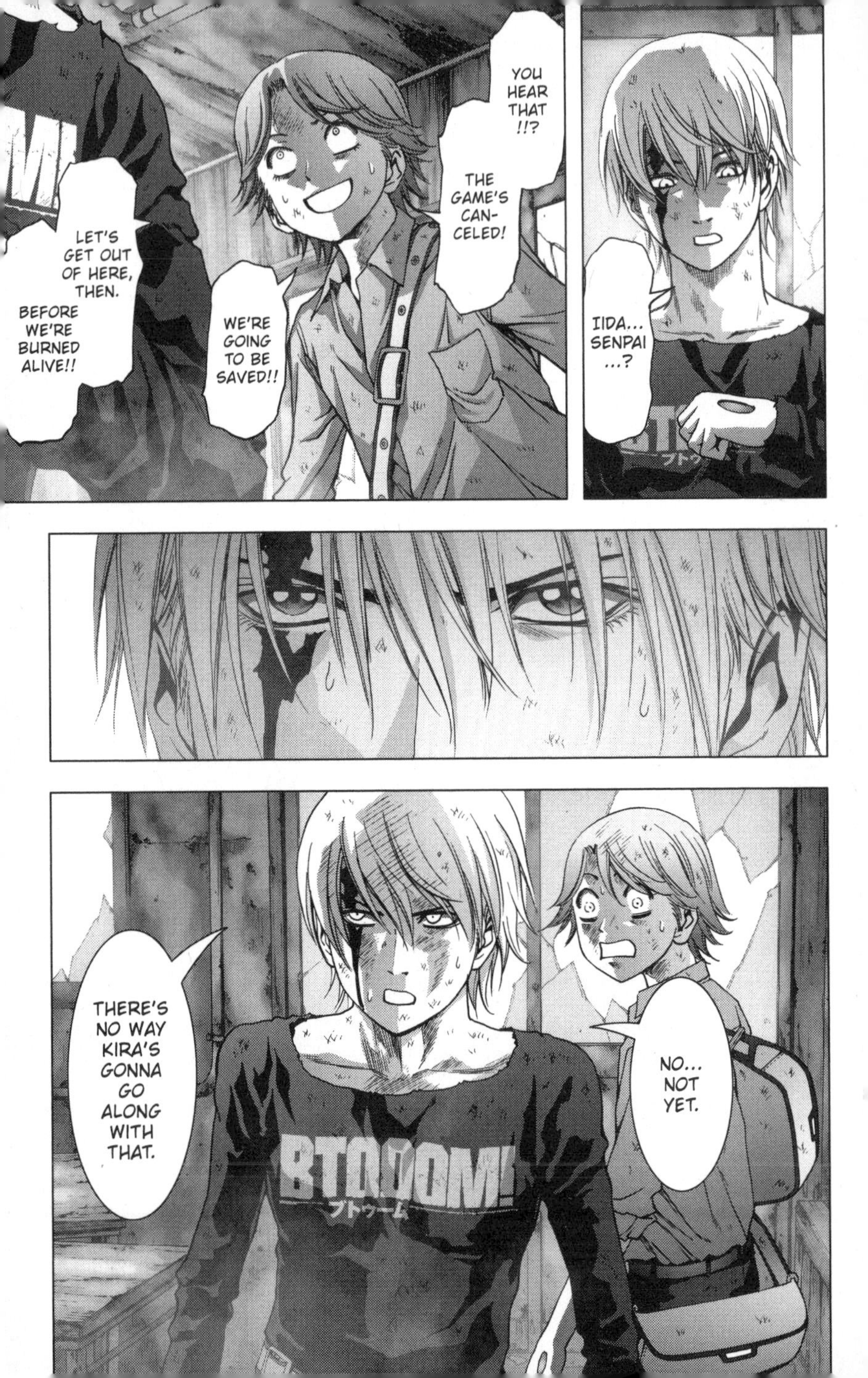
IIDA... SENPAI ...?
YOU HEAR THAT !!?
THE GAME'S CAN-CELED!
WE'RE GOING TO BE SAVED!!
LET'S GET OUT OF HERE, THEN.
BEFORE WE'RE BURNED ALIVE!!
NO... NOT YET.
THERE'S NO WAY KIRA'S GONNA GO ALONG WITH THAT.

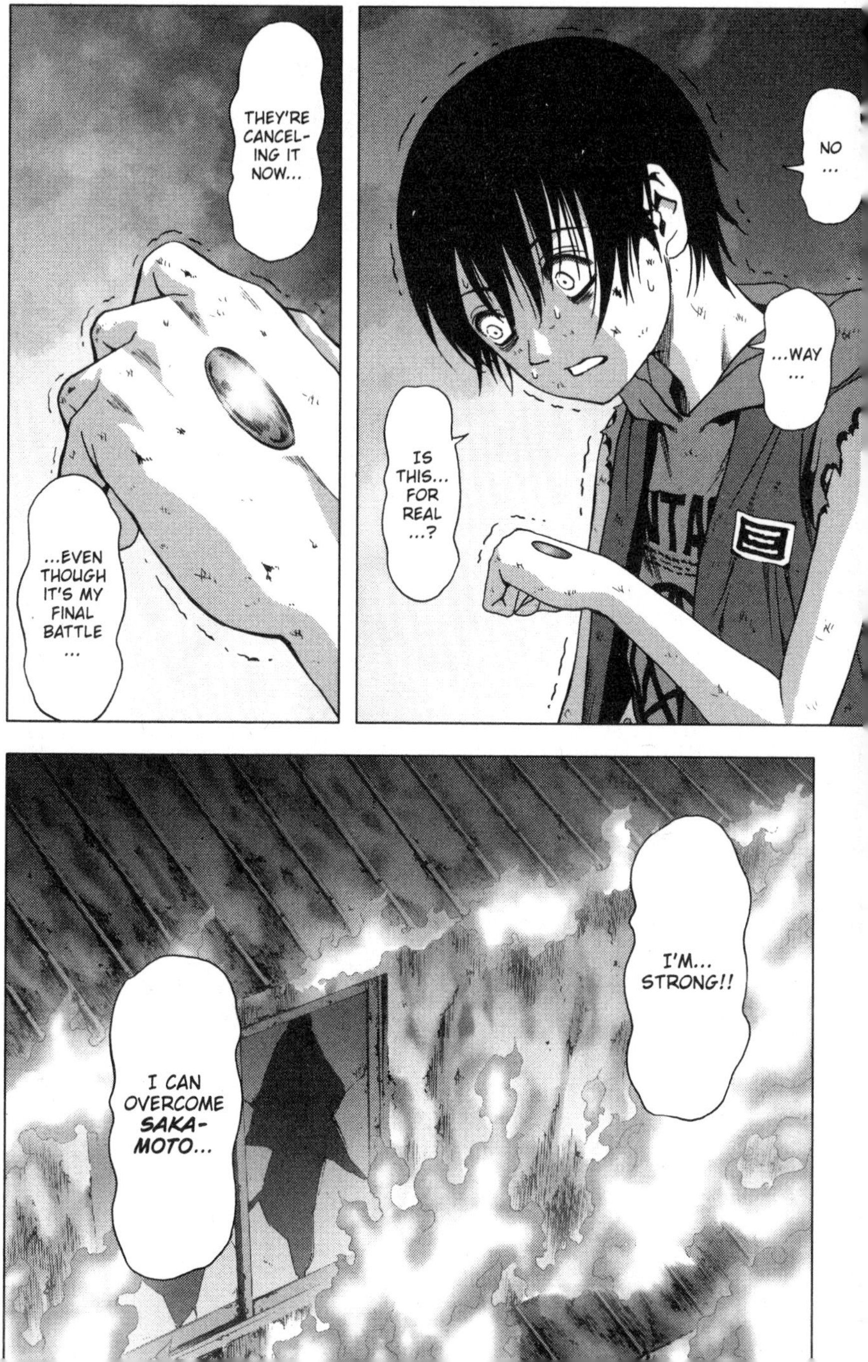
NO...
...WAY...
IS THIS... FOR REAL...?
THEY'RE CANCEL-ING IT NOW...
...EVEN THOUGH IT'S MY FINAL BATTLE...
I'M... STRONG!!
I CAN OVERCOME ***SAKA-MOTO***...

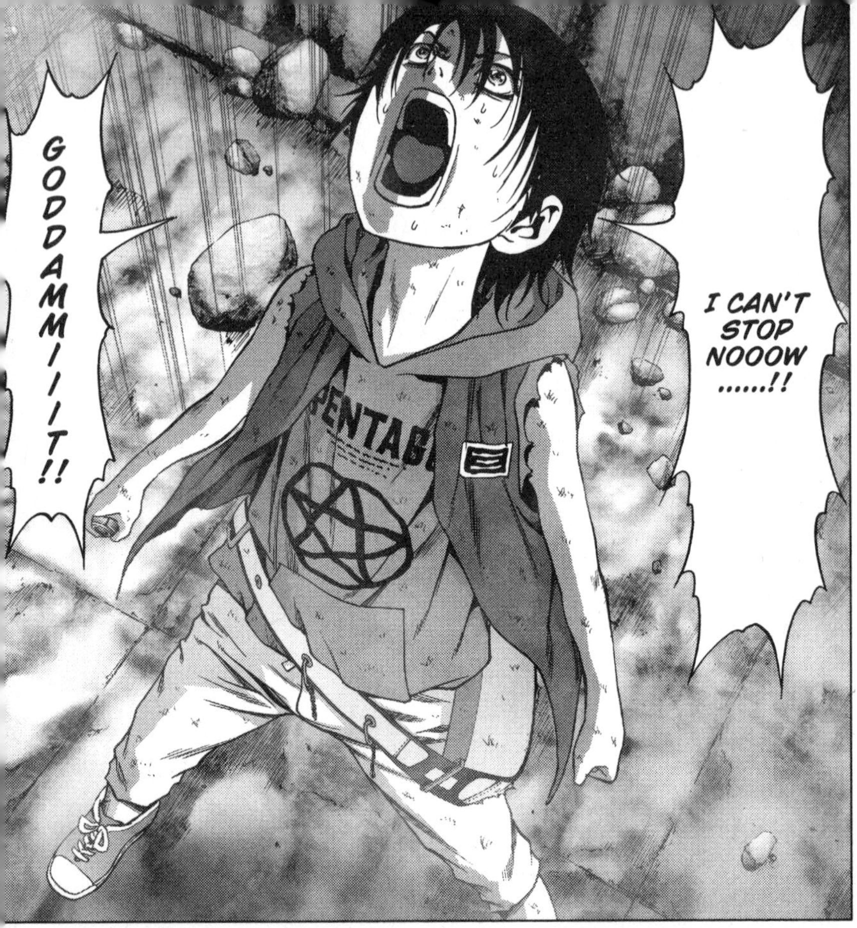
I CAN'T STOP NOOOW ......!!
GODDAMMIIIIT!!
PENTAGE

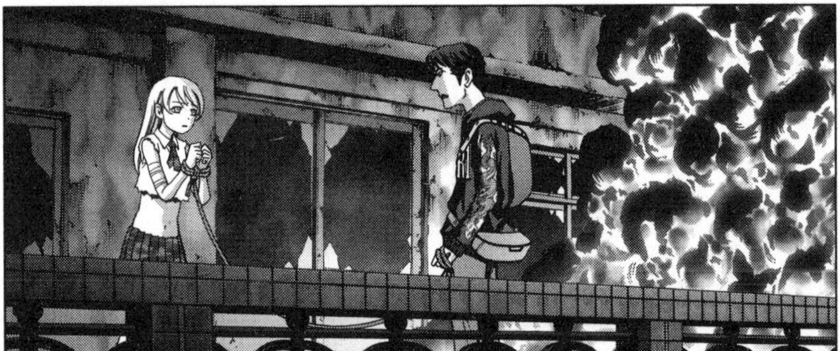

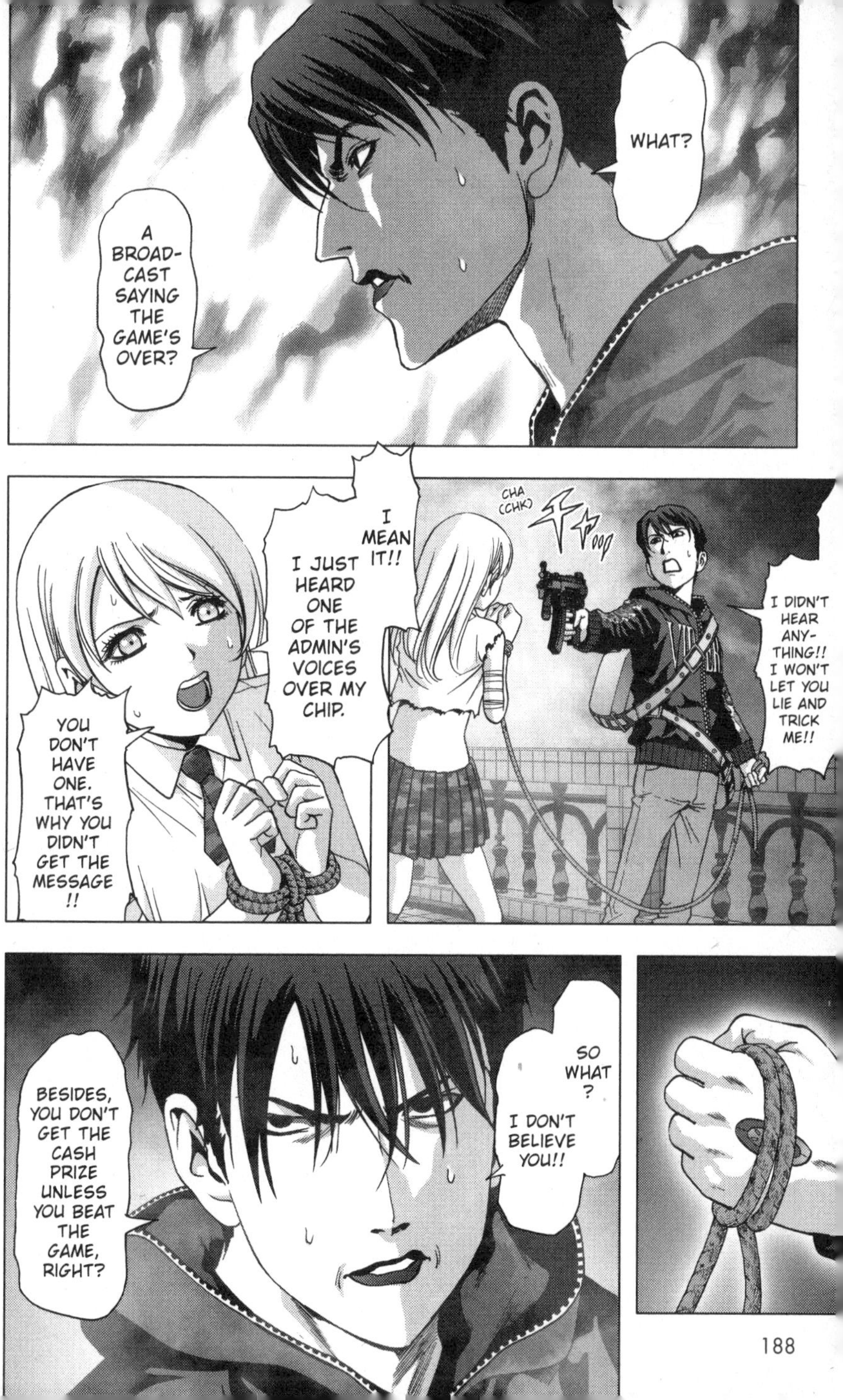
WHAT?
A BROADCAST SAYING THE GAME'S OVER?
CHA (CHK)
I DIDN'T HEAR ANYTHING!! I WON'T LET YOU LIE AND TRICK ME!!
I MEAN IT!!
I JUST HEARD ONE OF THE ADMIN'S VOICES OVER MY CHIP.
YOU DON'T HAVE ONE. THAT'S WHY YOU DIDN'T GET THE MESSAGE!!
SO WHAT?
I DON'T BELIEVE YOU!!
BESIDES, YOU DON'T GET THE CASH PRIZE UNLESS YOU BEAT THE GAME, RIGHT?

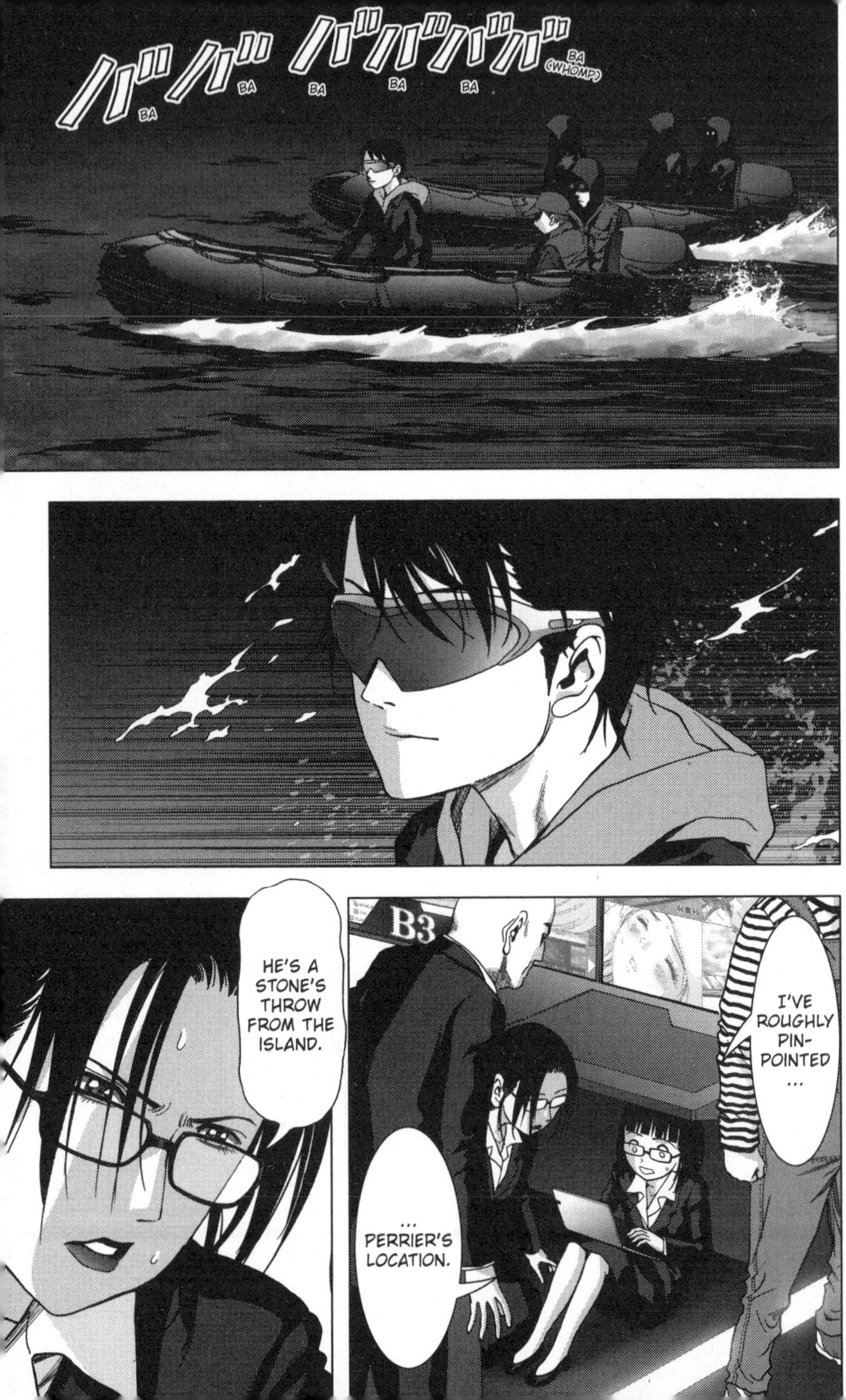

BA BA BA BA BA BA (WHOMP)
I'VE ROUGHLY PIN-POINTED...
...PERRIER'S LOCATION.
HE'S A STONE'S THROW FROM THE ISLAND.

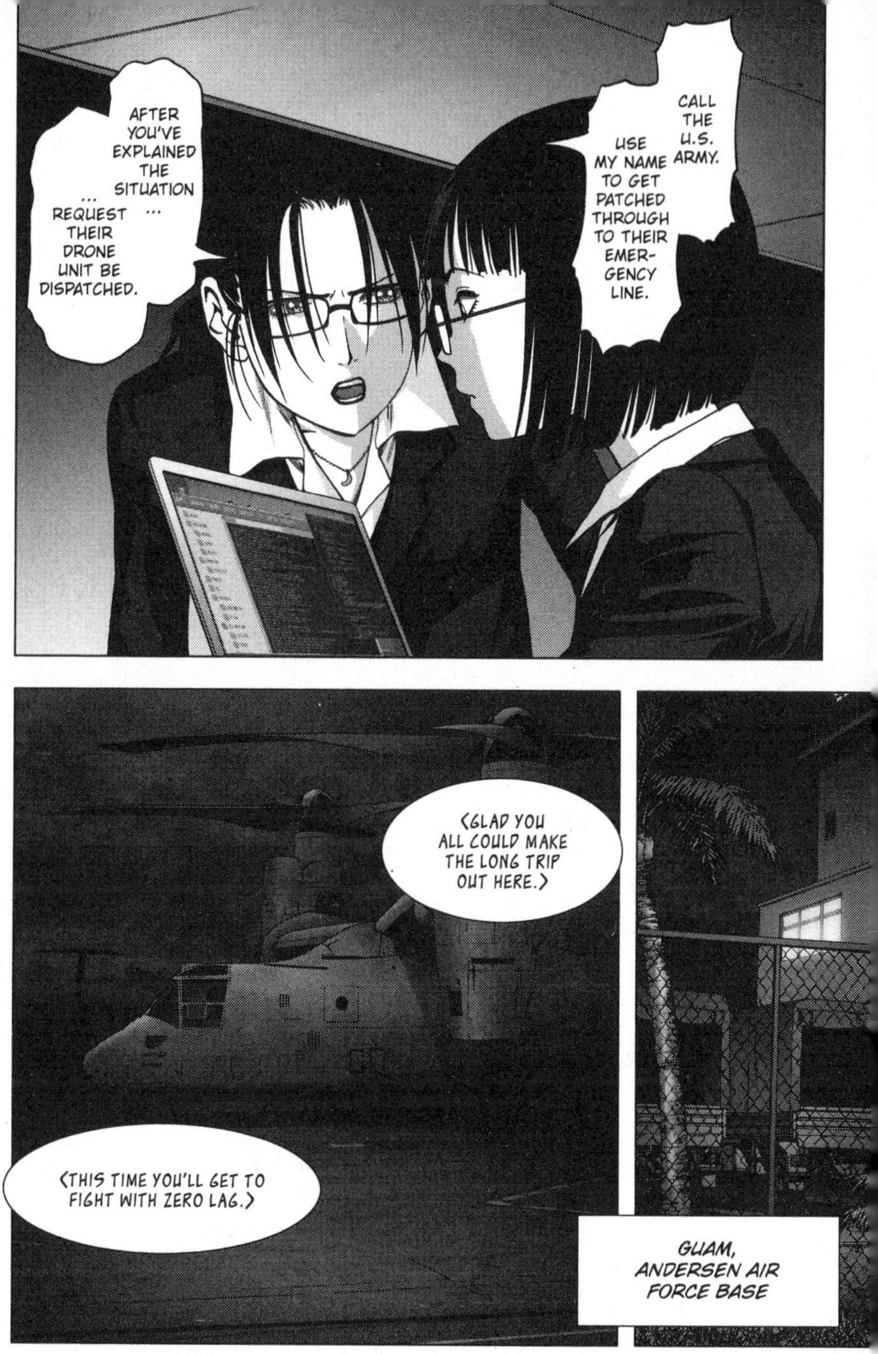
CALL THE U.S. ARMY.
USE MY NAME TO GET PATCHED THROUGH TO THEIR EMERGENCY LINE.
AFTER YOU'VE EXPLAINED THE SITUATION ...
... REQUEST THEIR DRONE UNIT BE DISPATCHED.
GUAM, ANDERSEN AIR FORCE BASE
‹GLAD YOU ALL COULD MAKE THE LONG TRIP OUT HERE.›
‹THIS TIME YOU'LL GET TO FIGHT WITH ZERO LAG.›

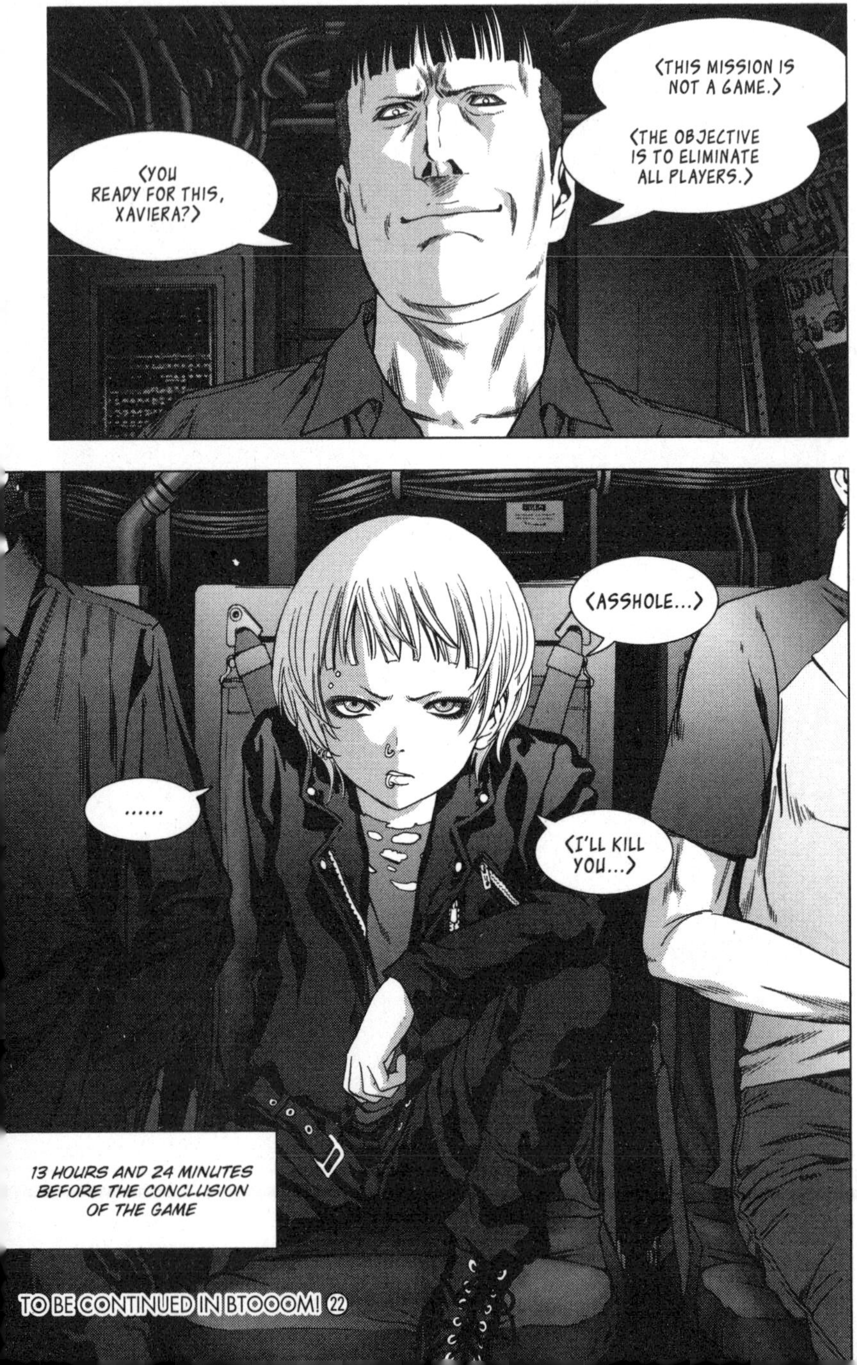
<THIS MISSION IS NOT A GAME.>
<THE OBJECTIVE IS TO ELIMINATE ALL PLAYERS.>
<YOU READY FOR THIS, XAVIERA?>
<ASSHOLE...>
......
<I'LL KILL YOU...>
13 HOURS AND 24 MINUTES BEFORE THE CONCLUSION OF THE GAME
TO BE CONTINUED IN BTOOOM! 22

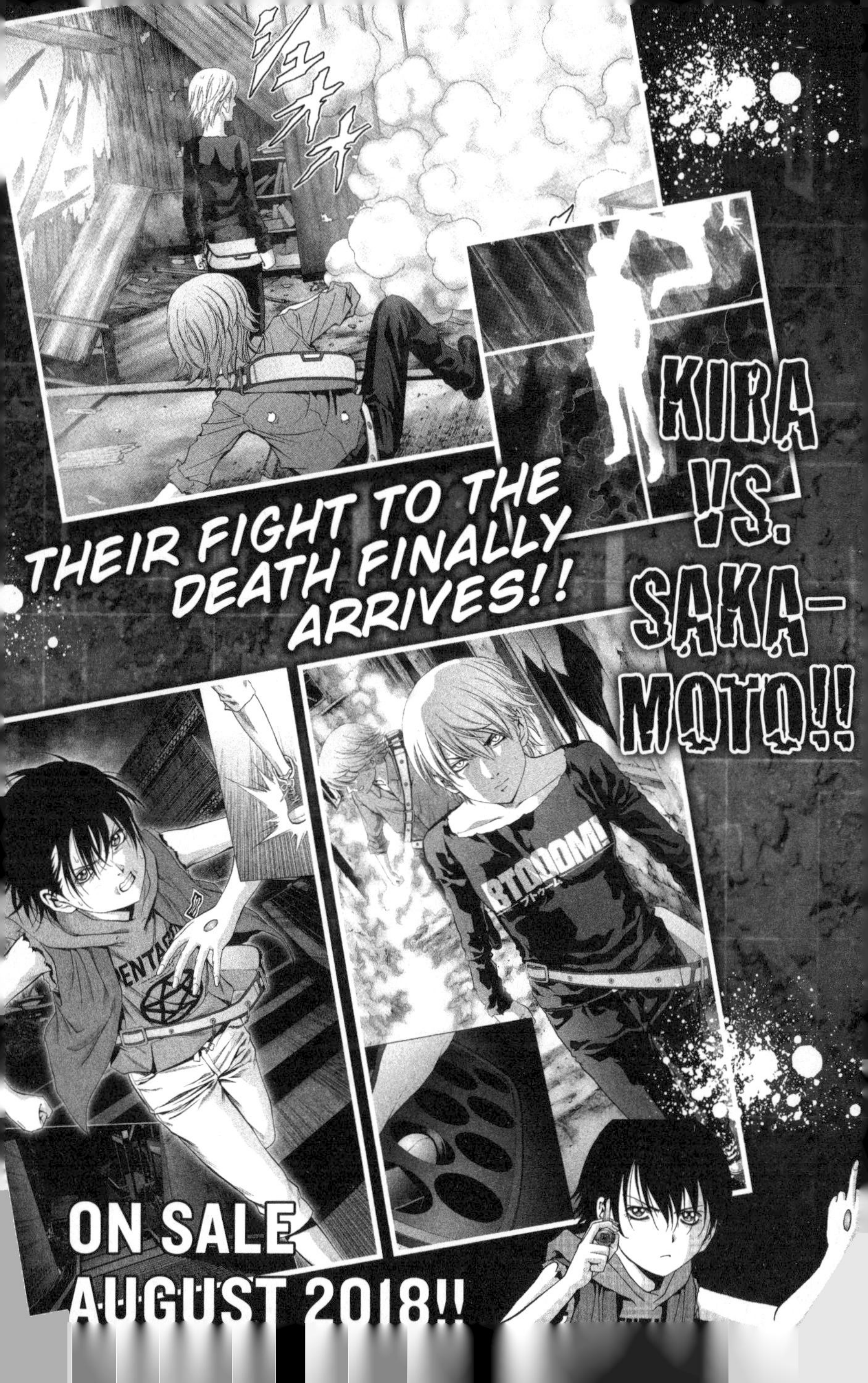

シュオオ
KIRA VS. SAKA-MOTO!!
THEIR FIGHT TO THE DEATH FINALLY ARRIVES!!
BTOOOM!
ON SALE AUGUST 2018!!

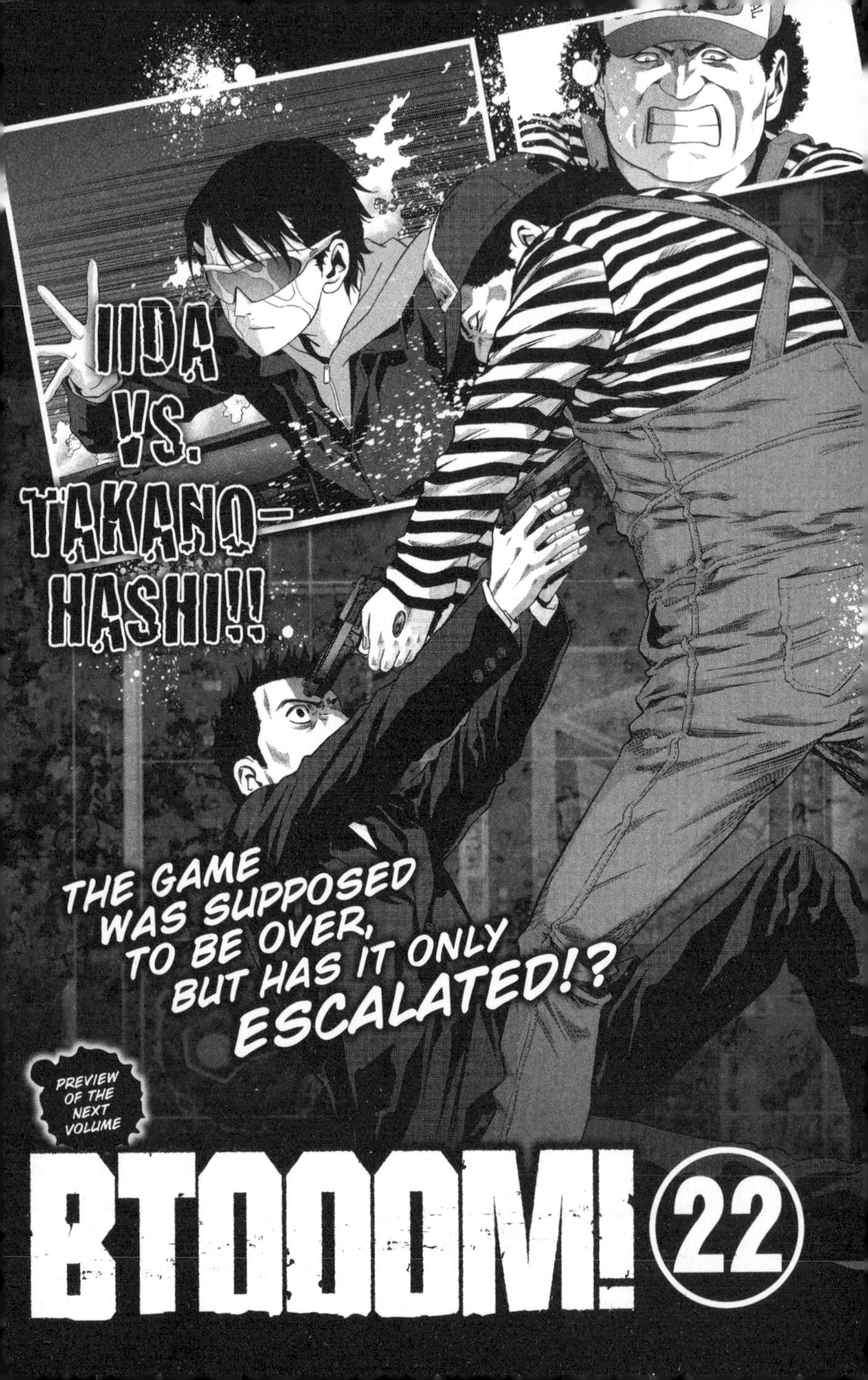
IIDA VS. TAKANO-HASHI!!
THE GAME WAS SUPPOSED TO BE OVER, BUT HAS IT ONLY ESCALATED!?
PREVIEW OF THE NEXT VOLUME
BTOOOM! 22

BTOOOM! 21

D0917533

Translation: Christine Dashiell

Lettering: Brndn Blakeslee

This book is a work of fiction. Names, characters, places, and incidents are the product of the author's imagination or are used fictitiously. Any resemblance to actual events, locales, or persons, living or dead, is coincidental.

BTOOOM! © Junya INOUE 2016. All rights reserved. English translation rights arranged with SHINCHOSHA PUBLISHING CO. through Tuttle-Mori Agency, Inc., Tokyo.

English translation © 2018 by Yen Press, LLC

Yen Press, LLC supports the right to free expression and the value of copyright. The purpose of copyright is to encourage writers and artists to produce the creative works that enrich our culture.

The scanning, uploading, and distribution of this book without permission is a theft of the author's intellectual property. If you would like permission to use material from the book (other than for review purposes), please contact the publisher. Thank you for your support of the author's rights.

Yen Press is an imprint of Yen Press, LLC.
The Yen Press name and logo are trademarks of Yen Press, LLC.

The publisher is not responsible for websites (or their content) that are not owned by the publisher.

Library of Congress Control Number: 2013497409

ISBNs: 978-0-316-52061-4 (paperback)
　　　 978-0-316-52062-1 (ebook)

10 9 8 7 6 5 4 3 2 1

WOR

Printed in the United States of America